D1378559

MODERN ART IN THE MAKING

MATISSE: *The Blue Window* (New York, The Museum of Modern Art).

MODERN ART
IN THE MAKING

BERNARD S. MYERS

Guest Professor of Art History

The University of Texas

McGRAW–HILL BOOK COMPANY, INC.

New York Toronto London 1950

Moore Institute of Art, Science & Industry

LIBRARY

PHILADELPHIA, PA.

709.03
M 992

c.2

MODERN ART IN THE MAKING

Copyright, 1950, by the McGraw-Hill Book Company, Inc. Printed in the United States of America. All rights reserved. This book, or parts thereof, may not be reproduced in any form without permission of the publishers.

v

82607 - 9/12/55 - BA/28 - V,30

To
S. L. M.
whose book this is
as much as it is mine

PREFACE

The relationship of painting in modern times to the contemporary history and social development of which it is so much a part has seldom been attempted in an organized fashion. Since, however, the art of any period is the result of the background factors of that age plus the personalities of its creative artists, it becomes as much an obligation to examine modern painting from this point of view as it has been with art of the past.

The story of modern art has been told before. Most tellings, however, do not include much discussion of the basic reason, or reasons, for the various stylistic changes of the past century and a half. To be sure, the plastic arts have a tradition of their own, of ideas handed down from generation to generation, but it will be found that the artist of one epoch borrows from the past or is influenced by that past precisely in the manner and to the degree that conditioning factors and personal predispositions demand. Thus the artist, in seeking his own historical and individual level, expresses both the demands of his era and those of his own creative character.

To stress personality factors at the expense of historical-cultural elements, as is so often the case with histories of painting, music, and other arts, would seem to be as fallacious as the kind of explanation that isolates the history of art in a cultural vacuum. Admittedly it is far simpler merely to observe, describe, and catalogue, but that does not release us from the duty of attempting some sort of honest analysis. The present volume undertakes to set forth for both student and layman the "why" of modern painting as well as the "how," outlining and examining the stylistic changes from generation to generation, together with a sequence of historical, social, and cultural sources of these developments.

The thread of our story is the increasing isolation of the modern painter in a society that no longer provides even a moderately secure type of patronage. The specific results of that isolation are a series of highly individualistic, escapist, and nonnaturalistic forms of expression. If the artist has become the whipping boy of those who fear progress or individualism, it is no more his fault than it is the fault of a social order that has grown too rapidly in material things to accustom itself to spiritual changes.

In a period marked by increasing pressures against personalized expression, a reexamination of the recent history of painting will show us how often this has happened in modern times, and for generally similar reasons. It is very easy indeed to attack a new form of expression, to dislike something that is strange and different, even if we pretend to be democratic in other ways. Nevertheless, it should be apparent that if we are to be consistent in our democracy we must give a new man the right to be heard. We are not forced to agree with him any more than he should be forced to agree with us.

If the modern painter has persisted in the face of the active hostility of the nineteenth century and the disregard of the twentieth, it is a great tribute to the strength and creative urge of the human spirit. Whatever remedies may be advocated for the situation, this volume attempts none. It merely gives some idea of what has been tried along those lines and opens up the possibility of further discussion.

In the telling of the story, the author has tried to be as straightforward as possible, using an absolute minimum of technical talk or the hyperaesthetic jargon which often disfigures otherwise useful books. Practical considerations as well as a desire for clearness and simplicity of understanding have led to the choice of those illustrations which may be most useful. They are always tied in very directly with the text.

The author would like to extend warm thanks to his various friends at The Museum of Modern Art and the Metropolitan Museum of Art for their valuable help. Miss Pearl Moeller has been both patient and kind in allowing him to use the photograph collection of The Museum of Modern Art. From Bernard Karpel, Librarian of The Museum of Modern Art, there has come good advice as well as excellent bibliographical aid. Thanks are also due to that museum's Department of Publications for making available a number of color plates for this volume. In this connection, it should be noted that *Life* has helped in the same way, as has Raymond Stites of the National Gallery of Art, who has very kindly consented to the use of a color plate from his book, *The Arts and Man*. Special thanks are due the author's friend Miss Alice D. Franklin of the Metropolitan Museum's photograph collection department, who has been more than generous with the material in her charge.

To the many collectors and institutions who have permitted the inclusion of their pictures in this volume, acknowledgment has been made in the credit lines.

Since it is impossible to thank each author from whom the factual material in this book has been amassed, the bibliography will indicate some of the chief sources of information in the English language. Authors such as Alfred H. Barr, Jr., R. H. Wilenski, F. Antal, J. T. Soby, René Huyghe, and Lionello Venturi may be mentioned as typical of those from whom the author has learned much. The bibliography is confined to titles in English for practical reasons, with an appended list of picture books and color portfolios. Since this is designed as a book for students and laymen, the author has not attempted any startling originality of stylistic interpretation, but has tried rather to amass the facts as they are generally known in the field today. Where there has been disagreement or a feeling of insufficiency the author has added his own ideas and explanations for both stylistic and background factors.

The warmest thanks are due the author's wife, who edited the entire manuscript, read all the proofs, and undertook countless other tasks in preparation for publication. Without this help and her constant advice and encouragement, this book would never have been.

BERNARD S. MYERS

AUSTIN, TEXAS
December, 1949

CONTENTS

LIST OF ILLUSTRATIONS

XV

COLOR PLATES

MODERN ART IN THE MAKING

1. THE FRENCH REVOLUTION: A BREAK WITH THE PAST

The revolutionary storm of 1789, a climactic point in the century-old struggle against feudalism, marks the end of an era for art as for social institutions. In France, the art capital of the world, it witnessed the end of royal patronage and the release of artists into the stream of free competition. Church endowments in the arts having disappeared long before this, the artist now became a creature without roots, without real function in the newer commercial society that was to decide his fate. For the patronage of the court and the sponsorship of the Royal Academy the Revolution substituted the somewhat erratic patronage of the middle class and the sponsorship of the ultraconservative nineteenth-century Academy. With these objective conditions established for the isolation and increasing in-dividualism of the artist, the story of modern painting really begins.

As for the new rulers—the middle class—their self-assertive voices had begun to be heard long before 1789 in the bourgeois drama, novels, and painting of the Louis XVI era. The eighteenth century as a whole is in many ways the story of the conflict between this burgeoning class and the already dying aristocracy—a conflict climaxed in the Revolution proper. Pre-Revolutionary idealist philosophers supplied an intellectual basis for the action undertaken by the various factions who felt it in their interest to participate, but the result of the attack on feudalism was to put the business-men on top. During the rest of the nineteenth century, this middle class would be busy solidifying its authority in the new democratic society.

Jacques Louis David (1748–1825), leading painter of the Revolution, was perhaps the first artist in the modern tradition to regard himself as a vital force in the world scheme of things—social, political, or intellectual. His Romantic self-consciousness was the first example in a long line of

I

1. DAVID: *Oath of the Horatii* (Paris, Louvre).

individuals such as Géricault and Delacroix, Courbet and Daumier, Degas, Van Gogh, Signac, Rivera, Orozco, and many others, men who felt that their work had a significance beyond painting as such.

At a time when many artists were still producing their pink-skinned Rococo figures, the *Oath of the Horatii* by David made its appearance in 1785 with the prophetic power of some great tragedy (Fig. 1). This sober classical group and the forces it represents are symptomatic of the entire political and social trend during the decade before the débâcle. Obviously it was meant to be a moralistic work reflecting the bourgeois virtues found in the literature of the time, in Diderot, Rousseau, and others.

The painting itself is based on the *Horace* (or Horatius) of the seventeenth century dramatist Corneille, a play in which two families of neighboring ancient Roman cities are related by marriage but divided by war. In the center of the stage the Horatii, who have been chosen to represent Rome

2

against their Alban brothers-in-law, are being pledged by their father. The tragic women include the daughter of Horatius, who is betrothed to one of the enemy, and his Alban daughter-in-law, who grieves at the fact that her husband and her brothers will soon be trying to kill one another. As a type, the old man is a descendant of the virtuous and moralistic fathers of Greuze's paintings a generation earlier; but the newer version is much more heroic in attitude and specifically classical in expression.

We can look upon the sentimentality in Greuze as the predecessor of the heroism in David, which becomes possible only with the nearness of the Revolution and the demand for a more civic and powerful type of expression. David's work is clearly more concentrated and naturalistic, while Greuze's allegories still show a degree of Rococo sensualism as part of the transition to the severe morality of the Revolutionary bourgeoisie.

The *Oath of the Horatii* shows a series of simple groups, straight lines, and a very sober Roman Doric architectural background that parallels the mood of the scene. The arches and columns set off the three groups, arranged with the coldness and sobriety of bas-relief. Gestures and postures are still reminiscent of the exaggerated emotions in the paintings of Greuze, especially the manner in which the arms are raised.

The picture is evidence of David's painstaking exactitude, both in the preparation of sketches for the picture and in the accuracy of small details such as the swords, sandals, and armor. Such works are part of his effort to re-create the republicanism of ancient Rome as accurately as possible in feeling and accessories. It may be accidental that the eighteenth century, through its immense curiosity and scientific attitude, had developed archaeology to such a point that a real antiquity could be offered to the public for the first time; but with this historical attitude established, it follows that David would attempt to conform to its ideals.

Somewhat ironically, the painting was ordered by the Royal Ministry of Fine Arts as a concession to middle-class morality and in the interests of patriotism. For almost half a century before, the government had encouraged a classical viewpoint. In the same way that the monarchy under Louis XIV had used classical subject matter to portray the glory of the new Roman Empire created by that king, the rulers of the second half of

3

the eighteenth century adopted this point of view to show their simplicity and nobility. Scholarships were given in the form of the famous Prix de Rome and in membership to the so-called School of Protected Pupils, both aimed toward teaching the principles of Greek and Roman art and development of the "noble style."

The attempt to straddle the issue by furnishing a yearly moral sop based upon classical antiquity proved ineffective, for things had gone much too far by this time. David's picture, instead of turning out to be merely moralistic and virtuous in the Greuze manner, was really patriotic, for it told the story of pious Romans to whom the state was more important than the family. Actually, this painting may be thought of as anti-Royal, as representing the attitude of the bourgeoisie against the moral looseness and political oppression of a court on the verge of destruction.

It is clear that the classical type of expression used by David was already characteristic of the pre-Revolutionary period. The radical-minded public simply turned this material to its own uses and interpreted ancient Rome in terms of its early republican virtues rather than its later imperial power.

How does it happen that the neo-Classical style became the repository of middle-class morality and rectitude? The excavations in Italy that made available so much of this material had begun as early as 1737, but it was not until the century was ready that the style was clearly formulated in its social meaning. The rationalism and scientific curiosity that helped produce these archaeological discoveries was balanced and even outweighed by a romanticism whose chief manifestation was the desire to escape into the past, either the Middle Ages or classical antiquity. The Rousseauist ideal of "original nature" was accompanied by the admission that this state of perfection could be found only in the past, preferably the classical past.

With the writings of Winckelmann (*History of Ancient Art*, 1764) and the painting of Mengs that resulted from this theorizing, the neo-Classical movement was given tremendous impetus and popularity. The more advanced British (advanced along the direction of middle-class development) preceded the French in this direction, as they were to do in connection with Romanticism, landscape painting, and other forms. Hamilton and West

4

produced many examples of neo-Classical paintings with sentimental qualities consonant with the typical middle-class attitude of that age. Even before the specific element of bourgeois morality was added to the formula through the paintings of Greuze, it was evident that such pictures as those of Hamilton and West (the latter with the prestige of George III's almost Victorian approval) were already exponents of a kind of upstanding purity of style, in sharp contrast to both the Rococo and the Eclectic styles of the eighteenth century. In other words, the new neo-Classicism represented a nonaristocratic, non-sensual, *i.e.*, middle-class viewpoint.

This neo-Classical process, then, naturally developed out of the moralistic and virtuous ideals of the eighteenth century and, aided by the patronage of the court and the official academies, was a generally widespread phenomenon of which David was but the climactic point. Following the development of his career and tremendous influence, the movement spread rapidly into architecture, sculpture, the minor arts, and even into costume. The tremendous prestige given to the neo-Classical style through its use during the most crucial period in French history helped it to remain an important opposition factor in nineteenth-century art. In fact, this style with its many subsequent variations symbolized for a long time the authority and respectability of the middle class.

The early training of David clearly foreshadows his later classical efforts. His education at the Collège des Quatre Nations in Paris stressed ancient languages and history, while his apprenticeship to the painter Vien (one of the pioneers of the neo-Classical movement) also pointed in this direction. After five unsuccessful efforts, David finally managed to win the Prix de Rome in 1776 and traveled there in the company of his teacher, who had just been appointed director of the French Academy in Rome. In Italy the classical development of David naturally was made easier, through such existing collections as the Vatican Gallery and the newly excavated centers at Pompeii and Herculaneum, both of which played such an important part in the orientation of the neo-Classical movement.

In the *Oath of the Horatii*, for example, the exactness of archaeological detail, plus a conscientious and sober sculptural quality, makes this picture more realistic than Rococo painting. We see in it the emergence of what

5

may be called naturalistic classicism, a combination of elements that undoubtedly accounts for the tremendous popularity of the work. A historical painting at that time had to be represented in a classic fashion, but the newer bourgeois ideal demanded a greater degree of realism.

There are definite indications that the monarchy of the pre-Revolutionary period was not unaware of the rumblings from beneath. A concession to middle-class morality is implied not only in ordering such a work as the *Oath of the Horatii* but also in a series of pictures showing the deeds of popular rulers of France, such as Francis I and Henry IV, and designed to increase good will toward the monarchy. These works approach in a very general way the classical compositions of David but are obviously much more Baroque in feeling (to stimulate emotional response) and display an even greater naturalism because of the concrete historical facts to which they refer.

An interesting example of this type is to be found in Vincent's *Molé and the Partisans of the Fronde* (1779, Paris, Chamber of Deputies). Reflecting a period when the monarchy of Louis XIV was allied with the middle class, this work was apparently meant to increase the prestige of the ruler and to impress people with the beneficent effects of his rule. In the active and Baroque manner of its execution, it appears to be a forerunner of a much later style, the Romantic historical effort of the 1830's.

An even more significant example of the pre-Romantic style is found in a sketch by Ménageot for a painting commissioned in 1781 of the *Death of Leonardo da Vinci* (he had died in the arms of his benefactor, Francis I). The composition and color of this work (Paris, Private Collection) bring us very close to Delacroix by using the typical theatrical effects of the Romantic period, the doctor described in pitch-black colors against a dark-green background.

The existence of such nonclassical works, out of their apparent art-historical place, shows that a purely stylistic examination of modern paintings without proper consideration of their *raison d'être* would not be particularly helpful in determining their chronological positions. An analysis of the stylistic development of David makes the importance of social background much clearer.

6

The first stage of his career shows him as a fairly typical Rococo artist of the century. A series of decorations for the house of Mlle. Guimard, praised by Fragonard, typify this phase of his activity. Under the impetus of the changing social and political conditions of the seventies and eighties, he developed the bourgeois naturalistic classic style already considered in the *Oath of the Horatii* (1785). A good many of his early works, like this one, were bought by Louis XVI; but David, reacting as always to the outstanding tendencies of the time (in a perhaps opportunistic fashion), threw himself into the Revolutionary movement in which he soon became a leading figure. Some of his paintings of this period, such as the *Paris ana Helen* (1788), done for the Count d'Artois, still show traces of the accepted Rococo tradition in softness of modeling and color as well as the general lack of social purpose, but they are not typical.

The public demand for more progressive tendencies in art is reflected in the *Death of Socrates* (1787) and then in the *Brutus* of 1789. In the very year of the Revolution, David again used the theme of the patriot, with the stern and unflinching Brutus facing the fact that his son had been executed for activities detrimental to the welfare of the state. Again a work commissioned for government purposes turned out to be a stimulus toward the frenzied patriotism of 1789. The significance of this painting for the Parisian public is illustrated by the fact that it was utilized as part of the curtain scene in Voltaire's *Brutus*, where the principal actor assumed the pose of David's hero. Both the play and the picture had a vital patriotic meaning for Frenchmen of that day, and when Mirabeau, the famous Revolutionary, appeared at the performance, he was hailed as the French Brutus, the destroyer of tyranny.

With the outbreak of the Revolution, David was carried away by its tremendous enthusiasm and in 1792 was elected a member of the Convention. In this capacity he voted for the execution of the King and for abolition of the Academy, of which he himself had been a member. His still extant speech on the latter subject almost indicates a personal grudge against the institution that trained him but took five years to award him his Prix de Rome. Similarly, his participation in the execution of the King, his earlier patron, may be looked upon askance, but his own favorite Roman characters

2. DAVID: *Oath of the Tennis Court* (Paris, Louvre).

would undoubtedly have approved since it was all for the welfare of the state. As artistic dictator of the time, David wielded a powerful influence both in deciding the character of Revolutionary art and in preserving the art treasures of the nation.

During the Revolution proper, the paintings of David avoided their usual classical references and turned toward a direct transcription of the situations of the day. Although some of them are "histories," they are not done in the so-called "noble" style but in a highly realistic manner. The important thing to observe in such a painting as the *Oath of the Tennis Court* (Fig. 2) is the fact that it violates the custom that a historical representation be rendered in antique costume and that it be executed in a restrained and impressive fashion. The deputies of the Third Estate, swearing not to leave their posts, are represented with more naturalism than ever before, even though arranged like a multiple version of the *Oath of the Horatii*.

This accurate record of a specific event gives us the different reactions of individual members of the group. Emotional effect is heightened by the blowing curtain at the upper left and the large empty space above the figures, suggesting Caravaggio and the early work of Rembrandt. David made a tremendous number of studies for the different personalities involved in the work, to help give the vividness of actuality to an event witnessed by the artist and painted in 1791.

In his political capacity David had the opportunity of observing the famous characters of the Revolution in action (he was a member of the Robespierre circle) and recorded his impressions graphically in a number of extremely vivid sketches such as *Danton* (Fig. 3) and others. These sketches, apparently made while the subjects were in the act of haranguing audiences, have all the immediacy of later reportorial graphic work and offer an interesting evidence of the fundamentally realistic character of David's art. If there appears to be a discrepancy between a casual drawing of this type and the definitely cold effect derived from one of the finished works, this is due to the prevalent mode of representation rather than to a fundamental deficiency on the part of the artist. In comparing the drawing of Danton with *The Death of Marat* (1793, Fig. 4), the spectator is aware immediately of the difference

3. DAVID: *Danton*—drawing (Lille, Museum).

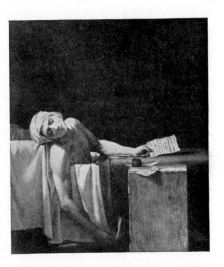

4. DAVID: *The Death of Marat* (Versailles, National Museum).

9

5. DAVID: *Portrait of the Flutist Devienne* (Brussels, Royal Museum).

between the actual field of action in which the former was done and the studio, with its artificial lighting, which is the milieu of the latter.

The last picture, however, when compared with the classical "histories" or even the *Oath of the Tennis Court*, shows the highest point of narrative realism reached by David up to 1793. If the *Oath of the Tennis Court* had been revolutionary in its representation of contemporary historical personages as they looked and dressed, *The Death of Marat* was even more so. David had seen Marat in his bath only the day before the assassination, so that the picture is the result of a very vivid memory image seen through the painter's sorrow and indignation.

The relative objectivity of the picture of the Deputies or the sketches of the Revolutionary characters gives way before a subjective and personal participation of the artist in this particular tragedy. One must not lose sight of the fact, however, that *The Death of Marat* is still a Revolutionary and patriotic picture in spite of the scrupulous accuracy of detail or that it is to be regarded as a symbol of the struggle, made more immediate by the personal contact between subject and painter evidenced in the dedication: "À Marat, David." The element of pathos is heightened both by the fact that the Revolutionary is struck down at the moment of working for the cause and by the specifically melodramatic (Baroque) light in which he is shown here.

The much disputed *La Maraichère* (Woman of the People), which may well have been done by David, would be one of the strongest evidences of the basically realistic inclinations of this artist. A portrait of a woman of the Marais district, this picture becomes a powerful symbol of the people of the Revolution. In this particular period of David's life, as before, he painted a number of dignified but very forthright portraits, occasionally (as in *Portrait of the Flutist Devienne*, 1792, Fig. 5) achieving an almost Chardinesque restraint and introspection.

After the fall of Robespierre's party, in which David had been active, the wealthier bourgeois appeared to take the place of the less important members of the middle class; and under the Directoire a fashionable society turned away from the austere Republican habits and ideals of the previous epoch. David was in prison for a time and during this interval he conceived his next large historical canvas, *The Sabine Women* (Fig. 6).

This work (1799), in which the Sabine women attempt to reconcile their Roman husbands and Sabine relations, is no longer as clear and as concentrated as the earlier Revolutionary works, but rather overcrowded and "posed." Instead of naturalism, a certain sculptural quality emerges, particularly as applied to the nude (proscribed under the previous Republican period). Natural only in details, these figures, posed somewhat like marbles,

6. DAVID: *The Sabine Women* (Paris, Louvre).

11

7. DAVID: *Mme. Récamier* (Paris, Louvre).

stress an artificial and elegant line deriving more from the Hellenistic art of Greece than the relatively sober production of Rome. Emphasis upon line seems to have derived from two other sources also: the early Italian Renaissance and Greek vase painting, so that this so-called neo-Greek style is a rather eclectic thing.

All these elements, particularly the softening, the nude, and the elegance, are in line with the shift in social emphasis of the time. The fashionable ideals of Directoire society produced certain types of furniture and costume that also began to appear in the paintings of David and others. Such a work as *The Sabine Women* no longer shows a definite political emphasis (except perhaps in the rather oblique and vague sense of the reconciliation of divergent political parties) because there is no urgent necessity at the moment.

The work of David during this period moves toward the combination of pleasantness with archaic elegance, shown particularly in the fashionable portraits executed by his entire school. Of these paintings the best known is that of *Mme. Récamier*, a famous lady of the time (1800, Fig. 7), whose portrait shows an elegant simplicity rather than the crude power of the *Horatii* or *Brutus*. The precise linear expression of her body is part of the severe elegance of the furniture specifically designed by David for this work, while the clear-cut and cameolike features of the lady are paralleled in the simple lines of her costume. If we contrast this kind of portrait with earlier works such as the *Devienne*, the change in David's style is seen more clearly.

Psychologically, the neo-Classicism of the Directoire period differs from that of the pre-Revolutionary epoch in the sense of greater affectation and stylization. No longer is it used to stimulate people to worthy emotions, but it is meant to be an ornament of society applied to such externals as furniture and clothes.

Shortly after, under Napoleon, David became court painter; and if it appears rather peculiar that the fiery Revolutionary could take this step, it must be remembered that he was not alone in his attitude. To a great many young radicals of the time (like Stendhal), the Emperor seemed to be the incarnation of the ancient rulers of Rome. David, to whom pompous attitudes and expressions were not entirely foreign, is said to have characterized Napoleon as a man "to whom altars would have been erected in ancient times."

If the aims of the new Imperial period appear to be a bit confused, with their mixture of military dictatorship, bourgeois ideals, enlightened despotism, and a revived court, the fact remains that this epoch put the final imprimatur upon the accession to power of the upper middle class, many of whom were now ennobled. A good many of these new barons are to be seen in David's great contribution to the period, *The Coronation of Napoleon* (1808, Fig. 8), a very large canvas commemorating the event and combining an almost classic simplicity with the naturalism of detail demanded by a contemporary occurrence. This rather imposing state occasion, like everything else during the period, is dominated by the presence and actions of the Emperor, shown in the act of placing the crown upon the head of his kneeling wife while the not too impressive "new" nobles look on. The

8. DAVID: *Coronation of Napoleon* (Paris, Louvre).

rather furtive blessing of the Pope, seated behind him, is only one evidence of the outstanding will of the little Caesar in the midst of his parvenu nobles. Here again, as in the *Oath of the Tennis Court*, the painter uses the Baroque empty space above the figures.

During this period David still continued to do historical paintings dealing with antiquity, such as the *Leonidas at Thermopylae* (1814), but apparently these subjects had outlived their usefulness, for here his classicism seems entirely devoid of vigor and power. The appeal that similar compositions had offered during the pre-Revolutionary period no longer existed, with the middle class now so firmly established in their new position.

The last decade of David's life was spent in an exile (in Brussels) imposed by the return of the Bourbons after Napoleon's downfall and their prejudice against an individual who had participated in the condemnation of Louis XVI. Here his last classical productions were of an ineffable softness, indicating the ultimate phase of their decay. The portraits of these last few years in the middle-class atmosphere of the Belgian capital bring back the realism of the Revolutionary portrait sketches and pictures of the *Devienne* type. This aspect of David's work constitutes his contribution to the later Realist movement. Pictures such as these show pretty clearly what David and others could have done had it not been for neo-Classicism.

In summing up the phase of David's work that must be regarded as his most typical, the neo-Classical, it must be admitted that, although it expressed the necessities of the time, it was done with the rhetoric and frequent pomposity of a parliamentary speech. As David moved out of his early Rococo phase into those works which follow Diderot's point of view that a painting should lend itself to reproduction in bas-relief, the eighteenth-century pinks of the flesh tones tended to give way to a coldness and hardness suitable perhaps to sculpture but hardly conforming to what is the common notion of pictorial quality. The lighting in his pictures is, more often than not, artificial and melodramatic to the point of being Baroque, as in *The Death of Marat*, or extremely cold, as in the *Mme. Récamier*. Although his characters are frequently posed in violent attitudes, they are hardly men of action but rather Ciceronian rhetoricians summing up their cases.

Perhaps the most characteristic of David's direct followers was Gérard (1770–1837), who is revealed typically in the well-known *Cupid and Psyche* (Paris, Louvre), an elegant idealization of nudity and extremely mannered in its method of execution. This picture may be said to parallel the Directoire and Empire classical works of David himself. Gérard, however, was better known as a portraitist and all the important people of the Empire and Restoration periods sat for him. Although his paintings are extremely decorative and even charming, and although Gérard himself was one of the most brilliant conversationalists of the age, his contribution to the evolution of art is not too significant. Other direct and indirect pupils of David will be considered in their proper places in the development of different movements during the early nineteenth century.

Although the artistic legacy left by David is not, on the whole, as significant as that of other leaders in the nineteenth century, the force of his example as an individualist is most important. It may be some consolation to point to his great naturalistic works, such as *The Death of Marat* and many of the portraits, and look to them as examples of what might have been. The fact remains that in the heat of the hour David could not have done

15

other than he did. If the painting of the Revolution is in many respects a step backward or away from the previously flourishing naturalism of the middle-class tradition, it is also an acknowledgment of the potential relation of art and society.

Again on the positive side is the fact that it swept away the Royal Academy as well as the Rococo style, and brought into being a new kind of *salon* open to all artists. Here the painter could be judged by his peers and by the public, unsympathetic though these two groups might turn out to be later. Even if the *salon* was to become a closed corporation slightly sooner than one could have hoped, the example of sweeping out the reactionaries had been set. In 1848, the old guard was to be turned out again as the by-product of a later Revolution.

2. GOYA, FORERUNNER OF MODERN ART

Goya, the "Old Master," was a contemporary of David. Like the French Revolutionary painter, he was involved in the political situation of his own country, a situation that was nothing if not revolutionary. He was not, however, an official leader of anything nor was he an exponent of middle-class political morality in the same conscious way as David.

Yet Goya was a rationalist, a typical eighteenth-century liberal who hated tyranny, especially that form of tyranny imposed from the outside, so that he could hate David's imperial master, Napoleon, with the most violent passion the world of art has ever seen. The liberalism which often led him into bitter, if veiled attacks on established religion did not prevent him from playing a somewhat opportunistic role with his royal masters, again suggesting the career of David.

More than anything else, Goya was the great individualist, the Romantic rebel who defied all canons of taste in subject matter and technique—and often in his personal life. In that sense he is the ancestor and analogue of the French Romantics of the 1830's, but on a much more intense level. A lifelong record of social satire, a consistent refusal to truckle to the still dominant neo-Classicism of his age and country, a violent sense of reality expressed through the vivid colors and dynamic rhythms of his canvases, make Goya the arch-symbol of self-expression carried to its highest and most significant point.

Whereas the art of David was symbolic of the break with eighteenth-century Rococo style and the interruption of middle-class Realism, Francisco de Goya (1746–1828) spans the two centuries in a different fashion. Standing on the threshold of the modern world, he embraces in his art the Romantic, Realistic, Impressionist, and even Expressionist points of view.

Though not too important as an influence in his own country while he lived (there were very few direct followers), he became known shortly after his death in France through publication of his extraordinary aquatints and lithographs. These were intimately known and copied by both Delacroix and Manet shortly after the middle of the century and by some anonymous artists as early as the 1820's. These specific influences on the leaders of the Romantic and Impressionist movements are easier to indicate than the general force of his powerful example toward realism and action. Yet it is the latter factor that holds Goya's real importance, for in that area he was not only far in advance of his time but had more to give than most artists of the nineteenth century.

Born in an age dominated by neo-Classical art, Goya never for a moment looked in that direction but insisted, rather, upon an intensely realistic and personal rendering of the civilization in which he lived. More than most artists of any period, he was a rebel and individualist, but it would be an exaggeration to consider him a political revolutionary in the modern sense, in spite of the obviously critical themes in his paintings and prints.

Goya undoubtedly had certain Romantic qualities apart from his anti-Classicism, but these never led him into the kind of "escape" subjects found so often in French Romanticism. The Spanish painter always retained his critical faculties, even when not able, as was often the case, to express a direct and open condemnation of what went on. That is why so much of his work is allegorical and imaginative, using weird monsters and animals to express his feelings. Goya's entire career was a protest against the conditions of his time. His special position at court enabled him to survive even the attacks of the Inquisition, so that perhaps he was in a better position than his French contemporaries to speak his mind.

There is little question that Goya was a social critic. The many veiled but palpable attacks on organized religion, the bitingly satirical portrayals of the looseness of aristocracy in his day, the lampooning of his royal masters, all point in this direction. Obviously, he was an enemy of many prevailing superstitions, of the lying and deceit all around him, the peculiar combination of lechery, corruption, and unthinking reverence for the past that marked that period.

Unlike David, however, he was not a political radical or revolutionary ready for extreme measures. His point of view may be best understood, perhaps, from one of his famous prints showing a young man resting his head on his arms, asleep against a table over which monstrous forms hover. The caption, *The Dream of Reason Produces Monsters*, tells the story better than anything else could. Politically, this is eighteenth-century Encyclopedist thinking.

In the face of such an extraordinary social document as his *Disasters of the War* (1810–1813) that reflects the French invasion during the Peninsular War, it may seem curious to say that Goya was not political-minded. Yet there is no direct evidence to prove that Goya did not believe in war as an instrument of political necessity. We use his material as vivid proof of the horrors of war, the mockery of decadent royalty and corrupt religion, but from what we know of his life, these things did not have the same meaning to him as they did to later artists using his pictorial ideas. His reaction to war was apparently more patriotic or anti-French than antiwar, although he reacted powerfully to man's inhumanity to man.

The relations of the artist to the ruling dynasty in Spain left him in a slightly ambiguous position. Although he seemed to detest them, he stayed on through thick and thin, even transferring his loyalties—at least for the sake of expediency—to Napoleon's brother, Joseph Bonaparte, and later to the candidate of Bourbon reaction, Ferdinand. Goya's connections with the clergy were apparently not too good, but the intervention of Charles IV saved the painter from the revenge of the Inquisition. Undoubtedly Goya was antireligious, but this is the hallmark of the eighteenth-century liberal and fits the pattern very well.

Basically, Goya must appear as a social annotator more interested in pointing out the evils and contradictions of society than in prescribing for those ills. Yet, when the time came, his powerful sense of reality struck sparks from the creative imagination of more political-minded artists like Daumier, Käthe Kollwitz, and others. From generation to generation, as the story of modern art unfolds, Goya will be many things to many artists.

Francisco de Goya was born in 1746 of peasant stock in Fuendetodos,

9. GOYA: *The Blind Guitar Player* (Madrid, Prado).

Aragon, and sent at an early age to nearby Saragossa to study art. Instead of devoting himself to work, the next six years (1760–1766) found the young man indulging in dancing, singing, fencing, bullfighting, love-making, and other extracurricular activities. A gang scrape sent him off to Madrid, where life went on in the same way, ending for the moment in his being stabbed almost to death. The next few years were spent in Italy, first in Rome and then in Parma, where he won an Academy prize in 1771. Then came an interval in Saragossa again, this time doing church decoration. Here he married Josefa Bayeu, who came from an influential artistic family, and returned to Madrid to begin his career.

Although Goya did not begin to produce significantly until he was past thirty-five, his exciting youth had furnished him with a wealth of vivid experiences and knowledge of humanity that were to emerge in his later work. Goya's belligerent individuality and his general directness of vision can be understood in the light of this background. The Spanish capital, where Goya soon became a leading figure, was dominated by an unusually decadent and socially useless royal family and aristocracy, and filled with adventurers, questionable characters, demimondaines, procurers, thieves, and other interesting types. Although most of these characters were ignored by Goya's neo-Classical contemporaries, it was from this rich, picturesque source that Goya was to draw some of his best themes.

Goya's first state work was a series of tapestry designs in 1776. Three years later he was made court painter and in 1785 became president of the Academy. The earliest work of the artist still bears the stamp of his indebtedness to the Rococo decorator Tiepolo in its general gaiety and charming color. However, realism and a sense of movement are the keynotes of most of Goya's production. From the very beginning, even in the more

20

decorative works, we find him recording the everyday things about him in a direct and positive manner.

The Blind Guitar Player (Fig. 9) is only a step removed from his picturesque tapestry designs but it is already filled with a sense of the dramatic and the vivid. This characteristic Spanish subject (Picasso in his Blue Period uses the theme again much later) is not set down for a moral reason, as Hogarth might have done during the same period, but rather for its psychological possibilities, its picturesqueness, and its possibilities of contrast. It remains an interesting subject to paint, made stark in the way it is revealed against the sky and monumentalized in contrast to the two gallants in the rear, who remain oblivious to the blind man and his music. An everyday subject has been singled out in a slightly Romantic fashion and made more "interesting" and significant.

Even at this early point in his career, Goya's figures are already beginning to emerge in terms of strong contrast between light and dark. Like many of his seventeenth-century predecessors, especially Velásquez, Goya is very conscious of the part played by light and atmosphere in rendering the mass of a figure.

Goya's relation to Velásquez is particularly clear, although at no point does the later artist lose his individuality. In addition to direct copies made as studies, Goya is often influenced by his Realist ancestor in many of his own creations. The portrait of *Carlos III in Hunting Dress* (Fig. 10) illustrates the relationship as well as the differences between the two great Spanish painters. In this work Goya has placed his subject against a low-lying landscape with the figure sil-

10. GOYA: *Carlos III in Hunting Dress* (Madrid, Prado).

21

houetted by the light that shines out around its edges, a technique that can be compared with Velásquez' portrait of *Philip IV as a Hunter* (Madrid, Prado). Here, the figure is also outlined against the light with only the head and hands modeled to any extent.

Although Goya becomes a link in the chain between Velásquez and Manet in the nineteenth century, it must be understood that in psychological objectivity Manet is closer to Velásquez than to Goya. Velásquez' king was painted in a completely detached way, avoiding reference to qualities of mind, while the subject of Goya, although as unattractive physically as the earlier king, shows a definite and successful attempt on the part of the painter to render its shrewdness.

The visualization of a figure in terms of silhouette used by Velásquez, Goya (not invariably), and Manet is bound up with their common conception of form as existing through light striking upon it in varying degrees and

11. GOYA: *Family of Charles IV* (Madrid, Prado).

22

depths. Goya, for example, was very outspoken about the nonexistence of the line in nature, and if we refer back to the *Carlos III*, it becomes clear that the form has been modeled by using light and dark rather than lines. Manet was to say considerably later that the most important person in a painting was the light.

Another aspect of this interest in light is found in Goya's celebrated group portrait, the *Family of Charles IV* (Fig. 11), his next royal patron. Here again we feel a link with Velásquez because of the importance of atmospheric light that has been poured into this canvas, as in the earlier painter's *Las Meniñas* or his *Tapestry*

12. GOYA: *Josefa Bayeu* (Madrid, Prado).

Weavers. Goya's painting seems to be based on the same technique of making a group of figures into a coherent unit by means of almost tangible air painted into the spaces between them.

Socially, the *Family of Charles IV*, described by Théophile Gautier as the "grocer's family that has won the big lottery prize," is one of the most scathing indictments of royalty ever painted. More remarkable is the fact that Goya painted this picture as court painter and that in spite of the apparent stupidity and depravity of its main characters, the work was acceptable. The bravura and dash of its color, the looseness of brushwork, and the flecks of brilliant unadulterated paint make this one of Goya's masterpieces, even without its psychological analysis. But the merciless analysis, to be repeated in many of his so-called official portraits, especially those of the libidinous queen, is one of the outstanding characteristics of this brilliant observer.

When Goya wished to be sympathetic and noncritical, as in his many characterizations of children, he produced such things as *Josefa Bayeu*, a portrait of his wife (Fig. 12). Although the handling of paint is similar

23

13. GOYA: *Rebellion of May 2, 1808* (Madrid, Prado).

here to his other works, Señora Goya has been portrayed with the same dignity and sympathetic understanding as Hendrickje Stoeffels in Rembrandt's paintings. Characteristic of all Goya's portraits are such details as the clumsily drawn hands (also feet in the full-length pictures) and the enlarged pupils that contribute so much to the interesting quality of the glance.

The three great branches of later painting that have been more or less directly influenced by Goya are the Romantic, the Realist, and the Impressionist. Indirect influences on the Expressionist and Surrealist movements should also be noted.

The turbulence and sympathetic feeling of Romantic painting, particularly the work of Géricault and Delacroix, are anticipated in Goya's *Rebellion of May 2, 1808* (Fig. 13). Here he tells the story of the reaction of the citizens of Madrid to occupation of the city by the French. In a composition reminis-

24

cent of the wild and diagonal action of the hunting pictures of Rubens and foreshadowing the turbulent action and color of many works by Géricault and Delacroix, Goya portrays the passionate revolt of the *Madrileños*. Although both Goya and the slightly later Romantics derived this form from Rubens, the Spanish artist seems to have done it before the French generally used the same manner.

Much more important, however, is the difference between the French type of battle picture and the Goyesque examples. Gros, for instance, in portraying the campaigns of Napoleon at Eylau, Arcola, Jaffa, etc., was concerned with glorifying the conqueror, for that was his job. Moreover, war emerged from his hands as something fine and noble, as an opportunity to die for the Emperor, whose soldiers are being attacked in the painting of Goya. Not only does Goya express his fierce hatred for the French here and in other works, but he is never particularly interested in showing war as anything but what it generally is— a brutalizing and sordid business.

It is well known that Eugène Delacroix, the outstanding Romantic painter, copied specific works of Goya, particularly some of the plates in the series of prints called *The Caprices (Caprichos)*. What attracted the French painter was their imaginative sense and their vivid use of light and dark contrasts; but, in all fairness to Goya, it cannot be said that the benefits derived remotely resembled the force and imagination of the originals. The influence of Goya on Delacroix, like that of the English painter Bonington, was primarily a matter of example, especially Goya's independence of spirit in breaking with the

14. GOYA: *Nadie se conoce, Caprichos #6* (New York, Metropolitan Museum of Art).

neo-Classical tradition. Again like Bonington, he offered strong evidence of what could be done with vivid and clean colors.

The specific connection between Goya and Delacroix can be localized in the former's print, *Nadie se conoce* (No One Knows the Other, Fig. 14), one of the *Caprichos* copied by the French painter from a set he owned. The unusually weird and diabolic effect of the print, with its brilliantly lighted figures against a sombre background, repeats itself in many works of Delacroix, especially his literary illustrations for *Faust, Macbeth*, and *Hamlet* (Fig. 34).

We may examine Goya's same print from another point of view: his manner of modeling the figures by means of abrupt transitions from a light area to a dark area. In this he foreshadows the method of the Realist Daumier for both his graphic work and his painting. Although there is only the slightest possibility of direct contact between the Spaniard, who visited Paris in 1824 (he died in self-imposed exile at Bordeaux in 1828), and Daumier, Goya's prints were known in France. The Spanish painter, like most of the great moderns, was more interested in expressive figures than in purely imitative ones. Combined with his feeling for violent movement, this play of interacting volumes, as well as the abrupt modeling already described, offer a very striking parallel to the manner of the great master of French Realism.

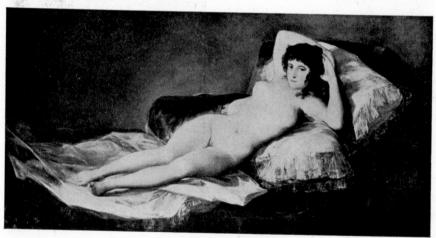

15. GOYA: *Nude Maja* (Madrid, Prado).

Goya's influence on the Impressionist Manet can be illustrated by the *Nude Maja* (Fig. 15), a direct ancestress of the French painter's *Olympia* (Fig. 82). The rather questionable person in Goya's painting—generally accepted as his mistress, the Duchess of Alba—is similar in her amoral frankness to the demimondaine of Manet, while the atmospheric quality in the two works and the use of fresh clear color are further points of resemblance.

In the case of *Majas on the Balcony* (Fig. 16), Goya has not only provided the prototype for the *Two Women on a Balcony* of Manet (New York, Metropolitan Museum) but has offered in a very interesting manner an unusually modern subject. Our attention is

16. GOYA: *Majas on the Balcony* (New York, Metropolitan Museum of Art).

caught first by the brightly dressed women, the *majas* of indeterminate social status, the men remaining silhouetted in the background as foils against which the clean colors of the dresses stand out brilliantly. The most interesting thing, however, is that, like the ladies of Manet or Renoir, these people are engaged in the absorbing city custom of vicarious participation in the movement of the street. This painting is early nineteenth century, but we may look upon it as pre-Impressionist in character, though in Goya's case this simply means an interest in the world about him.

It is always Goya's awareness of everyday reality that is so striking. This is nowhere shown with such vividness as in *The Bull Fight* (Fig. 17), dealing with a subject familiar to the artist from personal experience and interesting to him now because bullfighting had recently become a people's sport. The artist descends into the *corrida* to show the sport and its adherents with a sense of the momentary and an instantaneous vision entirely foreign to his age. The quick and powerful action of the bulls and their tormentors is seen against a sun-drenched arena surrounded by masses of spectators, who emerge as mere dabs of clean color. There is no intention to model these figures completely, because in brilliant sunlight people are not seen very clearly, especially at a distance. Those in the immediate foreground, therefore, are more clearly indicated than those further back, who become mere blurs of light. Here the artist uses more or less instinctively some of the clean color ideas later promulgated by painters of the 1860's and 1870's.

Similar to some of the more advanced Impressionists, like Renoir, Goya is not only interested in descriptive color. In this picture, for example, we have a good instance of color patterns skillfully arranged across the entire surface to achieve movement for formal rather than for purely decorative effect. Moreover, the apparent jumble of figures in *The Bull Fight* arranges itself into a flattened "X" described by the performers in the arena.

One striking difference between Goya and the majority of Impressionist painters lies in the fact that he is a man of action. Although they are indebted

17. GOYA: *The Bull Fight* (New York, Metropolitan Museum of Art).

18. GOYA: *Shooting of a Group of Citizens by the Soldiers of Murat* (Madrid, Prado).

to him for many things, their use of the material is more in the line of "sensations" of a visual nature than toward direct emotional expression. We have only to compare one of Goya's great masterpieces, the *Shooting of a Group of Citizens by the Soldiers of Murat* on the night of May 3, 1808 (Fig. 18), with the somewhat derivative *Execution of The Emperor Maximilian* by Manet (Fig. 84) to see the difference. Although the French painting owes a great deal to Goya, especially in the arrangement of the line of executioners, the Manet picture, in spite of bright and startling colors, remains a static thing. Its interest for us lies in the elements of patterning and silhouette, the vivid new color system that Manet is bringing forth, while the work of Goya is a wild Expressionistic rendition of a particularly horrible and moving scene.

There is no question of inferiority or superiority implied in these distinctions, but rather an attempt to understand the different purposes of the two painters. Goya is moved by the tragic plight of his country and his hatred

29

of the French into a fierce protest, whereas Manet's interest in the shooting of Maximilian in Mexico is primarily aesthetic. Whatever form elements exist in the painting of the Spaniard are there as part of his conception of a night piece, worked out under conditions of startling glaring light to show the wild expressions of the helpless victims in contrast to the pitilessly quiet purpose of the soldiers. In the painting of Manet the aesthetic elements are consciously inserted and the subject chosen for its pictorial interest.

More convincingly dramatic than Delacroix's *The Massacre at Scio* (Fig. 30) and more instantaneous in effect than Manet's *Maximilian*, Goya's work seems to leap over decades toward the twentieth-century Expressionists and their vivid outpourings of the human soul. Probably no other painter of the horrors of war and invasion has approached the universal tragedy depicted here. Callot in the seventeenth century was his logical ancestor, just as Daumier in the nineteenth and Käthe Kollwitz in the twentieth century are his just descendants.

In the series of prints known as the *Disasters of War* (1810–1813), Goya has elaborated the terrors of the French invasion of Spain shown in his *Shooting of a Group of Citizens*. Yet the motivation of the arrogant individualist emerging from a socially unselfconscious society was not a hatred of war as such, but rather a simple and fierce patriotism and love of country. So far as we can tell, these black-and-white pictures were not meant to arouse public opinion, and indeed could not have done so since they became known long after the event. The tradition of Goya's going out into the city after the massacres with lantern and sketch pad to see for himself what had happened can also be taken as an artist's fascination for the horror of his subject. Not until the rise of modern journalism and such social-minded commentators as Daumier will we find reference to the economic and social causes of war and a direct attack on war as an instrument of political necessity.

Goya was interested in the animal "man" and particularly excited and stimulated by some of his apparent stupidities, but he was not a reformer. Such a subject as the *Procession of the Flagellants* (Madrid, Royal Academy), showing a crowd of worshipers carrying the image of the Virgin through the streets while lashing themselves until the blood flowed, is implicitly critical. Although superstition, hysteria, and stupidity are often the subjects

30

of Goya's art, the *Flagellants* is also an opportunity for the artist to show an interesting and exciting subject.

Realism, movement, power, emotionality, and finally imagination are the important characteristics of Goya's epoch-making art. The macabre series of paintings he did on the walls of his own home, the so-called House of the Deaf Man, long after the death of Josefa and his Duchess, when his deafness had cut him off from the world, are in some ways the most bizarre and imaginative works he has left us. Nothing more fascinating and horrible in the purely abstract sense came from his brush than the *Saturn Devouring His Sons* (Fig. 19). Although there may well be some direct reference in this work, we must rather accept it for its gigantesque qualities, its stark color, and vivid imagination. With this series of works

19. GOYA: *Saturn Devouring His Sons* (Madrid, Prado).

he becomes more than ever a tower of light illuminating the art of the modern world.

3. EARLY ROMANTICISM

Romanticism, the traditional antagonist of neo-Classicism, is also the product of the late eighteenth century. During the incubation period of the latter movement, there were already pictures showing qualities opposed to the formalism, clear color, rigid compositions, republicanism, and collective morality of Davidian art. During the decade before the Revolution, Vincent and Ménageot produced paintings glorifying the monarchistic past in a Baroque and shadowy manner. The latter painter, especially, in his highly personal interpretation of the *Death of Leonardo* with its emotional color and vaguely indicated figures, foreshadows the nonclassical Romantic movement.

The most significant exponent of this pre-Romantic style is Anne-Louis Girodet (1767–1824) whose *Pietà* sketch (1787, Fig. 20) strikes a new note. In one of the most unusual pictures of the pre-Revolutionary epoch, the strong deeply receding background for Christ and the Madonna and the vivid light and dark effect relate this work to Baroque art in a moving and serious way. Its gloom, sense of mystery, violent lighting, and naturalistic handling—all designed to create religious feeling and pathos—seem out of place only two years before the Revolution. Yet there was a need for this kind of picture.

Eighteenth-century bourgeois art, as we know, presupposed not only naturalism but a high emotional content as well. In the art of David this emotional viewpoint, parallel to the moral excitement of contemporary literature, appeared to be subordinated to a certain extent by both his highly developed sense of realism and the general patriotic nature of his ideas.

Such diffused emotionality in a frame of political virtue is an interruption of eighteenth-century sentiment, wherein the individual had the right to express himself as an individual and not as a collectivist. The subjective attitude developed by Jane Austen, Goethe (*Sorrows of Young Werther*), and Rousseau (*The New Héloïse*) represented the middle class and its growing emotional reactions. Certain individuals, like Rousseau, also tried to find in nature reflections of their own strong feelings, thus fostering an interest in the wild, the picturesque, and the unusual. At a later and more developed stage, artists and writers of the Romantic school would express

20. GIRODET: *Pietà*—sketch (Montpellier, Museum).

themselves with further exaggeration in an exalted, pathetic, and sometimes macabre fashion.

The *Night Thoughts* of Young, of which the historian Grimm complained that "there were too many bells, too many chants, too many tombs, too many funereal cries, and too many phantoms," is a good example of the emotional indulgence popular in eighteenth-century England and, soon after, in France. In the latter country, physicians published treatises on melancholia, nervous diseases, and vaporous afflictions.

We see, then, that the most typical characteristics of later Romanticism existed in the second half of the eighteenth century. This developed individual viewpoint, together with the philosophical humanism of the time, produced a personalized emotionalism in Goethe and Rousseau. In the English "Graveyard" poets it goes further, resulting in constant reference to the "unusual," the "interesting," and the "macabre." With the introductions of German and English literature into France through translations and periodicals, French writing was stimulated in this direction.

The Germans exerted another influence in their accentuation of national cultures. Affected by their new-found unity under Frederick the Great, writers such as Herder and young Goethe showed great enthusiasm for their literary and historical heritage, the former through his collection of older German poetry and the latter in such medievalistic dramas as *Götz von Berlichingen.* Schiller and others in Germany soon followed suit, while Bishop Percy's *Reliques of Ancient English Poetry* represented the English movement.

Almost all aspects of the past interested these early Romantics, the classical as well as the medieval, since most of the old buildings were known to them in picturesque ruins and romanticized historical accounts. Thus the eighteenth-century neo-Classicists, reviving the spirit of ancient Rome, were just as Romantic as the medievalists. One tendency was just as escapist as the other, as much removed from actuality and, although they later come into conflict, both were oblique reflections of their age. Gradually, the Greek and Roman revivals in the arts became a standard, dull, academic practice, still utilized today, while the medievalists, although ending in the morass of Victorianism, at least in France kept open the path of individualism and revolt.

Artistically, the important characteristics of Romanticism are found in emphasis of the irregular over the regular, the picturesque over the formal, the vague over the clear, and the exotic and mysterious over the rational. In such a painting as the *Pietà* of Girodet, the artist has accentuated the irregular contour, the vague form, the mysterious background, and the unusual emotional quality, all foreshadowing the more developed Romanticism of Delacroix.

During the second half of the eighteenth century, emotionality and Gothicism had been synonymous. Rousseau, for example, speaking of *The New Héloïse* as done "in the Gothic manner," illustrates how the intellectuals of that day associated the Gothic past with emotionality. Here again we have a pre-Romantic symptom of yearning for a different environment, milieu, or local color. The later Romantics were to seek a new local color not only in time but in space, extending their interest in different atmospheres chronologically downward and geographically outward.

Interest in the Middle Ages is one of the signatures of the Romantic 1830's, but it existed much earlier. Gothic buildings, such as the Cathedral of Orléans, for example, were built in Paris during the seventeenth and eighteenth centuries. At the same time Voltaire, du Bellay, and Sedaine put into verse the stories of Tancred, the Siege of Calais, and Richard the Lion-Hearted. Although descriptions in these works are fantastic and picturesque rather than historically correct, this very fact indicates their Romantic character. Gothic structures existed in English and French parks and gardens at the end of the eighteenth century, while Paris offered exteriors and interiors in this style down through the early nineteenth century.

The same governmental attitude that had produced patriotic neo-Classical subjects in David's time also brought forth Lépicié's *William the Conqueror Disembarking in England* (1765, Caen). When in 1775 d'Angeviller, the minister of public works, had demanded subjects that would inspire patriotism, many themes such as St. Louis, Bayard, and the Citizens of Calais appeared.

One might assume that a period interested in Gothic history, literature, and cathedrals would be influenced by religion but this was only true in an emotional and universal sense. The ecclesiastical aspects of religion (developed during the Romantic period proper) could not yet appeal to rational bourgeois in the second half of the eighteenth century. These more advanced thinkers found their outlets in the feelings of *Brutus* or *The Death of Marat* (Fig. 4). For the less socially aware, the "different," the fantastic, and even the religious became possibilities. During the post-Revolutionary period, with a general reaction against rationalism, religious ideas were to burgeon again.

In painting, early Romanticism is a peripheral element that ultimately changes the mixture of which it is a part. It adds itself to Rococo art (whose theorists spoke of "sentiment"), to the somewhat Baroque historical painting of the time, the sentimental works of Greuze, and the classically naturalistic creations of the advanced groups. The *Pietà* of Girodet, then, would represent eighteenth-century sentiment raised to a more emotional and "interesting" level in the manner of later Romantic painting. In a typical example of the Baroque-Classical type of work ordered by the Church, the element of excitement and pathos has entered.

David, around 1787, was busy with his neo-Classical patriotic productions and would probably have refused this commission, but that merely indicates the difference between him and his pupil. Girodet seemed to be one of those people who must be original. While David was involved in the Revolution, Girodet spent his time in Italy, painting soft dreamlike works, such as the *Endymion* (Paris, Louvre), entirely without contemporary reference. This nonconformism in Girodet is another Romantic symptom. He returned to Paris during the Directoire and naturally became popular with the pleasure-loving, newly rich, upper middle-class society. The shift from standards of the previous period, noted in David's softer line and emphasis on contours, shows itself in the unintellectual Girodet even more radically. His *Danaë* (1799, Paris, Enriquant Collection) is a typical, if exaggerated, example in its obvious eroticism and personal references.

Of the Napoleonic period, Girodet's *Ossian Receiving the Generals of Napoleon* (1801, Fig. 20a) is an interesting and instructive work. Commissioned by the Emperor, it portrays Ossian, Fingal, and other heroes of Celtic myths receiving in their cloud home the fallen generals of the *Grande Armée*. During a period so much interested in the unusual emotion, the fantastic, and the uncanny, this picture expresses both the private interests of Napoleon, whose two favorite books were *Ossian* and *Werther*, and the emotional receptivity of the age. A combination of naturalism in the uniforms and unnaturalism in the bards, heroes, and virgins typifies the

36

confused thinking of this era. Girodet apparently wanted to be bizarre and unusual, so that naturalism here became subordinate and unimportant.

The Burial of Atala (1808, Fig. 21), his next large picture, shows the direction in which the period was heading. Inspired by Chateaubriand's poem, *Atala* (1801), it is also symptomatic of a religious revival arising out of the cultural necessities of the time and the newly arranged Concordat

20a. GIRODET: *Ossian Receiving the Generals of Napoleon* (Malmaison).

between the Napoleonic state and the Church. Following the *Atala* with its specifically Christian emphasis, Chateaubriand wrote his *Genius of Christianity* in 1802; while in 1810 Mme. de Staël published her *Germany* in defense of the Northern and Christian point of view. The field was now clear for a change from the generalized religious feeling of the previous period to a

37

21. GIRODET: *The Burial of Atala* (Paris, Louvre).

specific institutional emphasis. Anti-rationalism, as part of the reaction against revolutionary ideas, appeared most strongly in the works of Chateaubriand, one of whose favorite arguments for Catholicism was that it helped art and was so beautiful in itself.

Under the Empire, with the Church again legally recognized, Christianity came forward anew but in a much more conservative fashion. It represented a swing to the Right, away from the effects of the Revolution, with Chateaubriand's group adherents of the pro-Bourbon restoration.

Looking at the *Burial of Atala*, we can see how Rousseau's enthusiasm for free and untrammeled nature had been transformed into a strange macabre medium. The new poetry had created a novel and bizarre Catholicism, tinged with exaggerated emotionality and even with sensualism. Chateaubriand had Atala commit suicide to avoid losing her chastity to her lover, since her mother had dedicated her to the service of the Virgin.

38

Girodet's treatment of the exotic, faraway American tale of Christian Indians is reminiscent of his earlier *Pietà*. Even the story told in a cave and the tiny cross outside reappear but with a significant change. The later picture is less sincere and more theatrical, less Christian in spirit and more interested in showing the aesthetic possibilities of Christianity. With this mixture of religious fireworks and thinly disguised sensualism, we enter the land of the exotic subject, the far-off land that fascinated the later Romantics.

Exoticism, of course, existed earlier. From Louis XIV's Turkish visitors, through the later Persian envoys of 1714 and 1721, to the domestically produced Oriental tales of the eighteenth century, interest in the East had been evident. Travelers brought back silks, lacquers, and porcelains from the Orient to fill the palaces of Europe. In art during this period, bizarre scenes showed Frenchmen dressed as Turks, Chinese, or American Indians; while writers used imaginary Orientals to criticize contemporary manners, as in Montesquieu's *Persian Letters*. As knowledge of the East increased, artists and writers became more accurate. With the Egyptian campaigns of Napoleon, modern archaeology began, and the imaginary Turks of the eighteenth century disappeared.

Napoleon's campaigns stimulated two phases of Romanticism: the one which will emerge as Emperor worship and, more lasting, the contact of Frenchmen with so many alien cultures—Egypt, the Near East, central Europe, and Russia. This helped to crystallize the rather vague ideas of the eighteenth century. Idolatry of the Emperor was first due to his own desire for self-aggrandizement, reflected in the work of many official artists of the period; later, it became part of a nostalgic harking back to a period of great glory. Napoleon seemed extraordinary to non-Frenchmen as well. When Beethoven temporarily dedicated the *Eroica* to him, it was done out of Romantic exaltation of an unusual personality and the feeling that a new world hope had appeared.

This phase of Romanticism is best exemplified in the career of Baron Gros (1771–1835), another non-Davidian pupil of David. Reaching maturity at the height of the Revolution, Gros, unable to make a living in Paris, went to Italy. In Genoa he studied Rubens and Van Dyck, whose verve

and brilliant coloring are suggested in most of Gros' subsequent work. Through David he was introduced to the Napoleonic family and in 1796 he painted the still youthful *Napoleon at Arcola* (Fig. 22).

This work marks a serious break with the neo-Classical tradition in its violent realism, its freshness of attitude and color, and the brief momentary conception of action. The violent gesture of the future Emperor is paralleled by the Baroque composition, the rapid manner of applying colors, and the disordered hair that suggests both movement and emotional excitement. This heroic portrait, under the influence of

22. GROS: *Napoleon at Arcola* (Paris, Louvre).

Rubens, pleased Napoleon so much that he had the painting engraved and made Gros Inspector of Reviews, a rather vague but useful job that enabled him to mix with the troops and come into first-hand, but not too dangerous, contact with the war. In 1797 Gros was included in the commission appointed to loot the Italian museums, an important experience that familiarized him with many different styles, just as it was to do for future French painters examining these works in the Louvre.

After a series of harrowing adventures that showed him the war from close up, Gros returned to Paris in 1801, better equipped than any other artist of that day to paint war scenes. His painting of the *Battle of Nazareth*, in which General Junot had distinguished himself, was interrupted by a commission for *The Pest House at Jaffa* (Fig. 23), celebrating a visit to that sad institution by Napoleon himself.

Scorning ordinary military glory, the Emperor chose to have himself shown as a humanitarian and Christian, unafraid of the most horrible of deaths as he walks among the patients touching their plague sores with his bare hand. He stands there with the typical religious look that Gros gives him in these pictures, almost Christ-like in his abnegation and symbolically healing with his touch. To the heroic and highly personalized attitude of the compassionate conqueror, the artist has added the exotic atmosphere of a mosque courtyard and a series of strong contrasts of light and dark.

Unclassical in its abandonment of the bas-relief ideal, the composition is still well controlled, with the First Consul shown at the center of an ellipse of dead and dying. Although Gros had not witnessed this scene personally, he had obtained eyewitness accounts. Moreover, in the interests of what we can call Romantic Realism he changed the locale of the story from a simple hospital to a mosque, so as to convey the true local color of the Near East. What we have, then, is a contemporary, highly emotionalized, and piteous scene rendered in terms of an exact knowledge of the milieu and the people.

The religious character of this work is one of its most striking features, from the piety of Napoleon's attitude to the figures at the left distributing

23. GROS: *The Pest House at Jaffa* (Paris, Louvre).

bread, and the reverse symbolism of the doubting Thomas putting his fingers into the wounds of the Lord, as Napoleon touches the sick man. Without realizing it, Gros has given us one of the first "colonial" pictures. The waving tricolor on the hill is complemented by the Frenchman's pious assumption of the "white man's burden" as he deplores the sufferings of the conquered, sufferings of which he himself is the cause.

Gros' realism is shown not only in the perfection of local color but also in such details as the nude giant in the center foreground tearing his hair in agony, the blinded patient at the extreme right groping about, and the dying soldier seated immediately below him with the protective mask slipping from his mouth.

In his next important battle picture, *Napoleon at the Battle of Eylau* (Fig. 24), Gros chooses to show the aftermath of the conflict (February 9, 1807) with the same merciful figure as before. The mournful realism of the landscape suggests Victor Hugo's description of the snowy plains of Russia across which the *Grande Armée* would retreat five years later. Again the picture is built up around the idea of compassion, to which is now added the element of worship.

With his men looking on admiringly, the Lithuanians press forward to embrace Napoleon's knees. Even the horribly realistic dead enemy, lying across the body of a Frenchman and still clutching him about the throat, does not prevent the latter from raising his dying arm to salute the Leader. To the right of this snowy horror, another Frenchman tries to help a frightened Lithuanian, but the ungrateful Slav is more concerned with his own skin than with the benefits of French civilization. Through it all Napoleon sits on his horse, his eyes actually rolling heavenward, whites exposed, the picture of piety and pity.

As in the *Pest House*, the artist insists on exact detail, since this picture by a war-experienced man is meant to convey a specific message in his usual realistic terms. Romantically speaking, we have the distant milieu, outspoken nationalism, a feeling of pity, exaltation of the Emperor's personality, and a religious accent. Again paralleling the *Pest House*, where the personalities shown are definite people, we find here the picturesquely dressed General Murat mounted on a rearing horse to the right of Napoleon. This is the same

24. GROS: *Napoleon at the Battle of Eylau* (Paris, Louvre).

Murat who led the attack on the citizens of Madrid the following year (Fig. 18). It is interesting to note not only that Gros thought in terms of specific individuals, but that the public, in its response to these works, criticized them in the same manner. Moreover, it was not at all inconsistent to portray the rather distressing sentiment of the *Jaffa* or *Eylau* type together with the most outspoken realism. It should be clear by now that Romanticism is not incompatible with realism but rather the reverse. Whatever the artists in this category wish to depict, whether the propagandistic pity of Gros' pictures or the attempted escape into another environment of Delacroix, the effect is always more successful as the details are more convincing.

Although Gros' work up to this point was part of the contemporary situation, he soon fell victim to the taste for medieval bric-a-brac, part of the nationalistic interests of the time soon to be utilized by the Bourbons for their own propaganda. At the *salon* of 1812, Gros showed his *Francis I and Charles V Visiting the Abbey of St. Denis*, one of the first instances of a historical picture with all the Romantically theatrical accessories. All the famous people of the sixteenth century are shown in this work as realistically as the artist was able to paint them, but the element of conflict is lacking. There is no question of pity or other strong emotion, just a simple pious narrative with picturesque costumes. Pictures of this type are bound to be less interesting than the battle scenes.

From that time on, the career of Gros is less specifically Romantic, but interesting for personal reasons. Apparently the kind of man who needed an idol, Gros attached himself to the Bourbons after 1816, the year that David, because of his Revolutionary past, had to flee into exile. The "school" fell into the hands of Gros who, partly out of faithfulness to his old teacher and partly because there were no more battles to paint, tried to "open his Plutarch" again and paint in the "noble style." Obviously, the author of the *Jaffa* and the *Eylau* was in an ambiguous position, for both public and students clamored for more pictures like them. His singlehanded attempt to stem the tide of Romanticism gradually alienated pupils, public, and critics. By 1835 he was openly derided for his large mythological opus, *The Horses of Diomede*, and on June 25 of that year he committed suicide.

In spite of his swerve from the original path, the painting of Gros, like that of Girodet, is not only an important link in the Romantic chain but as perfect an expression of the Napoleonic period as can be found. Trained to do a specific job, he was lost when the necessity for his work no longer existed. We must turn to others for the story of the post-Napoleonic era.

4. GÉRICAULT AND DELACROIX

As the French Revolution swept away the monarchical state, it unleashed economic, political, and cultural forces that were ultimately to change the world. Its ideals left their mark in spite of the regressions of Napoleonic opportunism, a militaristic aftermath, and eventual political reaction. Occasionally the clock might still be turned back but not permanently. Whatever else happened in the years after the Revolution, the individual now moved forward conscious of his new-found freedom. Within a short time after, he was swimming in the tide of economic competition for better or worse.

Napoleon had given France internal security for fifteen years and great reforms, such as the *Code Napoléon*, an educational system, and efficient central administration. These benefits were vitiated by his desire to create a "new order" in Europe. His understanding with the Church was a by-product of this dictatorial purpose. We shall see both facts reflected in the art of that day.

The Napoleonic aftermath was a period of great confusion. From 1815 to 1851 we find various types of government tried in France as a result of the different social and political urges. On the extreme Right, there were many trying to wipe out the memory of the Revolution with a program of absolute monarchy supported by a cooperative aristocracy and clergy. These gentlemen showed their hand throughout the century as the unfailing enemies of reform and republicanism—and any new art forms. Slightly to the Left, the constitutional monarchists (aristocratic membership) stood near the constitutional monarchists (middle-class membership). Another important element of the political mixture during the first half of the century was the conservative peasantry, respecting king and Church, suspicious of

45

MOORE INSTITUTE
LIBRARY
SCHOOL OF DESIGN FOR WOMEN

Paris, and approving only the land reforms of the Revolution. Finally, there was the new working class without rights but literate. Although these workers believed in the Revolution, there was no party to express their point of view. At that time they strung along with the Liberals; later they were to become Socialist and even Communist.

For us, as for the French, the salient fact emerging from this period is a tradition of political instability. Security could only be maintained by coalition governments and then for no more than ten or twelve years at a time. Any group trying to rule France by itself failed—perhaps because of the Napoleonic example. As for the Church, its involvement in the politics of this period, and generally on the unsuccessful side, drove the lower classes away from it. At the end of the century it lost its political power completely, but still remained a factor to be reckoned with.

A general loosening of strictures during this period enabled artists to exhibit more freely, but now they had to please different and less informed patrons, the newly empowered middle classes and for a short time the Napoleonic nobility. The patrons of the post-Napoleonic era still believed however, that the only way for an artist to express himself was in the highly respected and traditional neo-Classical manner.

The dazzling speed with which the bourgeoisie had come to power left little time for the development of a middle-class art such as we find earlier in Holland. It was more rational for them to retain the antique style that had established itself during the latter part of the eighteenth century, particularly since this style symbolized respectability and tradition. The naturalistic middle-class art (Chardin) that had been started during the previous century did not possess the necessary dignity. Nor did the moral indignation of Greuze against the aristocracy fill the needs of a new situation where the virtuous had become the masters. Because of its inherent poise and balance, only the neo-Classical style—symptom of an earlier desire to find the ideal state—could fulfill the necessities of the new middle-class society and its crying need for stability.

What had been a progressive art form in the eighteenth century was now a tool of conservatism and of the desire to maintain the *status quo*. Every attempt to deviate from this prescribed norm was looked upon with suspicion and treated with scorn, hatred, and vilification. Neo-Classical and Renaissance art were to remain the symbols of respectability. It was only natural that the new middle class should be conservative; it is equally understandable that it should have expressed itself conservatively. On the other hand, we can also appreciate how this confused period of reactionary domestic politics, Holy Alliance police methods, and the beginnings of modern industrial problems should have produced new spiritual and cultural needs.

The intellectuals of the post-Napoleonic period had newer things to say, things that could not be expressed in the formal and austere technique of either Greco-Roman or Renaissance art. These things included, among others, nationalism, glorification of the Emperor (first as a symbol of freedom and then as a symbol of individuality), protest against the growing materialism of the age, hatred of oppression, sympathy for the downtrodden, and personal reaction to the vastness of nature. Such needs, let it be remembered, must be expressed by men and women who feel themselves free. For the expression of such ideas, the formal and prescribed patterns were too few and inadequate. Newer techniques and unused subjects had to be—and would be—developed. It is because of this conflict of views between traditional and more modern ideas that the artist would ultimately be isolated. Already during the Romantic period men like Géricault and Delacroix were made to feel outside the pale. The gap between the public and the artist becomes wider and wider, as the former refuses to accept and understand what the latter is doing. The artist in turn begins to express himself more and more in a language of his own, understandable to his own few followers and friends. In the time of Géricault and Delacroix it became perfectly clear that the conflict was primarily one involving the manner rather than the subject matter of painting.

The form of the artist's expression (for Romantics as for others) is conditioned to a great extent by techniques and subjects borrowed from those sections of the past and present that fit his needs best. It is not a conscious process in any case but rather a gradual finding of a particular mode that suits his personality or his aesthetic. Thus the conservative or academic painters refer back to the Renaissance and classical antiquity for their ideas while the Romantics lean toward the melodramatic art of the seventeenth century, the Baroque, for support. We may go one step further and note that in any period of the history of art, ancient or modern, the borrowings of any artist or school of artists are conditioned by the existing proclivities. The young men of the early nineteenth century walking through the newly opened Louvre could find on its walls almost anything they needed for direct or indirect expression of the new age.

The same considerations that condition the novel techniques of the "modern" painter also influence his choice of subject. New needs engender new subjects and these also compromise the position of the nonconformist artist. During the Romantic versus Classical period, the first half of the century, the conflict was more stylistic than anything else. In the third quarter, the emphasis shifted to subject. After that, it became mainly a quarrel over the proper means of painting.

The history of the nineteenth century became the story of the "ins" against the "outs," the constant and unending quarrel between "accepted" artists and the "declassed." Romanticism, perhaps the most important and original movement of the century, was dedicated to the dissolution, or at least the defeat, of the entrenched academies whose members received critical favor as well as public acclaim and commissions. In the minds of the conservative public and critics, the "new" artists were associated with intellectual and even political radicalism. Undoubtedly, Géricault and Delacroix sympathized with the oppressed, as did Byron, Hugo, and many others, but this defense of the rights of the individual could not properly be classed as political in the modern sense. Often the artist seemed to feel that his reaction to this great indignity was more important than the offense itself.

Above all, this was the century of the "I," the century in which the individual, because of his enforced isolation from society, began to think of himself not only as a special creature but as a genius. This attitude permitted and even forced him to express himself differently, to act differently. Eventually this led to the Bohemianism of the end of the century.

The uncongenial environment against which many of the Romantic artists revolted finally drove them into psychological isolation, into exploration of the cultures of the past as a means of escape. This was facilitated by the great advances in archaeology, the development of means of travel and communication that brought them more easily in contact with exotic places, and finally by the increased interest in comparative philology, literature, and religion. In this way, the artist had spread before him a variety of ideas and forms to which he might have recourse as compensation for his spiritual exile.

These tendencies are exemplified in the more dynamic viewpoint of Géricault and Delacroix, as contrasted with Girodet and Gros, who typified the picturesque piety and the military

25. GÉRICAULT: *Officer of the Imperial Guard* (Paris, Louvre).

expansionist tendencies of their time. The Romanticism of Géricault and Delacroix is a form of protest emitted in direct terms for a time, then retreating into a kind of escapism that is still rebellion against an uncongenial environment. While the earlier Romantics fitted into their background, these later exponents stand away from it in sharp relief.

At the 1812 *salon*, where Gros had shown his picture of Charles V and Francis I, a powerful equestrian portrait by the then unknown Théodore Géricault (1791–1824) was hung. This *Officer of the Imperial Guard* (Fig. 25), although in the same Rubens tradition as the large pictures of Gros, had nothing to do with the latter's type of glorification. As the first of a series of horse and rider studies, it stems from the painter's interest in horses and is part of his interpretation of the most important class of men of that time, soldiers. The horse springs up from the lower left-hand corner diagonally to the opposite side in a typically Baroque manner, the head of the animal slightly turned back while the body of the rider faces the spectator. Barely touching the ground as it bounds along, the tips of the horse's hind legs seem to strike sparks from the rocks beneath. If anything is being glorified in this picture, it is the horse.

49

Educated in the studios of Vernet and Guérin (the latter a strong classicist who trained a good many of the young Romantics), Géricault studied Rubens intensively, much to the despair of his teacher. The *Officer of the Imperial Guard*, a distinctly Rubensesque work, is not the product of any military experience but the result of his having seen an interesting dapple-gray in the course of his frequent visits to stables, race courses, and horse auctions. Using his friend Lieutenant Dieudonné as a model, Géricault finished this exciting piece of animal realism in twelve days. As a painting dedicated to force and movement, it strikes the keynote of his entire production.

Shortly after completing his *Wounded Officer* (1814), he left for Rome, partly because of a love affair and partly in search of local color. His almost mystical approach to horses expands in the picturesque *Riderless Horse Races in Rome* (Paris, Louvre), a work filled with passionate action and Michelangelesque physical striving. The men struggling with the horses move diagonally as before, their powerful muscles rippling under the skin. Man against the forces of nature, even in this somewhat symbolic form, is one of the constants of Romantic art. The visit to Rome, for Géricault as for other Romantics, had nothing to do with archaeological research. It was rather a sentimental thing similar to the nostalgic Italianism of Goethe's *Mignon*, as well as a search for the kind of local color we see in the *Riderless Horse Races*.

Géricault returned to Paris in 1818, when opinions were sharply divided over the disaster of the transport, Medusa, that had gone down off the coast of Africa leaving only a handful of survivors. In abandoning ship, the officers had taken the lifeboat and placed the crew on a large raft. For a few days they towed the raft over the torrid African waters and then set it adrift. Weeks later, when the raft was sighted by a passing vessel, most of the men had died of thirst or madness. It was this story that Géricault immediately decided to paint.

The *Raft of the Medusa* (Fig. 26), one of the most important paintings of the nineteenth century, is a monument of pathos and despair expressing in cumulative form the force and emotional power of the subject, the artist's anger at the suffering of his fellow creatures. The Michelangelesque

26. GÉRICAULT: *Raft of the Medusa* (Paris, Louvre).

strength of the tense seminude forms and the melodramatic lighting and receding diagonal pyramid, stemming from Baroque art (Caravaggio), are combined in a brilliant example of nineteenth-century eclectic Realism. With his characteristic energy, Géricault located the survivors in a hospital and got the ship's carpenter to construct a raft. Some of these unfortunate men were persuaded to pose together with friends of the artist—the bearded figure at the extreme left is supposed to be Delacroix. Not satisfied yet, Géricault haunted the Paris hospitals to study suffering and dying people. When the *Raft* was finally shown, there was a great deal of unfavorable criticism from official sources and shortly after Géricault went off to England.

As a painter of human suffering, Géricault is just as Romantic as Gros, except that now the group is shown as the hero instead of an individual. David had thought in terms of the individual and Gros had shown the individual emerging from the mass, but in the *Raft*, or in the *Liberation of the Negroes* and the *End of the Inquisition*, which are later works of Géricault, larger groups of people become the protagonists. Yet this does not

51

make Géricault any the less Romantic, since he still asserts his sympathy for the various forms of suffering. The real difference between Gros and Géricault lies in the fact that the latter protests, while Gros approved and glorified.

Géricault felt more at home in a comparatively liberal England and during his stay there produced a series of brilliant animal studies. These works demonstrate the fundamentally Realistic nature of this painter's art and foreshadow some of the horse pictures of Degas and Lautrec in their vividness, spontaneity, and momentary quality. *Derby at Epsom* (Fig. 27) marks a serious advance over the stylized hunting pictures of England; together with his lithographs of prize fighters, stable dogs, and certain disturbing but typically London scenes of misery, it reveals Géricault as the first modern Realist.

Upon his return to France, Géricault continued to seek out unusually Realistic subjects. An excellent opportunity came in a visit to a mental institution, where he set down the faces of some of the inmates. *The Mad*

27. GÉRICAULT: *Derby at Epsom* (Paris, Louvre).

52

Assassin (Fig. 28) is one of the more exciting pictures of the period—so vivid and psychologically Realistic that it removes Géricault from the conventional Romantic category. Pictures of this sort fit our loose definition of Romanticism by their unusualness and their interest in the fate of the individual and his misfortunes. Whether the artist understood madness as we do today, as a form of retreat from reality, is improbable, but it is clear that he felt the isolation of the unfortunate mad person.

28. GÉRICAULT: *The Mad Assassin* (Ghent, Museum of Fine Arts).

There was still no sharp dividing line between Romanticism and Realism after the time of Géricault (*e.g.*, Daumier and Courbet), but even a definitive classification of this painter is rather difficult. Like the novelist Stendhal, he was a keen observer and Realist far ahead of his time, indulging in the kind of social protest that was more appropriate to the middle of the century and after; and then, too, we find no painter as direct and meaningful as he. His popularity among modern painters arises partly out of this protest element but even more because of the violent emotional outpourings reflected in such works as *The Raft of the Medusa*.

It is interesting to speculate what would have happened if Géricault had not fallen from his horse at the age of thirty-three and died. Would his art have developed finally into the first full-blown example of modern Realism, anticipating the paintings of Daumier and Courbet? Keeping in mind the social conditions in France and the repressions of the time, it is much more likely that he would have been forced into the kind of psychological retreat represented by the work of his friend Delacroix. For his own period, even though Géricault shares with Gros an interest in human suffering and the general Romantic attention to details of local color plus a constant interest in force and motion, he stands away from the movement as a whole.

53

With Eugène Delacroix (1798–1863), the leader and most typical of French Romantic painters, the issue is somewhat clearer. The most discussed of artists even in his own day, his career brings into sharp relief the incipient conflict between the free artist and middle-class society. For the first time, the conservative viewpoint of moneyed people and the almost malevolent misunderstanding of critics, both implacably opposed to innovations in art, emerged to plague the future development of painting. Delacroix, who by the age of twenty-six had already painted his sensational *The Barque of Dante* (Fig. 29) and *The Massacre at Scio* (Fig. 30), was to remain for the rest of his life a controversial figure.

Today, when his genius as a painter is acknowledged and understood, Delacroix's other talents are much less known. For these, one must turn to the published letters of the painter and the rich and varied material of his famous *Journal*. Here his critical estimates of the artists, writers, and musicians of his time are worthy of a great literary man, and no less a writer than Baudelaire has testified to their merit. As a rule, artists are not notably articulate either as authors or as critics, but with Delacroix the painter and the writer are two different people. We would read the *Journal* even if it had been done by someone else.

The many-sidedness of Delacroix's culture extended to his wish to be a poet and musician as well. He is known to have had a very well-developed musical sense, particularly for the composers of the eighteenth century. In his paintings the wide variety of literary subject matter, from medieval history to Shakespeare, Scott, Byron, and Goethe, indicate again a well-nourished mind. Artistically, though we think of him as a figure painter, he was an outstanding landscapist, a water-colorist of rare delicacy (especially the wonderful papers done in North Africa), and one of the best illustrators of the nineteenth century.

Although titular leader of the Romantic school, Delacroix had no great respect for such poets as Lamartine, who impressed him as a child, or George Sand, to whom he referred as "poor Aurora." The only Romantic for whom Delacroix had a sincere admiration and love was Chopin, though their characters and intellectual attainments were markedly different. By the same token, few of the Romantic poets were impressed by him or his work, the explanation for these apparent paradoxes lying perhaps in the exaggerated individuality that prevented complete admiration and self-subjugation. Yet the association between artists and writers, begun at this time and solidified in the heat of conflict against a conservative society, was to continue to the present day. Delacroix himself wrote criticism for the *Revue des deux mondes,* the *Moniteur,* and others.

The duality in Delacroix's nature is based on his thinking of himself as a classicist—for example, his preference for Mozart over Beethoven. Although he acknowledged the importance of new and inspirational creations, they would have to be beautiful enough and consistent enough in character to take their place in the historical evolution of art. For an intellectual of this type to look upon himself as a link in the historical chain is entirely in character. Cézanne, a half century later, attempted to "re-do" Poussin in modern terms or, in other words, to make of Impressionism "an art as solid and as durable as the art of the museums." Delacroix's

29. DELACROIX: *The Barque of Dante* (Paris, Louvre).

55

work must be analyzed somewhat similarly, as an attempt to achieve final and definitive crystallizations of the Romantic point of view and technique—final for his own time, just like the work of Cézanne. The poet Baudelaire, a great admirer of Delacroix, said of him that "he was passionately enamored of passion, and coldly determined to find a means of expressing passion in the most visible terms."

Paralleling his written preference for the works of the Venetians and Rubens, the pictorial sources of Delacroix's mature style are to be found in these masters. His early work, like *The Barque of Dante* (Fig. 29), combines Baroque melodramatic lighting with the naked, writhing forms of his friend Géricault. Its accent upon pathos and conflicting emotions recommended it to Gros and Géricault, as well as to the famous statesman, Thiers, through whose influence it was purchased for the state.

Two years later his *The Massacre at Scio* (1824, Fig. 30), a scene from the Greek war of independence that had stimulated the imagination and sympathy of so many Romantics (especially Byron), brought his house tumbling about his ears. Even Gros, who had been one of his strongest supporters, turned away from him, referring to the picture as the "Massacre of Painting."

Neither the subject nor the grimly realistic treatment of suffering Greeks would have aroused this antagonism in a public accustomed to the horrors of Gros' battle pictures. Delacroix, however, had not only unbalanced the composition in the interest of additional emotional effect but he had enriched his palette in such a vivid and violent fashion that critics spoke of his painting as having been done with a drunken broom. The clear vibrant color with which he had loaded his brush, in contrast to the heavy impasto of Gros or even his own earlier work, was the factor that was regarded as revolutionary.

Delacroix's new color orientation was apparently due to the presence of a number of Constable's pictures at the salon of 1824, particularly *The Hay Wain* (Fig. 53). The story goes that on seeing Constable's brilliant landscape, Delacroix asked for permission to take his picture home and rework it in the cleaner colors of the Englishman. More likely, the young Romantic touched up his picture in the course of the "varnishing" attendant on such exhibitions; but the impact of Constable on Delacroix at this moment is fairly obvious.

For Delacroix's purpose of heightening emotion, the compositional and bravura effects of Baroque art could be amplified by the vivid highlighting and juxtaposition of complementary colors in the work of Constable. The

30. DELACROIX: *The Massacre at Scio* (Paris, Louvre).

technique of strengthening colors in this fashion was very interesting to Delacroix, whose observations of the bluish shadow on a yellow carriage or the mutually reinforcing quality of red and green were anticipations of later Impressionist practice. Although the specific effect of Constable on Delacroix is probably exaggerated, there are some tangible results in the landscape work of the Frenchman. Moreover, Constable did offer the artists of the first half of the century an independent and individualistic manner of seeing nature that was important for the development of modern painting.

57

Delacroix's interest was not in vivid color and action for their own sake but rather as a device for the expression of a psychological attitude. In the sketch for *The Death of Sardanapalus* (Fig. 31), one of the most exciting things he did and superior to the finished painting, he has shown the story of the dying monarch who wished his favorite people and animals to accompany him to the world beyond. The tragic horror of this idea is reflected in the energetic and powerful gestures of the executioners in contrast to the almost somnolent posture of the king. Bathed in luminous, broken, and shimmering color, the picture conveys the megalomaniac fury of the king in a highly disturbing Expressionistic manner.

In 1831 Delacroix presented an allegory of *Liberty Leading the People*, usually known as *La Barricade* (Fig. 32), reflecting the recent events of the Revolution of 1830. A powerful, symbolic, feminine figure dressed in

31. DELACROIX: *The Death of Sardanapalus*—sketch (Germantown, Pa., Henry B. McIlhenny Collection).

32. DELACROIX: *La Barricade* (Paris, Louvre).

flowing robe and revolutionary bonnet leads a group across the traditional barricades, a gun in one hand and the tricolor in the other. Although reminiscent of the battle pictures of Gros, the dramatically conceived and recumbent figures in the foreground are more suggestive of *The Raft of the Medusa* of Géricault or the *Shooting of the Citizens of Madrid* of Goya (Fig. 18), especially in their stark horror.

This combination of realism and symbolism is a Romantic expression of the general dissatisfaction of the time. It is socially conscious and revolutionary in the same general sense as the contemporary battle between the Classicists and the Romantics at the first performance of Victor Hugo's *Hernani*, when the respective factions actually came to blows. The former represented traditionalism and the latter rebellion and individualism, yet neither group was political as such but rather symptomatic of the opposing political trends of the day.

In spite of the trepidation of the government, *La Barricade* was purchased for the state at the instance of Thiers, a great admirer of the painter. The picture was apparently turned to the wall so as to do a minimum of political damage. It seems that a good many of Delacroix's pictures were bought for the nation through this support which, some assume, was a result of the artist's relationship to the great Talleyrand, whose illegitimate son he is supposed to have been. Similar pressure perhaps accounts for Delacroix's receiving the Legion of Honor (1831).

After 1830, the year of the second Revolution, protest subjects such as *The Raft of the Medusa*, *Greece Expiring*, *The Massacre at Scio*, and *La Barricade* were very rare. The only artists to speak up against reactionary government were the newspaper cartoonists and they were suppressed by 1835. Romantic painting took another direction.

Return of the Bourbons in 1816 had brought government encouragement of subjects taken from earlier French history which stressed the continuity of the royal house. This had ceased temporarily during the Revolution and the Napoleonic interlude. Now once again the past was glorified in such a way that not only historical paintings but also illustrations of literature dealing with the past became popular, as in Sir Walter Scott. With resumption of contact with the rest of Europe, foreign literature in general was joyfully received. This affection for the works of Scott, Goethe, Shakespeare, etc., gave the new movement its rather peculiar title, *le style troubadour*. To this school of expression belong Gros' pre-Bourbon picture of *Francis I and Charles V Visiting the Abbey of St. Denis*, Delacroix's later *Battle of Poitiers*, *Battle of Nancy*, and others, and his many literary illustrations.

After his success with *La Barricade*, Delacroix went to Spain, Morocco, and Algeria as part of a diplomatic mission (1832). From this trip he brought back many vivid impressions of Mediterranean sunlight and strange subjects soon to be shown in his exotic paintings. Paintings like *Algerian Women* (Paris, Louvre) are doubly important because of the exact rendering of local color and the psychological interpretation of characters. One has but to compare this work with eighteenth-century "Oriental" paintings to see how far it has come from the older masquerades in which Frenchmen were dressed as Easterners. Delacroix's work becomes possible because modern

33. DELACROIX: *The Tiger Hunt* (Paris, Louvre).

economic and political expansion permit the direct contact and observation necessary for accurate painting of environment, physiognomy, and character.

Many vivid and exciting studies of exotic animals and hunting scenes stem from this same contact with the Near East. *The Tiger Hunt* (Fig. 33) although reminiscent of Rubens in its dash and diagonal emphasis, is much more Expressionistic in feeling and more loosely painted. Although we are not too sure that Delacroix witnessed an actual hunting scene of this sort, he re-created the local color after a lapse of many years. Greater importance lies in the feeling of frenetic energy expressed in this and indeed in most of his paintings. In spite of the influence of Rubens, he had little of that master's ability as a draftsman. Actually, he was interested in color rather than in drawing, and his most convincing works are the result of a sparkling color applied in a highly individualistic manner. Sometimes, in a completely immobile subject such as the *Christ on the Cross* (Paris, Louvre), we feel the lack of solidity. The more his figures move about, the more successful

61

the picture. We are told that his models were allowed to walk around while he painted them in action. Sometimes, in fact, he did not begin to work until they had left.

As a typical Romantic, Delacroix was very much interested in historical, especially medieval, subject matter derived either directly from history or from historical novels. The choice of subject was always influenced by the "unusual" possibilities of the scene, as with *Tasso in the Madhouse* or the *Entry of the Crusaders into Constantinople* (Paris, Louvre). In the latter painting, for example, instead of the more conventional entry into Jerusalem, he brings them into the most "marvelous" city of the Middle Ages, Constantinople. Again emphasis is placed upon pathos as the old man pleads with the soldiers to spare him and his family. The picturesque spectacle of the already burning city forms a background for the Gros-like contrast between the elegance of the crusaders and the misery of the people.

Delacroix's interest in literary illustrations is best exemplified by his famous series of lithographs for Goethe's *Faust*, which drew considerable praise from the giant of Weimar. The French artist goes beyond mere illustration, developing the story in his own personal fashion. Typically

34. DELACROIX: *Hamlet and Horatio* (Paris, Louvre).

Romantic, he chooses from literature the things that allow the greatest individual or "unusual" development. *Hamlet and Horatio* (Fig. 34), for example, developed from the well-known gravedigger scene, shows a distinctly mournful landscape, cloudy skies, and a wind that blows the clouds as well as the plumes in the hat of the melancholy Dane. Types like Hamlet, Ophelia, and Macbeth appeal to Delacroix because of their psychological problems, their conflict with the world.

One of the outstanding intellectuals of the period, Delacroix was on terms of intimacy with its leading writers, artists, and musicians. His portrait of the celebrated violin virtuoso, *Paganini* (Fig. 35), is one of the painter's most personal and Romantic pictures. Though it is not a portrait in the ordinary sense—many of his "portraits" are emotional studies rather than transcriptions of physiognomy— the *Paganini* is one of his most vivid and Expressionistic efforts. The unusually tall, mysteriously swaying figure here seems part of the painter's desire to show an otherworldly force and power as well as a continuity of sound. Light falls sharply on face and hands in contrast to the darkness on the body. The exaggerated length of the figure, the enlarged head, and the

35. DELACROIX: *Paganini* (Washington, Phillips Memorial Gallery).

enormous hands engulfing the violin add to a feeling of power and mystery and of a vibrant and unusual personality, the strange effect produced by the playing of this great fiddler.

The emphasis on movement in the work of Delacroix can be contrasted vividly with the neo-Classical and neo-Renaissance attitude of this time. Ingres, for example, did a portrait drawing of Paganini, but in his treatment (Fig. 40), instead of the frightening absorption of Delacroix's figure, we see a placid and serene individual, clearly and precisely drawn, the violin tucked under his arm, posing for his picture very calmly. On the other hand, the Romantic painter's picture with its extremely personal and psychological quality, its vague and mysterious mood, rendered with arbitrary lighting and vivid color, sums up his own work and the neo-Baroque phase generally.

The year 1832 marked the dividing line in the career of Delacroix. For one thing, it was the end of his pictures of protest. Moreover, his trip to Spain and North Africa offered him a fulfillment of the Romantic's desire to be part of an exotic milieu. Its effect on his art was twofold: first, it gave him a subject matter to which he returned for the rest of his life, and then it reinforced whatever ideas he had had concerning luminous color. In the brilliant sunlight of Algiers and Morocco he became particularly conscious of the effect of complementary colors, thus forging the first link in the chain *From Eugène Delacroix to Neo-Impressionism* (title of the much later book by Paul Signac).

The final importance of 1832 in the chronology of Delacroix was the beginning of a long series of important mural commissions. Whatever the antagonism of critics and public, whatever the reluctance of the official art hierarchy to admit him to its ranks, the fact remains that building after building was enriched by his broad and sensitively felt wall decorations. The Palais Bourbon, the Luxembourg Palace, the Gallery of Apollo in the Louvre, the Salon de la Paix in the City Hall, and his last work in the Church of St. Sulpice were produced from 1833 until a few years before his death in 1863. Perhaps the shadowy influence of Talleyrand and Thiers accounts for his receiving these assignments, but in an age filled with academic and formal wall paintings the work of Delacroix stands out as one of the most important contributions of the nineteenth century.

It is in these creations that we feel the affinity between Delacroix and the Venetian decorators of the sixteenth century, Veronese and Tintoretto. The rich coloring, the occasional flying figure suspended in air or moving rapidly to accomplish its purpose, the relationship between painting and wall space, the feeling for human problems, all relate him to the finest traditional muralists without impairing his personal expression. At the same time, the murals reveal Delacroix as an artist with a feeling for patterned movement in the modern sense, as well as a colorist far in advance of his time. The St. Sulpice paintings, finished in 1861, show large and separated brush strokes designed to blend at a distance and to add brightness and strength to the color in a pre-Impressionist fashion.

The domination of the French school by Ingres throughout this time made it very difficult for Delacroix. It was not until after the Universal Exposition of 1855 that the great Romantic was to receive official recognition, although by that time he was already suffering from the disease that ultimately killed him. But his enemies at the Academy still kept after him as a symbol of everything they did not like, and he remained isolated until his death. Discounting the perhaps apocryphal legends surrounding the antagonism between Delacroix and Ingres, who was official leader of the conservative wing, it is still clear that the former symbolized individualism and revolt while the latter represented the *status quo*. This conflict was to plague the rest of the nineteenth century.

5. INGRES AND THE ACADEMICIANS

Although the pattern of development in modern painting would be much clearer if we could say that such and such a movement ended Tuesday and another began Wednesday, things are not quite that simple. Nor, by the same token, is it practical to assign general reasons for the emergence of a particular style and let it go at that. In the history of ideas—as in history itself—new forms result from the mutual reaction of a number of older ideas from which the new one finally emerges.

The chronology and mythology of the nineteenth century are full of accounts of the titanic struggle between Romantics and the so-called Classicists. Incidents such as the memorable battle between the two groups at the opening performance of Victor Hugo's *Hernani* in 1830 where, as some would have it, blood actually flowed, highlight the long drawn-out conflict.

If, as seems today fairly clear, both groups of artists portrayed subjects derived from religion, the early history of France, the Near East, and literature, the reasons for the quarrel might seem farfetched. When we note that the Classicists also show many of the emotional symptoms of the Romantics, such antipathy seems downright nonsensical. Yet when we examine the work of the warring groups, a profound difference in technique emerges, a difference that could not but cause trouble, especially in the light of the men involved and what they represented.

The return of the Bourbons in 1816 and the exile of David left a vacuum in French art which the newly born Romantics with their flaming emotionality and subject matter rushed to fill. For a while Gros attempted to stem the tide, but the painter of battles, try as he would, could not paint like David. Nor did the gradual diversion of artists from subjects such as

The Raft of the Medusa toward histories in *le style troubadour* solve the problem for the artistic and governmental authorities worried by Romantic individualism. It was not until 1824, when Ingres exhibited his *Vow of Louis XIII*, that a possible counterweight to the Romantics appeared.

To be sure, 1824 was a peculiar year in French art, what with the simultaneous exhibition of Constable's *The Hay Wain*, Delacroix's *The Massacre at Scio*, and the Renaissance-derived *Vow of Louis XIII* by Ingres. Even though for the Romantics this last-named picture was anti-Davidian, for the disorganized Classical painters it was clearly non-Romantic in its clarity, balance, and restraint. At any rate, a new leader was born.

Ingres became the spearhead of a movement dedicated to using the technique and, in many cases, reviving the spirit of the Italian Renaissance. Partly as a result of his example, partly because of the Christian revival that took place under the bourgeois monarchy in France, and for other reasons in England and Germany, neo-Renaissance painting was to become a European phenomenon. At its best, it produces the marvelous draftsmanship of an Ingres or the serene and subtle compositions of a Puvis de Chavannes; at its worst, it gives us the photographic illustrations of Couture or Delaroche. The difference between the good and the bad, here as in other forms of derivative painting, lies in the use to which the borrowed material is put. If a man dips into the past for a creative and dramatic purpose and emerges with something personal and formalistically meaningful, no one can begrudge him his borrowing. On the other hand, a mere pastiche of Renaissance or any other style, whose only purpose is telling a story that anyone can read, adds little to the sum total of art. It is this latter type of borrowing which we call academic.

The transition from the Doric severity of David to the Renaissance lineality of Ingres is bridged by such artists as Gérard. His art was affected by two different currents and softened thereby. The archaizing elegance of late Greek art seen in his *Cupid and Psyche* (Paris, Louvre) is also evident in the Directoire phase of David's painting and in the early work of Ingres. Renaissance chiaroscuro, which came to him through the example of Prud'hon (1758–1823), is an important ingredient in the work of other Davidian pupils who leaned toward Romanticism: Guerin, Girodet, and

Ingres himself. The example of Prud'hon is particularly important for our purposes here since his borrowing from the Renaissance includes both subject and technique, as in the *Rape of Psyche* (Paris, Louvre). In this picture Prud'hon, who had spent six years in Italy studying such masters as Leonardo and Correggio, gives us a combination of the sensuous charm of the latter master and the delicate haze with which Leonardo enveloped his figures. The motif of the goddess carried through the air by smiling cupids makes the derivation complete. This self-conscious emulation of the artists of the Renaissance, although perhaps questionable in its results here, is more successful in the work of Ingres.

Jean Auguste Dominique Ingres (1780–1867), one of the greatest drafts-men of the French school, came from an artistic family in the south of France. To them he owed not only his interest in painting but a love for music as well. His early flair for the violin, on which he gave a number of concerts as a boy, is reflected in his famous portrait drawing of *Paganini* (Fig. 40).

At the age of seventeen he was admitted to the studio of David, where he did very well. After a short time, however, serious differences developed and Ingres left in 1800. For one thing, Ingres felt that painting should be free of political implications—an altogether understandable sentiment for the later autocrat of French art. The fact that David preferred the specifically sculptural art of Rome with its hard contours, whereas Ingres as a boy of twelve had already been initiated into the mysteries of Italian Renaissance drawing, made the conflict sharper. The young pupil's interest in the ideas of *Les Barbus* (The Bearded Ones), a group of Davidians with a Romantic interest in the classical past, was the final element in the break between the two men.

Although Ingres was awarded the Prix de Rome two years after leaving David's studio, it was not until 1806 that the government had the money for the trip. He stayed in Italy a long time (Rome, 1806–1820; Florence, 1820–1824) because of the unfavorable criticism of works he sent to the annual *salons* in Paris. His interest in the nude, a lifelong preoccupation in spite of public apathy, irked the critics. His luck changed when he got the commission to paint *The Vow of Louis XIII* (Fig. 37) for the Cathedral of

Montauban. This picture was shown at the famous 1824 *salon*, together with Delacroix's *The Massacre at Scio* and Constable's *The Hay Wain*.

Preceding *The Vow of Louis XIII*, his first important work, *Oedipus and the Sphinx* (Fig. 36), had already shown the difference between his approach and that of David. Not only did Ingres soften the older man's forms but he already showed that interest in linear quality which marks so much of his work. At this early stage he was influenced by Greek vase painting, whose precise outlines are reflected in the figure of Oedipus. The vogue for this ancient art was due to

36. INGRES: *Oedipus and the Sphinx* (Paris, Louvre).

the work of the English painter Flaxman. As a theme, *Oedipus and the Sphinx*, like most of Ingres' classical subjects, differs from those of David in that it is more immediate and anecdotal. It uses the specific theme out of classical mythology to accentuate personal problems and relationships. This stress on the individual rather than the collective point of view makes it more Romantic than the work of David.

Although Ingres claimed he was interested in nature rather than ideal beauty, this painting shows the difference between what an artist says about his work and what he actually does. The setting is romantic and even dramatic with the cave atmosphere of Girodet and the figure at the right moving off in its flying drapery, but the form of Oedipus is much more ideal and typical of his later works. Some sort of Davidian influence is still perceptible because of the bas-relief effect rather than the accentuation of space.

Moving away from this combination of Greek drawing and Roman bas-relief toward the Renaissance, Ingres' conception of space—under the influence of Raphael—becomes more realistic and his line more flowing and sinuous. *The Vow of Louis XIII* (Fig. 37), where the king offers his

37. INGRES: *The Vow of Louis XIII* (Montauban, Cathedral).

crown and scepter to the Virgin, is romantically conceived and reminiscent of Raphael's *Sistine Madonna* (Dresden) in the drawn-back curtains, the beautiful quality of the Virgin, and the pyramidal composition.

Although the beginning of Ingres' public career coincided with Delacroix's, the reception accorded *The Vow of Louis XIII* was much more enthusiastic than that received by *The Massacre at Scio*. The Classicists approved because it tempered the extravagance of the "obnoxious" Romantics; while the latter, including Delacroix, wished it well since it seemed to give the death blow to the style of David. Yet *The Vow of Louis XIII* must be looked upon as part of the officially supported resistance to Romanticism that was to continue for a long time. It is no accident that the subject is monarchistic, that it not only glorifies the reigning dynasty but allies it quite clearly with the Church. Although well composed in the Renaissance sense, it is rather saccharine in sentiment and obviously derivative. Color in Ingres is almost invariably restrained and discreet, unlike that of the neo-Baroque Romantics, and more in keeping with the Classical point of view.

In spite of its defects—perhaps because of them—*The Vow of Louis XIII* marked the turning point in Ingres' career. From that moment he was destined to become one of the dominant figures in the art world of Paris, particularly since David was in exile, Girodet dead, and Gros going through the motions of being Romantic and Classic at the same time. In spite of his acknowledgment as head of the Classical group, the unenthusiastic reception of some of his pictures led him to accept the directorship of the French Academy in Rome.

When Ingres returned after a few years, there was no question of his domination of the school. For almost forty years he ruled with an iron hand, with pious respect for the neo-Classical point of view and high regard for authority and tradition; in his case this meant the Italian Renaissance, particularly Raphael, although he copied other masters as well. From earliest youth he had been taught to revere these masters whose qualities he now translated into nineteenth-century terms.

If David stands for solid sculpturesque forms and Delacroix for emotional color, Ingres is the archrepresentative of linear beauty. He is credited with once having said to his "enemy" Delacroix that "line is probity itself," which was supposed to put that purveyor of fire and brimstone in his place. Judging by the lack of recognition for the latter painter, perhaps it did. Ingres' positiveness and autocratic behavior in the art world admitted of no contradictions at all. It would be unreasonable to blame the stagnation of so much of French art during this period on him, as much as on the conditions that permitted such an individual to control the art world of Paris. Yet he himself was a great painter.

One of his most typical works is the *Odalisque* (Fig. 38), an exotic theme expressed in soft and undulating rhythmic lines carried in a half circle from

38. INGRES: *Odalisque* (Paris, Louvre).

71

the upper left to the upper right side of the picture. A certain classical reticence is shown in the nude turning away from the spectator, while the careful control of elements, as the line of the arm flows into the curtain, develops this idea further.

The *Odalisque* is a harem subject both in title and in the turban, fan, and jewels. Here, and in many works such as *Turkish Bath* and *Odalisque and Slave*, Ingres, the Romantic Classicist, illustrated exotic themes. But this is not done in the turbulent manner of Delacroix nor with that artist's feeling for local color. It is rather an aesthetic experiment in design and linear expression. Thus the fact that the woman holds the curtain has no particular psychological significance or inner meaning, though it is good for the swing of line. The aesthetic nature of the picture is emphasized by the head of the odalisque, so clearly derived from Raphael's *Madonna of the Chair* with its analogous interest in linear rhythms. As for the body, here the painter went back to the French Renaissance and its elongated Venuses of the Fontainebleau school, a mingling of elements that Raphael himself would have approved. Ingres' relative coldness is shown both in the hyperaesthetic treatment of a theme deliberately chosen for these possibilities and in the use of color purposely subordinated to his justly famous draftsmanship.

Scrupulous analysis of individual parts of a composition as well as the intensely detailed treatment of the whole tend to make the painting of Ingres more realistic than the art of David. Their common archaeological interests, however, place them in a similar neo-Classical position.

Ingres' classical borrowings have been noted in *Oedipus and the Sphinx* and its archaic line. More obvious examples may be found in his well-known *The Bather* (Fig. 39), the even more famous *La Source* (both in Paris, Louvre) and the lesser known *Stratonice* (Chantilly, Musée Condé). In the last-named example, not only has the painter borrowed from Greek pottery but in this instance he has lifted a whole composition intact from a krater now in the Munich Museum. As in the case of the *Odalisque*, the early work merely served as a point of departure for the creation of a personal and characteristic work that, from its showing in 1841 until the painter's death, left him the undisputed master of the French school.

In *The Bather*, Ingres again took a harem type and set her upright in an

72

Oriental interior, her back to the spectator, posed like one of the figures on a Roman sarcophagus that Napoleon brought back from Italy. This sculpture shows a Nereid riding a Triton in the same position as Ingres' bather, a bit of cloth similarly rolled about her elbow to give a comparable contrast between the rumpled cloth and the smooth skin. This very fact probably led the painter to choose the subject, for it gave him a fine opportunity to show the soft and undulating lines of a woman's back and its smoothness of surface. *The Bather* is warmer in quality than the *Odalisque* and closer to the flesh quality found in Raphael.

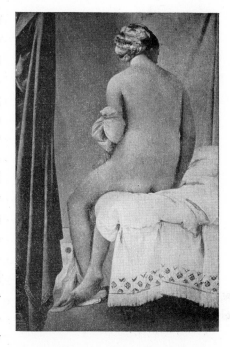

39. INGRES: *The Bather* (Paris, Louvre).

Although it is regarded as the most hackneyed of Ingres' paintings, *La Source* is interesting because of its academic borrowings. The classical composition framing the head between the arm and the urn goes back as far as Phidias' Amazon type and has survived in various gems and bas-reliefs. Ingres' version is apparently derived from the French Renaissance relief sculpture by Jean Goujon on the Fountain of the Innocents in Paris, where a draped figure holds a water jug in almost the same position.

The portraits of Ingres represent one of the most creative aspects of his art, both the numerous sensitive pencil sketches and the fine paintings. A great many of the drawings come from his youth in Italy where he made his living doing portraits of this kind for residents and tourists. The beautiful three-quarter-length *Paganini* (Fig. 40) is one of the finest examples. Dated "Roma, 1819," it comes from that period in his life when he was very friendly with the future virtuoso and even played in string quartets with him. Later in life, when the brilliant Italian had developed his characteristic pyrotechnical style, the strictly classical Ingres refused to have any-

40. INGRES: *Paganini*—drawing
(Paris, Louvre).

41. INGRES: *M. Bertin* (Paris, Louvre).

thing to do with him. The purity of line in Mozart (a second Raphael to Ingres) must not be sullied by the "ostentatious" cadenzas of the flashy Italian.

The contrast between the Ingres and Delacroix (Fig. 35) versions of Paganini, referred to earlier, may be understood better by observing the technical approach of the more conservative artist. Although apparently static, this drawing, like most of Ingres' works, has an inner movement and rhythm that comes from the flowing quality of line. Both violin and bow are arranged to parallel or continue the lines of the arms, forming a closed circle about the body. The emphasis is not placed on any unusual or emotive quality but rather on the fine and precise modeling of the head. In the Renaissance tradition of similar drawings by Holbein and Clouet, the nineteenth-century painter accentuates the head at the expense of the rest of the body. This example varies from his norm to the extent that he has wished to single out the violin that characterizes the individual. Beyond the linear arrangements, the *Paganini* consists of a series of recurrent dark accents from top to bottom that finally disappear in the thinly sketched trouser legs. This type of drawing, linked to the

74

Renaissance in method and mood, forms the basis for the early portrait drawings of Degas.

The *Portrait of M. Bertin* (Fig. 41) brings out the highly developed descriptive faculties of Ingres. Here he shows with fine psychological insight the typical man of affairs of that age, the ponderous but energetic businessman in a characteristic posture, the extremely personalized hands on the knees. Motion within the figure is again achieved through the lines of the vest and the creases in the sleeves. Even the tousled hair has a certain movement comparable to the *Paganini*, while the circular pattern of the arms repeats the flowing contour of the chair back, with countercurves offered in the lines of the open coat.

More characteristic of Ingres' portrait production are his many studies of women, such as *Mme. d'Haussonville* (Fig. 42). In a severely mannered fashion reminiscent of the sixteenth-century paintings of Bronzino, Ingres sets his elongated figure into its space very cleverly, rendering the personality of the sitter with a strikingly objective naturalism. Although Ingres did not consider his portraits important, these paintings are a fine and sensitive record of the upper middle class of his day.

In spite of Ingres' preoccupation with formal analysis or individual parts, like most great artists he represents a form of abstraction and a movement away from obvious naturalism. The precise and carefully controlled outlines are no less important for this purpose than the frequently attentuated forms.

Among the followers of Ingres, the work of Théodore Chassériau (1819–1856) presents one of the most curious mixtures of all derivative painters in the nineteenth century. In spite of this and despite the small number of his surviving works—he died at thirty-seven, and his most important creations were destroyed during the Commune—he is, like his master Ingres, one of the few justifications of the academic process.

An extremely precocious individual, Chassériau entered the studio of Ingres at thirteen and within three years was represented at a *salon* exhibition. Although his early work was modeled after the subjects and technique of his teacher, he was also directly influenced by the Renaissance, as in his *Sleeping Venus* (Avignon), apparently derived from Giorgione. His personal background, however (he had been born in Santo Domingo), made

42. INGRES: *Mme. d'Haussonville* (New York, Frick Collection).

43. CHASSÉRIAU: *Peace* (Paris, Louvre).

the relative coldness of Ingres not entirely satisfactory. After a visit to Algiers, both subject matter and method began to show the influence of Delacroix, a "betrayal" that hurt Ingres deeply. Though a fusion of the opposed styles of Ingres and Delacroix may seem implausible, Chassériau's importance lies in just that fact. The fragment in the Louvre known as *Peace* (Fig. 43) is a warmer and more intense version of the fine draftsmanship of Ingres, endowed with a much better feeling for composition and action, and full of that languorous ardor so characteristic of the Creole temperament. This decoration is not the usual cold studio arrangement of his first teacher but an atmospheric and convincing evocation of a bygone and imaginary age.

Although many of Ingres' pupils worked in the Paris churches, it is no exaggeration, judging even from the pitiable fragments of Chassériau's creations, to say that he was one of the most inspired decorators of the century. Certainly when he is compared with men of reputation like Besnard who filled the public buildings of the capital with their careful and precise work, we see just how impressive is the decorative art of this master. In this field he can only be compared with Delacroix.

Public decoration is necessarily one of the strongholds of academic practice. In this area experimentation is only for extremely individualistic artists, since jobs commissioned by the government are bound to be weighted down with tradition and respectability. It was only natural that the recently enthroned middle class would favor the more established point of view. Even Delacroix, in spite of the relative freedom of even his mural work, in some instances felt it better to temper his style toward a more "acceptable" manner, instead of indulging in the "free and original expression of each painter's peculiar qualities."

Yet, if most nineteenth-century decorators of public buildings produced nothing more than uninspired repetitious borrowings from the past, there was one painter who within the limits of Renaissance-derived art produced a type of plastic expression that justifies the method. Pierre Puvis de Chavannes (1824–1898), like many of the neo-Renaissance artists, is a combination of restrained technique and Romantic yearning for the glories of the past. His paintings with their meticulous and carefully handled out-lines, their delicate subdued coloring, take us back to the early Florentine muralists. Yet he is not as forthright and sculpturesque as, for example, Giotto or Masaccio. His art suggests rather the more lyrical restrained qualities of Fra Lippo Lippi, for it is always thoughtful, always serene. He has been called a "thinker who paints" and in such wall decorations as *The Sacred Wood* (Fig. 44), one of a series for the Sorbonne in Paris, the almost mystical quality of his art is revealed.

Product of a period still dominated by the personality of Ingres, Puvis de Chavannes naturally went back to the early Renaissance for many of his formal ideas. Nevertheless in the abstractly patterned effect of his paint-ings he is more suggestive of the moderns than the photographic and detailed manner of many of his contemporaries. It is not without reason

44. PUVIS DE CHAVANNES: *The Sacred Wood* (Paris, Sorbonne).

that Gauguin, beginning his career toward the end of Puvis de Chavannes' life, found in the work of the older man the very decorative qualities, the linear rhythms, and almost Orientalized space that were to distinguish his own work.

For a long time it was fashionable to decry the deliberately delicate manner of this serene decorator; in an age overwhelmed by the violent expression of the great experimenters of the post-Impressionist period, it was perhaps natural. Yet it is not altogether without significance that Gauguin found in him what he needed or that Seurat and Lautrec admired him as well. It is even believed that Lautrec used to keep a large-size reproduction of *The Sacred Wood* in his studio.

Our own interests in the twentieth century have gone beyond the allegorical and philosophical figures and ideas that constitute Chavannes' vocabulary. It is still possible for us, however, to understand his emotional approach and technical contribution. *The Poor Fisherman* (Fig. 45), one of the best known of his easel paintings and a work that could just as easily have been a mural, is designed with the same regard for space pattern effects which we have seen before. Like his larger works, it consists of a series of more or less vertical areas inserted one behind the other. In this example, the alternating land and water spaces suggest the stylized space of Oriental art.

As for the emotional quality of *The Poor Fisherman*, a pious and restrained feeling is combined with the sense of psychological isolation and other-

79

45. PUVIS DE CHAVANNES: *The Poor Fisherman* (Paris, Louvre).

worldliness. Although its primitive Christianity may seem artificial for the late nineteenth century, it does fit in with a whole movement, not only in France but elsewhere. The fairyland atmosphere of Fra Lippo Lippi or Fra Angelico is re-created here in the ascetic praying figure of the man and the woman bending over the child, suggesting an Adoration composition. It is easy to see, though, how this French "pre-Raphaelite" feeling, less sensitively expressed, could become the banal emotion of the English, German, or French neo-Christian works at the end of the century.

By the time of Puvis de Chavannes, when the Romantic versus Classical conflict was only a memory, the respective preferences of the two schools had developed into a single, monotonous, academy practice. Both exotic and classical subjects were now precisely rendered in artificially controlled studio light. These academic painters catered to a very uninstructed public, turning out hundreds of infinitely detailed works, some Oriental in subject, others ancient, a good many historical, and a few mildly erotic in character. The only difference was the subject; otherwise, they all insisted on a detailed photographic story that could easily be understood in terms of the simplest illustration. The story was the important thing; of formal vitality and volume tensions, of compositional structure, these artists knew little and cared less.

What happened to the historical and exotic Romanticists of Delacroix's type is illustrated by the work of Hippolyte Delaroche (1797–1856), a student of Gros who felt himself closer to Ingres. His careful drawing allies him more to Renaissance drawing than to the tempestuous colors of the Romantics. With the public of Louis-Philippe's time his popularity was due to the fact that he was a sort of corrected or subdued Delacroix, able to offer "interesting" subject matter with a "correct" technique. *The Murder of the*

46. DELAROCHE: *The Two Princes in the Tower* (Paris, Louvre).

Duc de Guise, *The Execution of Lady Jane Grey*, or *The Two Princes in the Tower* (Fig. 46) show his so-called romantic ideas exploiting the melodramatic, the sentimental, and even the cheap. Some of Delaroche's "historical" paintings are not even factually accurate, though they are so "correctly" drawn.

An even more exaggerated instance of the academic approach is found in the work of Jean Louis Ernest Meissonier (1815–1891). The immense popularity of this artist, when weighed against his labored, illustrative technique, exemplified the taste of the second half of the century. Although he had experienced war at first hand as an officer in the Franco-Prussian War, his observations, judging by the famous *1814* (Fig. 47), are far removed from the vital emotionalized pictures of Gros. Meissonier, a miniaturist at heart, shows the final moments of the *Grande Armée* with the painfully photographic and scrupulously detailed manner of most academic historical painting. The sweep and force of Gros' Napoleonic material is lost here because Meissonier is more interested in showing the appearance of the army rather than the effect of the army.

47. MEISSONIER: *1814* (Paris, Louvre).

This difference between the emotive quality of Romantic art and the purely narrative interests of the academic historians was demonstrated rather dramatically in the 1938 Knoedler exhibition: "Gros, Géricault, Delacroix." Here a seldom shown and incomplete painting, Géricault's *The Retreat from Moscow* from the collection of the Duc de Trevise, shows a series of Expressionistically agonized figures writhing across the canvas. Without benefit of photographic detail, this study tells the story of that agonized march as excitingly as Victor Hugo's great poem with its vistas of endless snowy plains as the background for man's suffering. Where Géricault and Hugo symbolize the tragedy of defeat, Meissonier gives us an army on parade led by a surly general. Vollard describes a visit to Meissonier's studio where an assistant is preparing "the field of battle" with rice powder and boracic acid for snow over which toy ammunition wagons, guns, and soldiers are placed. Meissonier himself tells them: "When I painted my *Retreat from Russia*, instead of boracic acid I used caster sugar. What an effect of snow I obtained!" But when the bees came for the sugar and the mice for the flour, he had to finish his picture from imagination. "It almost looked as though I should have to wait for the snow to fall if I wanted to paint a winter landscape."

The so-called "historical" point of view was varied with classical narratives. Couture's famous *Romans of the Decadence* (Paris, Louvre) shows an antiquity just as carefully representational as the various academic treatments of the Middle Ages or the Renaissance. Nothing could be as dull or uninspired as this orgy or more minute in detail.

The fate of the exotic and Near Eastern subject is revealed in many pictures during Delacroix's own lifetime, works reduced to the same bright exactitude as in the so-called classical or medieval themes. Henri Regnault (1843–1871) illustrates this type with his *Execution without Trial under the Moorish Kings* (Paris, Louvre), where the primary concern of latter day Orientalism is to see that the accessories are easily legible. In the standard, cold, clear light of academy practice someone has had his head removed. Without the elaborate title the reason for this picturesque butchery would be somewhat obscure.

Perhaps the last major effusion of the academic spirit took place during

83

the second half of the century in England. A group of high-minded men, none of them, unfortunately, real painters, undertook to liberate England from the gross materialism of the Victorian period. In their idealistic attempts to glorify the higher values, the things of the spirit, they ignored the world about them. At a time when Daumier, Courbet, and Manet were dealing with the world of visible reality, they produced the pre-Raphaelite movement.

The very title indicates the technical source of their inspiration, the early Italian Renaissance when, theoretically at least, the Italian artist had not yet been contaminated by worldly Rome or carnal Venice. Led by such noble spirits as the poet Rossetti, Burne-Jones, Hunt, and Millais, the group attempted to re-create the unspoiled spirituality of the later Middle Ages in Italy. This attitude of the pre-Raphaelites was still part of the neo-Christian movement of the early part of the century, the period of Chateaubriand and Mme. de Staël. In Germany a group of painters, later consolidated as the Nazarenes, produced a somewhat similar pictorial philosophy.

During the course of the Romantic movement in France neo-Christian symptoms had developed as part of the trend toward medievalism. As a strong and steady undercurrent beneath the steady flow of medieval poetry, novels, cathedrals, and paintings, this spirit had flourished with originality and individuality as its keynotes. It was more an inspiration from the Middle Ages than an attempt to copy that period.

With development and hardening of the Renaissance-academic viewpoint, with growth of the photographic attitude toward the past, the artist began to look for a transcription rather than an interpretation. A nineteenth-century person attempting to express himself as a man of the fourteenth or fifteenth century appeared no more ridiculous to such Frenchmen as Jean Hippolyte Flandrin, "the modern Fra Angelico" (1809–1864), than to the slightly later English group.

England during the second half of the century was moving toward a powerful spiritual movement partly as a reaction against its somewhat gross materialism. Unfortunately, the movement was to be cluttered with the bric-a-brac of conventional historical painting, together with its meticulous technique, which thus obscured what could have been an important contribution. Dante Gabriel Rossetti (1828–1882) is perhaps the most original member of the group. His *An-nunciation* (Fig. 48) illustrates the virtues and defects of the pre-Raphaelite movement. Its cold harsh light suggests the painting of the French academics, as does the sharp and precise drawing. Emotionally, however, this picture is on a much higher level than the French, as illustrated by the exaggerated, almost psychotic reaction of the shrinking Madonna. This otherworldly feeling runs through much pre-Raphaelite painting and ultimately distinguishes it from the milder and more illustrative efforts of a Flandrin or an Ary Scheffer. For English painting as for French this movement represented a dead end in spite of its many followers. The contribution of the English school was to emerge in the work of Constable, Turner, and others and bear fruit across the channel.

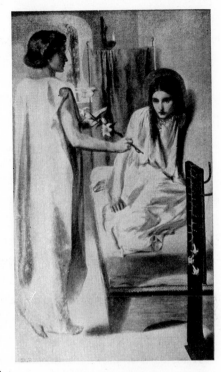

48. ROSSETTI: *The Annunciation* (London, National Gallery).

Although academicism in general represents a conservative rather than a progressive and constructive phase of art, the majority of artists belong to this category or, at best, to the "middle of the road." For every innovator there are fifty conservative, even reactionary painters and critics ready to annihilate him. Yet the radical movement of one era becomes, through the dubious magic of academic repetition and transcription, the accepted practice of a later period. We have seen here how the personalized original art of Delacroix or Ingres turned into the standardized narrative picture of the end of the century. In the same way many later movements, such as Realism, Impressionism, post-Impressionism, and beyond, all go through their baptism of critical disapproval and emerge a generation later as "respectable" forms of art.

6. THE ENGLISH CONTRIBUTION

We have already seen the important role played by eighteenth-century England in the development of neo-Classicism and Romanticism. Because of its very early middle-class revolution in Cromwellian times, it had swept forward during this era to the first climax of the Industrial Revolution, giving rise to a variety of highly developed bourgeois attitudes. The virtuous neo-Classical paintings of Hamilton and Benjamin West, important predecessors of Davidian art, represented one aspect of this development; the more contemporary and individualistic emotional reactions of Jane Austen, Richardson, and their colleagues denoted another side.

Also, as a response to the emotional needs of the conquering middle classes, the eighteenth century produced early forms of pre-Romantic Gothicism, as in the *Night Thoughts* of Young and the medievalistic architecture of Strawberry Hill. Part of this development was also a great vogue for Nature in her more moving and unusual aspects, her most picturesque and broken forms.

In addition to its contributions to the classical revival of the late eighteenth century and the Romanticism of the early nineteenth, England was to affect continental and American art through two other forms. These two movements, including the social criticism of Hogarth and Rowlandson and the Romantic-Realistic nature painting of Gainsborough, Crome, Constable, and Turner, stem from the same environment as the previous British contributions. Although the two latter categories are part of the general Romantic development of the age, they carry us toward the post-Romantic period, toward the Realism of the middle of the nineteenth century—and even beyond, to the Impressionism of the 1870's.

The advanced nature of British middle-class art, its aggressive condemnation of the aristocracy, stand in sharp contrast to the contemporary moralities of Greuze in France. William Hogarth (1697–1764), though often looked upon as a preacher of virtue, is in reality a devastating critic of manners, a keen observer of weaknesses in the society of his day. His penetrating portrayals of upper-class foibles, lower-class weaknesses, and the general cruelty and heartlessness of this brawling, lusty period of English history raise to extraordinary heights the genre painting of his Dutch predecessors. More important, it points to the later development of social satire in his own country in the early part of the nineteenth century, as seen in the work of Thomas Rowlandson and the later pictures of manners and customs offered by Daumier, Guys, and others during the middle of the nineteenth century in France.

Hogarth's fame is often obscured by the superficially entertaining nature of many pictures in the different series of anecdotal paintings he produced. Such stories as *The Rake's Progress* and *The Harlot's Progress*, painted in progressive incidents and engraved for general widespread sale, may be amusing but they have an importance far beyond this. They represent the first concrete effort to analyze and evaluate a society, an effort preceding that of Goya in Spain and Daumier in France. Some of his work, to be sure, gives off an aura of ultrarespectability in its indication of the rewards of virtue and the punishment of vice, but this is its least important aspect in spite of the fact that it is so middle-class in character. From a purely formal point of view, the art of Hogarth points to a highly developed type of Realism; from the psychological side it is even more incisive than contemporary literary social criticism.

Hogarth's awareness goes beyond the mere use of type weaknesses as material for pictures—although he also did a good deal of that kind of thing—and pours over into attacks on weaknesses in the social structure. The scene entitled *The Visit to Bedlam* from *The Rake's Progress* (Fig. 48a) showing the visit of some fashionable women to a madhouse to enjoy the peculiar remarks and antics of the inmates is critical of the women as well as the society that permits such depraved entertainment. Similarly, the first scene of *The Harlot's Progress*, showing the arrival of a country girl in London and her reception by a procuress and her client, the notorious

48a. HOGARTH: *The Visit to Bedlam, Rake's Progress Series, #8.*

Colonel Charteris, is an editorial against all that these vicious people represented.

Though Hogarth's work met with considerable success with one segment of the population to the degree that the engravings made from the serial paintings were widely bought, he was constantly at odds with the art experts, the purveyors of traditional painting, and their customers. This controversy, too, places him directly in the line of later development, both in his own country and in France, when Modern versus Traditional becomes an even more serious issue.

More directly comparable with the rich productivity of Daumier is the slightly later Thomas Rowlandson (1756–1827), an artist who has been called the greatest of British caricaturists. Covering every aspect of English life, this French-trained draftsman becomes a link between the French eighteenth-century print makers of *galant* subjects and fashionable themes and the nineteenth-century analogues of Daumier and his contemporaries, especially Constantin Guys. Like Daumier, Rowlandson uses certain stock types who reappear again and again in his pictures of society: duchesses, soldiers, butchers, promenaders, gamblers, artists—even types from other countries that he visited. Apart from this elaborate cast of characters for his comedy of manners, Rowlandson also constructed a series of bestial types, gross and monstrous beings who revel in cruelty of all sorts and suggest in a general way the more exaggerated figures of Goya.

Before considering our second important and influential area of British art, and without forgetting the earlier neo-Classical and pre-Romantic works, it should be noted that a good many original and highly gifted men like William Blake and others fall outside the compass of this narrative of development and influence. Nor need the portrait school of the late eighteenth and early nineteenth century detain us. Although it did produce innumerable capable craftsmen and some superlative painterly talents like those of Gainsborough, the bulk of this school had little to say that had not been said better before by both the Venetians and Van Dyck.

The influence of the British landscape school is as important to the modern tradition as that of the English social critics. Although the effect of the artist-commentators was considerable and quite direct, that of the nature painters was more far-reaching. The latter were to influence French Romantic art in general and the Barbizon school of landscape in particular. Finally their work was to reach across generations to the Impressionists in the latter part of the nineteenth century.

Like the various emanations of British eighteenth-century art we have considered so far, the interest in nature also stemmed from the increasing emotional attitude of the middle classes, their interest in the emotive, the picturesque, and the sublime. A relatively mild example of this phenomenon is found in the work of Thomas Gainsborough (1727–1788), whose sympathetic personalized treatment of nature offers an instrument for the expression of a diffuse Romantic attitude.

As part of the eighteenth-century interest in the picturesque, his loosely painted *Landscape* (New York, Metropolitan Museum of Art, Fig. 49) is in strong contrast with the classical arrangements of Poussin, where

49. GAINSBOROUGH: *Landscape* (New York, Metropolitan Museum of Art).

people and background are integrated. The pictures of Gainsborough, rhythmically rather than architecturally arranged, combine the figures and background much more casually. His work stands somewhere between the picturesque-genre tradition of the Dutch and the picturesque-Romantic tradition exemplified by Salvatore Rosa. The fuzziness of his trees suggests Watteau, just as the often doll-like figures bring to mind contemporary French engravings. In spite of the rather mechanical way Gainsborough prepared his landscapes, with models built of bits of cork and coal, dabs of sand, clay, moss, and even broccoli, they have a charming quality quite his own.

Although Gainsborough's method is less photographic than Dutch landscape painting, his treatment of atmosphere is as convincing in its way. The Dutch for the most part had retained a relatively brownish tint that muddied their effects, while the English painter took the first step toward a "greenness" of nature whose full possibilities were to be realized in the work of Constable. With Gainsborough a soft atmospheric quality adds to the inherently Romantic nature of his approach. At a time when many Englishmen were addicted to the still-life type of Dutch landscape, he created something different.

The new softness and brightness in his work are undoubtedly reflections of the strong popular water-color tradition in England. Although amateur in character, this movement was very important in its influence on the taste for loose and casual construction. A good deal of public interest in landscape may be traced to this activity in which young ladies as well as men participated. Ultimately it may be the reason for the individual quality of English landscape painting since it accentuates light colors in whose presence the browns of Dutch painting soon disappeared. These water-colorists, led by the little-known Thomas Girtin (1775–1802) whose natural-istic and emotive works were the envy of such craftsmen as Constable and Turner, gradually accustomed the English to coloristic truth in landscape.

The real contribution of Gainsborough's *Landscape* is not its realism but rather the relationship established between the wayfarer on the road and nature. This bond is essentially Romantic in its creation of a melancholy twilight mood and in the subjugation and anonymity of the person: "The plowman homeward plods his weary way And leaves the world to darkness and to me."

John Crome (1768–1821), commonly known as Old Crome, was fond of the work of the Dutch Hobbema but not as much influenced by this source as is frequently believed. His pictures, for the most part of his native Norfolk, are endowed with a force and majesty that the Dutchmen in general seldom achieved. The typical *View of Mousehold Heath* (Fig. 50) implies a distance much deeper than the usual seventeenth-century produc-tion. Its lifelike colors show even stronger divergence from the older tradition, its greens, yellow-greens, silver grays, and delicate blues betraying an altogether fresh and novel luminosity. Emotionally the picture is related to Gainsborough in its reticent quality; the tiny figure at the upper right shows his companion an even smaller group moving along the winding

50. CROME: *View of Mousehold Heath* (London, National Gallery).

path into the landscape. These paths again distinguish English paintings from their classical French predecessors. Here the spectator is invited to come into the picture through the winding road, as in Dutch landscape, and to participate, as it were, in the action. In the classical pictures we feel that the carefully planned environment is meant to be looked at but not entered, no more than we would think of walking into a piece of stage scenery. In spite of the element of participation in the English landscape, however, the individual is symbolically subordinated to the vastness of nature.

The principal colors of *Mousehold Heath* are supplemented by little touches of adjacent color that help to strengthen the generally bright effect. At the same time, the realism and grandeur of still-life conception of the plant forms at the lower left anticipate some effects of the later Barbizon painters. This mingling of the general and the particular is an outstanding characteristic of Crome and other English landscapists. They achieve it by allowing the spectator to break through the immediacy and interest of the object in the foreground toward what is going on further back in the picture.

Historically, *Mousehold Heath* stands between the Dutch tradition and nineteenth-century Romantic landscape. Like the pictures of Holland, the Crome painting shows a still-life interest, as in the flowers at the left. But this interest, we have seen, is subordinate to a concept of nature—or part of nature—as an emotionally moving scene accentuated by the curving sweep of road, the silhouetted bent figure of the shepherd, and the mass of clouds, which all carry us into the desired distance.

Crome wrote to one of his pupils: " . . . Trifles in nature must be over-looked that we may have our feelings raised by seeing the whole picture at a glance, not knowing how or why we are so charmed." Or again: " . . . Do not distress us with accidental trifles in nature but keep the masses large and in good and beautiful lines, and give the sky, which plays so important a part in all landscape, and so supreme a one in our low level lines of distance, the prominence it deserves, and in the coming years the posterity you paint for shall admire your work."

In 1802 Crome founded a school of landscape painting at Norwich, perhaps the first example of an art colony dedicated to the study of nature. This forerunner of the Barbizon and Pont-Aven groups in France is an interesting example of a nonurban art, in this case provincial and sincere throughout its existence. Some of its members, like Morland and Ward, were interested in animal painting, thus linking the Dutch and the nine-teenth-century Barbizon schools again.

The short-lived Richard Bonington (1801–1828) is interesting for both figure and landscape painting. In the former field, he did such historical Romantic subjects as *Francis I and the Duchesse d'Étampes* in the manner of his friend Delacroix. As a landscape painter, he stems from the water-colorists, reproducing their spontaneity and transparency in oil to give his pictures an interesting atmospheric and broad quality. Bonington's long sojourn in France seemed to influence the later Barbizon school, especially Daubigny. *Mantes on the Seine* (Fig. 51) is typical of the Englishman's interest in atmosphere, especially in melancholy and quiet twilight effects. Like many of his countrymen, he stresses the intimacy of a given scene, but also insists on rendering the larger aspects of the landscape or seascape. As a colorist, Bonington shows skillful use of little spots of color to heighten broader areas, somewhat in the fashion of Crome. The prevalent feeling, however, is emotionally spontaneous and free in accordance with the avowed aim of all Romantics.

The full naturalistic possibilities of landscape were discovered by John Constable (1776–1837). He may be called the first great naturalistic landscape painter of the nineteenth century since he was the first to discover the atmosphere as a motivating and moving element. It was this aspect in landscape that became the main component thereof and Constable's particular preoccupation.

His approach to nature was basically new in its consciousness of the ever-changeable appearance of objects under the shifting and shimmering quality of light and air. As the wind moves a branch, the light necessarily falls upon it differently and changes the color of each particular spot and its adjacent ones. Here again there can be little doubt that Constable's true inspiration for lightness and brightness of color came from the water-

51. BONINGTON: *Mantes on the Seine* (New York, Metropolitan Museum of Art).

52. CONSTABLE: *Salisbury Cathedral* (London, Victoria and Albert Museum).

color painters of the previous generation, the group led by Girtin, Cozens, and their fellows.

The curious thing about the work of Constable is not that it is so essentially lively—one can almost take this for granted—but that no matter how long he worked at a particular subject it always retains its freshness, always looks like a spontaneously improvised work. Where he painted sun, the spectator feels as though he were bathed in that element; when it is rain, there is almost a parallel reaction. One presumably witty painter is supposed to have opened an umbrella at a Constable exhibition.

Constable has left a number of versions of his favorite building, *Salisbury Cathedral* (Fig. 52). These pictures, done at different periods in the artist's life and painted at different times of the day under various conditions, suggest a similar procedure by both Daubigny and the later Impressionist painter Claude Monet. Since most artists in Constable's day painted their landscapes late in the afternoon or early in the morning to avoid too strong illumination, this round-the-clock approach of the English painter represents a new practice.

Scenically, however, Constable enjoys a striking advantage over the French Impressionists who have nothing quite like the picturesque English combination of complicated civilized architecture against a beautiful natural background; French cathedrals are almost always surrounded by other buildings in fairly large cities. In the *Salisbury Cathedral* Constable was shrewd enough to use the building as a background dramatically seen through a Gothic arch formed by trees. The light comes from within the picture and is only sensed on the inner sides of the monumental trees as it filters down through the upper foliage. As we move further back into the painting, Salisbury emerges in a brilliant light under fleecy skies that add immeasurably to the sense of movement and fleeting shadows. Paintings of this particular type show an interesting technique of small spots of thick color to reinforce a larger area. For such details as the bark of a tree, where the patches of light falling on the trunk are shown as flecks of white, this method lends greater conviction.

The most spectacular of Constable's works is his celebrated *The Hay Wain* (Fig. 53) painted in 1821 and shown at the so-called English salon of 1824 together with more pictures by Constable and other English artists. We have already seen the effect of *The Hay Wain* on young Delacroix and his supposed retouching of the *The Massacre at Scio* (Fig. 30) under the influence of the Englishman's lively and vivid colors. In no other work had the English painter shown such an unusual sense of the momentary and broken quality of landscape with its shifting and contrasting lights. Delacroix quotes Constable as attributing the vividness of his greens to the fact that he used a variety of shades of that color for his meadows. Similarly, he accounted for the dullness in ordinary landscapes by observing that artists generally painted in one uniform green.

Instinctively perhaps, Constable was also aware of the fact that certain colors had the quality of reinforcing or complementing each other (*e.g.*, red and green or orange and blue). By this use of color he achieved a greater degree of luminosity for his grass and sky. It was that quality more than

53. CONSTABLE: *The Hay Wain* (London, National Gallery).

anything else which so impressed the young Frenchman. On the other hand, it will not do to say that the influence of Constable on all Romantic painters was either direct or very considerable, except in the sense that he helped to further the spirit of individuality and a sense of movement. To a generation still under Davidian influence this meant more than we can realize today.

English landscape is never reduced to a series of clichés, as happened to some Barbizon painters of the generation of 1840–1870. Although some critics argue that to reduce the spontaneous and perhaps rough technique of the English to a usable mechanism by the French is a service of value, it would seem that the contrary were true. We are seldom bored by Constable and his countrymen, but "understandable language" or not, Barbizon landscapes can often be rather tiresome.

The specific message of Constable, then, was not to his own period in France but rather to the generations following. First he affected the Barbizon school, where a similar naturalness of expression before nature was the

97

ideal. More specific—and perhaps more important—was the effect on the Impressionists, who were very much interested in clean, broken colors and temporary effects. In his own country, the influence is his development of a method for unifying a landscape by saturating the picture with atmosphere. Here he undoubtedly touches the art of Turner.

Intelligent critics and painters in France were aware of the fact that pictures like *The Hay Wain*, seen close up, were primarily a series of dabs of rough color that blended into the desired form as one moved back. Unquestionably, the method of out-of-door painting of the 1870's was anticipated here. Yet it must not be overlooked that the return to nature, even in this honest and direct English fashion, was essentially Romantic and parallel to the nature poetry of the early nineteenth century.

The work of Joseph Mallard William Turner (1775–1851) is the logical consequence of all that had come before in the English school. Although it is difficult to classify his works in regular chronological development, one finds almost every type of landscape picture in his repertoire. Beyond the obvious virtuosity and versatility is the purely personal and individualistic creativeness of this man's art. To the intrinsic merit of his great Romantic personality must be added the influence of his vivid atmospheric painting on the generation of 1870 in France, on such men as Monet, Pissarro, and Renoir.

The two main streams of traditional landscape painting, the picturesque-Classical and the picturesque-Romantic, form only part of Turner's rich heritage. Both trends stem from the seventeenth century, the former from Claude and Poussin and the latter from Rubens and the Dutch landscapists.

In a somewhat Romantic fashion, Turner set out to rival the earlier men, particularly Claude Lorrain, whose famous *Embarkation of the Queen of Sheba* is recalled in the Englishman's *Dido Building Carthage*. What interested Turner in the pictures of Claude was their atmospheric treatment, a technique that, in addition to its purely descriptive possibilities, also helped to convey a mood. In other words, the Claude who had gone out of doors for his inspiration, who was able to suffuse his pictures with an allover light and at the same time convey the "feeling" of an early morning or a melancholy episode, was the very man Turner needed for his own art.

Though Turner soon dropped the geometrical quality of Claude's classical composition, the example of the earlier master was never completely out of his sight. He even insisted on having the *Dido* hung next to Claude's *Queen of Sheba*, an ostentatious but significant gesture.

The picturesque-Romantic tradition is reflected in such works as *Childe Harold's Pilgrimage—Italy* (Fig. 54) which, although Rubensesque in its diffuse handling of nature, is more distinctly contemporary in its reference. As subject matter, it comes from the poetry of Byron, paralleling in that sense many paintings by Delacroix. Its technique, however, much as it may be in the picturesque-Romantic tradition, is also contemporary in its typically English emphasis on atmosphere (out of Constable). Even more significant is its use of picturesqueness and roughness in this scene as a foil for the emotions of the characters in the *Pilgrimage*. Nature here, as in the poetry of the Romantics, is used to express the feelings of the artist and becomes a reflection of his struggles.

Subjects such as *Dido* or the *Pilgrimage*, however, are relatively rare in

54. TURNER: *Childe Harold's Pilgrimage—Italy* (London, Tate Gallery).

99

Turner's work. For the most part, he was concerned with the phenomena of visual reality translated into his own powerful atmospheric symbols. The most important part of reality, so far as he was concerned, was the power of the elements: the sea, the air, the rain, the reality of movement.

The Fighting Téméraire (Fig. 55) is a good instance of Turner's translation of a naturalistic theme. An old warship is being towed to her last berth by a fussy little tug with the symbolic sunset and moonrise for background. The last rays of the sun stealing across the water may suggest similar effects in Claude Lorrain; here, though, we no longer have the balanced regularity of the classical painter but rather a diagonality of composition in which the masses are as cleverly placed as in a modern painting.

The idea of a gallant old ship of the line going to be broken up is sufficiently romantic with its overtones of mutability and gentle melancholy. Even more, it has a symbolic quality indicated by the setting sun and the

55. TURNER: *The Fighting Téméraire* (London, National Gallery).

56. TURNER: *Rain, Steam, and Speed* (London, Tate Gallery).

rising moon, with a heavy impasto cloud effect thrown over the former. It is the end of one era and the beginning of another; the machine has bested the sail.

Turner's interest in symbolism went much further, however. In some of his more vibrant pictures, such as the *Snow Storm* (London, National Gallery), the *Whale Ship* (New York, Metropolitan Museum), or *Rain, Steam, and Speed* (Fig. 56), a more dynamic factor emerged. He tried to invent a new art form consisting of symbols for forces without form, forces like rain, steam, or speed. Although Impressionist in the type of color used, the total effect is rather Expressionistic in its portrayal of the inner meaning of a given idea.

Turner deals with a modern subject in *Rain, Steam, and Speed* only through the accident of living from one age into another, for this picture's importance does not lie in its representation of a train crossing a bridge. The fact that it is a violently moving object, that it sheds clouds of steam as it races like a startled ghost through the fog, has more significance in terms of Turner's wish to set down the meaning of these forces. Like his contemporary Delacroix, who was determined to find a systematic method for showing Romantic emotion, or perhaps more like the later Futurists, who delineated the visual effects of dynamic movement, Turner wished to symbolize the elements.

Thus his paintings dedicated to the elements, because they tried to portray phenomena that are essentially formless, tended themselves to become increasingly without form in a purely descriptive sense. Yet in the modern Expressionistic usage of abstract volumes moving back and forth within a picture space to convey restlessness or tragedy, the symbolic paintings of Turner achieve form in the most basic manner.

Although Turner's greatest influence is on the Impressionists of the seventies and eighties, he has already gone one long step beyond them to a point where color and atmosphere are used not merely to describe a specific moment in time and space—but time, space, and the physical elements within them.

7. THE ROMANTIC LANDSCAPE IN FRANCE

French culture is Paris—the culture of a great metropolis speaking in a variety of sophisticated accents. England, in spite of the dominance of London, had other smaller centers; Norwich, Bath, and similar provincial cities played an important role in the development of English art. In these cities and towns artists and amateur artists were constantly in the presence of nature. Under such circumstances landscape painting in both water color and oil naturally flourished.

In France, or in Paris, the artist was almost automatically away from nature unless he lived in the suburbs—and it was there that landscape flourished when the time came. Between the seventeenth-century pictures of Poussin and Claude and the early nineteenth century, there was no school of landscape painting except the Rococo-picturesque works of Hubert Robert and Fragonard. When Constable came to Paris for the famous *salon anglais* of 1824, he observed that though the French painted landscape, they knew very little about it. To use his words, they knew as little of nature as a cab horse does of meadows.

Whatever interest the French had shown in nature during the eighteenth century had been nipped in the bud by the rising tide of neo-Classicism. The subsequent Romantic movement with its interest in faraway things again removed the artist from direct contemplation of nature as such. Although there had been Dutch landscapes in French collections as early as 1750, they were paid little attention. It was not until the post-Empire period, under the influence of the English, that Frenchmen became conscious of this tradition.

The French-British relationship in art began with the 1802 visit of Thomas Girtin, the famous water-colorist and friend of Turner. Glover, Haydon, and Wilkie continued the chain down to Bonington and the Fielding brothers, who settled in Paris. In the reverse direction, Géricault and Delacroix visited England, the latter apparently interested in clothes as well as in art.

The most important element is the permanent residence in Paris of the almost completely Gallicized Bonington, from whom the French derived (as they also did from Thales Fielding) a knowledge of water color and its possibilities. To French artists still under the influence of the plastic forms of David or the sinuous linear style of Ingres, it was interesting and instructive to observe that a fresher view of nature could be attained not with line but with fresh spots of color. Delacroix, later to be influenced by Constable, was friendly with both Bonington and Thales Fielding. Bonington especially must be credited with first transposing for the French the fluidity and purity of water-color tone into oil painting. The precocious Bonington, who died at twenty-six, paved the way for the success of the *salon anglais* of 1824, the final stimulus to development of landscape in France. There the sensational appearance of three Constable pictures, one of them *The Hay Wain*, was to make artistic history.

Among the French landscape painters who arose in the 1820's were Corot, Rousseau, and Dupré. Later, others were added and by the end of the 1830's they were thought of as a group. Certain things they held in common: their interest in nature itself (Constable had criticized French painters for studying nature from pictures), their poverty, and their lack of success in a hostile environment. On the other hand, their leaders showed markedly individualistic approaches to nature in the true Romantic sense.

Although the group is spoken of as the Barbizon school, since many members were driven there by poverty from a city that was not interested in their art, it is a "school" only as a matter of convenience. Some of its members, like Rousseau, Diaz, and Millet, did spend a good deal of time in the little village on the edge of the Fontainebleau forest. Others, like Dupré, Daubigny, and Troyon, visited less frequently, while Corot, financially independent, preferred his own place at the Ville d'Avray.

Their personal emotional reaction to nature was the thing that bound them together and that enables us to refer to them as a school.

Probably neither the Dutch nor the English influence would have turned the French toward landscape had it not been for the broadening effect of Romanticism which enlarged the feelings of individuals. The relationship between man and the forces of nature had been one of the main elements of the Romantic movement. Delacroix in his *Shipwreck of Don Juan* and Géricault in the *Raft of the Medusa* (Fig. 26) had stressed the struggle of man against his environment. A more pantheistic attitude, that was to be characteristic of French landscapes for a long time, emerged in many English paintings as well as in the poetry of the early nineteenth century. Crome's lonely heaths with man reduced to tiny proportions and little importance are mirrored in such poems as Lamartine's *The Lake:* " . . . and I am like a withered leaf, Carry me away, O stormy winds!"

The smallness of the individual before the majesty of nature is a purely Romantic phenomenon that had been best expressed pictorially by the British. Certain of the Barbizon painters showed this quality also, although generally their emphasis was on the more particularized aspects of nature, upon as naturalistic a rendition as possible. At the same time, each painter was interested in the creation of a mood that came to be recognized as typical of him alone.

Reduction of the individual's importance was bound up with the diminishing place of classical humanism. Man became merely part of the universe and not the yardstick by which it was measured. This may have been a negation of the supposedly increased consequence of man in post-feudal society, but it was also an indication of the escapist or Romantic attitude of the Barbizon movement. Even in the art of Millet, where human beings seem to have a more prominent part, the emphasis is upon man as an emanation of nature. Not only are the shepherds of Corot or the peasants of Rousseau reduced to this minor role, but frequently they are eliminated completely and the artist achieves his emotional effect without them. It becomes possible for a large tree or rock to be substituted for man and his problems.

Occasionally the Romantically inclined painters used picturesque or

57. DIAZ DE LA PEÑA: *Descent of the Bohemians* (Boston, Museum of Fine Arts).

pseudo-historical people in their landscapes. These are most often found in the works of Corot, whose nostalgic reminiscences of Italy are occasionally peopled with nymphs and such old standbys as Virgil. Diaz de la Peña, in his *Descent of the Bohemians* (Fig. 57), fills the scene with a number of colorful vagabonds that suggest characters in the picturesque Romantic landscapes of the seventeenth-century Salvatore Rosa.

The work of Camille Corot (1795–1875), in its evident Romantic sentiment, hazy quality, and feeling for atmospheric values, reminds us in a general way of the earliest and non-naturalistic English landscape painting. His characteristic silver-gray haze enveloping the figures and trees does not vary much from Italy to the Île de France or Provence. These places are all represented in accordance with the prevailing sentiment of the artist—atmospherically they are all alike.

The well-known *Souvenir of Italy—Nymphs Dancing* (Paris, Louvre) has the same diffused and fuzzy quality as *Two Men in a Skiff* (Fig. 58), probably a scene from the neighborhood of his beloved Ville d'Avray. Nothing could be more Romantic than the *Souvenir of Italy*, which is not only part of his constant and personalized reaction to nature but also a reinterpretation in terms of bucolic poetry derived from some vague antique source. Although critics often refer to Virgil and Theocritus in speaking of Corot, it is doubtful if the painter was more than generally familiar with these authors. Anyone who had lived in Italy could easily acquire the idea that this classic land had once been peopled with nymphs and satyrs. Corot's interpretation, however, is not that of Renaissance masters like Titian or Correggio but rather a vague and misty florescence of the Romantic imagination, of the soul that looks for a far-off land, for the fabled Italy in this case. The light that Corot throws about his scenes belongs to twilight or early dawn. Very seldom do we get the impression of a specific time of day, for we are dealing here with states of feeling rather than literal representations of nature.

Corot's work may be divided into three groups. During the early part of his career, especially the two years in Italy, he painted a series of precise

58. COROT: *Two Men in a Skiff* (New York, Metropolitan Museum of Art).

and clearly lighted landscapes with architecture seen across a long vista stretching between the spectator and the buildings. The artist rendered the scene as though it had been viewed through a telescope, an effect accentuated by the distance across which we have to look and by the clear impression of detail. Pictures like the *View of the Roman Forum* (Fig. 59) are apparently a result of the strict self-training of the painter (he did not have much formal art schooling). They encompass a wide variety of scenes from Italy, Provence, the Île de France, and Normandy.

This aspect of his work is also Romantic through its visible interest in historical monuments and old cities existent in a present-day environment. Separation of the painter from the architectural scene, indicated by the telescopic distance, places him in a world of solitude where it is impossible to reach the particular building that represents the past. This almost Surrealist removedness that symbolizes the past is connected with the present through realistic painting of a contemporary landscape. Apparently the distance was deliberate (a fact revealed in Corot's later painting of streets and buildings from close-up) and, it must be believed, was part of his feeling for the scene. As a form of personal experience, there can be little question that these emotive landscapes have a much greater value than the fuzzy middle-period works already discussed.

From the viewpoint of modern painting, this earlier category of Corot's work has further importance. The *View of the Roman Forum*, in addition to the qualities noted, shows a manipulation of planes and an arrangement

59. COROT: *View of the Roman Forum* (Paris, Louvre).

of geometrically shaped volumes that suggest the work of Cézanne. Study of Poussin may have led him in this abstract direction: " . . . the only staff which he may carry from time to time to strengthen his steps is an occasional glance on the best masters . . . Poussin, Lesueur, Claude, Hobbema, Canaletto." In any case the results are significant for the student of modern art.

In later pictures, we have seen, the forms are diffuse and instead of the sharp, clear colors of the "travel pictures," we have grays and silvers reminiscent of Watteau. Occasionally, Corot throws a bit of white impasto on the bark of a tree to indicate the penetration of sunlight, but generally the atmosphere is as indeterminate as can be. Corot's Hellenism, mentioned before, differs from that of the neo-Classical painters since they insist on a humanistic point of view which makes man the measure of all things. The Romantic landscape painter, however, makes his people or nymphs pure emanations of the spirit of nature, their formal character determined by atmosphere.

The third important category in Corot's art is his figure painting. Here his interest in the past is closer to that of the neo-Renaissance artists. The *Woman with the Pearl* (Fig. 60), though it uses the cleaner color range of the nineteenth century, suggests *Mona Lisa* in its pose, placing of hands, expression, and triangular composition. Although Corot is not supposed to have considered his figure paintings very significant, they are nonetheless a most important part of his work that will bear comparison with the best painting of the century. Aside from their luminous color, sensitive mood, and fine feeling for form, they are also part of the long tradition which encompasses David, Géricault, Ingres, Courbet, Renoir, Derain, and Picasso.

From the standpoint of public taste and sales, the misty landscapes are still the preferred aspect of his production in spite of their frequently monotonous and repetitive character. For the serious student, the clear and precise works of the early period with their almost untraversable space and abstracted buildings are much more interesting. Late in life, Corot took up the architectural idea again. This time, as in the *Belfry of Douai* (Paris, Louvre), the spectator is brought close to the building and only has to cross a street to reach it. Spatial quality of this kind can be compared with the street paintings of Utrillo in our own times.

The work of Corot, as we have seen, is much too varied to be included within the rather narrow limitations of the Barbizon school. Even in the circumstances of his life Corot was different. His sojourn in the country near Fontainebleau (actually he preferred Ville d'Avray) was entirely a

60. COROT: *Woman with the Pearl* (Paris, Louvre).

matter of choice since he was financially independent; he sold a great many pictures and was probably the most successful landscape painter of the century—at least commercially. Emotionally, Corot seems to have been different as well, for he remained very simple and even naïve throughout his life. The great esteem in which he was held by his fellow artists was not only due to his characteristic generosity. "Papa" Corot was revered as an independent and sweet soul, a good man in every sense of the word.

Most members of the Barbizon school, living in their simple rustic way near Fontainebleau, had at least their poverty in common. Each painter, however, had his own psychological attitude toward nature, his own form of Romanticism. Diaz de la Peña (1809–1876) we have already seen in his picturesque view of a nature peopled by interesting and colorful creatures (Fig. 57). Perhaps more than any of the others, he was lyrical in his approach. His softly sad feeling is markedly different from the tragic moods of a Dupré or the monumentality of a Rousseau. Diaz' light is artificial in its focus on a few spots designed to accentuate dramatic contrasts of light and dark. This controlled illumination helps him to raise the emotional level in a gentle but positive manner.

If we contrast such pictures with the usual production of the British, we find that this painter (if he can be called typical) is more specific than the English. He takes a much smaller portion of nature for his stage than do Crome, Constable, and the others, who offer a combination of broad and detailed effects. In the *Descent of the Bohemians* the spectator is placed within a limited section of melancholy forest. We are forced to look intently at the trees and, in fact, prevented from looking beyond them. This not being able to see the forest for the trees is true not only of Diaz but extends to the other Barbizon men as well.

Théodore Rousseau (1812–1867), the acknowledged chief of the "school," exemplifies this attitude even better. His *The Sunlit Oak* (Fig. 61) shows intense and immediate naturalism in a very striking way. His accentuation of the personality of tree, rock, or stream is part of the pantheistic attitude so clearly seen in Dupré, Corot, and others of the group. Strong concentration on the reality of the chosen object is balanced by a general allover effect to avoid distraction at any one point.

Rousseau thinks of Nature in terms of stratification, of her more permanent features rather than temporary light sensations as in Constable and Turner. His preoccupation with the substance of the thing under consideration tends to make him more objective than most of the Barbizon painters. In his almost frantic desire to find out everything, he seizes too many details that other artists would indicate generally and more pictorially.

The art of Rousseau, in one sense, is a form of documentation not concerned with transitory light phenomena. These had to be sacrificed in the interests of permanent likeness. The anecdote about his standing in the forest for hours until the birds perched on his shoulders will illustrate his approach. Not only is the individual completely submerged in Nature, but he studies her so intently and absorbs so much that he becomes a biographer rather than an interpreter. Even broader and more typical compositions, such as *The Edge of the Woods* (New York, Metropolitan Museum of Art), show intense concentration on the objects in the foreground with the vista cut off by a monumental tree and high ground line.

The work of Jules Dupré (1812–1889) is much rougher in character and

61. ROUSSEAU: *The Sunlit Oak* (The Hague, Mesdag Collection).

62. DUPRÉ: *Setting Sun after a Storm* (Paris, Louvre).

more Romantic than Rousseau's painting, since he adopts a specific emotional attitude toward nature instead of an objective viewpoint. Just as Delacroix used historical and literary subjects for his passionate expression, so Dupré utilizes landscape to show certain moods such as rage or sadness. Although it is not necessarily easy to identify the particular emotion intended, there is always some reaction from the spectator. *Setting Sun after a Storm* (Fig. 62) illustrates his viewpoint in a rough and broken technique very suitable for the subject. Often the palette knife is used to create projections and roughnesses that increase the sense of disorder, and the subjects are frequently chosen with an eye to their possibilities in this technique. In spite of the Romantic character of Dupré's analysis of nature, color is still traditional with browns, blacks, and grays in his palette.

Charles Daubigny (1817–1878) was the poet of the group, the gentle painter, and yet the only member of the school to paint directly from

63. DAUBIGNY: *Evening* (New York, Metropolitan Museum of Art).

nature. His work, often reminiscent of the diffuse quality of Bonington, is dedicated to Nature in her milder phases in the twilight hours. The atmospheric *Evening* (Fig. 63), typical of the kind of mood he creates, also demonstrates the rather limited vistas of his pictures.

Historically, Daubigny is responsible for popularizing the Barbizon type of painting. The reasons for his success are not too difficult to find, for his work is the most understandable of the group and (with the exception of Corot) the most inoffensively emotional as well. In fact, the landscape taste of the latter part of the century was influenced more by his particular brand of sentiment than by any other single individual—again excepting Corot. Although still Romantic, the instrument could easily become academic, for nothing is as easy to stereotype as a gentle, sentimental reaction. Yet both Corot and Daubigny were important influences on the evolution of Impressionism during the early sixties because of their atmospheric interests. The fact that the latter artist worked outdoors and was interested in the "impression" which a particular scene made on him is not without significance in the same area.

At the end of its development, the Barbizon tradition tended, as we have seen, to become a formula attractive to many members of the middle class. Although it had lost the freshness of its original English inspiration, it remained the avenue by which the French artists in modern times were brought back to nature, out of the studio and into the forest and field. Its connection with later Impressionism is quite clear, especially in the case of Daubigny, Diaz, and Corot. Even if most of the brotherhood only did their sketches out of doors and painted the pictures in the security of their studios, they had gone outside for their ideas, which they then translated into the vocabulary of their own Romantic personalities. More than anything else, their work underlines the need for the modern individual to get away from the city if he is to understand Nature. What they did in this regard would be repeated many times later in one form or another.

While it retained its emotional vigor, as in the work of Rousseau and Dupré, Barbizon painting remained an important cultural aspect of the Romantic movement; later, its sentiment was to degenerate into material for art merchants and the cheaper forms of reproduction.

8. THE REALISTS: MILLET, COURBET, DAUMIER

We have already seen that French politics during the first half of the nineteenth century were extremely confused. After a period of readjustment to modern economic conditions marked by the Revolutions of 1830 and 1848, Louis Napoleon was elected first president of the Second Republic in 1848. Gaining control of the army and support of powerful financial interests, he "putsched" his way to imperial power in 1851. For a period of twenty years France was to be stable.

Universal suffrage was encouraged—even though with prearranged slates—and public education fostered. French bureaucracy, so succinctly represented by Daumier, achieved its real development during this period. Most important for our story, the regime welcomed the Industrial Revolution by government aid to business and at the same time tried to help labor through better working and living conditions. However one may feel about the benevolent despotism of this regime, the materialism of the age was better organized than it had ever been before.

Under these circumstances the Realist movement in art reached its full flower during the reign of Napoleon III but it was also conditioned by the previous era. The miserable state of the peasantry and also the suffering of the new working class and the lower middle-class individual during the confusion of the first half of the century formed a background for the painting of Millet, Courbet, and Daumier. During the very period that the followers of Ingres and Delacroix still debated the proper method of painting literary, historical, or exotic subjects, and while the Barbizon school was in full flower, this new point of view emerged.

The three men we group under the Realistic banner, however, although profoundly stirred by the everyday world, are not only Romantic in feeling but stem directly from that tradition. In Romantic art, Realism had been an integral, if secondary element. The Romantic painter was interested in two things: first, his own emotions, and then the particular fragment of reality which caused the emotion. This fragment—a battle scene, a shipwreck, or a scene in a harem—was done with scrupulous attention to the facts, as we have seen in the work of Gros, Géricault, and Delacroix.

Contrary to classical doctrine, the Romantics maintained that a subject not inherently beautiful or moving could be made beautiful, moving, or both. *The Raft of the Medusa* (Fig. 26) and *The Massacre at Scio* (Fig. 30) exemplified this point of view. The Realists, especially the literary men (Balzac, Zola, Flaubert), went one step further to maintain that every aspect of life is beautiful. Reacting against the emotionality of the Romantics, they also insisted that the recording of this reality must be as objective as possible, since the facts portrayed are more important than the emotions of the artist. In our group of Realists, the only one to adhere to this principle was Courbet, although somewhat later Manet and the Impressionists also exemplified the same, almost scientific attitude. We shall see, then, that the Realists of the fifties and sixties are a bridge between the Romantics and the Impressionists both in time and in character.

If Millet, Courbet, and Daumier cannot properly be called a movement, they do exemplify a clearly marked tendency toward concern with the everyday world which they glorify in their various ways. By its very nature as a luxury commodity, painting cannot be as far forward in its choice of theme as literature. Thus the Realistic movement in art is neither as widespread nor as extreme. We may compare, if we like, the art of Daumier with the writing of Balzac, the painting of Courbet with the work of Flaubert, and the peasants of Millet with those of George Sand. Except in the case of Daumier, the comparison is superficial and true only in the most general terms. The point at which Daumier touches Balzac is his work in the field of newspaper illustration (his paintings were not for public consumption). Yet it cannot be doubted that the existence of the work of these Realist writers had an important influence on the emergence of our three painter Realists. With the writers, as with the painters, the transition from Romantic Realism to Realism is a logical one, each period expressing itself in the language most appropriate for it.

Whereas the creative artists of the early nineteenth century had revolted emotionally and individualistically—in other words, Romantically—against the injustices of their time, later men and women reacted differently. Misery and exploitation resulting from the rapid growth of urban centers, domi- nance of the profit motive and the commercial spirit brought in their wake a new examination of the world of that day. Social philosophers like Malthus and Ricardo observed and analyzed society, while writers were similarly moved to record its annals. Some of the writing was still in the form of Romantic sympathy, as in George Sand and Victor Hugo; a good deal of it became analytical, as in Balzac, Flaubert, and Zola. The painting of the Realists, although slightly later in date, is part of the same movement.

One real contribution to the subject matter of art is a new series of city themes, especially in Daumier. Here again we are reminded of the great debt to Goya, for in modern times he was perhaps the first one to sound the song of the city with his gallants and ladies, balcony groups, processions, water sellers, blind beggars, and many other subjects.

Daumier's beggars, street singers, actors, washerwomen, strollers, artists, and scores of other types show us the changing face of the big city. *Third Class Carriage* (Fig. 78) is a scene from modern city life, a cross section of its social strata. Courbet's *Young Women on the Banks of the Seine* (Fig. 70) is our first example of city people coming back to nature by train or bus for a day's outing. Both pictures are evidences of the effects of megalopolis, the city so large that people have to travel considerable distances to get to work and even further to get to nature. It is only one short step from here to a new and more nervous conception of nature, the Impressionist method that will render it in a momentary fashion as though seen from some moving vehicle carrying people to work or to an outing in the country.

It was no accident that Realistic literature emerged in the reactionary and poverty-stricken 1830's and 1840's when the Realist painters were forming their respective styles. But it was not until after the Revolution of 1848 that both Millet and Courbet came forward with their Realist paintings. The opening of the *salon* to all artists made it possible for them to show their work more freely than had been possible earlier. On the other hand, the great World's Fair of 1855 accepted only one of Millet's pictures, while the Imperial Director of Fine Arts condemned works of this nature as "the painting of democrats, of those who don't change their linen. . . . " The rejection of two of Courbet's most important pictures at this Exposition caused the latter to open his Pavillon du Réalisme, a magnificent failure.

In spite of critical disapproval in the reactionary period following the assumption of Imperial authority by Louis Napoleon, these two painters maintained their point of view. As for Daumier, his paintings, too, do not figure in our story until after 1848, if only for the reason that he does not seem to have painted before that time. His political caricatures were forbidden in 1835 under the general law curtailing freedom of the press. From that point on, his criticism was social rather than political.

Although these men were all labeled "socialist" for the subjects they chose to paint, each represented a different level of social and political thinking. Millet was definitely uninterested in politics and conservative in his outlook. Courbet, in spite of his friendship with the socialist philosopher Proudhon, did not seem to understand too well the ideological basis of his actions. Since he was the symbol of artistic revolt, he was pushed into a position of leadership. Although he had always felt the unfairness of the public toward new art, especially as it hit him personally, it was not until the sixties, when he became involved in politics more directly, that he appreciated fully what was going on. As for his "socialist" subject matter, the foundation for this belief is found both in the writings of Proudhon, who used Courbet to illustrate the social function of art, and in the savage attacks of the critics. Though Courbet did not hesitate to show poor people in his pictures if he felt like it, his work is more concerned with his reactions to reality. Direct political and social commentary, such as we find in the lithographs and paintings of Daumier, does not exist in the work of Courbet, who was interested in realistic subject matter for its own sake. Daumier, on the other hand, was the great and conscious social critic of the group, analytical in his approach, critical in his attitudes.

Yet each of these artists in his own way is part of a movement of protest, a strong reaction to the increasing materialism of the age, which each interprets in a fashion consonant with his particular personality. Moreover,

119

their work represents the victory of the artist's right to paint what he likes, whether it sells or not.

Jean François Millet (1814–1875) liked to refer to himself as "a peasant of peasants." Of rugged Norman farmer stock, he was a fairly well educated man whose name could more justly be associated with classical literature than Corot's. One of the most important influences of his youth was the religious teaching of his grandmother. This simple Christianity furnishes the explanation for a good deal of Millet's work. A man brought up in the tradition of the Bible, French religious writers, and such poets as Robert Burns, would naturally produce the powerful and profound expressions of the Christian ideal that place him beside Tolstoy.

After a few efforts to learn art near his native village, Millet at the age of twenty-three went to Paris. Enrolled in the atelier of the academic Delaroche, one of his fellow students was Couture, who was destined for illustrative immortality for his *Romans of the Decadence*. Millet was not particularly happy here and left to study the masters of the Renaissance on his own. To help make a living, he painted Biblical subjects as well as eighteenth-century style nudes for which there was a good market. In 1847 he was admitted to the sacrosanct *salon* with a classical subject, *Oedipus*. The revolution of the following year, with which he was not in particular sympathy, opened the *salon* to everyone, and Millet began to exhibit the pictures for which he was later to become famous. Even this did not make him happy nor did it provide a living, and Millet moved to Barbizon with his already sizable family. What he had to offer could not compete with the Boucher-type nudes the public preferred.

The Barbizon period, although the most fruitful of his career, was marked by intense privations, fortunately relieved to some extent by faithful French and American friends. (The most outstanding Millets are today in America.) It was not until the great Paris Exposition of 1867 that he began to receive adequate recognition, and within a few years his pictures were selling for considerable prices. By that time he was too ill and old to enjoy his success.

The roots of Millet's art are embedded in French tradition, in the simple mood and monumentally ennobled peasants of the seventeenth-century Le Nains. But the modern Frenchman adds a peculiarly pious "thankfulness

for daily bread" attitude, admirably illustrated in *The Gleaners* (Fig. 64).
Here he tells with Old Testament seriousness and dignity of the right of
the poor to follow the binders of sheaves and pick up what they let fall.
Because of the artist's belief in the inherent dignity of man, his peasants
rise above their difficulties. Millet does not deny that his peasants, here
and elsewhere, have a difficult life—in this sense he shows the life of his
time—but by covering their problems with a kind of Christian resignation,
he minimizes those problems.

His characters take on a symbolic quality because he chooses to leave
them anonymous, with deliberately darkened faces and generalized features
that make them into types rather than individuals. Emphasis is placed on
strength and hardness, the farmers and their women shown with powerful
bodies, limbs, and hands, as though they are part of the soil with which they
constantly struggle. One result of this generalization is to give the figures
an almost abstract quality that brings us close to the "modern" forms of

64. MILLET: *The Gleaners* (Paris, Louvre).

121

Daumier. Many of Millet's figures will stand comparison with those of Daumier from this general point of view (*e.g.*, Millet's *Quarriers*, in the Toledo, Ohio, Museum). Moreover, his figures, in spite of their concrete actions and realism, are still Romantic in their pantheism, in their identification of man and nature. In this sense they are as much emanations of the soil as the nymphs and picturesque personages of Corot.

65. MILLET: *The Sower* (Boston, Museum of Fine Arts).

Millet's self-imposed museum training gives his art a certain formal academic discipline in space arrangement and drawing. *The Gleaners* is a typical example of his carefully arranged composition, the actors disposed in a series of increasingly bent forms. The almost classical drawing is an index to the Old Master training of artists like Millet, Courbet, and Daumier in the public collections. In these respects, as well as in his drab and hard colors, Millet is still academic and typically nineteenth century in his attempts to utilize techniques of the past for needs of the present. The stiffness and formality of many of his works no longer appeal to us, although they may have been "different" when they were first shown; nor are we attracted by the sentimental and pious overtones of such paintings as *The Gleaners* and *The Angelus*. Even more unfortunate was the later adaptation by academic artists of what had undoubtedly been a sincere expression in Millet.

Many of Millet's other paintings, prints, and drawings are more exciting and moving in a true Romantic sense. *The Sower* (Fig. 65), composed diagonally against a stark background, moves through the fallow earth with the primeval strength of Michelangelo's symbolic figures. Clothing or drapery are almost unnecessary for this powerful, expressive form. Once more man is pitted against nature, as in the heroic works of Géricault, without the earlier "dignity of labor" sentimentality. Pictures like *The*

Sower and *The Man with the Hoe* exemplify the relationship between man and his environment in arbitrary arrangements and by significant gestures. Their sincere feeling and pathos link them with Rembrandt on the one hand and Van Gogh on the other. Like the former artist, Millet paints with a heavily loaded, "fat" brush that leaves a thick but porous surface on the rough canvas in keeping with his themes. His subject matter and sincerity are important in the development of Van Gogh, who copied such pictures as *The Noonday Rest* (Boston, Museum of Fine Arts) both for exercise in drawing and for the strength of theme.

Generally speaking, Millet's color leaves a great deal to be desired, particularly when he ventures into the open air. In the large figure pieces this is not so apparent, but in his Barbizon-type landscapes there is a certain unconvincing color quality. He seems to be genuinely interested in the achievement of the fleeting changing quality of open-air effects without knowing how to go about it. Once in a while, however, as in *The Path through the Wheat* (Fig. 66), he scores. Here an almost Impressionistically treated section of a field, with a man proceeding through the grain as though wading in water, conveys the effect of flashing tips of wheat, brilliant sunlight, and movement.

That Millet almost starved to death because of his relatively new approach emphasizes the growing gap between the artist and public in his day. France's later attempt to stem the tide of American buyers would be funny were it not so tragic for the painter. It is not strange that the America of Edwin Markham and Walt Whitman should have been interested in the work of Millet. Americans such as Morris Hunt and Quincy Shaw were among the first to appreciate his work and to buy it. In spite of the tremendous competition that arose between France and America for his paintings—after he had died—there are a great many fine examples of his work in the United States today.

If Millet was ignored during most of his lifetime, the same can hardly be said of Gustave Courbet (1819–1877), the stormy petrel of the Realist movement. From the beginning of his career to its miserable end in exile, he was the recipient of vilification and abuse. In part, the trouble was due to an aggressive personality, as many surviving anecdotes indicate. But these same stories are only symptoms of his fanatic insistence on maintaining his own integrity and independence as an artist. More concretely, this meant the right to paint what he chose, the things of the everyday world.

Although a self-trained painter, Courbet was very much dependent on tradition, especially the more Realistic masters of the seventeenth century. From such teachers as Velasquez, Ribera, Zurbarán, Caravaggio, Frans Hals, and Rembrandt he acquired his strong feeling for the material facts of existence and for atmospheric treatment. Like some of these men, we find Courbet often more objective than analytical. This is entirely in line with the Realistic doctrine of objectivity enunciated by Balzac and others. Yet the reactionary period after 1848, when his work first appeared, associated him with socialism, partly because he painted simple subjects, and because the philosopher Proudhon hailed his work as an example of the social mission of art.

66. MILLET: *The Path through the Wheat* (Boston, Museum of Fine Arts).

67. COURBET: *After Dinner at Ornans* (Lille, Palace of Fine Arts).

Courbet probably painted as he did because of his vital, powerful personality that placed him almost inevitably against the established order. The circumstances of that period made it possible and even necessary for independent people like Millet, Courbet, and Daumier to react to the evils of society. Their protest ranged from the Christian socialism of Millet through the misunderstood but sincere socialism of Courbet to the vibrant social consciousness of Daumier.

If Courbet often exaggerated the size of his pictures and further enraged a public that could only allow allegories and histories in those hallowed dimensions, it must be remembered that Realistic art almost naturally tends toward life-size figures.

The year after the Revolution of 1848, Courbet appeared on the scene with two paintings that were to keynote his entire career: *The Stone Breakers* (Paris, Louvre) and *After Dinner at Ornans* (Fig. 67), both dealing with simple homely subject matter. The former picture is in no way extraordinary, either in color or in composition (composition was never Courbet's long suit), but it did indicate the trend of his thought toward an everyday realism, an almost deliberate ugliness.

In *After Dinner at Ornans*, however, the painter has given us a wonderfully atmospheric interior permeated with the quiet mood and idealization of the Le Nains in the seventeenth century. This idealization won a prize for the picture, while *The Stone Breakers* in its theme and treatment made people suspicious. Until unfavorable reaction to his "socially conscious" subject matter turned the public against his art as a whole, peasant subjects like the *After Dinner* were very well received, undoubtedly because of their gentle mood and reticence.

This duality in Courbet, combining his rebellious insistence on mundane subjects and his equally Romantic development of pictures of mood, produces in many of his paintings a peculiarly mixed quality. Together with his constant emphasis on the materiality of forms and substances, we find a quiet introspective feeling that gives his art its own special character. Even those works which were attacked in their day for Realism, the famous *The Studio of the Painter* (Fig. 69) or *The Burial at Ornans* (Fig. 70), bear that special psychological quality.

68. COURBET: *Portrait of a Man with a Leather Belt* (Paris, Louvre).

This thoughtfulness of the painter negates a good deal of the usual critical insistence on his objectivity, uncompromising materiality, and the like. Even the most casual examination of portraits like those of Berlioz or Mme. Boreau shows a real, if restrained, emotional quality. In some pictures there is withdrawal from the world, as in *The Young Women on the Banks of the Seine* (Fig. 71), *The Woman with a Mirror* (New York, Metropolitan Museum of Art), or *The Awakening* (1864), that slightly erotic and disturbing vision.

69. COURBET: *The Studio of the Painter* (Paris, Louvre).

In Courbet's self-portraits (he did more than any other artist except Rembrandt), we are immediately impressed by the independence that shines from his face and pose. The feeling of the artist as an important personality comes through forcibly in his *Portrait of a Man with a Leather Belt* (Fig. 68), one of the finest self-portrayals of the century. In this admirably posed figure the arrangement of the various angles suggests the great Baroque portraits. Reminiscent of Michelangelo, one hand moves down toward the belt, while the other goes self-confidently in the opposite direction to caress the sensuously painted hair.

Again and again he affirms his individuality and independence, the aware-ness of his worth as a human being and as an artist. No more aggressive asser-tion of the ego can be imagined than the famous *Bonjour, M. Courbet* (Montpellier, Musée Fabre) or the even more fantastic but marvelously painted *The Studio of the Painter* (Fig. 69). In the former picture he is shown on a walking tour in the south of France to visit his patron M. Bruyas. This worthy greets him with all the deference due to a great painter, while the manservant at the left worships, hardly daring to raise his eyes. The widely caricatured, pugnaciously upthrust Assyrian profile of the bearded Courbet,

127

and the deliberate contrast between his rugged "simplicity" and independence and their bourgeois deference, explain why he was such fair game for the critics. Painted in harsh dry colors to simulate the character of the landscape, this unusually balanced composition is primarily concerned with the relation of artist and patron. In no previous or subsequent work has an artist had the temerity to show himself in quite this attitude toward his source of income, but we are dealing with an unusual man.

The Studio of the Painter (Fig. 69), tremendous in its size, is the painter's apologia for his art, with various models at the left and literary and other friends at the right. The center of the stage shows Courbet painting a landscape with a small boy and a nude model watching as though water were being turned into wine. It takes a certain kind of obtuseness to conceive such a picture, but it also takes a special painterly ability to do the fine strapping nude and the creamy cloth she holds or the charming landscape on the easel. In spite of the convincing quality of its atmosphere, one still wonders why anyone would want to do a picture of this kind— and in such heroic proportions. Small wonder that Courbet was a *succès de scandale*, shown in caricatures with his signature half as high as the picture on which it was placed.

Only the subjects with which he was personally familiar interested him, as witnessed by the famous story of his refusal to paint angels because he had never seen any. As a result he was labeled "Realist," which for 1850–1870 was as bad as "Communist" at a later period. The worst that can be said of him, if indeed it is bad at all, is that he was powerfully stimulated by reality and moved to paint it. Other artists are moved by ideas or emotions, but Courbet reacted to visual and tactile stimuli that were as important to him as allegories and histories to other men. This was beyond the public of that day, and when Courbet painted the simple, straightforward *Burial at Ornans* (Fig. 70) almost life size, there was a great "to-do."

Apart from its size, which glorifies a simple subject, there is nothing revolutionary about the groups of priests and mourners in this picture. Compared with the average religious burial scene, there is little pomp or symbolism here; but it was this very everyday quality that irritated critics and secured him the Realist label. As an objective picture of provincial society,

70. COURBET: *The Burial at Ornans* (Paris, Louvre).

the *Burial at Ornans* with its restrained and unspectacular emotionality has an unusual character. Neither grief nor piety are emphasized and no one looks at either the cross or the grave. People are distinguished not through characterization but rather by costume. The long, curving composition is as regular and monotonous as the people themselves, many of them counterparts of characters in Flaubert's *Madame Bovary*, typical middle-class provincials.

An even more striking theme is the *Young Women on the Banks of the Seine* (Fig. 71) showing two Parisians under a tree on a hot summer day, their boat pulled up on shore. This is probably the first example (1856) of the "vacation" picture popularized by the next generation of Realists, the Impressionists. It illustrates the new relationship of man to nature brought about by the growth of large cities from which the individual escapes in the occasional and casual contact of a Sunday outing. The Impressionists will come to nature in this temporary fashion, for which they will develop a fleeting technique. Although Courbet's picture anticipates them in theme, it is far from Impressionist in manner because, like the majority of his landscapes, it was painted indoors in his typical dark style and traditionally composed.

Courbet was one of the frankest sensualists in art but not in the slightly dubious manner of Ingres. A tremendously vital being, he was stirred by the physical qualities of matter, all matter. Very often, as in *The Young Bather* (Fig. 72), he seemed to consider the human body as a piece of still life, with interest concentrated on the tactile qualities of his subject. To an Ingres-trained public this must have been maddening, especially since many people have always identified themselves with the characters in a story or picture. This painting has very little of Ingres' kind of idealization, the artist having permitted the surface of the ample body to retain its natural oiliness. The landscape background in such works is frankly that of the studio.

Courbet's *Bather* of 1853, praised by Delacroix for its power in spite of its "vulgarity," was described by another critic thus: "This creature is such that a crocodile wouldn't want to eat her." Yet it would be a serious mistake to minimize the idealizing tendency in Courbet's art, even in these

71. COURBET: *Young Women on the Banks of the Seine* (Paris, Petit Palais).

130

inedible nudes. They have his own personal quality of glorifying the flesh and monumentalizing the figure. No more impressive female nude can be found anywhere than the model standing before Courbet's easel in *The Studio of the Painter*.

In his reactions to nature, Courbet is still Romantic. These subjects again emphasize the physical power and vividness of his art, especially his sea paintings. Such pictures as the *Stormy Sea* (Fig. 73) reveal the painter at his most virile, giving a clear sensation of the substance of foam and waves as well as the power of that great natural force with which he loved to wrestle.

72. COURBET: *The Young Bather* (New York, Metropolitan Museum of Art).

As Courbet moved toward the end of his career, colors tended to become brighter and cleaner. The idea of "clear painting" was in the air and Courbet certainly knew the work of Manet. His treatment of snow in a brilliantly gleaming white, flaky manner is an indication of his virtuoso handling of paint.

Aesthetic considerations apart, Courbet is important in modern times for having maintained with considerable courage the artist's right to express himself. Organizing his own exhibitions when it was impossible to exhibit otherwise, refusing to bend the knee under the worst circumstances, he stands out very impressively in spite of personal foibles. As a pioneer in the field of modern objective representation, he turned men's eyes more than ever before to the materiality of the world we live in. As with most real artists, his materiality was transmuted by a personal idealism and emotional quality that remove his work from competition with the camera.

As early as 1848 he had joined the *Artistes Républicains*, an antimonarchist group, while during the Commune of 1870 he became president of the

73. COURBET: *Stormy Sea* (Paris, Louvre).

Artists Federation. Its members, among them Corot, Millet, Daumier, and Manet, believed that artists should be free of governmental interference in artistic matters (no more Rome Academy, no *salon* medals, liberalized School of Beaux Arts, government commissions by competition, etc.). One of the Federation's first acts was to pull down the Vendôme Column, a symbol of past tyranny. During the terror following the return of the Versailles party, Courbet was sent to Sainte Pélagie for six months— Daumier had been a guest there earlier. Later he was condemned to rebuild the column at his own expense. He escaped to Switzerland where he died a few years later. The subsequent exclusion of Courbet's paintings from public exhibition was instigated by reactionary artists under the leadership of Meissonier, a fact which speaks for itself.

Honoré Daumier (1808–1879), the third member of the Realist "school," was more socially conscious than perhaps any other artist up to that point. In his "one must be of one's time" attitude he left far behind the somewhat one-sided art of Millet and Courbet, with a tremendous awareness of the misery and corruption of his era.

His early newspaper experience brought him into contact with a then anonymous hack writer, Balzac, later famous as the author of the *Comédie humaine*. Daumier's four thousand lithographic plates that comprise the artist's picture of nineteenth-century society are a fitting parallel to Balzac's great series of novels. As a cartoonist for the journals of the day it was Daumier's job to furnish two plates a week, the captions supplied by someone else. For generations almost, until he ultimately went blind, Daumier continued this soul-straining activity, regularly turning out satires that occasionally fell flat but were almost always well drawn and brilliantly designed. Finding very little time to paint, he still managed to produce some of the most significant pictures of the century, today acknowledged as considerably in advance of their time.

Since he did not draw very well from life, the themes of Daumier's paintings and lithographs were culled from a wealth of memory images from the everyday life of Paris. From this source came the inexhaustible series of Parisian Types, Conjugal Customs, Bathers, Bohemians of Paris, Men of Justice, Pastorals, Summer Pictures, Railroad Pictures, Difficult Moments of Life, and many others.

Born in 1808 the son of a glazier from Marseilles, he was forced from earliest childhood to help support the family. As clerk and errand boy he acquired a wide familiarity with the seamier side of life. At twenty he published his first lithograph and three years later joined the staff of *La Caricature*, a well-known satirical paper. During the thirties Daumier was the Royalist party's most determined opponent in a series of violently personal caricatures climaxed by the famous *Gargantua* representing the king. Daumier was given six months in Sainte Pélagie Prison. When in 1835 the press was forbidden the right of political criticism, he turned to a milder form of critique through the social subjects listed above.

Of his early period of political activity the most famous print is *Le Ventre législatif* (The Legislative Belly), setting out in stiff but mordant fashion the members of the Chamber as seen from the visitors' gallery. We are told that instead of drawn sketches he made little clay figures from which

133

the lithograph was prepared. This procedure may explain a good deal about the technique of Daumier, whose forms always have a sculptural quality and bulk. In many paintings and prints the abrupt transition from one plane to another makes his figures look as though modeled in clay. That Daumier was a sculptor to be reckoned with can be seen from the still existing models for *Le Ventre législatif* or the bronzes made from them.

If Daumier was aware of the hollow mockery of the Chamber of Deputies, he was no less conscious of the economic misery of the time. The celebrated lithograph, *Rue Transnonain* (Fig. 74), has often been reproduced, but we are seldom reminded of its significance in the social and political scheme of the early nineteenth century. When during the nationwide unrest of 1834 a general strike was called at Lyons, the workers in Paris showed signs of joining in. During suppression of the April riots in the capital, while soldiers were patrolling the streets, it was claimed that snipers had fired on the troops from numéro 12, rue Transnonain. True or not we do not know; but the soldiers marched into that building and killed every man, woman, and

74. DAUMIER: *Rue Transnonain*—lithograph (New York, Metropolitan Museum of Art).

child in it. A few weeks later Daumier's print appeared with the eloquently simple title, *Rue Transnonain, April 13, 1834*, to describe the event about which Baudelaire had said: "Under this cold mansard, silence and death reign."

Apart from the characteristically abrupt black-and-white contrasts there is a brutally shocking quality here reminiscent of the more macabre portions of *The Massacre at Scio* (Fig. 30) and similarly effective. The outspread legs of the figure against the bed is a Baroque motif also used by Delacroix in the latter's *St. Sebastian* of 1836.

75. DAUMIER: *La République* (Paris, Louvre).

During the forties Daumier spoke out against the Napoleonic group and after the Revolution of 1848, to which he may well have contributed, political caricature was again permitted. That very year his first identifiable painting, *La République* (Fig. 75), appeared in connection with a competition for the Hôtel de Ville, which Daumier did not win. Symbolic in subject matter, with the slightly mature boys suckled by the robust figure seen earlier on Delacroix's barricade, *La République* is typical of Daumier's emphasis on powerful and expressive form. As always the accent is first upon design and then upon form expressive of an idea, as in post-Impressionism toward the end of the century. In this regard Daumier breaks sharply with the ordinary Realist point of view, for his art is the least descriptive and the least objective of the group. Although the physical is always subordinate to the spiritual, in the feeling of "exuberant carnality" he far outstrips Millet and Courbet.

As for the sources of Daumier's style, although we know very little, it is customary to compare him to Géricault. The fluid plasticity of the children in *La République* seems to be the same loose version of Michelangelo's physical force that we found in the earlier painter. Another point

135

of comparison is the series of abrupt transitions from light areas to dark as modeling devices. Although this method does occur in the painting of Géricault, it is a much more constant factor in the aquatints of Goya, which were surely known by this date, especially to artists interested in black-and-white media.

Later paintings of Daumier (and most of them are later, though undated) reveal a number of modern qualities that are quite striking and far in advance of their time. *The Drama* (Fig. 76), one of his many representations of theater scenes, combines bulky and plastically powerful figures with an emotional purpose. Expressiveness is achieved first by the device of looking over the heads of a number of figures in the foreground—an Oriental mannerism much used by the later Impressionists. In his characteristic way, Daumier also alternates light and dark spots so that, on the one hand, we are drawn back into the body of the picture and, on the other, the emotions of the spectators are brought into relief. This patterning of light and dark spots for plastic purposes, creating movement in space, is again a modern but this time post-Impressionist device. It is not for nothing that the art of Daumier, although known through his first exhibition in 1878, achieved its first critical approval only after the post-Impressionists had established the modern aesthetic.

76. DAUMIER: *The Drama* (Munich, Staatsgalerie).

The constant movement in the paintings and prints of Daumier is a joint result of manipulation of the lights and the various directional lines, tugging volumes, and overlapping planes. Moreover, the aesthetic devices contribute considerably to emotional conviction, with the patterned light and dark effects, not decorative but plastic in their purpose, creating movement and reflecting the emotions of the spectators.

Aesthetic considerations aside, subjects such as *The Drama* are part of

136

the vast *comédie humaine* which he was painting and drawing during his entire lifetime. All subjects were grist for his mill but never from an objective viewpoint. Daumier was always interested in why people do certain things and have certain feelings. In this picture the audience, which in a similarly composed Impressionist picture would be merely a steppingstone to the stage, is the protagonist. The collective reaction to Hamlet on the stage is more important than the play itself.

There is no single word to describe Daumier's approach to subject matter, even though many people still think of him only in terms of social satire. Daumier was as many-sided in his approach to people as one could be—sometimes as gentle as Millet, as romantic as Delacroix, or as brutal as Goya. Whatever his mood, the technique is vigorous and economical to the point of parsimony, yet rivaling Rubens and Michelangelo in the creation of powerful forms. His awareness of bulk and contour ranged over the chubbiness of children, the haggard faces of the old, or the lean and avid faces of his hated judges and lawyers. In the contrastingly thin Don Quixote and plump Sancho Panza we have another example of his use of the human body as a vehicle for emotions. The frequent use of this theme—and the world often seemed divided into Sanchos and Quixotes—illustrates his still Romantic use of literature as a source of inspiration. Unlike the true Romantics, however, he used these themes in a more cosmic fashion as comments on the world and man.

In the prints, subject matter is not only varied but, general opinion to the contrary, extremely sympathetic as well. Even where the intent appears humorous (assisted by the caption writer), Daumier remains a curious mixture of crass Realism and pathos. No one has understood the miseries and foibles of the middle class as well as he. His bourgeois pictures do not represent individuals as much as symbols of a class, like the Rougon-Macquarts of Zola, the typical family of the Second Empire.

One of these lithographs shows a middle-class man and wife at a window in the morning, still in their nightgowns and piously watering flowers, with the caption: *"For thirty years they have cultivated virtue and flowers"* (Fig. 77). If we fail to look beyond the caption, it is merely funny, but for Daumier people like this represent the little man living in a dark tenement

LES BONS BOURGEOIS

77. DAUMIER: *For Thirty Years They Have Cultivated Virtue and Flowers*—lithograph (New York, Metropolitan Museum of Art).

and finding a measure of release in a flower box. Examined from this point of view, the print takes on a touching quality wherein the artist may smile at the pathetic eagerness of these poor people but feel compassion at the same time. For the things he disliked, however, Daumier had the sharpest of eyes and the bitterest of comments: dishonest lawyers, false philanthropists, scandalmongers, and others of the same breed.

Daumier will always be remembered as the artist of his own class, the poor. In such pictures as *Third Class Carriage* (Fig. 78) he brings together a variegated group of people in a typically fluid and changeable modern background. These people in the train will not remain together very long as they move from station to station, but while they are there they symbolize the various strata of the lower middle class and the poor. Like most of his pictures, these economically painted forms are arranged with regard to compositional rhythm and colored in subdued but expressive tones. Unlike Courbet but more like Millet, he prefers to work in generalized forms rather than particularized details, subordinating these to mass effect. His quick summaries of form are not only abstract in the modern fashion but always part of a decorative pattern as in Oriental art. Such effects are often pointed up by the arbitrary use of outlines which supplement Daumier's sketchy modeling.

In *The Uprising* (Fig. 79) powerful and broadly expressionistic figures move diagonally into the left side of the painting to give in an isolated, architectural fashion the idea of action. Although the placing of the figures so far forward in the composition might conceivably have overweighted the front of his picture space, the reduction of background to almost a single plane acts as a kind of backdrop to close off the space. The contrast between

138

the leader of the group and his soberly painted followers not only adds to the feeling of volume but is part of the basically decorative character of Daumier's work. His forms express ideas rather than realistic facts, in which respect his art is on a different level from that of Courbet and closer to the post-Impressionists of the end of the century.

Although we are more concerned with painting than with prints, it must be remembered that Daumier as a print maker with a social purpose forms a very important link in the chain between the Hogarth-Goya-Rowlandson group and more recent practitioners such as Forain, George Grosz, and Käthe Kollwitz. His graphic political observations are a mixture of the satire of Hogarth and the brutality of Goya but more socially conscious than either. It was only during the more politically and socially aware nineteenth century that a man like Daumier could inveigh against specific evils and offer remedies. We cannot picture Hogarth or Goya lambasting the munitions makers and stock manipulators, not only because those things did not exist in their day, but because social criticism had not developed far enough.

78. DAUMIER: *Third Class Carriage* (New York, Metropolitan Museum of Art).

79. DAUMIER: *The Uprising* (Washington, Phillips Memorial Gallery).

It is fairly clear that Daumier understood the times in which he lived better than Courbet; yet, apart from his graphic protests against the social order, he was much more restrained. Courbet's refusal of the Legion of Honor in 1870 was a public demonstration of his independence; Daumier also refused, but not noisily, merely pointing out that it was too late for it to mean much to him.

The last few years of Daumier's life, after his eyes had failed him, were wretched and poor. Had it not been for the kindness of the ever-generous Corot, who bought the house in which the Daumiers lived as a present for them, they would have been out in the street. For whatever it may mean in terms of Daumier's feelings about the inequities of his times, the painter was buried in a pauper's grave. The hundreds of paintings that were in his little house at Valmondois disappeared into the vaults of a group of unscrupulous dealers who paid next to nothing for them. A half century later they were to reappear, heralded among the predecessors of the modern movement.

9. FROM MANET TO IMPRESSIONISM

Two decades of Napoleon III ended in the defeat of France by Germany and the Revolution of 1870. The Left wing, still trying to carry on the war, was mercilessly crushed by the conservative National Assembly that preferred Prussians to the Commune. After a number of abortive attempts to install a king, the disorganized Assembly was dissolved in favor of a genuinely national body that formulated the 1875 constitution. Many later difficulties of France stem from this period. A figurehead president was installed—they had become wary of dictators—to share authority with a parliament of five hundred individualistic members, divided into some ten to twenty political parties.

The danger from the Right (Royalists and conservative Church elements) was to remain an ever-present challenge. Only two years after the signing of the Republican constitution, the conservatives struck back and tried to take over by a *coup d'état*. When the Royalist "putsch" failed, Republican candidates were swept into the Chamber and Senate. From that point to the middle of the next decade the liberals managed to hold on. Although the Impressionist movement suffered considerably from the Right wing attempt to create a "Red" scare in 1877 and 1878, the temporary victory of the Republicans, who continued in office for almost ten years, made things better for the modern painters.

The conflict between artists and the public had reached its first climax during the fifties in the violent reaction against the work of Courbet. During the following decade, this notoriety was shared by Édouard Manet, initiator of the new painting. Manet marks the end of one era and the beginning of another. As part of the Realist movement, he had exhibited together with Courbet and was attacked on the same grounds; but he is also a bridge from

Realism to Impressionism. From the very beginning, Manet's kind of Realism is more concerned with technique than with subject matter. His themes, even though drawn from the world of fact and painted in the clear light of day, were pictorial motifs rather than exaltations of materiality or studies of mood. In other words, Manet was more concerned with how to paint rather than what to paint. This is the dividing line between the art of the earlier nineteenth century and modern art as we know it.

The literary Realists had shown the way during the fifties by insisting that every aspect of reality was suitable for the creative artist. Although they were not quite as objective as they imagined, they did pave the way for a new art. As for the pictorial Realists, they had been intensely subjective —theme had been all-important. Moreover, they had not abandoned the technical devices of the past; a figure by Millet or Courbet, although challenging in theme, was still done in the traditional chiaroscuro and with the conventional dark underpainting.

To Manet and the Impressionists, however, all subjects were worth while (the Realist credo) provided they lent themselves to the method these people evolved. Not only is this an extension of the Realist attitude, but it also means an intensification of the artist's right to express himself. Moreover, as we shall see, the new technique is bound up with the scientific attitude of the age.

Literary Realism had grown out of the intense materialism of the period, the writer's reaction to it, and finally his protest against it. But authors— and artists—were still affected by personal involvement in the situations they portrayed: anger, exaltation, pity, or disgust. In that sense they were still Romantic. With the next generation of artists, however, the personal emotional factor diminishes and even tends to disappear. More and more, the painter becomes an objective observer setting down without comment in his new language the subject as it appears to him.

The development of highly individualized technique is also an extension of Realist doctrine. If any subject is of itself interesting and worthy, especially in terms of the artist's right to self-expression, his method of observation is equally his own affair. We find sympathetic people making it a point to defend men like Manet, even though they may not care for or understand what he is doing. Zola, for example, as part of his championing of Impressionism, took up the cudgels to defend Cézanne whose work did not appeal to him.

The fight for artistic freedom upheld by Baudelaire, Zola, and others is part of the general tug of war between progress and reaction throughout the century. Although there is no step-by-step artistic parallel to the continuous political struggle between Right and Left, generally the defenders of the right of free speech in art are lined up on the liberal side.

Even though many of the artists are nonpolitical, they are often attacked as subversive. Any rebellion against authority, even the authority of the *salon* or Academy to prescribe techniques and subjects, is clear evidence of nonconformism. The feeling in our own times that modern art is a form of radicalism is a carry-over from the nineteenth-century attacks on Realism, Impressionism, and post-Impressionism as politically suspect movements. Just as Courbet had been labeled "socialist" long before he knew anything about politics, the Impressionists were called "communard" in spite of the conservative politics of Degas, the monarchist, and Cézanne, the devout Catholic. The fact that these men were definitely not radical and that their associates, Manet, Renoir, Monet, and Sisley, were not interested in politics, could not save them from attack when the political situation became ripe. (Pissarro was the only one with radical ideas.)

Essentially, the Impressionists were perfecting a middle-class art, glorifying the life of the big city, and portraying in a gentle lyrical fashion the various aspects of nature outside the city. It took the wealthy public a generation to catch up with what they were doing. By the middle eighties, modern painting was moving off to its next point of development, leaving Impressionism to the "connoisseurs" and art lovers.

From a historical point of view, Impressionism represents the full flower of urban art. Not only does it give us the subject matter of the big city in Manet, Degas, Lautrec, Renoir, and others but presents it in a newer and more nervous manner than the still solid painting of Daumier and Courbet. In a similar fashion, it brings us back to nature from the city. We have only to compare a traditional landscape with the landscape of the "new painting." The development of swifter and cheaper forms of travel

143

made people see nature differently. In the past the artist had built for himself a wide panoramic scene and observed it without hurry as though from a nearby hill, whereas the modern method was more dynamic. Instead of classical balance or infinite extension into space, we get a more rapid and disjointed point of view resembling flashes of scenery from a moving train. It would follow almost inevitably that for this sort of concept the artist would have to evolve a more casual and broken method of painting, the Impressionist method.

With travel cheaper and more available, the average city dweller is brought back to the country but he returns only temporarily, as a picnicker on Sunday afternoon. Courbet had sensed this in his *Young Women on the Banks of the Seine*, but with the Impressionists it became a favorite theme. The Impressionists saw other subjects in the same momentary fashion: scenes in cafés, streets, theaters, stores, and other places. A feeling for spontaneity was stimulated also by development of the camera, whose effects many artists tried to emulate. Some even used photographs as the basis for their "accidental" and momentary studies.

The final element necessary for the evolution of Impressionist technique is scientific interest in the phenomena of light, the results of color mixing, and the effect of colors on the eye. For the Impressionists the development of physics and optics, begun as early as the first quarter of the century, was an important aid in their thinking, even though their use of the material was far from scientific.

Édouard Manet (1832–1883), considered by many as the spiritual father of Impressionism, was the son of a well-to-do bourgeois family. Although intended for a practical career, he soon showed so much interest in art that his family sent him away at sixteen on a long voyage to Rio de Janeiro to cool him off. From 1850 to 1856, however, he was a pupil of Couture, a famous academic master who could not agree with young Manet because the latter insisted on painting things as he saw them. Couture's pitying remark that if Manet were not careful he would be the Daumier of his time, tells the story. Manet left this conventional studio for a period of travel in Belgium, Holland, Germany, and Italy, where the painting of Frans Hals and Velásquez seemed to affect him considerably. Hals is reflected in Manet's

144

later loose application of bright and startling tones, and Velásquez in the Frenchman's interest in atmospheric light and the use of flat, broad areas of color. Later the example of Goya would reinforce the effect of Velásquez.

80. MANET: *Lola of Valencia* (Paris, Louvre).

The Romantic element in Manet's early work is shown in the appearance of Spanish themes even before his trip to Spain. These themes apparently had little to do with his interest in Velásquez or Goya but rather with the bright color potentialities of the subjects as well as the appearance of a troupe of Spanish dancers in Paris in 1861. That year he painted the *Spanish Ballet*, *The Guitar Player*, and *Lola of Valencia* (Fig. 80). Unlike the theater paintings of Daumier and Lautrec, these works were less psychological than aesthetic, less due to an interest in the theater than to the aesthetic possibilities of the brightly dressed Spaniards. Instead of making sketches on the stage, Manet had the subjects brought to his studio to pose. In fact, he even dressed friends and family in these exotic costumes and painted them, as in the *Young Man in the Costume of a Majo* (New York, Metropolitan Museum). Many of these pictures look awkward and stiff, obviously posed, and not in action.

They were designed to create a sensation of light and the appearance of the transitory. Painted in startlingly bright tones, they were received with the same lack of enthusiasm accorded to every one of his works. Lola, for example, is placed against an artificial stage "flat" and is revealed in an intensely vivid and novel light. Pink, red, and black are applied in large broken splashes for the ornaments and bold flat areas for the body, which is modeled as little as possible. The form exists as it does in actuality because of the contrast between light and dark areas.

145

This visual method, practiced earlier by Velásquez, was repeated in Manet's great *succès de scandale*, the so-called *Luncheon on the Grass* (Fig. 81). It was first offered to the *salon* in 1863 and was refused, together with the works of Whistler, Jongkind, Fantin-Latour, Pissarro, and many others, and with them was placed in a nearby Salon des Refusés on orders of the Emperor Napoleon III.

What were the objections to the art of Manet that were to make him "as famous as Garibaldi?" Like Courbet, he gave the same elaborate treatment and importance to a naturalistic subject as others did to allegory or history. More serious was the intensely novel color that, since it was unexpected, was undesirable. Critics referred to his usage as the caricature of color. Traditionally, artists had worked gradually from a dark background to the highlights where necessary. Manet, on the other hand, painted from initially indicated light areas into which half-light and darker tones were worked while the light portions were still wet. In this way the painter felt he could convey the feeling of a surface charged with light.

81. MANET: *Luncheon on the Grass* (Paris, Louvre).

In *Luncheon on the Grass* Manet had brought together one nude woman, two fully dressed young men (one talking very matter-of-factly), and one partially dressed young woman. Although composed in the conventional Renaissance triangle, the work violated all accepted canons of subject matter. When Manet and his friends pointed out that Giorgione had used the same theme, they were told that the Italian painter had idealized his treatment, whereas anyone could see that Manet's people were real. Actually, the young lady was his model Mlle. Victorine, one man his brother, and the other his brother-in-law Laenhoff. The casual attitude of the nude was unpalatable to the public, while the idea of food being eaten under these dubious circumstances made the offense worse.

For us, the picture is interesting as an illustration of his flat technique, the silhouetted figure of the nude emerging against the stark blackness of the young man's coat. Colors are bright and clear, with the studio landscape diffused in intensity to concentrate our attention on the figures. Yet when the Emperor and his Empress visited the Salon des Refusés and saw the painting, the noble gentleman remarked: "This picture is an offense to modesty." The experiment of a "Salon of the Refused" was never repeated; artists had to wait until 1884 and the Salon des Indépendants for a similar opportunity to exhibit.

With these facts in mind we can understand more easily the public reaction to Manet's *Olympia* (Fig. 82), offered in 1865. The unidealized nude young woman receiving her daily offering of flowers from an admirer of the moment, and staring at the spectator with a bold, forthright glance, brought crowds ordinarily reserved for fires or public executions. Some enthusiastic detractors tried to destroy the picture and guards had to be set over it. Manet, somewhat more thin-skinned than Courbet, went to Spain for a while, where he met his future biographer and apologist, Théodore Duret, who was later to write a *History of Impressionism*. (His first defender had been Baudelaire: "But one sees gleaming in Lola of Valencia, the unexpected charm of a pink and black jewel.")

On his return Manet became friendly with Émile Zola, who was then starting a journalistic career. The latter, urged by his friend Cézanne, wrote an enthusiastic review of Manet's work that brought in so many letters to the editor that young Zola almost lost his job. One of the pictures singled out in this article was *The Fifer* (Fig. 83). In addition to the usual bright color and almost complete absence of shadow, the painting shows a highly stylized, almost Persian figure revealed in brilliant contrast against a less intense background. Only the hands and face are definitely modeled, with the rest of the body left relatively flat, thus accentuating the function of light in rendering a momentary and instantaneous vision of the subject.

With Manet, as with Velásquez, forms were considered as though they had just appeared through an open doorway—or against the sun—where only the face and possibly the hands would be seen with any degree of clarity. The momentarily less important body would remain a silhouette during this first quick visualization. As in Velásquez, *The Fifer* shows no specific outlines but rather the end of one color area and the beginning of another. The Oriental flat quality of the picture, already evident in its composition, is accentuated by the absence of a ground line.

In 1867 the jury of the Universal Exposition refused Manet's paintings, and he had recourse to a private exhibition at the Fair, as did Courbet. Like

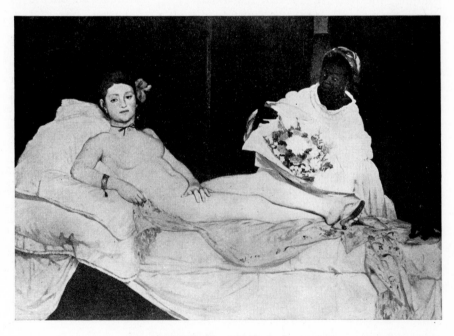

82. MANET: *Olympia* (Paris, Louvre).

148

his earlier show at the Martinet Gallery (1863), it was hardly worth the trouble. The following year he thanked Zola for his help by painting the author's portrait against a background wall showing a Japanese print and screen, a photograph of Velásquez' *Los Borrachos*, and a sketch of the *Olympia*. This picture and the somewhat earlier *Woman with the Parrot* (New York, Metropolitan Museum of Art) were sent to the *salon* of that year. The latter painting is one of the artist's most aesthetic productions, where objects not in themselves related are brought together in a composition of lemon-yellow, brown, and green. A woman holding a flower, a parrot on a stand, and a lemon on the floor are presented

83. MANET: *The Fifer* (Paris, Louvre).

in a completely objective manner without any psychological implications.

The period following Manet's trip to Spain shows the effect of Goya's painting on the Frenchman. Pictures such as the *Matador Bowing* and *The Bullfight* are generally influenced, while *The Balcony* (1868) is directly derived from *Majas on a Balcony*, and Manet's *Execution of the Emperor Maximilian* (Fig. 84) from Goya's *Shooting of a Group of Citizens* (Fig. 18).

This series of direct influences and borrowings are no reflection on Manet—he made no bones about this aspect of his work—but are illustrations of the primarily aesthetic nature of his painting. Reworking the ideas of an older master and use of an earlier work of art as a steppingstone or point of departure happen with increasing frequency in modern art. Manet's interest in the art of Goya is parallel to his study of Velásquez or Hals, but more useful in this later period of the Frenchman's development through its offer of more brilliant and exciting color as well as an abstract type of arrangement.

149

84. MANET: *Execution of the Emperor Maximilian* (Mannheim, Kunsthalle).

Comparing the two *Execution* pictures, we are more impressed by differences than by similarities. The Spaniard, under the stimulus of anger and hatred, produced a violently emotional work filled with Romantic sympathy for the suffering. Manet, on the other hand, treats his theme as an opportunity for brilliant color and light effects, deliberately avoiding the picturesque and Romantic elements in the tragic story of Maximilian. This attitude is in line with the Realist credo of objectivity to which no one adhered more rigidly than Manet. It is inconceivable that any Romantic-Realist painter, like Courbet or Daumier, could have shown this scene in such a detached fashion. But while they were still Romantic in their Realism, the intellectual Manet was able to rationalize himself into a reportorial objectivity that leaves him the only complete exponent of the Realist viewpoint. This lack of psychological content is not so much a defect as a consciously developed technique in the process of seeing things as they are, without comment.

After the dynamic paintings of the Romantic and the Realist schools, the work of Manet is startling in its lack of both feeling and movement. Manet seems to have been unable to resolve the problem of showing his figures in clear light and in motion. In this respect he adheres more to Velásquez than to Goya. His desire to show people at a given moment in time and space led him to suspend all movement, to leave them as they would presumably appear to us at the first instant of visualization. Though Manet pioneered in this method of seeing things, he could not proceed beyond this point, nor could Monet, Pissarro, and even Renoir, all of whom show the same arrested motion. Degas and Lautrec, on the other hand, solved the problem by means of other devices.

The response to Manet's *Execution of the Emperor Maximilian* was aggravated by political considerations. Since the reactionary government already looked upon these new artists as declassed creatures, the ban against a picture that dealt with the shooting of the French candidate for the throne of Mexico was a foregone conclusion.

Manet was the ideological leader of the period preceding the War of 1870. His contribution in demonstrating the value of pure colors and the importance of light was equaled only by his steadfast example of independence in the face of persecution. A charming personality and sharp wit formed the background for the discerning comments on art that drew young artists and writers of the period to the Café Guerbois, where they held their meetings until the outbreak of war. Manet remained fundamentally a studio painter, emerging out of doors only on occasion. Although he painted a view of the International Exposition in 1867 and some sea and beach pictures in 1868, this type of work was only a small part of his production. The other members of the group, Monet, Pissarro, Sisley, Renoir, and Guillaumin, with these works as a point of departure, devoted themselves to the outdoors exclusively.

Even though the open-air experiments of Manet do not yet make use of the rainbow palette developed by Claude Monet and his associates, they are as "accidental" in conception and as quickly finished as any of the later conventional Impressionist pictures. In paintings of this early type, the artist tried to see his subject as a pattern of varying intensities of light, just as the camera does. Some of Claude Monet's pre-rainbow-palette pictures are done in this way too, and the technique is still widely used by conservative painters. Manet's so-called conversion to outdoor painting after the war is relatively unimportant to the history of art, for his contribution had already been made. Although he remained in the city to paint in the studio and the others placed themselves directly in the presence of nature, the debt they owed him was not denied. Fantin-Latour's *Un Atelier aux Batignolles* of 1870 paid homage to the father of Impressionism and the last of the Realists. The picture shows Manet painting at an easel, with Monet, Renoir, Bazille, and Émile Zola grouped around him.

The future out-of-door painters are first encountered as a group in the studio of the academic Gleyre, where Monet, Renoir, Bazille, and Sisley were students as late as 1863. That year, the double impact of the Salon des Refusés and Manet's private showing at the Martinet Gallery led them to leave Gleyre and work on their own. Monet introduced Pissarro, and the latter brought Cézanne.

In 1864, Monet, who had already had outdoor painting experience, took his friends, Sisley, Renoir, and Bazille, out to Chailly, fairly near Barbizon. For most of Monet's companions this was the first real contact with nature, a contact soon fructified by their meeting with certain Barbizon masters. Sisley, Pissarro, and Berthe Morisot were very much interested in Corot. Renoir vacillated between Corot and Courbet, though he was much encouraged to paint light by Diaz, whom he introduced to the others. Of all the Barbizon painters, Daubigny was the only one working directly from nature, and it was his influence that affected Monet. Not only Daubigny's interest in the "impressions" he got from nature but even specific compositional ideas of his were borrowed by the group during that year.

Within the next few years, round about 1866, the group began to meet regularly with Manet at the Café Guerbois. Although he took the lead in many discussions, the café atmosphere promoted a kind of give-and-take in which everyone could voice his own ideas. When Manet had brought them his shadowless painting and clear tones, Corot and Courbet were still considered very advanced and in some circles even Delacroix was suspected. Renoir's *Bather with a Griffon* (Fig. 88) of 1870 still shows Courbet's influence. Manet had upset the traditional idea that every bright color should have its complement of shadow, that lively colors must be introduced through intermediary half tones—the system that held figures in semi-obscurity. His unidealized nudes taken directly from life and painted almost shadowless in clear colors on other clear colors were bound to create excitement. Instead of the traditional shadowy transitions, he used less intense but still clear tones that were always in value. Manet's influence was to extend even further, for his outdoor pictures, as we have seen, were broken in color and "accidental" in conception and composition.

Until the war, various members of the group were admitted to the *salon* but ignored for the most part with the exception of Manet. They were still not well enough known to be disliked. With the outbreak of war in 1870, Monet and Pissarro went off to London to escape service and Cézanne to the south of France for the same reason; Manet and Renoir served in the army. For Monet and Pissarro and by indirection for the rest of the group, the contact with the work of Constable and Turner was decisive in its crystallization of their interest in atmospheric and vibratory color. The broken and complementary colors of Constable, highlighted with the spotted whites that the Impressionists were to find so useful, and the shimmering tonal paintings of Turner made a tremendous impression on the Frenchmen.

After the war, Manet's leadership continued on a reduced scale at the Café Nouvelle Athènes. In 1872 and 1873, all the group members except Berthe Morisot were refused at the *salon* and they decided to put up their own exhibition the following year. Almost every future Impressionist was represented at the 1874 exhibition set up in the studio of the photographer Nadar: Pissarro, Degas, Claude Monet, Sisley, Renoir, Cézanne, and Berthe Morisot, together with a number of non-Impressionist artists who helped pay expenses. Manet, always a bit on the conservative side, did not take part—perhaps organized opposition seemed too radical. He had always maintained that the "new painting" should fight its way into the official *salon.* The fact that he himself had scored there in 1873 with the Hals-like

Le Bon Bock (Philadelphia, Tyson Collection) may well have influenced his decision to abstain. Manet's refusal to paint outdoors, his fine manner, social contacts, and wealth tended to remove him from the leadership of the increasingly rebellious Batignolles group. Yet he persisted in painting his "unacceptable" Realist pictures. As far as the critics were concerned, his abstention did not help for he was damned with the rest.

Although the press and academicians attacked the first exhibition of the Independents (the name Impressionists was fastened on them by one of the critics), the show was not without its small successes. A few enlightened collectors appeared, one or two dealers bought pictures, and a group of critics lent their support. Among the visitors was the liberal-minded publisher Georges Charpentier, a stalwart among Impressionist patrons, and the stockbroker Paul Gauguin. The poor financial results of the exhibition, however, coupled with a generally bad economic situation, led to an auction in 1875 at the Hôtel Drouot. In his reminiscences the sympathetic dealer Durand-Ruel noted the tremendous hostility of the audience and the fantastically low prices at which pictures were "knocked down." Renoir apparently came out worst.

The second Impressionist exhibition in 1876 was hardly more successful than the first. Albert Wolff in *Figaro* set the tone with his oft-quoted: "There are some people who can burst with laughter before these things. I, on the other hand, am bitterly grieved by these so-called artists who call themselves Intransigents, Impressionists. They take canvas, color and brushes, throw a few tones about carelessly and sign the result."

Although Degas, Manet, and Cézanne had no serious financial worries, the situation was not so pleasant for Monet, Renoir, Sisley, and Pissarro. The latter group arranged with a restaurant keeper to feed them in return for pictures, while *Père* Tanguy made a similar arrangement with them for colors and canvas.

The third exhibition in 1877 was organized with the help of Caillebotte, a wealthy naval architect and painter who participated in it and ultimately became one of the important collectors of Impressionist painting. In many ways this show represented the high point of public hostility to the new movement. The Party of Order, engaged in a plot to overthrow the Republic, agitated against the "Red" menace. These tactics had their effect on the few supporters of the "intransigent" Impressionists, and purchasers were even scarcer than before. Very few people had the courage to resist the propaganda that referred to "communard art" and similar accusations. The 1877 exhibition was attended by a politically hostile group that did not hesitate to show active dislike of what it saw. Efforts by Caillebotte and some of the friendly critics to explain the pictures to individual visitors were met with insults.

The auction held a few months later in the midst of an election campaign was the victim of organized heckling, and pictures brought as little as forty-five francs—for a Renoir. Repercussions of these attacks were felt for some time; even the courageous Durand-Ruel withdrew his support until things got better. The Impressionists had really become notorious; they were the subjects of newspaper caricatures and music hall jokes, and there was even a play about an Impressionist painter.

Renoir, who could do portraits, received a commission from the Charpentier family. He also profited from sympathetic purchases by Mary Cassatt and Gauguin, who bought pictures from the needier members of the group. In general, however, things were so bad that some of the members drifted away and began to send paintings to the *salon* again: Sisley, Cézanne, Renoir, and finally even Monet. By 1880 the exhibitions were no longer really Impressionist. The group was definitely split. Only Pissarro and Caillebotte carried on, while Degas was bringing in second-rate artists to swell the roster. The last real Impressionist exhibition was organized by Durand-Ruel in 1882.

Gradually, by the middle eighties, Impressionism began to take hold. There were more purchasers, particularly Americans, and eventually foreign imitators as well. Official opposition, nevertheless, went on for a long time until other, more "advanced" forms of painting had to be attacked. Eventually, it should be noted, Impressionism became an academic procedure, a routine method of brightening a canvas. By that time, no one objected, and Impressionist pictures became conventional collector's items. In our own day, no other form of painting has had the same appeal for the middle class.

During the period of gestation, however, the members of the Impressionist group were extremely discouraged. After Manet's *Bar at the Folies Bergères* was shown in the *salon* of 1882, Albert Wolff, author of the famous 1876 "blast" in *Figaro*, wrote him a congratulatory letter. The painter replied: "Thank you for your kind remarks. But I confess I should be glad to read in my lifetime the fine article you will devote to me—as soon as I am dead." A year later this actually happened.

In order to understand the reaction of hostile critics during the early career of Impressionism, we must see that it was no longer as much a question of theme as of technique. Unlike the opposition to Courbet's "gross" and "realistic" subjects, the antagonism to the Impressionists was based on procedures so new to the public that they could not be ignored or forgiven.

What the "new painting" really represented was the logical conclusion of the Realistic process that had been going on since the Renaissance, when artists had occupied themselves with learning all they could about the visible world. During the seventeenth century, especially in Holland and Spain, this viewpoint was intensified through the visual painting of Velásquez and Hals and the magnificent genre works of Vermeer. The latter painter had even noticed that adjacent objects cast colored shadows on each other, and that painting from a fixed point of view without moving around the object gave him unusual perspective and pattern effects. But this development had been so gradual as to be almost imperceptible.

The modern painter had to contend with the fact that most people came to art and to nature with preconceived notions. The struggle of Constable to prove that foliage was green and not brown shows the conditioning effect of older art on people's minds. Today we realize that under certain conditions of light, foliage may even look violet, but this was too much for the public of the 1870's. The "truth" for a given moment in time may indeed call for violet, although this will be a violation of the permanent fact. Monet and the other out-of-door painters were not interested in permanent fact but in the momentary appearance of an object against brilliant and natural light.

In their search for the best way to simulate the effect of sunlight, they realized that no green paint alone could give the intensity of that color under sun nor could any bright yellow substitute for the sun itself. They soon found that a primary color like yellow, reinforced by its complement, violet (*i.e.,* a combination of the other two primaries, red and blue), would be much more intense than bright yellow by itself. The same relationship held true for green plus red and for blue plus orange, other important outdoor combinations. This meant that the three most important colors for landscape painting, blue, green, and yellow, would now have to be strengthened by complementary spots of orange, red, and violet, respectively.

Further, these complementary colors were found most effective in an uncombined or "divided" state with their constituent tones left on the canvas for the eye to integrate. Thus, instead of touching yellow with violet, the painter could use dabs of red and blue, the components of violet, to heighten the yellow. The Impressionist was also aware that objects are visible not only in their local or immediate color but also with reflections from adjacent objects. These factors all would necessitate a series of vibrating spots that described the light on the object rather than its form, which became less important and often shapeless. Monet, Pissarro, and Sisley reveal these qualities with individual differences.

Claude Monet (1840–1926) is not the only exponent of outdoor Impressionism. He developed the style together with Renoir; but Monet soon became the leading landscape painter in the new method.

As the son of a merchant family, Monet was brought up in Le Havre where he knew the landscape painter Boudin, whose cloudy atmospheric effects were an important early influence. In 1862 Monet was at Le Havre with Boudin and Jongkind. The latter is important in our story for his open-air sketches and water colors and for his impressions of a particular scene under different conditions of atmosphere. Here he anticipated some of Monet's later experiments with haystacks, lily ponds, cathedrals, and so forth. Between 1864 and 1865 came the Barbizon contacts, especially with Daubigny and his atmospheric impressions and the influence of Courbet whose broad landscape technique and use of the palette knife for bold effects were very impressive.

By 1866 Monet began to use spots of clean color as well as complementary and unmixed tones, but forms were still solid and the later shimmering atmospheric effects were not yet there. Here we may note that in 1867 Pissarro's color still shows a dull green comparable to Barbizon painting. During the sixties also, Monet became acquainted with Manet, who was then vacillating between tonal outdoor pictures, such as the *Universal Exposition* with its broken color effects, and his more characteristic flat area works, such as *The Fifer*.

Around 1866 Monet joined the Café Guerbois group where Manet, at that time under the nervous strain of public disapproval, engaged in frequent arguments that sometimes led to quarrels and in the case of Duranty even to a duel. To these gatherings came writers such as Zola, Astruc, Duranty, and Duret, artists like Braquemond, Bazille, Fantin-Latour, Guillemet, Degas, and Renoir, occasionally Alfred Stevens and Constantin Guys, and Cézanne, Sisley, Monet, and Pissarro when they were in town, away from their nature painting.

As early as 1867 the hostile reaction of the *salon* to their aims led these painters to speak of an independent exhibition, but they did not seem able to raise the money. In 1868 the friendship of Daubigny, who was on the *salon* jury, got many of their pictures into the exhibition: Pissarro, Monet, Manet, Degas, Morisot, Renoir, Sisley were all in, though badly hung. This had very little effect, however, on public acceptance and, more important to painters like Monet and Renoir, the question of a living. For longer than one cares to think, the economic problems of these two men were really frightful. Constant lack of such elementary necessities as food, clothing, and paints did not prevent them from continuing along the path they had laid out. Monet was a tower of strength during this period, encouraging Renoir in the dark days.

The study of water was an important element in the formation of Monet's style during the latter half of the sixties. His *The River* (1868, Chicago, Art Institute) uses the water as the center of interest, presenting an opportunity to develop reflections and shimmering effects. *The River* is perhaps the earliest Impressionist "vacation" picture and the first to show the threefold derivation of the color of a given form: its own color, the colors reflected on it, and the atmospheric color. Somewhat earlier, snow

158

had offered these artists a means of studying shadows that were colored instead of bituminous and were affected by the color of the object casting the shadow.

Monet and Renoir worked together for a while at Bougival during the period immediately preceding the war. In the main, the latter's color seems to have been brighter and cleaner than Monet's at that time. The year 1870 found Monet, Pissarro, and Sisley (a British subject) in London. It was there that Monet met the dealer Durand-Ruel through Daubigny. This famous picture merchant, who had been the chief agent for the Barbizon group, was to become a decisive influence in building up a market for Impressionist painting.

Of the London period, Pissarro later said that the water colors of Turner and Constable and the paintings of Crome influenced them—even though the older artists, especially Turner, had no understanding of "the analysis of shadow." The important thing to note is that the future Impressionists were arriving at their colored shadows, rainbow palette, and unified atmospheric effects before they came to London.

During the postwar period, Monet and Renoir were together again, this time at Argenteuil, where the river with its bridges and boats furnished the final stimulus for their development of the sensation of nature, using little dots of color. The similarity of their styles around 1873 is so striking that there can hardly be any question of priority in development. They often painted the same subject and, as John Rewald indicates in his *History of Impressionism*, their treatment of such themes as the *Duck Pond* is almost identical. That same year Cézanne and Pissarro were working together at Pontoise.

Although it is still fashionable to consider Monet's painting as "scientific," this is an unwarranted exaggeration. In spite of the logic in color relationships and the search for transitory effects, the total effect of a Monet landscape is gently lyrical. Like most of the Impressionists, he subscribed to the idea that a picture should be painted to give an "accidental" quality—as though the artist just happened to be there at that moment. This would mean that the scene would have to be recorded at once and in the case of landscape necessarily out of doors. With some members of the brotherhood,

159

like Degas, the feeling of a camera-like rendition is very strong, as well as actual dependence on that machine for compositional ideas.

Monet's *Isle on the Seine near Giverney* (Fig. 85) shows the main characteristics of this type of outdoor painting. Not only have the forms of the trees become broken and diffused because of the many small patches of pure color, but the original color of trees and water have both been changed. We see that the greenness of the tree is a fusion of the tones constituting green and also that under brilliant sunlight objects are rather difficult to see clearly. The original simple green and the very form of the tree yield to component tones and the added complementary and contrasting spots of color. If we stand close to the painted trees, they break down into the various contributory colors; moving away from the subject, we find the eye begins to fuse the various tones into more understandable forms, which still continue to shimmer as a result of constant ocular adjustments.

85. MONET: *Isle on the Seine near Giverney* (Columbia, S.C., Mrs. B. Duvall Chambers Collection).

The destruction of local color in this picture is best shown in the water, which consists largely of reflections from the trees and from the sky. These shadows from outside the water reveal the further fact that shadows are not merely the absence of color but rather a combination of the color of the area affected and the object from which the shadow comes.

It is unfortunate if the relative formlessness of Impressionist painting and its fragmentary technique were to give us a feeling of casualness in workmanship. The very name Impressionism, wished on the group by an unfriendly critic, also conveys the idea of a picture polished off in a few hours. Actually, men like Monet worked very hard trying to adjust the various color relationships so that they would blend in the eye of the spectator, stepping back for almost every spot added to test the effect. That the final result approximates a momentary, almost "accidental" glimpse at nature is a tribute to their careful work. On the other hand, we should not get the idea of artists working with color charts of the spectrum in their hands. These color combinations become as instinctive as chords to a musician, yet the possible relationships are so diverse that they have to be tested as the artist proceeds.

The tendency in French landscape ever since the Barbizon painters to concentrate on a given section of scenery reaches a climax in many of the Impressionist works. In the *Isle on the Seine near Giverney*, for example, Monet is clearly interested in a particular part of the river at a specific time, as the title and composition both show. Yet the Impressionists were interested in their own kind of space representation, achieved by building up the picture around a foreplane and rear plane separated by an empty space in the middle. This space not only represents ordinary perspective distance but is supposed to tie the picture together through the evenly spread atmosphere with which it is filled. The *Isle* omits the foreplane, but the rear plane and the atmosphere are still there.

The main character in Monet's pictures is unquestionably the light—as had been the case with Manet also. Human beings are distinctly secondary and, where they occur, take on a certain immobility already seen in the painting of Manet for perhaps the same reason—the interest in light and atmosphere above all else. This is equally true of many pictures by Pissarro and Renoir. Subjects like the *Isle* seemed to be chosen deliberately for the waving grass and rustling leaves that lent themselves so well to the fleeting effects desired by the artist.

About 1890 Monet developed a "serial" technique for showing the same scene or object under different conditions of light and atmosphere. Whereas Constable had occasionally utilized the same subject at different times, and Monet's friend Jongkind had indulged in this practice once in a while, it became an important part of Monet's production. Version after version of poplars, lily ponds, haystacks, or the façade of Rouen Cathedral poured from his brush with almost the prodigality of a Hokusai and his many *Views of Fuji.*

Monet would come out to the scene of action armed with a large number of canvases. Beginning on the first of these, before the Cathedral of Rouen (Fig. 86), for example, he would paint until the intensity of light had changed, or at least until that change was perceptible to his sensitive eye. This would not be very long—between an half hour and an hour—after which the artist would begin all over again on a second canvas under the new conditions of light created by the shifting sun. Proceeding in this way from hour to hour and from canvas to canvas, the end of the day would leave him with a number of canvases, each with less than an hour's painting on them. Coming back to the same spot in the days following, the process would be repeated, each canvas getting its daily layer of work at its apportioned time, until there would be a series of completed pictures showing the Cathedral, haystack, poplar tree, or other theme.

Although this may well sound like the *reductio ad absurdum* of the Realistic process and an attempt to do a rather mechanical job, such an impression is due to the fact that we never see a given group or series together. People who have seen exhibitions in which an entire series was presented have testified to their stunning impact in the feeling for atmosphere and hour-by-hour change. It is equally true, however, that some of the serial paintings are among Monet's poorest efforts especially in terms of form. The haystack series is perhaps the worst offender. In his intense concentration on the effect of rapidly changing light, Monet worked very quickly, paying attention to the external quality of the light—not light as a form-building quantity. Moreover, the very visibility of the brush strokes tends to accentuate the formless effect.

Monet must have been aware of the fact that the very objects he chose to paint were broken and shimmering even before he painted them; in fact,

86. MONET: *Cathedral of Rouen* (New York, Metropolitan Museum of Art).

he seems to have chosen them deliberately so as to increase the sense of movement in his light and air. On the other hand, he and the other Impressionists were faced by the constant and paradoxical problem of the creation of form and space with atmospheric color whose primary effect was to describe only the surface of an object and destroy its solidity. As we have seen in the *Isle,* Monet's atmosphere could create a reasonably

163

effective space over the distance between foreground and rear plane, but the forms of individual objects such as haystacks and poplar trees had to be sacrificed.)

Although the geographical range of Monet's work covers England, Holland, France, and Italy, it leaves us with a generalized lyricism and sense of color exaltation reminiscent of the fuzzy paintings of Corot, similarly done all over Europe. For one unacquainted with Monet's life, it would be difficult to gather any clear idea of his personality from the paintings alone, except perhaps that of a healthy, if slightly Romantic, attitude. Compared with the violent emotional and physical approach of Courbet, Monet's art is much more objective, more concerned with external effects. Yet Cézanne's estimate of Monet, "He is only an eye, but what an eye!" is not altogether fair, because it leaves out the gentle and lyrical character of Monet's sensations of nature, his poetry so much in the tradition of French art, the poetry of Corot and Watteau.)

The work of Camille Pissarro (1830–1903) is even today not fully appreciated. In his own time, the alleged similarity between his paintings and those of Millet caused many people to look on his efforts as imitations of the Barbizon painter. Yet, as we shall see, he was one of the leaders in modern painting.

Born at St. Thomas in the West Indies of a French-Jewish family, Pissarro was sent to Paris at the age of twelve to complete his education. He learned to draw at boarding school and when he returned home several years later to go into the family business, his interest in art began to interfere with work. In 1855, the year of the Universal Exposition, he went back to Paris where he came face to face with the paintings of Delacroix, Courbet, and the Barbizon painters: Corot, Daubigny, and Millet. Corot interested him so much that Pissarro went out to see the master at Ville d'Avray to get some good advice and the sort of encouragement that the younger man would, in turn, give later to Cézanne and Van Gogh.

Although he went to the official ateliers for a while to please his father, Pissarro soon turned to the outdoors and for the rest of his life remained a painter of nature. His early work, influenced by Corot's atmospheric quality and Courbet's firmness, still showed a fairly dark color system. In 1863 he participated in the Salon des Refusés with Manet. Gradually his colors became brighter, in keeping with the general trend. These ideas were reinforced when he met Monet, Cézanne, and a few others and participated in the discussions at the Café Guerbois. Within the next few years his colors reached their most characteristic purity.

The Franco-Prussian War drove him out of Paris to London, where he encountered Monet again. They were introduced to Durand-Ruel by Daubigny and together they studied the paintings of Turner, Constable, and Crome. Returning to Paris after the war, Pissarro found that his studio, in the direct line of the Prussian advance on Paris, had been stripped of most of the pictures he had produced before leaving France.

In the twenty years following the war, Pissarro's career, like that of the other Impressionists, was a constant struggle to assert his right to the simple, frank representation of man and nature that was his self-appointed task. Pissarro now lived at Pontoise and became friendly with Cézanne, who had been drawn to the nearby town of Auvers by the sympathetic personality of Dr. Gachet. This contact between Cézanne and Pissarro led the former directly to nature and drew him at least temporarily into the Impressionist orbit. The relationship between the two men had its reciprocal effect on the painting of Pissarro, whose works always retained a higher degree of solidity than those of Monet or Sisley.

The financial difficulties of the period, occasionally alleviated by Durand-Ruel and *Père* Tanguy, were continued for Pissarro through the entire series of Impressionist exhibitions. As late as 1890 things were still difficult for him, but he persisted. In 1882 he began to suffer from an eye complaint that prevented him more and more from working outdoors. From this period on, he turned toward city scenes: the Boulevard des Italiens and the Pont Neuf in Paris, and the old streets and bridges in Rouen.

The work of Camille Pissarro is much more diversified than that of Monet, both in the variety of media he practised and in treatment and subject matter. Pissarro is one of the few open-air painters who was a print maker— ordinarily, Impressionism's emphasis of color over line did not lend itself to such a linear medium. There are over a hundred of his etchings and lithographs that have become known to the general public only within recent years. He was an accomplished master in pencil, pastel, gouache, and water color and used these techniques in most cases to catch some passing scene on his paper.

Pissarro's friendly nature may be seen in his relationship with the shy Cézanne, the morbid Van Gogh, and the egotistical Gauguin, and his generosity demonstrated by the fact that he introduced his friends to one of his few sources of income, *Père* Tanguy. In his socialist youth (he was the only political-minded member of the Batignolles group) a few of his lithographs, *Homeless*, *The Wood Carriers*, and *The Laborer*, were published in a socialist daily called *New Times*. Later in life his political views changed to a kind of benevolence, a patriarchal quality that made everyone love him. Cézanne said of him: "He was a father to me. He was a person to consult and something like the Lord." When Pissarro died, even the anti-Semitic Degas broke down with a heartfelt tribute.

Although associated in many minds with Millet, there was nothing Biblical about his approach; "Millet is Biblical, I am only Jewish." The self-conscious dignity of the Barbizon painter is completely absent from Pissarro's work, which does not conceive of the relationship between man and nature as a struggle. Every subject was grist for Pissarro's mill, not only the impressive ones—an Impressionist rather than a Romantic attitude. There is a definite sense of enjoyment in the paintings of Pissarro that suggests the *joie de vivre* of Renoir. It is a frankly visual thing tempered by tenderness. Although Pissarro was certainly aware of what was going on in the world, this did not interfere with his art, which is emotionally serene.

In landscape painting, his fully developed work, although generally similar to that of Monet, is quite individual and easily distinguishable from the other, as in *L'Isle Lacroix, Rouen* of 1882 (Plate I), a typical example of Pissarro's lyrical mood. This slightly atmospheric picture—it is supposed to be a misty impression—enjoys all of the color qualities of plein-air painting but the "touch" is that of Pissarro and not of Monet. With both artists the reaction to color relationships is bound to be personal and instinctive, and we may be certain that even if they were to treat the same motif the results would be different. The important difference between

Plate I.   PISSARRO: *L'Isle Lacroix, Rouen* (New York, Durand-Ruel Collection, color plate, courtesy of Art Foundation, Inc.).

Pissarro and Monet is found in the relative solidity of the former painter's work, even in landscapes. This difference is illustrated in Pissarro's *Peasants Resting* (Fig. 87), a very unpretentious picture of people outdoors under bright sunlight. The forms hold together very clearly, although the light is not concentrated on any particular spot but falls evenly over the entire surface, whereas in Monet the same diffusion of light results in a relative formlessness. If there is any explanation for this different result, it must rest on the fact that Pissarro is not so much the atmospheric virtuoso (at least in pictures like this) as Monet, that he is more interested in people.

87. PISSARRO: *Peasants Resting* (Toledo, Ohio, Toledo Museum of Art, Libbey Collection).

One might make an analogy between Pissarro and Renoir, both extensive users of pastel and water color. They show the same gentle, tender, lyrical approach to humanity, both consciously avoiding the ugly and presenting their subjects in the most favorable light. If the painting of Renoir reflects a profound joy in living, Pissarro might be considered a kind of rustic Renoir.

During the eighties, Pissarro was attracted by the more systematic divisionist practices of Seurat and for a short time produced a number of pictures in this technique. Afterward, because of the eye trouble already mentioned, he changed his locale as a painter from the country to the city. Some of these views of boulevards and other city scenes suggest the early work of Monet along this line; others, perhaps because of the association with the more solid manner of Seurat, have an entirely different quality. He died in Le Havre, watching and painting from his window the docks and ships, the movement of that great port.

10. RENOIR

Although Renoir was a "founding father" of Impressionism, he is often considered one of the last Old Masters. In his monumental conception of humanity, particularly in the works of his last period, we find the same breadth of execution and the same emphasis on more permanent values as in great painters of the past.

To the casual observer, the paintings of Renoir are significant only in so far as they portray the sentiments and qualities of orthodox Impressionism. But this is not his only importance, even though the momentary and pleasurable phases of existence are recorded in a charming fashion that outdoes the efforts of Monet and Pissarro. No one in modern times has sounded the song of the flesh with the same intensity and sheer physical pleasure as Renoir. If we think of his painting in terms of an insistently joyous materiality, the psychological side of his creativeness becomes clear.

Yet he is not a Realist in the Impressionist sense of recording externally a series of visual images, even though his brilliant colors seem to be another interpretation of that point of view. As he himself once put it, " . . . with Nature one can do nothing," if it is the artist's desire merely to reproduce her. It was to the art of the museums that he pointed as a source for pictorial inspiration, for concepts of form and composition. Using the new rainbow palette of brilliantly clean, divided colors which he had helped develop, he applied himself to the study of the masters of the past: the Venetians of the Renaissance, the eighteenth-century French, and his own immediate predecessors. With these materials he produced an art at once a reflection of his age and a link with the older plastic tradition of western Europe. He was fond of saying that he only "continued what others had done— and much better—before me."

Auguste Renoir (1841–1919) was born at Limoges of a poor family. When still an infant, he was taken to Paris and at the age of thirteen given a job painting porcelain, which may account for the lovely blues of his pictures somewhat later. After five years hand-painted porcelain was driven from the market by a machine-made product, and young Renoir turned to painting awnings, window shades, and fans. Frequent use of the then still popular Rococo subjects for these things may account for the close affinity between the mature art of Renoir and eighteenth-century painting.

During 1861–1862 Renoir studied in the atelier of Gleyre, where he met Monet, Sisley, and Bazille. His first *salon* entry in 1864 was still Romantic in feeling and subject, *Esmeralda Dancing by Moonlight*, inspired by Victor Hugo's *Notre-Dame de Paris*. During that same year the four future Impressionists began to turn to nature. This so-called Fontainebleau period introduces a series of new influences on the work of Renoir: Corot, Courbet, Diaz, Cézanne, and even Fantin-Latour. In the main, however, this phase marks a turning point toward a more Realistic art. The *Lise* of 1867, painted in the open air, still shows the silver tone of Corot, although here and in the portrait of *Sisley and His Wife* we feel the influence of Courbet's solid forms. Yet Renoir's application is individual and he achieves form through modeling and the interplay of colored shadows. At this early stage of his career he is already interested in reflections and vivid splashes of light as they come through foliage. During 1869 he was working with Monet at Bougival, both developing a brighter type of color, though Renoir was still ahead of Monet at that point.

Although the works of this period mark a shift toward themes of everyday life, Renoir is still too much concerned with technique to be able to express himself freely—unable to integrate the various influences. From this point of view, the *Bather with a Griffon* (1870, Fig. 88) is one of the most interesting of his early paintings. It shows the kind of monumental figures that Courbet preferred, as well as the latter's interest in surface texture and tactile quality—an emphasis on the materiality of the flesh. A certain stiff wooden effect suggests derivation from sculpture, with the composition of the nude similar to the *Cnidian Venus* of Praxiteles. From a more modern point of view, the two young women evoke the spirit of Courbet's *Young Women on the Banks of the Seine* (Fig. 70). The atmospheric light in which they are bathed reflects the influence of Corot, while the luminosity of the figures themselves reminds us of the color of Manet.

For a few years Renoir participated in the development of open-air painting, working side by side with Monet during 1872–1873. Together they achieved the full evolution of the rainbow-palette, broken-color method. In fact, at certain times during this period their pictures are almost indistinguishable in style. For a time, then, Renoir's work was part of the objective Realist Impressionist effort and concerned only with atmospheric problems. He participated in the First Impressionist Exhibition at Nadar's in 1874, sending among other pictures *The Loge* (1874, Fig. 89). The unusual angle of vision through the railing of the box, the figures cut off at right and left, and the momentary casual gesture of the man with the opera glasses are characteristic Impressionist details that add to the sense of impermanence these artists desired. As to the subject, it is one of a long series of typical themes in the theater, the café, the race track, and the home that were to be repeated so many times by the members of this school for both their realistic content and their "accidental" possibilities.

The typically sleek and physically attractive Renoir types of *The Loge* relate the picture to the artist's beloved Venetians, especially Veronese, while the rich, deep black suggests the same period. From a purely technical point of view, this painting marks a serious advance over earlier and more typical Impressionist efforts. The two figures in the box here begin to show Renoir's personal approach toward monumentality and permanence achieved through expressive color. The velvety blacks are far from Impressionistic and have fuller value as contrasting elements that help make his forms more meaningful, while the subtle variations of color are much better integrated than before.

88. RENOIR: *Bather with a Griffon* (Basel, Museum, photograph courtesy of Lionello Venturi).

In the paintings of the next few years, Renoir reaches the full realization of his early personal style with such works as *The Swing* (1876) and *Moulin de la Galette* (1876, Fig. 90). These two offerings at the Third Impressionist Exhibition in 1877 represent the sort of pure lyricism ordinarily associated with this painter and, for the average person, the justification for his existence. For the student, however, they reveal a more highly developed personal color sense, a loosening of forms, a suffusion of the canvas with a unifying pearly quality that arranges misty blues, greens, and

89. RENOIR: *The Loge* (London, Courtauld Institute).

pinks into highly complex color compositions. We feel an almost Fragonard-like delicacy of expression in many pictures of this period. *The Swing*, for example, represents a popular eighteenth-century subject brought up to date by the sprinkling of light through the trees and reflections of green and other colors on the faces of the subjects—a shimmering Impressionist treatment handled in Renoir's unique manner.

The quiet youthful joyousness of *The Swing* is even more strongly felt in *Moulin de la Galette* (Fig. 90), a scene in a Montmartre café. In a typical Impressionist composition, the foreground is built up by a group of figures obliquely arranged and cut off at the side and bottom. Casualness and informality are stressed, with all the participants presented in the painter's usual good-looking healthy manner. Although the subject prescribes movement, there is a curiously quiet and suspended quality in the scene, especially in the immobile dancers. This poetic languor in modern costume recalls similar qualities in the art of Watteau and the Venetians.

Psychologically and formalistically, the paintings of Renoir from this point on represent a bridge between the simon-pure Impressionism of Monet and Pissarro and the work of artists like Degas and Lautrec. In terms of mood, pictures like *Moulin de la Galette*, *The Swing*, or the famous

171

90. RENOIR: *Moulin de la Galette* (Paris, Louvre).

Luncheon of the Boating Party (Fig. 92) part company from the objective work of Monet and his group. Renoir is interested in establishing a mood, half lyrical, half sensual, that pervades so much of his art. Where the out-of-door men concerned themselves solely with the effects of light, Renoir inserts the element of personality. Even though this brings him closer to the aims of Degas, the latter artist did not like him the better for it. From his own linear and sociological point of view, Degas disapproved of Renoir's cult of beauty as too flabby and lyrical. Nevertheless, the art of Degas, though by no means subjective, is still interpretive like that of Renoir but with a different purpose. As to Lautrec, the element of subjective reaction to the Realist-Impressionist material becomes very important.

From a technical standpoint, Renoir attempted to solve the inherent contradiction in the Impressionist dogma: the creation of volume through an atmospheric color that helps to disintegrate the very forms it colors.

As early as *The Loge* it was evident that Renoir was going to try to retain solidity in his forms, in spite of the broken-color system and small brush strokes. *The Loge* is still overtly traditional in its derivation, with its Venetian coloring and tightly filled space in the Titian manner; however, it did not take Renoir long to amalgamate the old and the new.

The Swing and the *Moulin* also owe a great deal to tradition, the tradition of the eighteenth century, but by now the past had been thoroughly digested and absorbed into the painter's system. Although we feel the Rococo character of so much of Renoir's work, the borrowings are not at all obtrusive. Overt or no, the fact remains that Renoir's figures, whether from Titian, Tintoretto, Watteau, Fragonard, or other sources, retain their solidity. Combining this museum-derived solidity with the rainbow palette which he himself had helped develop, Renoir gives us a new version of Impressionism.

Renoir had never been entirely relieved of the burden of poverty, but since joining the Impressionists, the day of deliverance seemed further away than ever before. The problem was solved to a certain extent during 1878–1881 by his friendship with the wealthy but liberal publishing family the Charpentiers, publishers of Zola. From them and from others Renoir soon had portrait commissions. Although some of these are a bit tighter in drawing and soberer in coloring than his development warranted, the resultant financial security allowed him to revert to his more characteristic and daring color combinations.

The group portrait of *Mme. Charpentier and Her Children* (1878, Fig. 91) illustrates the mild conservatism of this phase. Composed with a Renaissance pyramid as base, this painting is perhaps the closest modern approximation extant of Venetian upper-class portraiture. Renoir must have been familiar with the work of Veronese in the Louvre, a fact suggested by the similarity of the modern painter's grouping of the little girls and their dog to the Italian master's treatment of the donor's family in *Christ and the Pilgrims at Emmaus* (Paris, Louvre). The colors in the modern picture have been toned down, the blacks reminding us of the earlier *The Loge*. Perhaps the best parts of the impressive Charpentier portrait are a brilliant still life at the right and the creamy blond coloring of the little girls. Through the influence of the lady who was its chief subject, this painting was admitted to the *salon* of 1879. Renoir did not participate in the Fourth Impressionist Exhibition that year, but M. Charpentier became a leading proponent of Impressionist art at this point—especially that of Renoir. He started a magazine, *La Vie moderne*, to further the cause, helped arrange exhibitions in the building where the magazine was printed, and soon became an important factor in promoting the "new painting."

During the early eighties Renoir continued his outdoor paintings, using increasingly brighter color arrangements, as in the famous *Luncheon of the Boating Party* (1881, Fig. 92). Not only had his interest in light increased, but some of the pictures at this point have a more decorative quality as well. The *Boating Party* is typically Impressionist in its casual informality,

91. RENOIR: *Mme. Charpentier and Her Children* (New York, Metropolitan Museum of Art).

92. RENOIR: *Luncheon of the Boating Party* (Washington, Phillips Memorial Gallery).

its ease, and lightness of mood. More than ever before we feel the sense of relaxation, of vacation, of city people out in the country for the day. Some of the men still retain their stiff city costumes; others are in sport shirts and more relaxed. Yet, as in the paintings of Degas and Lautrec, this work has been carefully arranged and posed so as to achieve the "accidental" quality cherished by the Impressionists. Like most of Renoir's pictures showing people in the open air, forms are stressed at the expense of land-scape, either deliberately or because the artist felt it impossible to do the figures as solidly as he wished and still retain the maximum of atmospheric shimmer. This also applies to the many characteristic nudes he painted out of doors during this period.

By 1885 a significant change had taken place in Renoir's style. Partly as a result of his two trips to Italy, made possible by his portrait commis-sions, he abandoned the sketchiness of his earlier works and their rainbow palette. In pictures like *Les Grandes Baigneuses* (The Great Bathers)

(1885–1887, Fig. 93), we find more carefully worked out contours, more precise modeling of the figures, smoother brush technique, and a less shimmering but more uniform tonality binding the various parts together. Instead of his former vibrant and gay transcription of reality, we find here a carefully considered, almost monumental work.

Although the subject immediately suggests the bathers of Boucher or those of the sculptor Girardon (in the well-known bas-relief at Versailles), Renoir's *Baigneuses* are more robust than the former and less obviously arranged than the latter. As the examples pile up for both Renoir and other painters during this period, the striving for a more ordered type of picture becomes evident. Both Seurat and Cézanne were already changing Impressionism into something beyond the mere impermanent appearance of things seen under natural light. Thus, in the *Baigneuses* Renoir concerns himself rather with the rhythms of his powerfully outlined and modeled forms and their architectural unity than with his previous titilation of the senses.

93. RENOIR: *Les Grandes Baigneuses* (The Great Bathers) (Philadelphia, Carroll S. Tyson Collection).

The very year that Renoir painted this picture (1887) he was working at L'Estaque with Cézanne, whose painting had already forsaken the Impressionist path. Like Cézanne, Renoir at this time turned toward a coloristic reinterpretation of the past, not only to solidify his forms as he had done earlier, but now in the interests of almost abstract design. It is tribute to Renoir's integrity as an artist that he devoted himself to this experimental phase of painting at a time when he could have capitalized on his popularity. By the middle eighties Impressionism had become relatively respectable, and certainly Renoir's work

94. RENOIR: *Children at the Piano* (Paris, Louvre).

had already achieved acceptance among his wealthy patrons.

After this phase of classicistic picture building, Renoir reverted to his earlier Impressionist manner and from 1888 to the end of the century he seemed to waver between one procedure and the other. Although, for the most part, his pictures show his standard light and personal Impressionism, there are a good many examples that indicate the new direction. The *Children at the Piano* (1892, Fig. 94), a Fragonard theme out of the eighteenth century, has been transformed in the hands of Renoir into a new kind of mood. Obvious charm yields to a less pretty and more blunt kind of physical attraction. Colors change also, and instead of the shimmering rainbow tones, he begins to run over into warm browns and earth colors. This can no longer be called an Impressionist picture because the artist has abandoned the transience and impermanence associated with that style for a quiet, almost classical concentration.

The little girls seen here are the same ones the artist shows in scores of pictures, differently posed, following their development from adolescence to womanhood. One blonde and the other brunette, they offer a kind of cross section of Renoir's art during this period.

177

95. RENOIR: *Nude Woman Seated* (Paris, Élie Faure Collection).

At the very end of the century, in 1899, Renoir suffered the first attack of an arthritis that ultimately crippled him completely. The remaining period of his life, spent in the attempt to make himself physically comfortable in spite of increasing difficulties with his health, marks the final crystallization of his powers as a painter. During this interval the tendency toward the monumental becomes more clearly expressed; the accent upon attractive color gives way before extreme concentration on the achievement of plastic forms and volumes. Instead of the pearly surfaces he had employed before, Renoir makes extensive use of reds and browns, as in the *Children at the Piano*.

Because of the increasing stiffness of his fingers, he had to paint more broadly and even clumsily. He was forced to ignore drawing in the conventional sense and to create his forms through the use of a highly developed structural color from which the figures appear to emerge as if by magic. In the *Nude Woman Seated* (c. 1914, Fig. 95) Renoir has increased the quietness of the *Children at the Piano* to an almost brooding monumentality expressed in the form of a woman as powerful as a goddess. It is almost paradoxical that while Renoir was painting with the brushes strapped to his paralyzed fingers, he was able to create the magnificent and robust forms that are as impressive in their physical vitality as those of Rubens. The broad strokes of hot reds and browns are not as overtly appealing, perhaps, as the lyrical forms and charming colors of his earlier paintings but the resultant impression of strength is more than adequate compensation. With the fewest possible indications of drawing, the figures are created and vibrate out of the amazingly limited palette he now uses.

In stressing the manner of painting rather than content or subject, Renoir abandoned his characteristic lyrical feeling in favor of a powerful reaction to the form possibilities of his motifs. From 1904, when his last phase crystallized, to the end of his life in 1919, Renoir reworked all of his old subjects in this new vein. If his figures rival those of Cézanne in monumentality and his landscape rhythms those of Gauguin and the later Fauves, it is perhaps because he actually was living through these further developments in the history of modern painting. Moving across the Impressionist field, he had rebelled instinctively against formlessness and temporary values. With the integration of traditional art into this pattern, he proffered the first solution; with the simplified and abstracted forms of his last period, he stepped into the twentieth century.

11. LINEAR IMPRESSIONISM: DEGAS AND TOULOUSE-LAUTREC

Although striking and effective as a combination of momentary theme and appropriate technique, Impressionism carried within it the seeds of its own destruction. Monet's small sections of broken landscape were undoubtedly suited to his shimmering and evanescent color system; but like all the outdoor painters he was plagued by an atmospheric color that almost automatically destroyed form.

Neither Monet nor Pissarro was able to resolve this contradiction, although Renoir had more success, using traditional color as a basis on which Impressionist divided tones were placed. Moreover, none of these men had been able to set their figures in motion, a somewhat paradoxical limitation in an art of avowed spontaneity and casualness. In spite of the fact that the painter wished to give the impression of happening accidentally upon the scene, his preoccupation with light and its effect on the figure made everything stop. In fact, had the action not stopped, the figures would have dissolved completely.

Both difficulties were to be resolved to a great extent through the linear approach of Edgar Degas (1834–1917). One of the original Impressionists, the accidental quality of his brilliantly colorful work differs markedly from the creations of other members of the group. To begin with, he was not interested in nature and almost never painted landscape for its own sake. Degas was, rather, a painter of the city scene: cafés, theaters, dance halls, workers, dancers, and people generally. Accenting spontaneity, he reminds us of the Realist writer who rode the Paris busses with a notebook in hand, jotting down fragments of conversations he happened to hear. Although there are no conversations as such in Degas' painting, there are gestures and quick actions equally fragmentary and caught on the wing.

Most important in distinguishing Degas from the other Impressionists is the fact that his people exist on canvas or paper by virtue of his powerful and supple line rather than because of twinkling color components. Since he expresses his Impressionist feeling through the movement of forms rather than the movement of light over forms, Degas' choice of subjects is completely appropriate. These themes had to be shown in such a way that the forms would not disintegrate as soon as they began to move—hence the strong silhouette that could contain form in any position or gesture.

His views of Paris are a far cry from the lyrical interpretations of Renoir, toward whom he felt a certain natural antipathy both as man and artist. Degas is principally the biographer of a sober and realistic environment, painting his subjects more out of intellectual interest than for the sheer pleasure of it, as Renoir did so often. Moreover, the linear painter's camera-like spontaneity is the result of a carefully labored and studious process. Elements are carefully chosen for their effectiveness and compositional value, everything laid out in terms of the final effect in whose interests nonessentials are sacrificed.

Since he thought of painting as a "conventional art," the study of nature was unimportant to him. Technique, on the other hand, was vital: "It is infinitely more important to learn to draw after Holbein." He said of himself: "No art was ever less spontaneous than mine. What I do is the result of reflection and study of the great masters; of inspiration, spontaneity, temperament I know nothing." The great difference between Degas and the other Impressionists was not simply one of technique or the use of line instead of color, but further, that they represented just what they saw, while he arbitrarily selected what he felt to be important. For this reason he painted mostly from memory.

The ballet dancers, milliners, laundresses, and café sitters for which this artist is generally known appear only with his maturity. In the beginning this son of a wealthy banking family thought of himself as a historical painter, partly because of his severely academic training and also because during his youth archaeology had been very much publicized. The investigations in Assyria, Egypt, and Persia even attracted Realist writers like Flaubert and Gautier, the former writer's *Salammbô* paralleling Degas' early *Semiramis Raising the Walls of Babylon* and *Young Spartans Provoking Each Other to Combat*. Although pictures of this sort are usually considered part of Degas' academic period, especially the somewhat dreamy *Semiramis*, the fact remains that the *Young Spartans*, like *Salammbô*, is a vigorous Realist interpretation of antiquity.

The true relationship between Degas and the academic painters of this period may be found in a fine psychological portrait group, *The Bellelli Family* (Fig. 96). Here the fine linear accuracy of the thoughtful heads suggests Ingres, whose pupil Lamothe had taught Degas for a while. The patterned design is Degas' own, but the cameo-like features of the mother are strikingly reminiscent of the older master, while the atmospheric treatment suggests traditional French portraiture. In 1865 Degas had the good

96. DEGAS: *The Bellelli Family* (Paris, Louvre).

182

97. DEGAS: *The Cotton Exchange at New Orleans* (Pau, Museum).

fortune to meet the aged Ingres socially. The eighty-five-year-old painter advised the young man to "do lines and more lines, from nature or from memory, and you will become a good artist."

Between 1860 and 1870 Degas became very friendly with Manet, whom he had met at the Louvre, and was gradually converted to the new Realist point of view. Here and there we begin to get a racecourse subject or a theatrical theme, but for the most part the period is full of marvelously precise and formal portraits painted in subdued but very warm tones.

Degas' career was interrupted by the War of 1870 in which he served as an artilleryman. After his return we find him increasingly involved with the Café Guerbois group. The transition from formal subject matter to realistic material is seen in *The Cotton Exchange at New Orleans* (Fig. 97), result of a visit to relatives in that city shortly after 1870. Although this painting is still precise in drawing and somewhat cold in color, it is an everyday scene observed at first hand and viewed from the Impressionist high vantage point (high and to the side).

A more serious change in Degas' work is found in such themes as *The Pedicure* (Fig. 98), the beginning of his characteristic "keyhole" art. Here,

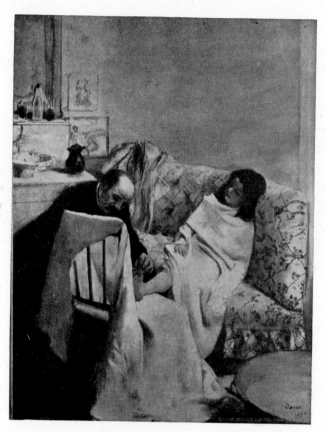

98. DEGAS: *The Pedicure* (Paris, Louvre).

he is already the observer of society that Edmond de Goncourt admired so much. Pictures of this type remove the walls from houses and look in to see people engaged in intimate activities, catching them off guard in their most natural postures. The characters in this painting are as completely unposed, as "accidentally" seen as any casual outdoor landscape by Monet, except for the fact that the latter artist does not trouble to rearrange nature, while Degas is always "arranging" the facts for design purposes. But the purpose of both Impressionists is to record something they "just happened to see" at a given moment and in a given spot. Just as Monet concentrates on a particular section of landscape, in Degas' painting we find ourselves in part of a room. Instantaneity of vision is inferred not only from the fragmentary view but also by the steep and diagonal perspective induced by the high vantage point.

This unorthodox perspective view is part of the influence on Degas and the Impressionists of Japanese colored prints. This material had been "discovered" by Bracquemond in the fifties. In 1862 the famous Porte Chinoise, a shop dealing in Orientalia, had been opened and soon became a gathering place for artists. The International Exposition of 1867 had given final acceptance to the art of the East. From Degas' point of view, Japanese art was attractive because of the off-center placing of the principal character, the subtle linear style, decorative sense, and abrupt foreshortening. Unlike some painters of this period, he did not utilize these subjects for their picturesque qualities but absorbed their method. The unusual angle of vision in *The Pedicure* and many later works stems from this source, as does the type of subject itself, which was very popular in Japanese art of the late eighteenth and early nineteenth centuries. Most important, artists such as Degas, Lautrec, Whistler, and others derived from the Japanese a sense of abstract patterning that makes every subject a problem in design. Just as the outdoor painters chose subjects for their broken contours, artists like Degas chose themes for their pattern possibilities.

The Degas of legend and anecdote, the surly intractable terror of the drawing room, had not yet appeared. We find, rather, a man keenly interested in the artist's problems and a leading organizer of the First Impressionist Exhibition. In spite of his best efforts, Manet could not be persuaded to join the others. Two years later a second exhibition at Durand-Ruel's gallery produced among other things a pamphlet on modern painting by Edmond Duranty, an early Realist novelist who saw in the work of Degas something akin to his own interest in everyday life. This booklet, which Degas may even have helped to write, is devoted mainly to that painter's art and indicates that line is the only thing that matters; color is distinctly secondary. The social function of the painter is stressed. Some of the Impressionist brethren were annoyed with Duranty—and with Degas, too.

Ballet Rehearsal on the Stage (Fig. 99) is a good example of Degas' approach to subject matter. Instead of taking advantage of this theme's inherent charm, he has chosen to show the hard work, the more sordid side. The girls who may appear ethereal and lovely from the other side of the footlights are often thin overworked creatures, like the gaping and yawning girl near the conductor. This is not a theater of glamour but a behind-the-scenes interpretation revealing the artistic and financial problems in getting a production together. The gentleman seated casually at the right, a strong portrayal of the backer or producer type who controls the show, demonstrates Degas' keen understanding of what was going on. Typical of Degas' compositions is the way he places the dancers far away from the spectator and makes them visible over the heads of the foreground figures.

Some people are only partially shown, others appear in strained momen-

99. DEGAS: *Ballet Rehearsal on the Stage* (New York, Metropolitan Museum of Art).

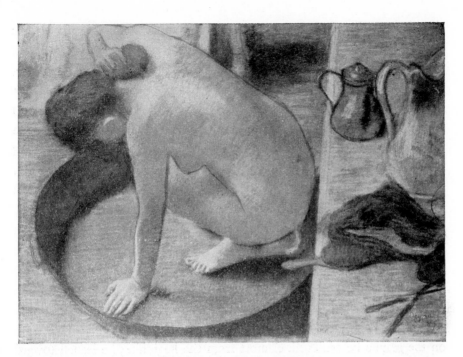

100. DEGAS: *The Tub* (Paris, Louvre).

tary positions, like the girl scratching her back, the one yawning, or the young woman stretching her arm along the "flat" projecting from the wings. This casualness and intimacy and the arrangement of chief figures off center, visible over the heads of nearer forms, are part of Degas' artistic heritage from the Japanese. Catching his subjects in this "candid camera" fashion reminds us of the fact that Degas, like Manet before and Lautrec after, used photographs to help him "set up" many of his pictures.

Unquestionably, the opportunities for interpretation through movement were greater in this environment of the ballet than anywhere else. Ballet dancers had interested him as far back as 1868, and by 1874 he knew a tremendous amount about them, on stage and off. His choice of the less attractive moments in their lives—utterly unlike the Renoir approach—is deliberate in that it offers a greater possibility of analysis.

The love of intimate and "unposed" subject matter is best expressed in his many "keyhole" paintings of women in various stages of dressing, bathing, combing their hair, etc., such as *The Tub* (Fig. 100). Pictures like

187

this illustrate Degas' attitude as an artist. In the words of his friend Duranty: "In the representation of a back we wish to see revealed a temperament, an epoch, a social state; in a pair of hands we ought to express a magistrate, a merchant; and by a gesture an entire series of emotions." Yet we must keep in mind that like most Impressionist painting, *The Tub* is not as accidental as the theory dictates—nor are most of Degas' pictures. The existence of a prop bathtub in his studio, together with innumerable dancing costumes and other appurtenances, shows clearly the intellectual character of his art. The scene of this pastel is visualized in the briefest manner, a woman caught in a momentary awkward posture that will soon have to be relaxed. The resilient character of the pose stems from Degas' skilled line, his sensitive draftsmanship. This kind of picture is related to Japanese art through the closeness of the subject to the spectator, the flowing line, type of subject matter, attractive and unorthodox color combinations, and finally the sharply sloping perspective.

Degas' most frequently used medium, pastel, had an important influence on the results he achieved. Almost from the beginning he leaned toward pastel and by 1890 had abandoned oils completely. We are told this was due to increasingly severe eye trouble but it seems connected rather with the fact that he preferred drawing to coloring in the ordinary sense. By the use of the pastel crayon he was able to draw in color and thereby achieve two ends simultaneously. One of the curious effects of the attractive medium is a striking contrast between the ordinariness of his subjects and the beautiful quality of the colors in which they are shown. Nonidealized scenes, such as a sponge bath, a laundress pressing, or a shopgirl carrying a hatbox, induce a curiously ambiguous reaction. Some of the more intimate bathing pieces demonstrate this in startling fashion.

In a sense, Degas represents the obvious conclusion of the Realist method that had begun with the sentimentalizations of Millet and the monumental interpretations of Courbet. The Impressionists, logical successors of the Realist movement, had taken ordinary subject matter and given it the lyrical treatment of Monet, Pissarro, and Renoir. Ugliness was completely absent. In the work of Degas, themes are chosen with deliberate emphasis on their ugliness, as in *The Laundresses* (Paris, Louvre), or on their commonplace

188

101. DEGAS: *The Millinery Shop* (Chicago, Chicago Art Institute, Coburn Memorial).

character, as in *The Millinery Shop* (Fig. 101). The artist-draftsman has been able throughout to seize the essential character of a gesture to make us believe that the actors were unaware that they were being painted. The Impressionist character of such pictures is naturally heightened by the most brilliant coloristic effects. In all of Degas' paintings, whether of dancers, shopgirls, laundresses, or bathers, the artist is concerned with the momentary gesture and the sharp unusual perspective that increases this sense of movement. The patterned cut-off composition, which forces the eye to move beyond the frame, also adds to the sense of motion and impermanence.

In his desire to show us the life of the big city, he takes us into every sort of environment but always from the viewpoint of the outside observer. We are shown a number of unsavory female types relaxing in a house of prostitution, a pair of girls waiting at a table in his *Café, Boulevard Mont-martre* (Fig. 102)—subjects similar to those done by Degas' great admirer Toulouse-Lautrec. Yet it is difficult for us to decide Degas' own sentiments concerning the people he paints. There is no discernible sympathy for the lower-class characters nor is there any overt criticism of the so-called evil person. We see the face of Paris but not what its people think and feel. That was not the job of the sociological description to which Duranty subscribed and which was practiced by writers like Zola and painters like Degas. The mere fact of recording the shifting metropolitan scene, noting its endless movement and frequent sordidness, sufficed. But these exercises gave Degas the same pleasure as Renoir derived from describing the tender dancing scenes at Bougival and the Moulin de la Galette. That much the brilliant pastel tells us.

Personally, Degas stood apart from the Impressionist group and from people generally. They enjoyed the sense of fellowship that came from mutual experience and struggle, whereas his background and wealth put

102. DEGAS: *Café, Boulevard Montmartre* (Paris, Louvre).

him into a special category. His unfriendliness socially cannot be attributed only to the facts that he was a bachelor and had trouble with his eyes. Nor do these things account for his conservative politics. It may seem curious that the painter of so many apparently social subjects was a Royalist and a violent anti-Semite, but these are matters of record. During the Dreyfus affair, of all the Impressionist group only Degas and Cézanne were anti-Dreyfusards. Degas, moreover, opposed making art available to the lower classes.

To those unacquainted with his numerous drawings, Degas appears the great painter of volatile subjects, the quintessence of the Impressionist manner. We must remember, however, his severe academic training and also that until the age of thirty he aspired to be a historical painter. Exacting discipline had ingrained the habits of the academic studio with its many careful drawings and precise compositional plans. The drawings he has left show not only innumerable preparatory sketches of his bathers and dancers but even that proportions were sometimes determined on paper ruled off into squares. Such a painting as *At the Races* (Fig. 103), for example, seems to be a bright and charming rendition of nervous movement in a thoroughbred race horse. Yet his many versions of this theme are not the result of exciting afternoons spent at the track but of careful planning in the studio from casual sketches done on the spot and from his wooden studio horse that could be set in any position.

Although the bulk of Degas' work belongs to the Realist-Impressionist stream, there are occasional later paintings, such as the *Danseuses roses* of the later eighties (Boston, Museum of Fine Arts), or the somewhat earlier *Woman Ironing* (New York, Metropolitan Museum of Art), where he underwent the influence of the abstract movement known as post-Impressionism. In these works we have a combination of representational and abstract procedures analogous to the method of Cézanne and others.

Unlike many members of the Impressionist group, Degas was not faced by the problem of making a living from his art. In fact, he often refused to sell his works and when he did sell, tried all kinds of stratagems to get them back. Many which were sold went out of the country, so that the general public in France remained relatively unacquainted with his production.

103. DEGAS: *At the Races* (Paris, Louvre).

It is equally interesting that the prices his pictures fetched were probably the highest achieved by any nineteenth-century artist during his lifetime.

If the background of Degas had been in many ways bourgeois, that of Henri de Toulouse-Lautrec (1864–1901) was extremely different. Born at Albi in the south into what was probably the oldest family in France, Lautrec's upbringing was enlivened by a father descended from the counts of Toulouse, a queer mixture of amateur artist, sportsman, and hunter. From the beginning, love of movement and interest in art are present. Although young Lautrec would have liked to join the family at riding and hunting, his frail health and fragile bones made this impossible. In 1872 the family settled in Paris for a while, where Lautrec senior made his restless and peculiar personality felt by somewhat eccentric gestures.

During the future painter's fourteenth and fifteenth years, both his thighs were broken. The fragile bones did not set well, and he stopped growing,

192

although his keen mind developed very rapidly, particularly his sense of observation. While the others hunted and rode, he had to sit about and fret. In later life, Lautrec showed a keen dislike of the country but he always remained interested in animals, especially horses. The animal painter Princeteau, who was a family friend, coached him in drawing and took him to the Paris zoo to sketch animals. His father's interest in modeling statuettes of horses and dogs gave him further stimulus.

Lautrec might conceivably never have become an artist had it not been for his physical handicap, for that kind of family could well have objected to art as a profession. Since, however, there was no necessity for him to make a living and since there could be little thought of marriage, he was allowed to follow his own bent. Thus, in 1882 he was admitted to the studio of the academic Bonnat, because his family (like that of Pissarro) felt it would be a good idea for him to learn from an established master. A few years later Bonnat gave up his studio, but Lautrec had already gone over to Cormon, where he met Vincent Van Gogh. With both his teachers Lautrec had studied the nude in repose, but this was not what he wanted. Ever since childhood, his main interest had been in action and movement— horses, human beings, anything. By 1885 he had thrown himself into the full tide of the exciting night life of Montmartre with its interesting and dynamic types.

At this time he was sharing a studio with his friend Granier in the same block where Degas had his studio. Although there is no provable personal contact between the two linear Impressionists, Lautrec showed a great admiration for the older man and in this particular period changed his own style and methods considerably. From what we are able to tell, Lautrec set out not only to imitate Degas but to rival him as well. The younger man's *À la Mie* seems to have been designed to compete with Degas' *L'Absinthe,* just as the various pictures of women at their toilet were done for the same purpose.

In reverting to scenes of everyday life, Lautrec was merely taking up again a type of subject he had temporarily abandoned during the Bonnat and Cormon period. At the time that Lautrec was starting his Montmartre subjects, Degas was beginning to shift from oil to pastel. In adopting this medium, Degas had solved his personal conflict between drawing and paint-

193

ing since the chalk enabled him to combine the two. Lautrec had felt the same difficulty about "spoiling" his lines with color; and to preserve the boldness of his draftsmanship, he adopted a rather unusual technique.

For pictures of ordinary size, Lautrec worked on cardboard with very thin color, a curious method justified by its results. The turpentine and oil were naturally absorbed by the porous thick paper and the color left smooth and matt on the surface. In *The Clownesse* (Fig. 104), showing one of the performers in "this fatal and fascinating abode of sin" he liked to portray, painting as such is destroyed. But the chalky quality of the resultant picture is well suited to the peculiar pallor he wished to get in these faces that combine hatred and love. Lautrec applied his paint in hatchings, a rather laborious technique when worked on a large scale, which may account for the small size of many of his works. Small or not, his pictures have a largeness of design exemplified by *The Clownesse*. The hatched technique of the painting has its own particular virtue in that it emphasizes the Impressionist character of the subject matter.

104. LAUTREC: *The Clownesse* (Gates Mills, Ohio, William Powell Jones Collection).

Lautrec's color is entirely different from the rainbow palette of the Impressionists. Color relationships are not bland like theirs but exist in a series of abrupt and startling contrasts typical of poster design—a field in which he was a master. *At the Foot of the Scaffold* (Fig. 105), a poster done for *Le Matin* in 1893, typifies his vivid and bold draftsmanship over large flat areas of color. Distinctively Impressionist in feeling, the characters are partially revealed from the same close position and abrupt perspective as in Degas, the general effect violent and striking. The drawing is intensely economical and the figures silhouetted, thus giving the casual and immediate

194

effect of a Japanese print. The relationship to Oriental art is so clear in the works of Lautrec that it may seem superfluous to point it out, yet so pervasive is this influence in the Impressionist movement that we may look at it again.

Instead of using the European eye-level perspective, the Oriental artist prefers to place himself above or below his subject, while standing closer to it than is customary with us. In Western art, it is the usual practice for the artist to suppress the foreground of a landscape in favor of the middle or background to which the eye is drawn. Japanese art, however, exaggerates the importance of foreground and even its shape, so that one always knows the

105. LAUTREC: *At the Foot of the Scaffold*—poster (New York, F.A.R. Gallery).

point from which the artist observed a scene. Lautrec often does the same thing, as in the poster just mentioned. His simple frank coloring is again the result of Japanese influence. Working as a decorator, he appears to have no use for subtle modifications of tone or lights and shadows to suggest depth. The flat tone, often brilliantly crude, projects the silhouette of the forms in a characteristically momentary fashion.

From the point of view of later post-Impressionist art, it should be kept in mind that Lautrec's posters generally have a quality of rhythmic design and abstraction considerably different from his more photographic paintings and lithographs. The element of simplification so necessary for poster design has, at least in this form of expression, led to a more advanced and "modern" approach. Although originally printed on the cheapest paper for a very transient advertising purpose, these posters, because of their Oriental decorativeness, find a permanent place on the walls of many modern homes.

195

While obvious technical similarities exist in Lautrec and the Japanese (examples could be multiplied indefinitely), their respective emotional attitudes are completely different. The oft-quoted remark of the French-man: "If I had had slightly longer legs, I should never have been an artist," gives us a hint of his motivation in art as a kind of revenge on life. His Oriental creditors, on the other hand, had no such impulses. In their attitude we find rather a parallel to the lyricism of the color Impressionists: Monet, Sisley, Pissarro, and Renoir. Impressionism, as we have seen, is a pleasant surface expression and, like Japanese art, not concerned with deep psycho-logical problems.

Lautrec, despite this Oriental influence, shows a cruel and frequently sadistic expression. He apparently derives great joy from mental and moral weakness, especially in those who are active and agile. At the same time, he seems to dislike inactive people and pointedly contrasts the supple movement of dancers, clowns, and acrobats with the stolid bourgeois who watch them, as in the drawing, *Chocolat Dancing* (Fig. 106). The lithe grace of the Negro dancer and the womanly fragility of his accompanist are opposed to the heavy-set waiter and the lumpy background figures of the audience. Like all his drawings and lithographs, this work is distinguished by its economy of means, that suggests rather than actually describes in detail. But the scene itself is not joyous and the café patrons take their pleasures very seriously. They are not dancers of the Moulin de la Galette as Renoir had shown them; the light and lyrical feeling is gone and in its place we have an almost brooding melancholy. The Impressionists proper, like the Japanese, have a far different attitude.

There is an interesting contrast between the albums of the Oriental artists, Harunobu and Shunso, showing the *Beauties of the Green Houses*, and the album of Lautrec lithographs known as *Elles*. The Yoshiwara girls, even in the most erotic scenes, never show the marks of vice and degradation found in the faces of Lautrec's women. If the art of Harunobu and his contemporaries seems joyful and almost childlike, it is probably the result of peaceful conditions in Japan during the late eighteenth century and the mass market for which prints were made. The periphery of Paris, as de-scribed by the isolated and individualistic Lautrec, smells of absinthe, stale cigars, and sweaty bodies. While the Japanese painted "the joyful luminous mornings of Tokyo, his domain was Paris and its sad nocturnal gaieties."

That is the spirit of his paintings. Examining *At the Moulin Rouge* (Fig. 107), we are overcome by a feeling of immense tragedy reflected out

106. LAUTREC: *Chocolat Dancing*—drawing (Albi, Museum).

of Lautrec's life and environment. The picture is distinguished by Lautrec's characteristic green, one of the predominant tones used here to convey a melancholy and bitterness suggesting El Greco. It is not the gay sun-drenched green of the outdoor Impressionists but a color dedicated to the evening, to a twilight sadness that pervades the painting. The background and face of the woman at the right have been rendered in this tone which underlines the artist's reaction to the subject here as elsewhere in his work.

197

107. LAUTREC: *At the Moulin Rouge* (Chicago, Chicago Art Institute, Birch Bartlett Memorial Collection).

In the far background, silhouetted in sharp color contrast, are two men and two women. The masculine pair consists of a very tall individual, Lautrec's cousin, accompanying a tiny dwarf-like figure in a bowler hat, the artist himself.

The effect of contrasting color, in painting as well as in posters, is one of the most characteristic features of Lautrec's art. With it he gains not only the momentary Impressionist quality but also the emotional needs of the composition. Arthur Symons has said of him: "His exasperating sense of contrasting colors is one of the qualities of his macabre genius. Nothing revolts him; he paints beauty and ugliness with a superb indifference; he paints vice and ignoble and exotic and atrocious and obscene creatures with the absolute insolence, the utter cynicism of some Satan or

198

some God who created in mutual antagonism the cruel and adorable world we live in."

One of Lautrec's most vivid commentaries on Montmartre life is the famous *La Goulue Entering the Moulin Rouge* (Fig. 108), showing the "Glutton" arm in arm with her sister and another feminine *habituée*. In perhaps no other painting of the nineteenth century have the clear indications of vice and degradation been presented as they are here. In Symons' words, these women "bear upon them the stigmata of their sins." *La Goulue*, "with a vampire's face, the profile of a bird of prey, a tortured mouth and metallic eyes," is contrasted diabolically with the "purely impure" fresh young face at her right.

Lautrec's reaction to a given situation is very intellectual; although the spectator is aware of a quick emotional response to the scene, it is the result of careful planning by the artist. In this sense, the pictorial historian of the *fin de siècle* is in direct opposition to the color Impressionists. The latter are charmed by their subject, approach it in an extremely informal manner and, most important of all, convey to the spectator almost nothing of their own personalities. Comparison of Monet, Pissarro, and early Renoir with Lautrec shows the sharp difference between a predominantly sensual art and one of thought and criticism. We cannot fail to note, although many of Lautrec's subjects deal with dancing, music, and drinking, that gaiety and joy are usually absent. Although we realize that a good deal of what went on at the Moulin Rouge and Moulin de la Galette was much less than genteel, the fact is that Lautrec deliberately sets out to demonstrate the vulgar qualities—and worse. Renoir's café atmosphere, on the other hand, possesses the completely different feeling of charm.

Although Lautrec's art is photographic and instantaneous in revealing momentary fragments of people and their activities, usually his works are better composed than the average Impressionist's. As a studio painter he can choose to paint what he wishes; the artistic factors are under his control. Moreover, he has benefited tremendously from the Orientals and Degas in fine composition and careful planning for effect. Like Degas, he makes frequent use of photographs as a basis for composition, although the results are not always so rewarding. In the architectonic sense, the pictures and

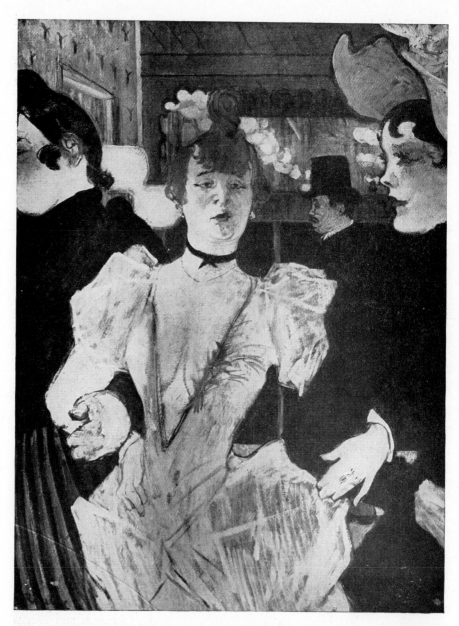

108. LAUTREC: *La Goulue Entering the Moulin Rouge* (New York, Dr. and Mrs. David M. Levy Collection).

prints of Lautrec fall far below those of Degas, who is the Impressionist planner par excellence. From the viewpoint of emotional significance and expressiveness, Lautrec has more to offer.

His desire to make his work emotionally meaningful, in contrast to the deliberate objectivity of Degas, leaves him less interested in the purely aesthetic and compositional side. Basically, Lautrec is a manipulator of the lithographic crayon or pencil. With these in his hand, he can perform miracles of economical statement, bringing a form or an emotion to life with a few brief strokes. He is not restrained by the academic compulsions of Degas—and to that extent he is more spontaneous, although less polished.

109. LAUTREC: *Yvette Guilbert Singing* (from *Le Rire*, 1894).

Notice the drawing he did for *Le Rire* of Yvette Guilbert singing her famous "Linger-longer-loo" (Fig. 109). Here the sensitive line of the Japanese artist has been utilized for a new and more modern purpose. What is further important, even though the famous *chanteuse* leans forward with all the grace of Harunobu's young women, the whole approach is sketchier, more Impressionistic. Where Degas achieves a sense of movement through the suppleness of his outlines, Lautrec's broken and quickly applied strokes arrive at a similar result. This picture, although small, has all the major characteristics of Lautrec's art: boldness of design, flat contours, and vantage point perspective, with the brilliant decorative quality and cynical feeling that are his chief contributions to the Impressionist movement.

Although Degas thought of himself as the portrayer of an epoch, his approach was basically too objective to make us feel his characters. The emotional involvement of Lautrec in his subjects, an involvement that allowed him to caricature his friend Yvette Guilbert, gives us in some measure a comprehension of one side of French life. Whereas Degas and Manet followed the Realistic doctrine of objectivity to its ultimate point, Lautrec combined a high degree of Realism with an equally intense feeling for the period in which he lived.

12. CÉZANNE AND POST-IMPRESSIONISM

Post-Impressionism, an attempt to reorganize plastically the spontaneous practices of the Impressionists, emerged against a background of great confusion. From the middle eighties to the end of the century, France was bedeviled by one crisis after another.

In 1886 there developed an ultrapatriotic movement to fight any form of cooperation with Germany. With the help of the League of Patriots led by the picturesque Boulanger, the conservatives tried to take over the government. By 1888 this Right wing movement reached its climax. In 1889 the boycott of the centenary of the Revolution marked the end of their agitation and Boulanger fled. Reflecting this second defeat of the Right in ten years, Manet's *Olympia* was accepted for the Luxembourg Museum in 1889, twenty-four years after its first showing.

The coalition of professional politicians and businessmen controlling France then produced the Panama scandal of 1892. In the course of this gigantic project (an irresistible temptation for the crooks) money had disappeared right and left. The guilty ones corrupted everybody they could reach to divert criticism, but when the storm broke, more than a hundred members of the Chamber of Deputies were involved.

On the Left, May Day had been established in 1890 as an official working-class holiday. The following year in the course of a demonstration, reported in the press as a "riot," troops shot at the participants. This was soon answered by the anarchist bombings of 1892 and 1893, apparently stimulated by *agents provocateurs*. In 1893 Roujon, director of the Beaux Arts Ministry, who had earlier refused the Caillebotte bequest of Impressionist paintings, told Gauguin: "I decline to encourage your art. It is revolutionary, and it repulses me. I refuse to create a scandal at the Beaux Arts by buying your pictures."

By 1894 a few more adventurous artists and critics showed sympathy for the anarchist movement, Félix Fénéon contributing a number of articles to their papers. The anarchists, in return, professed themselves admirers of all forms of "advanced" art, since these were symbols of revolt against constituted authority. The assassination of President Carnot that year resulted in the outlawing of anarchist propaganda and thirty people were put on trial, including the painter Maximilian Luce and Fénéon. Luce was sent to prison and almost all the others released.

The Panama scandal had given the enemies of the Republic an opportunity to point the finger not only at the government but also at those Jewish bankers who had been involved. In 1894 the Dreyfus affair began, with the Right wing press, including the anti-Semitic *La Libre Parole* (one of Degas' favorite newspapers), howling for revenge. Again the government was blasted, this time for allowing such Jewish officers, etc. France was divided into two camps by the railroading of Dreyfus to Devil's Island for alleged treason, the Revisionists agitating for a change in the sentence and the anti-Revisionists resisting fiercely. Cézanne and Degas belonged to the latter group.

A year after the trial, in 1896, the Christian Socialists proposed a political program amazingly similar to the later fascist ideology. In 1898, Zola wrote his famous *J'accuse*, following the acquittal of Esterhazy in the attempt to clear Dreyfus. Zola was tried for libel and condemned, while anti-Semitic riots took place all over France. With the confession of Colonel Henry a new trial was ordered, but the League of Patriots again incited reactionary elements to overthrow the government. The Liberals, however, were strong enough to pardon Dreyfus and to proceed against the Royalists and Rightists, who were either jailed or exiled. By 1900 things had quieted down and Liberal reform was able to proceed. Although there was still agitation from both wings, the net effect of the *affaire Dreyfus* was salutary in that it showed up the Royalists for what they were.

At the beginning of this period, Impressionist art had yielded to the flow and movement of the age of industry and let itself move toward an art of motion, an art as fragmentary as the kaleidoscopic world it viewed. The reaction of its artists had been physical—or rather visual—since they did not allow themselves to become emotionally involved. With representation as their excuse, they confined themselves to the way things looked rather than the way they felt. Perhaps in their attempt to escape the life of the city, they would not allow themselves any other reaction. Whatever the motivation, they produced an art without depth, either psychologically or formalistically. Nature was viewed as though from a canoe or path along a river bank, intimately and casually, rather than from a high hill in permanent and classical fashion.

When we speak of the post-Impressionist movement as a reaction against the formlessness of Impressionism, we mean against its lack of both emotional and plastic form. In a self-conscious way artists like Cézanne, Seurat, and Gauguin (to a lesser extent Renoir and unconsciously Van Gogh) tried to resist the pull of contemporary life toward aimless and empty pictorial gestures. They tried to organize reality, to formalize and arrange what they saw and felt into patterns and symbols. In this process they froze the iridescent twinkling colors of Impressionism into the sculpturesque volumes of Cézanne, the immobile forms of Seurat, and the controlled patterns of Gauguin. Van Gogh's art showed the explosive possibilities of the situation when he used neo-Impressionist pointillism, or dotting technique, for his own emotional purposes.

What we are trying to say is that both artistically and psychologically the artists of the last quarter of the century felt the need for trying to control an environment that had long since gotten the better of them. Using the tools at hand but with the traditional French balance and poise uppermost in their minds, they reformulated the Impressionist idea in this new way. Not without meaning is the fact that each of these men existed apart from his fellows: Cézanne carrying on his lonely experiments at Aix, Seurat working at night in his studio, Gauguin running away to another civilization, and Van Gogh escaping into the slightly disordered realm of his own mind. Essentially, they escaped from the environment which their art sought to control. Their individual idiosyncrasies are revealing only to the extent that they show in aggravated form the artist at odds with the world. The first three consciously tried to reestablish some sort of rational basis for art, Seurat and his school even attempting to create a socially useful tool that everyone could use. In his own way, Van Gogh also appealed for logic, the logic of decency, and an art that reflected the times.

The triple paradox—an evanescent technique for permanent purposes, artists trying to express their world while in complete isolation, and the irresistible force of modern mechanized society—helped to change their art into its next form, to shatter it into the various modern techniques of our time. When, as a result of impending war, the situation grows sufficiently acute, the planes of Cézanne reassemble themselves into the individualized experiments of Picasso's and Braque's Cubism or the color forms of Fauvism. From Seurat's intervals of space and cylindrical forms we move logically into Futurism (also influenced by Impressionism) and later to Purism. Gauguin's controlled rhythms become freer as Fauvism; and Van Gogh's still regular spots of color pour over into the inchoate mass of Expressionism. In this way, post-Impressionism becomes an important bridge between the nineteenth century and the twentieth. What is more, its paradoxical nature as a form of modern expression yields to these various emanations of the machine age and reacts against them. The twentieth-century artist will respond more directly to the machine environment than his post-Impressionist predecessors.

With post-Impressionist art we take the final step in the growing preoccupation with technique that ever since Manet had marked the evolution of modern painting. The group discussions at the Café Guerbois had been concerned with the Realistic problem at the same time that the "how" of painting grew increasingly important. Certainly a good deal of violent criticism had been leveled at the method of the Impressionists and their indifference to traditional procedures.

By the 1880's Cézanne and Seurat were working with "motifs," technically suitable or arrangeable material, rather than subjects with narrative implications or psychological value. Geographically separated from each other, Cézanne, Seurat, Van Gogh, and Gauguin concerned themselves with a method of painting, sometimes with such concentration as to depreciate the human element. This is truer of Cézanne and Seurat than of the other two, but in the main it does describe the post-Impressionist approach and that of the French before the First World War. It is no longer a question of Realist-Impressionist objectivity, nor does it mean that in order to fit into this category emotion must be obliterated, but it does signify a greater preoccupation with formal problems than ever before.

These circumstances are perhaps best reflected in the art of Paul Cézanne (1839–1906). In his old age Cézanne is quoted as having said: "I have wanted to make of impressionism something as solid and durable as the art of the museums." For the student of modern painting this statement underlines Cézanne's importance as a "full stop between impressionism and the contemporary movement in painting." Like Seurat and the mature Renoir, Cézanne may be regarded as a reaction against the loose and often nonstructural methods of the Impressionists. Renoir, by skillfully mixing traditional with modern procedures and subject matter, had achieved a distinctly solid art, a process completed in the wholly non-Impressionist works of his last period. In Cézanne's art the break with Impressionist method is just as radical; but the customary literary effusions about his sculpturesque qualities and well-ordered compositions, true though they are, do not explain how Cézanne arrived at these desirable effects.

Impressionist outdoor painting had stressed a relatively objective and unemotional approach to the motif as expressed in the lyrical tone of Monet and Pissarro. Their art sprang from an intuitional approach to color relationships existing momentarily in time and space, whereas the painting of Cézanne took a completely different tack. Although he was indebted to them for his knowledge of divided colors (particularly to Pissarro), his application of these rules was more precise and studied. While they had sought the momentary and evanescent, he looked for the permanent; they had attempted to render the temporary brilliance of a small section of nature, while he devoted himself to a never-changing summation of a larger part of the world under natural light.

It is often said that there is not one modern painter of importance who is not indebted to Cézanne. Certainly it is only in recent years that we have realized his influence on the twentieth century. Yet it is somewhat difficult to prove his direct relationship with the present, especially from an ideological point of view. The real contact lies between the actual paintings of Cézanne and the younger artists of the new century. As for his ideas that are supposed to have had such a great effect, Venturi indicates quite clearly that Cézanne never expressed a general theory of art. Chance utterances or sentences in some of his letters have been quoted by the ubiquitous Vollard, the dealer who was among the first to see the possibilities in his art, or the not too understanding Bernard, so that they were presented as aesthetic law.

The favorite quotation from the pseudo-aesthetic of Cézanne comes from a letter in which the painter said that all the aspects of nature are contained in "the cylinder, the sphere, the cone." This is used to explain his presumably geometric painting and offered also as the theoretical basis of early Cubism. There is little question of Cézanne's influence on Cubism. As for his own art, if the quotation were given in its entirety it would show that he was not so much interested in the underlying geometrical quality of objects as in a general order and system.

Although Cézanne's art is infinitely more systematic than that of the Impressionists, the fact remains that he spoke too often of "sensations" for us to believe that his painting was inspired by geometry instead of nature itself. We must rather think of his work as a series of interpretations resulting from prolonged meditation upon the figure, still life, or landscape. It must be kept in mind that his landscapes were not done as memory images but directly on the spot. In fact, photographs of the places represented in his pictures show very clear resemblances to the paintings themselves. In other words, we may assume that Cézanne started with life and allowed his extremely sensitive vision to absorb the character of the thing studied until he was certain that he had understood it visually. His main purpose, however, was not to record its atmosphere and impermanent light, as the Impressionists had done, but to render the permanent aspects of nature, ignoring the accidents and momentary effects which had interested his predecessors.

We have spoken of "sensations" as an important consideration in Cézanne's painting. This apparently intuitional approach to art may seem at variance with the strict order just indicated but it is a very important element in both the art and personality of this man. Whatever biographical material is available amply indicates that Cézanne was not a cold and detached scientist. Although there has been a great deal of exaggeration about his life, enough facts exist to show that he was a shy, introverted individual, suffering from a variety of complexes. Seated at the tables of the Café Guerbois, he spoke scarcely a word. Friendless, suspicious of most people, he struggled throughout his life almost without advice or help in his art and its peculiar problems.

Cézanne was the son of a middle-class family in Aix-en-Provence where, except for a short time in Paris, he spent most of his life. The most interesting part of his youth was the friendship with Émile Zola, early defender of Impressionism, whose novel, *L'Œuvre* (The Work), was based on the struggles of Cézanne and other members of the group. For a number of years Cézanne resisted the efforts of his banker father to put him into the business. Cézanne senior finally gave in and allowed the young man to go off to Paris to join Zola.

Through Zola, Cézanne met Manet and was drawn into the Realist movement. He was particularly attracted by the painting of Courbet. His earliest paintings, dated between 1858 and 1871, are part of his academic and Romantic period. In their sharp contrast of light and dark they suggest the Romantics, whose influence on these works was combined with the powerful modeling of Courbet. Such subjects as *The Poet's Dream* (Paris, Pellerin Collection) or the *Christ in Limbo* (Paris, Lecomte Collection) show the emotional nature of his art during this period. He even copied Delacroix's *Bark of Dante* at this time.

Cézanne's dependence on the solidity and heavy impasto of Courbet and Daumier during his formative period is illustrated by *The Man with the Cotton Nightcap* (Fig. 110) or *The Man with the Straw Hat* (New York, Metropolitan Museum of Art). Works of this early phase accentuate strong black-and-white contrasts carried out against a neutral or gray background. Such pictures indicate that in spite of a great emotional drive, his artistic impulse led him toward sound Realistic representation. From the very beginning, then, there is this conflict between sensation and organization.

During his stay in Paris, Cézanne met Pissarro and was initiated into the methods of Impressionism. Just as Courbet had driven Romantic subjects out of his art, this contact now drew him toward the newer Realist-

110. CÉZANNE: *The Man with the Cotton Nightcap* (New York, The Museum of Modern Art).

Impressionist methods of the 1870's. A few years earlier he had shown the influence of Manet in still-life painting, such as the *Still Life* of 1865 (New York, Simpson Collection), but he did not get to atmospheric landscape effects until after 1870. His well-known *The House of the Hanged Man* (Fig. 111) is one of the earliest examples of Cézanne's Impressionism; however, unlike most of the other practitioners, he always made the reservation that there was a difference between nature and art. In his own words: "To paint from nature is not merely to copy the object, but to realize sensations." Thus, *The House of the Hanged Man*, although painted in 1873 and shown at the first Impressionist exhibition, reveals the artistic personality of Cézanne more than the technique of the group as a whole. Although he had accepted their subject matter and their general method of seeing things, this early work already shows a more solid type of painting.

The House of the Hanged Man, like *The House of Père Lacroix* of the same date (New York, Chester Dale Collection), exhibits a change from the diagonal perspective of the Impressionists toward a point of view parallel to the picture plane. It also begins to arrange a series of planes behind each other to create space, instead of the continuous atmospheric Impressionist space. The main purpose here, as later, is not to draw the eye across a space in a perspective dictated by the photographic lessening of black-and-white contrasts as one moves back. At this point the artist is already beginning to guide the eye into a pattern (still somewhat on the surface), and for this purpose, instead of a jump through space, our vision is blocked by the solid houses. Finally, it should be noted that there is less dissolution of form in even these early Impressionist paintings of Cézanne than in the pictures of his colleagues.

His association with the Impressionists definitely places him among the dissidents of that day and leads to his own investigation of color relations in natural light. A certain objectivity appears, which he did not previously possess, and a concern with motif rather than Romantic or Realistic subjects. After the unfortunate results of the first few Impressionist exhibitions, Cézanne left Paris for good and settled more or less permanently at Aix. The death of his father shortly afterward made him financially independent and he was able to pursue his now fanatic attempts at visual analysis without worrying about selling pictures or pleasing the public. For almost twenty years (1877–1895) he isolated himself, resolved to work in silence until, as he put it, "the time that I felt myself capable of defending theoretically the result of my efforts."

To the provincial and narrow society of Aix, this strange painter fellow was not so much of an enigma as a madman and fair game for the jeers and

111. CÉZANNE: *The House of the Hanged Man* (Paris, Louvre).

211

stones of small boys. The general lack of understanding and sympathy forced him to turn inward upon himself. In later life this isolation developed into irritability and misanthropy, which gave rise to some of the more fantastic stories associated with him. The people of Aix may have thought him mad, but we must consider him as a most unselfish artist and the finest type of creator and investigator in that he was never satisfied with present results but looked ahead to the time when he would "realize" better.

When romantic biographers tell us that he left his canvases in the most peculiar out-of-the-way places, in forest and field, or in his child's room, or that his little son was permitted to cut holes in the windows and doors of these now sacred works, we may take it either as anecdote or as evidence of his constant search for a more complete method. The abandoned canvases, or those used by the maid to clean the stove, were merely steps in the developing process toward his own peculiar means of synchronizing his "sensations" with a grandiose and logical concept of the universe.

Accordingly, we approach the actual basis of Cézanne's technique and its elaboration of Impressionist method. In subject matter, like the Impressionists, Cézanne treats the figure, both indoors and out of doors, landscape, and still life. As we have already noted, however, his main interest is in the lasting effect of light, an aim more penetrative and analytical than that of the Impressionists. Where Monet or Pissarro created a momentary and somewhat lyrical effect upon the sensibilities of the spectator, Cézanne conveys finality and completeness. Monet, for example, showed us the Cathedral of Rouen, lily ponds, or haystacks at various times of the day and from different positions—time and place were both variables. Cézanne's light does not indicate any particular time of day nor is he interested in the superficial perspectives that enabled the Impressionists to view their subject matter from various positions. His light, like his compositions, is completely stable and so uniformly distributed and balanced that the intensity of illumination on one part of the canvas is definitely related to the strength of light on any other spot.

This, in itself, would suggest a totality of effect and an organization completely different from the Impressionist atmospheric perspective. Willard Huntington Wright very cleverly suggests the experiment of manipulating the light that enters a room where a Cézanne canvas is hung and finds that "it will darken or brighten perfectly, logically, proportionately with the outer light."

The Impressionists had taught Cézanne that divided spots of color would impart the intensity of light much more effectively than pure colors by themselves, for example, that yellow light reinforced by its complement, violet, would be much more vivid if the violet were rendered by a combination of red and blue. The violet formed by these two primaries would be the shadow around the object represented. They then proceeded to sketch in very rapidly the individual spots of color that, when complete, offered a series of contrasts by means of which the light was made to stand away from the object itself. In other words, they were satisfied with a relatively simple relationship between the yellow of light and the violet of shadow.

Cézanne, on the other hand, was not content with this but studied the many gradations away from the surface of the object touched with yellow. This warmth he followed in its gradual diminution to the cool shadows. In so doing, he became aware of specific laws of change from warm to cold that could always be followed provided that one began with white objects.

Since very few things are white, Cézanne had to go further to find out how diminution of light intensity and absorption are varied by the local or immediate color of the object itself. If he began with a blue object, there would be an entirely different result optically than if he began with a red object; but in either case the fundamental laws of color gradation from warm to cold remained the same. He was, therefore, able to paint in such a way that he reproduced the very effects of nature, the manner in which *solidity* is conveyed to the eye by the light which causes an object to exist in space. This may help to explain why the colors in a Cézanne painting move forward or back together. As in music, we deal here with a transposition of key.

To Cézanne, color was the only thing that caused an object to be visible; for him there were "no lines in nature." He drew or colored with his brush, meticulously observing these considerations, attempting always to achieve

213

the greatest intensity of coloristic expression. "When color is at its richest," he said, "form is at its fullest." His method may be summed up in his own words: "One should not say 'to model,' one should say 'to modulate.' Drawing and color are not distinct; as one paints one draws. The more the colors harmonize, the more precise is the drawing." By "harmonize" here he means to follow the processes of nature. Let us look at some of the results.

The painting of Cézanne can be divided according to subject matter, for as he treated the human figure, the landscape, or still life, his relative success may be said to vary. A method as precise and studied as his was not too suitable for painting the human figure since sitting for him necessitated a more than human patience. Yet even with this important drawback, the portraits of this artist or his figure studies have a monumental quality akin to sculpture. The merely decorative or anecdotal had no attractions for him.

112. CÉZANNE: *The Card Players* (New York, Stephen C. Clark Collection, photograph courtesy of M. Knoedler and Co.).

In such a painting as *The Card Players* (Fig. 112) men are grouped about a table without any specific reference to the activity of playing cards but rather as symbols of solidity and rhythm. We have no definite sense of cards passing back and forth, for these men, like his other human figures, are merely opportunities for realization of his sensations of form. Light is no longer focused on any particular spot but evenly spread over a composition that is carefully arranged in rhythmic pattern. Restrained in mood, it conveys an almost classical feeling, its architectural quality emphasized by the columnar effect of the curtain and the smock on the right-hand figure. Perspective here is directed from the rear to the front, as all glances converge at an imaginary point on the table, which becomes the formal as well as the psychological center of the picture. In this painting we are reminded of the traditional art from which Cézanne drew so much of his inspiration—and which he attempted to emulate—in this case, the Le Nains of the seventeenth century.

Cézanne's *Les Grandes Baigneuses* (The Great Bathers) (Fig. 113), on which he worked during the last years of his life, offers an interesting contrast with the picture of the same name by Renoir (Fig. 93). Although the latter had already forsaken his usual light Impressionist manner, Renoir's *Baigneuses* is still animated by a characteristic playfulness and enjoyment of fleshly beauty. Moreover, the meaning of bathing as an activity is still apparent. In the later work of Cézanne, on the other hand, there is no longer any reference to the act of bathing, nor are the figures based on models. As the forms arrange themselves under the Gothic arch of the trees, it becomes evident that they are only a motif. All the components of this picture: the nudes, the trees in their deliberate pattern, and the various horizontal accents, are treated without subjective meaning but rather as part of Cézanne's eternal rhythm and plastic design. To serve this end here, as in his other works, the painter does not hesitate to distort certain elements, the nudes, and the shapes of the trees. The general blue tonality is aesthetic rather than descriptive, in this fashion anticipating the form and color of later abstract painters, as Matisse in *The Blue Window* (Frontispiece).

Cézanne's characteristic timidity with models—part of his general misanthropy—made portrait painting a real problem. Moreover, his meticulous and probing method, the constant search for the correct relationship of one tone to another, required a phenomenal amount of patience in sitting for him. Although there are a number of portraits of different individuals during Cézanne's maturity, most of the pictures in this category are of his wife, who seems to have been the only one with adequate moral stamina. Here again we cannot think of portraiture in the ordinary sense of psychological interpretation. From this point of view the pictures have little, if any, interest but as examples of his method of realizing forms they are comparable to his *Bathers*, *The Card Players*, or any other regularly done motif. Generally, as in *The Card Players*, absolute symmetry is avoided and the artist deliberately deforms or distorts one side of a figure to prevent monotony. This expressionistic handling may be looked upon as part of Cézanne's "feeling,"

113. CÉZANNE: *Les Grandes Baigneuses* (The Great Bathers) (Philadelphia, Philadelphia Museum of Art, Wilstach Collection).

216

114. CÉZANNE: *Landscape, Mt. Ste. Victoire* (Washington, Phillips Memorial Gallery).

rather than his organizational or purely plastic intentions, and is repeated by artists of different schools in the early part of our own century.

In landscape or still life, the problem of models did not arise, and it is commonly felt that Cézanne expressed himself more completely in these areas. The transition from *The House of the Hanged Man* to his mature landscape style is shown in the *Landscape, Mt. Ste. Victoire* (Washington, Phillips Memorial Gallery) (Fig. 114). Although there is still a remnant of the Impressionists' hollow space, pictures of this type are basically quite different. For one thing, the conception of nature here is classical in both the finite closed space (as in Poussin) and the general parallelism of content to the picture plane. Moreover, the picture is closed to the spectator; unlike the average English, Barbizon, or Impressionist picture, we are not invited to enter and stroll about.

These things, however, would hardly have worried the public of the

217

eighties. Just when they had become accustomed to the dematerialized forms of the Impressionists and their photographic space with diminishing contrasts of light and dark, along came Cézanne with a new non-Realistic technique. His consistent refusal to use the methods of the Impressionists was taken as incompetence. It made no difference that the lack of atmospheric perspective, as in *Mt. Ste. Victoire*, kept the background forms related to those in the foreground, or in this case the emotionally powerful tree looming at the right, tied in with the curve of the mountain, became part of the general foreground pattern.

Since Cézanne was not concerned with ordinary appearances and the production of realistic illusion, he abandoned all the devices of that method. What interested him was not the momentary change in local color of objects affected by light but rather a permanent and pervasive light, glowing with the highest possible intensity and retaining the integral forms of all objects involved. Similarly, he arranged the pine trees in this picture to help close the intermediate space and remove it from our consideration—again a manipulation of the facts of nature for purposes of design. These factors contribute to a situation in which the background plays two roles: first, it contributes to the closed space, shutting off the view of the spectator; second, it becomes part of the foreground design as well.

The movement from foreground to background is effected by the relationship of the trees to the mountain, as well as by the deliberate directional diagonals and horizontals. In the first case, the left-hand tree and its associated foliage are joined by a mass of leaves and branches curving across the picture to the other tree in the middle ground and the mountain in the background. Recession between the two trees is also marked by foliage more or less horizontally arranged. From this point on, a series of rising diagonals lead to carefully placed solid color areas (little houses), bringing us through a group of lightly indicated straight lines to the horizontal aqueduct at the base of the mountain. All in all, this moving back and forth effects a characteristic combination of distance and nearby overwhelming largeness that is rather disturbing until we are able to follow its aesthetic reasons.

It is instructive to compare such a landscape with actual photographs of the same scene. The difference is revealed between recorded fact and aesthetically arranged nature; and also, it shows that the painter has been strongly moved in a visual and intellectual sense by what he has seen. It is this sensation of form, this feeling for the solidity and permanence of nature under brilliant unvarying light as "durable as the art of the museums," that Cézanne has tried to give us.

Cézanne never used his color with the small touches of Impressionist painting. In his landscape, like other subjects, color is applied in a series of small areas or planes moving from one intensity to another to resolve or define the form. Sometimes we find white spaces on a canvas or water-color paper where the intermediate tones have not yet been inserted, but the main outlines of his form-building color are always evident.

The *View of Gardanne* (1886, Fig. 115) marks a further step in Cézanne's abstraction of nature. Here there is no longer any question of middle ground but rather a decorative and dynamic surface pattern of planiform arrangements. Painting technique has changed toward a series of loosely applied and spaced strokes. These successively placed but not joined planes suggest rather than give volume. Alfred H. Barr, Jr., in his analysis of the origins of Cubism, assigns considerable importance to this painting as a forerunner of the later technique.

As separate entities the houses no longer matter; they are part of the rhythmic volume pattern, without meaning apart from augmenting the feeling of mass. Verticality is stressed; the eye is led upward, not inward. The raised horizon line again brings the background objects closer than they would be in reality. As in *The Card Players*, we feel the perspective, such as it is, moving from inside out—in this case, outside the picture proper.

Although one cannot base the existence of later schools on any one picture, the procedure used by Cézanne in his landscape painting will find outlets in the rhythmic painting of Matisse and the Fauves as well as in the dynamic, flattened plane analyses of Picasso and Braque, as in Picasso's *Portrait of Braque* (Fig. 151) or his *L'Arlésienne* (Fig. 152).

To reintegrate the forms of nature, to communicate the painter's intuitional response to their plastic qualities, was a task that often fell short of realization. For the average person, many of Cézanne's landscapes are not as interesting as the Impressionists', because the former are admittedly more difficult to understand. In his old age, Cézanne wrote to Émile Bernard: "I am too old, I have not realized and shall not realize now. I remain the primitive of the method I have discovered." He had begun his serious

115. CÉZANNE: *View of Gardanne* (1886, New York, F. A. Hirschland Collection).

experiments with the plastic function of light only after he was forty and, although he felt dissatisfied with the results achieved, his work marks a significant point in the evolution of modern painting.

On still life, where he was completely unhampered by the presence of human beings or the fluctuations of outdoor light, he could concentrate the full force of his intuitional eye. These pictures of fruit and utensils are highly personalized translations of inanimate form, similar to the monumental still-life pictures of Chardin. But Cézanne had the advantage of a knowledge of natural light and was able to make his forms more convincing and profound than the earlier master, to seek out the essence of an object as its shape was created by the light falling on it. Whereas Chardin had aggrandized specific objects of utilitarian importance, Cézanne's arrangements are compositions of unrelated objects, motifs painted to attain a permanent and cosmic form sensation.

His *Still Life with Apples* (Plate II) is a typical example of this phase of his work. Seen at closer range, it shows certain elements of distortion. These are generally meaningful, either for rhythmic purpose or to avoid the possible monotony of a too symmetrical effect. There is also a more practical explanation. Cézanne's attempt to convey all the gradations of light on a surface as small as an apple would necessitate using more spots of color than that small area could logically hold. In this fashion it may have come about that the forms of his still life or his people are frequently distorted. In this picture, too, surface arrangement makes for verticality of treatment. Perspective again moves forward rather than away from us. Part of that reaction is due to the arrangement itself, but it is the massive quality of each object which really gives the feeling of space.

Since 1877 Cézanne had been absent from the artistic quarrels of Paris. His name was brought forward in 1889 when Choquet forced *The House of the Hanged Man* into the Universal Exposition that year. Although by this time Monet and Pissarro were considered respectable, Cézanne's picture had to be pushed in. In 1895 the question came up again with the disposal of the Caillebotte collection which had been willed to the Luxembourg. The conflict between academicians and new painters, in the course of which the authorities refused to accept the pictures for the nation, was finally resolved by acceptance of forty paintings including two Cézannes. Partly as a result of the hullabaloo, Ambroise Vollard, then a young dealer, gave Cézanne his first one-man show.

Gérôme, the arch-conservative who had not yet gotten over the effects of Impressionist painting done by "anarchists and madmen," distinguished himself further on this occasion. "Time," he said, "will avenge those who try to paint without spending time on their work." History repeated itself, and Zola's earlier prediction that Manet's work would ultimately hang in the Louvre was now reiterated for Cézanne by the critic Gustave Geffroy. In any case, Cézanne's work, hitherto hidden in his studio at Aix, was now known to the world of art and could take its place as an influence in the evolution of painting.

To the art-minded public, the so-called amateurs, and the dilettantes, however, the painting of Cézanne was still unimportant. When in 1895 the collection of *Père* Tanguy, the sympathetic color merchant, was disposed of, six landscapes by Cézanne were sold for a total of six hundred francs.

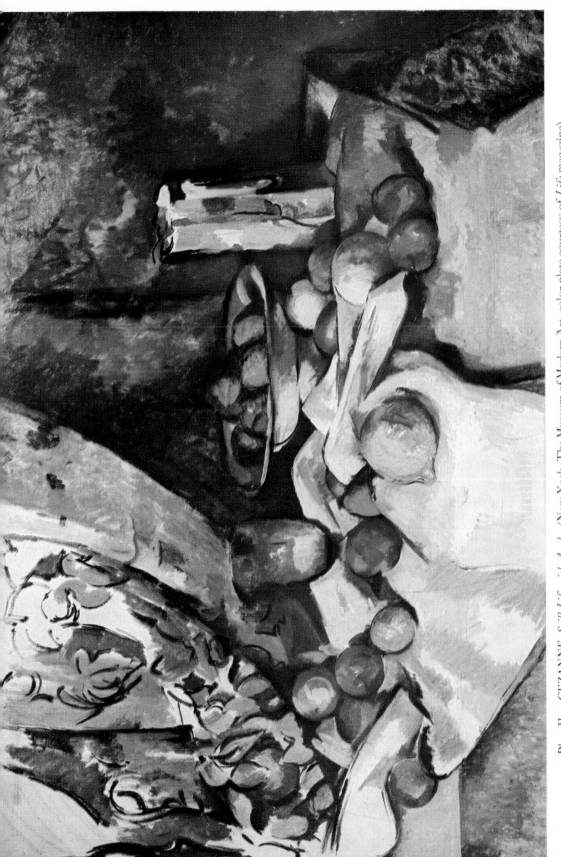

Plate II. CEZANNE: *Still Life with Apples* (New York, The Museum of Modern Art, color plate courtesy of *Life* magazine).

13. THE NEO-IMPRESSIONISTS: SEURAT AND SIGNAC

The Manet Memorial Exhibition of 1884 foreshadowed the end of the Impressionist struggle. Held at the École des Beaux-Arts, it added immeasurably to the prestige of the school and the prices it could now command.

That same year a group of young artists, including Seurat, Signac, Cross, and Redon, joined with some others to form the Society of Independent Artists. For a small entrance fee any artist could exhibit his pictures; there was no jury. This democratically run organization continued to function unchanged until 1914 and contributed greatly to the development of a free art in France. Its lineal descendant of the same name was organized in the United States in 1917 and until the Second World War held similar nonjury exhibitions each year.

In 1886 the first Independents exhibited together with what was left of the original Batignolles group in the last Impressionist exhibition. For one reason or another, Renoir, Cézanne, Monet, and Sisley did not participate. The sensation of this exhibition was the work of Seurat and his circle, which enraged the conservatives. Here again a friendly critic came forward, this time Félix Fénéon, to explain the aims of the new development as Duret had done for the Impressionists. Another period of struggle had begun.

From that point on, with Impressionist exhibitions no longer presented, it became the function of the *salons* of the Independents to carry the banner of progressive art for themselves and others. For example, in 1886 at the second of their *salons* the *douanier* Rousseau showed for the first time. The lack of Impressionist exhibitions, it should be noted, meant that the former rebels were accepted for the most part; newer ideas were now to be attacked.

What the Impressionists had tried to do with their instinctive approach to color and light, the neo-Impressionists, led by Seurat and Signac, attempted to reformulate into a series of rational and codified practices. In their sometimes smugly scientific attitude toward art, they wished to prove that painting could be produced by formula. With few exceptions—notably Seurat—the neo-Impressionists merely proved the superiority of Impressionist spontaneity. The theoretician of this new movement was Paul Signac (1863–1935), whose well-known book, *From Eugène Delacroix to Neo-Impressionism*, contains the main points of dogma. His own paintings, though perhaps the most typical of the movement, are by no means the best.

The Impressionist period had shown the possible effects of scientific progress on art as, for example, in the use and influence of the camera, that symbol of the new and speedier way of looking at things. More important, both for Impressionism and neo-Impressionism, was a large body of material on optics and color theory which derived from the great strides in nineteenth-century biology, physics, and chemistry. These developments, including the studies on color mixing, had affected Impressionism to the degree that they were useful in creating a casual realism and lyrical beauty opposed to urban drabness. But they were to be utilized more directly by a whole group of slightly later painters, including Georges Seurat, Paul Signac, Theo van Rysselberghe, Henri Edmond Cross, and others.

The main contribution of these neo- (or "new") Impressionists (also known as Divisionists, Pointillists, and Chromo-Luminarists) was their revolt against what they felt to be the formlessness and aimlessness of their Impressionist predecessors. They realized that the outdoor painting of Monet and his group had been primarily an intuitional and sensuous thing. Similarly, they believed that, because the earlier men had not been scientific, they had been unable to achieve maximum luminosity. What they set out to do, then, was to reduce the spontaneous technique of outdoor Impressionism to a series of formulae in order to make it more effective and more in keeping with an advanced state of scientific knowledge. In effect, this meant putting into words and rules what the Impressionists had felt and practiced, albeit casually—a somewhat risky procedure at best.

As early as 1838 the French scientist Chevreul had published *On the Law*

of the Simultaneous Contrast of Colors. This work, together with the subsequent *Color* by Rood, helped to focus attention on color theory. Although
the Impressionists had been aware of the existence of these ideas, it was not
until neo-Impressionist development that the final application took place.
It is true, of course, that the experiments of Rood, Chevreul, Helmholtz,
and Superville were done with pure light (sunlight or daylight), while the
neo-Impressionist painters attempted to apply these ideas with necessarily
impure pigments. Moreover, in spite of the good intentions of the scientists,
some of their facts—and hence some of their conclusions—were faulty.
In these circumstances a "scientific" art, based on a still experimental and
inconclusive science, had a somewhat limited chance of success.

Signac's book points out the opposed character of the Impressionists'
approach and his own method. Not only did the Impressionists portray
something fleeting and impermanent but they did not understand scientific
color relationships and possibilities. What he meant was that instead of
painting what they saw and felt, the Impressionists should have recorded
what science teaches us are the harmonies and contrasts of colors. When the
Impressionists had the fleeting sensation of a red in the shadow cast by a
greenish object, they should really have used the exact—and not the ap-
proximate or merely sensed—complement of that color. Signac states that
the shadow of any color is always lightly affected by its complement. He
forgets to indicate, however, that because of the changing quality of light
or reflections from adjacent forms, it is almost impossible to determine
accurately the local or immediate color of an object. If the starting point is
inexact, how can he hope to achieve an exact complement?

Signac's painting, *The Harbor of Marseilles* (Fig. 116), is a typical instance of his absorption with the qualities of brilliant, clean, and divided
colors. He shows here his characteristic use of regularly shaped spots of
pigment carefully placed side by side in complementary and contrasted
relationships. Tiny spaces are left between the spots of divided color so that
each lozenge of pigment can have its own optical effect. No mixture of any
sort is permitted under these rules; the eye is the instrument for achieving
the heightened color effect, as it combines the separate impulses coming
at it. This idea was apparently derived from one of the experiments of Rood,

116. SIGNAC: *The Harbor of Marseilles* (Paris, Luxembourg).

who had placed two colors side by side on a circular disk and then by rapidly revolving the disk caused them to blend. The fallacy of using this experiment on painting lies in the fact that only spots of limited size will blend at a distance, while most of the neo-Impressionists used such obtrusively large spots of mosaic-like paint that they defeated their own purpose.

Signac and his colleagues made the further error of using all their colors in the most intense form at their command, forgetting that luminosity, like everything else, depends on *relative* contrasts. Where every tone is used at maximum intensity, the force of differentiated color strength, which had made Impressionist painting so effective, is almost completely lost.

The art of neo-Impressionism, as explained by Signac, was to have a social purpose as well. Not only was it to serve as a brilliant decoration for the relatively dark interiors of public buildings but it was to be the sort of expression that could be practiced by anyone. Between the carefully prescribed color rules and equally precise and regulated dots of paint, the formula was so simple that a child could follow it. Signac even went a step further to regulate the kind of composition that would be appropriate for different subjects. For an exalted or gay theme, the compositional lines should be pointed diagonally upward and for a sad subject diagonally downward. Similarly, the mood of the picture could be suited by correspondingly warm or cool colors.

There can be little question of Signac's sincerity, of the fact that he was not trying to make a sensation. His devotion to the cause of the radical political movement in France for the greater part of his life explains his social viewpoint as an artist. But rigid adherence to any aesthetic formula is always dangerous—and Signac did follow his own prescription. If many of his paintings fall short of the expressed intentions of the artist, it is not for lack of trying but because the premises themselves are faulty and because there simply cannot be a recipe for good painting. The other neo-Impressionists follow for the most part the technique of Signac, although often rather academically.

Whatever we may say in criticism of this phase of nineteenth-century painting, the highly developed self-consciousness of the neo-Impressionists is typical of the theoretical interests of the modern painter. Their concern with methods of expression and with the problem of a new basis for painting shows the existence of a crisis in artistic thinking. When the Impressionists had shown a conscious desire to fit their art to the needs of the period, they had been laughed out of court. Their exhibitions, away from the *salon* which they could not enter, were designed to reach as many people as possible, even though most of the audience came to laugh. The neo-Impressionists felt even more strongly the need for reaching people, in spite of all the intervening obstacles and authorities. It is significant that Signac made a great point of the fact that his formulae for painting permitted the greatest possible participation on the part of the public, both as spectators and as practitioners. Of course he was talking far over the heads of the public at large, who could not be so sensitive to minor color variations as a professional painter.

Although neo-Impressionist painting may be more accurate scientifically, that does not make it great art or art more easily understood. For the student, however, its contribution lies in the fact that, like the work of Cézanne, it turned artists' minds to problems of form and structure. Even though their chief interest may still seem to be brilliant light, their paintings are more rigid and carefully controlled than Impressionist pictures—and in that sense more abstract or nonrealistic.

The real justification of the neo-Impressionist method is found in the work of a young artist who, in the short space of thirty-two years, produced some of the most significant paintings of the century: Georges Seurat (1859–1891). With Seurat we reach the complete negation of casual and loose Impressionism. Nothing in his painting is accidental or pseudo-accidental; everything is carefully worked out, studied, and composed with regard to spatial values and compositional rhythms. No one worked harder than he on the relatively few but precisely and monumentally planned works that mark his production. Night and day he applied himself to the meticulous technique imposed by the neo-Impressionist approach but unlike Signac and the others he had a sense of individual and composite form that is still the despair of many artists. The tiny spots of color, although visible on close examination, are used as constructive elements to create the abstract and monumental figures that people his paintings. These figures, in turn, are arranged to create rhythmic patterns, as well as profound extensions into space, what Seurat called "hollowing out the canvas." It should be noted that this post-Impressionist artist had studied with Lehmann, himself a pupil of Ingres and a fierce defender of the academic tradition. From the very beginning, then, Seurat applied himself to the problems of composition as had Degas, another modern stemming from similar traditional sources.

The art of Seurat is a curiously depersonalized thing because it is so carefully controlled and because the painter does not appear to have been interested in the emotional possibilities of his themes. Like Cézanne, he was preoccupied with his "sensation" of form; even more than the master of Aix, he controlled his medium to the point where all sentiment was squeezed out of his sculpturesque cylinders. Everything in these pictures assumes a profoundly solid and three-dimensional quality, even the landscape and the water. Although it cannot be explained just how he achieves the feeling of depth in a body of water, it is there for all to feel.

In the famous *Sunday Afternoon on La Grande Jatte* (Fig. 117) we find a most highly developed example of his method. Daniel Catton Rich's monograph on the picture tells us that this work, which took two years to complete (1884–1886), is the product of about seventy preliminary drawings, oil sketches, and other studies. During a period "when many paintings were done in a day by brushes priding themselves on cleverness . . . ," the painfully laborious technique of Seurat stands out in vivid contrast to the spontaneous method of the Impressionists.

Though *La Grande Jatte* shows a typical "vacation" theme of the Renoir type, Seurat is not concerned with the casual or joyous aspects of the scene or with creating the accidental quality so much favored by the previous generation. His middle-class Parisian crowd, set out against the lazy sunlight of a summer afternoon, is not an experience in relaxation so much as an exercise in design. Proceeding from the figures in the foreground, the space is built up step by step as we work our way back into the picture, each form deliberately placed to augment the space composition, as in the

117. SEURAT: *Sunday Afternoon on La Grande Jatte* (Chicago, Chicago Art Institute, Birch Bartlett Memorial Collection).

works of Raphael or Masaccio. Light in such paintings is not merely an illumination or atmospheric agent but serves to build up the various shapes. At the same time, by virtue of the recessive qualities of some colors and the advancing qualities of others, the sensation of moving into the picture and out of it is increased. The final function of color here is to create an atmosphere between the various figures, to help tie them together.

Working along these lines, Seurat developed an art form parallel in meaning to that of Cézanne, where the vantage point perspective of Impressionism and its other "accidental" devices have been eliminated. In their place we now stress permanence of effect in an arbitrarily set-out space which the artist proceeds to fill with connected patterns of line, form, receding and advancing color, atmosphere, and careful spotting of interest-creating figures in the various planes of the picture. In *La Grande Jatte*, as in other works, we begin in the foreground with a series of figures parallel to the picture frame and seen in profile. This not only establishes the front plane in a manner similar to that of Cézanne but, in keeping with the neo-Impressionist symbolic composition of upward, downward, or straight lines for different moods, sets the quiet tone of the story.

From this foremost plane, heavily accented in color, we move to the second important plane consisting of a series of figures that begin at the left and move straight across the picture surface. Between the primary and secondary planes, however, we find a few carefully placed transitional forms, the two seated girls and the mother and child facing us. In addition, a number of curved arrangements, the tree with branches bending left, the shore line, the sail in the left background, the umbrellas, and the foliage, all play their parts in carrying the eye back and forth within the picture. Directional movement is finally stopped by the wall in the extreme background that completes and delimits the picture space with an emphasis parallel to our front plane. Wherever we turn in this scene we are inevitably brought back to the geometrical center and the fullface mother and child, a point of rest like the arrangement often found in Cézanne's art. Such stability is contrary to Impressionist procedures, just as filling the center of a picture (the usual Impressionist vacuum) shows a new viewpoint.

At the joint exhibition of Impressionists and neo-Impressionists in 1886, the reception given this enormous canvas was doubly bad. Not only was it attacked and mocked by the critics and public, but the Impressionists also felt that Seurat had gone too far. It was perfectly evident to them that the newer painting deviated from Impressionist aims, but they were unable to ascribe any virtues to what Seurat was trying to do. As we have indicated elsewhere, most of the post-Impressionist painters were to endure this joint rejection from the public and the Impressionists or their supporters, the new collectors. It is quite understandable that the Impressionists should have been irritated with the extremely scientific method of Seurat; it is something else that they should have been as intolerant as many of them were. Of the entire group, the pliable Pissarro was the only one to whom the new technique appealed and for a while he worked along with the neo-Impressionists.

Seurat, who had carefully studied the painting of Delacroix for its use of complementary colors, limited the palette in his own painting system to four basic colors set forth by the scientist Chevreul: blue, red, yellow, and green. To these were added the various intermediate tones, such as blue-violet, violet, violet-red, red-orange, yellow-green, and green-blue. All these colors were mixed with white to increase brilliance but the colors themselves were applied separately.

Composition in the art of Seurat is so important that it overshadows everything else, even the neo-Impressionist pointillist method which, in his case, is not so obtrusive as in other members of the group. Compared with the larger and more discernible color spots of Signac, the small color areas of Seurat are not so big as to call attention to themselves nor are they so small as to preclude the possibility of their blending in the eye of the spectator. In *The Bathers* (1884, London, National Gallery), done a few years before *La Grande Jatte*, we have a somewhat simpler compositional method with all the people, except one, looking to the right in somnolent immobility. Once again enjoyment has been reduced to solemn formalized terms, while the composition may be analyzed in the same way as with the later picture.

In the paintings following *La Grande Jatte*, Seurat's forms become increasingly abstract and flattened to fit his arbitrary design ideas. *La Parade*

118. SEURAT: *La Parade* (New York, Stephen C. Clark Collection, photograph courtesy of The Museum of Modern Art).

(Fig. 118) exemplifies the flattening of figures that takes place in a very restricted space. Although we still look over the heads of the audience, the arrangement is perfectly horizontal and symmetrical, with the foreground figures establishing the front plane and a series of elaborate patterns showing the degree to which the painter bends realism to his abstract will. The movement from one flat plane to the next and the vibration from one area to another illustrates how Seurat, in pictures of this type, anticipated the Cubists. In the same way, the mechanization of forms suggests the post-Cubist paintings of Léger and even later artists.

Since Seurat's life lacked the biographical interest of such men as Van Gogh, Gauguin, and others, the general public is still relatively unaware of his contribution. It seems clear that he helped reconstruct painting after the comparatively formless work of the Impressionists, that he as much as anyone else showed the new abstract and nonrealistic direction. Whatever the degree of his effect on the early Cubists, they did admire in him the perfect structure and feeling for intervals and space. Together with Cézanne, he is one of the important influences on the growth of the analytical idea in our times. During his life and for some time later, his importance was dimmed by the tremendous fame and prestige of Cézanne. Beginning with the Cubists, however, he began to achieve recognition that grew in force with the approach of later Cubism, Futurism, and Purism. All this importance may seem a great deal for a painter who has left no more than seven major works, but the debt has been acknowledged in both deed and word.

His belief that the merit of a painting depends upon the relations and harmonies between tones (lights and darks), colors, and compositional lines, is always vindicated in his finished works. His is one of the few cases of an artist whose theory and practice are inseparable—and visible to all. With the exception of Cézanne, no other artist of this period is as much concerned with the mechanics of painting and as little concerned with the emotional content of his themes. Pictures like *La Parade* or *Le Chahut* (Otterlo, Rijksmuseum Kröller-Müller) are evidences of his about-face from the joyful mood of Renoir, Monet, and the others. Such scenes, taken by Seurat from contemporary French life and formalized into abstract Byzantine or Egyptian symbols of humanity, mark the turning point on the road to the twentieth century. In the painter's own words: "While certain critics see some poetry in my work, I paint by my method with no other consideration."

Yet, in spite of the apparent objectivity of this painter, we find that his marvelous black-and-white crayon drawings contain elements of spirituality unexcelled by other artists of his century. These masterpieces of tone in their subtle modulation of dark and light values convey a degree of mystery and mournfulness that lie beyond "method with no other consideration." Doubtless such drawings were studies for more elaborate compositions. Here, before elaboration and refining had eliminated emotional content, we still feel the artist's initial sensation of form. In the same sense, the many *croquetons* or oil sketches done on location for later finished studio works have far more Impressionist spontaneity than the final results.

As to the general idea of codification of rules for painting, it is something essentially foreign to our Western European tradition. There have been prescriptions aplenty from Leonardo and Dürer to Hogarth and Reynolds, but in the main we find relatively little connection between formulae and finished works. In the light of these facts, the nature of neo-Impressionist approach becomes even stranger. If we look on it as an effusion of scientific enthusiasm applied to art we have one possible explanation. The social aspect of the theory that it was usable by everyone may make sense in an age where the artist finds himself at odds with society and without a public. Consciously or otherwise, then, the artist-theoreticians apply a "scientific" method for "social" purposes in a reminiscently Eastern fashion.

The many striking analogies between the color lozenges and hieratic forms of Seurat and the mosaics of Byzantium may well be accidental. Yet it is interesting to note that the latter were also worked from a rule book, the *Book of Mt. Athos*, which prescribed the necessary forms and proportions. The artists of India also worked from set *sudras*. In an era characterized by great concern with Oriental art (Japanese and Chinese, to be sure), it is not too surprising to find this Near Eastern—and medieval—analogy. During our study of the twentieth century we will become particularly aware of the revitalizing effect of Oriental, Near Eastern, and various medieval arts on our own tradition. The process of using these ideas in a non-Realist, non-Impressionist fashion begins in this period, as we know from the art of Gauguin; the work of Seurat may well be another example.

Although only one important painting by Seurat remains in France today, and that one willed to the French nation by an American collector, Seurat is an important link in classical French tradition, the tradition of Poussin and Ingres. Whatever he did, whatever means he used, they were for the purpose of creating a controlled and reasoned architecture, a painting of the mind. It is a striking thing about French culture—particularly its art—that changing fashions in technique, no matter how extreme, do not alter its predisposition to logic. Even among the "advanced" artists, the reasoned turbulence of Delacroix, the plastic architecture of Cézanne, the measured intervals of Seurat, and the flowing but controlled rhythm of Matisse, all spring from the same desire for system and regularity, for an ordered universe.

14. VINCENT VAN GOGH

The excitement of Van Gogh's life, the pathos of his letters, and the capital made from this material by enterprising promoters have all obscured to a certain extent his importance as an artist. In the United States the sudden interest in Van Gogh after the Museum of Modern Art exhibition in 1935 and the best-seller novel on his life was diverted into other channels until the 1949 show at the Metropolitan. But whether or not reproductions of his works are so popular, Van Gogh's place in the evolution of modern painting is still the same. Beyond the fact that his art is the reflection of a tortured and unhappy personality lies its influence on the highly emotionalized contemporary method known as Expressionism. During the decade before the First World War, his effect was at its strongest, particularly in Germany where the Expressionist movement developed.

More than most of his post-Impressionist contemporaries, Van Gogh was aware of what was going on about him. This awareness is revealed in a sympathetic treatment of lower-class subjects and in the many thoughtful and warm letters addressed to his brother Theo. It is impossible to ignore the connection between what he painted and what he felt or wrote. Even if we were to hold with those critics who do not rate Van Gogh's painting too high, the vivid emotional reactions recorded in the letters can rank as literature. What he had to say about the position of the artist in society—what he had to say about the society itself—constitutes one of the important documents of that period. Although he had no fixed political viewpoint, his violent personalized reactions against the existing order are in line with the intellectual anarchism of the time. Basically, however, Vincent's approach to life was conditioned by profound religious sentiments, by a primitive kind of Christianity.

Vincent Van Gogh was born on March 30, 1853, the son of a clergyman at Groot-Zundert in Holland. From the very beginning his unfortunate appearance and shy, almost morbid temperament made him a creature apart. At sixteen he was taken into his Uncle Victor's firm, Goupil and Co., internationally known art dealers. Beginning at their Hague branch, he was transferred after a few years to the London division. His brother Theo, the well-beloved recipient of the famous letters, served the house of Goupil in Paris.

Vincent was working as a picture salesman, but his unusual temperament showed up in the slightly unorthodox advice he offered customers. Then the keen disappointment of being refused by his landlady's daughter upset him so much that he was no good to the firm at all. This time he was shifted to Paris. For about two years he shuttled back and forth between Paris and London, but his increasing interest in religion made it impossible for him to tell the lies necessary to sell pictures and he was finally dismissed for good in April, 1876.

This period of the artist's life is referred to in a later letter to his brother: "I am sure that many rich people, who for some reason or other buy expensive pictures, do not do so because of the art value they find in them, for such people the difference which you or I see between a tulip and a picture is not visible. They, the speculators, and blasé drunks, and many others, would buy tulips now as formerly, if it were but fashionable."

Van Gogh's religious interests grew even greater than before; he felt he had received the call. During 1876 and 1877 he tried to prepare himself for such a career, but school discipline was not made for him. Instead he left his studies in 1878 and volunteered as lay preacher among the miserably poor coal miners of the wretched industrial region, the Borinage section in Belgium. With his characteristic emotional intensity he threw himself into the work of comforting the stooping blackened people of the little town of Wasmes. Sharing their lives in every way, his "unorthodox" conduct created a certain uneasiness in official quarters, and after six months Van Gogh was dismissed. He continued the work unofficially in the nearby mining town of Cuesmes. In August, 1880, he began to draw from the life around him.

Although it is interesting to note the early influence of Millet, the work of Van Gogh, even from the beginning, is the result of his own emotional

236

approach, his passionate love and sympathy for the poor unfortunates who were his friends. A typical example of this first phase is found in the drawing of a *Dead Woman* (1879–1880, Fig. 119). The dramatic light and dark contrasts, the ugly angularity of the form and features against the stark poverty of the surroundings, strike the keynote of Van Gogh's work during that period in Belgium and Holland. Exaggerations and distortions of this kind, the profound feeling of inner emotion poured into the form, make the young artist an unselfconscious Expressionist whose approach will be mirrored again and again in the work of the painters of twentieth-century Germany.

Theo, who was in Paris, began to send him money and Vincent was definitely launched as a prospective painter. But he was to suffer a second great emotional shock in the summer of 1881. During the course of a visit home, his cousin "K" refused him in such a manner as to damage irreparably his already highly disorganized nervous system. Vincent left for The Hague and studied for a while with his cousin Anton Mauve, the animal painter, working very hard, eating very little, and generally ruining his health.

During 1884 and 1885 Van Gogh was back with his parents at Neunen.

119. VAN GOGH: *Dead Woman*—black crayon and water color (Otterlo, Rijksmuseum Kröller-Müller, photograph courtesy of The Museum of Modern Art).

237

From this period come the unusual paintings and drawings based on the lives of peasants and weavers, done in the artist's "green soap" manner. The best of these modern Rembrandtesque works is *The Potato Eaters* (1885, Fig. 120). Here he shows "the dirty linen table-cloth, the smoky wall, the dirty caps in which the women have worked in the field, all this *when seen through the eyelashes* in the light of the lamp, proves to be *very dark* grey, and the lamp, through a yellow reddish haze, is lighter still. . . . " He says further: "I have wanted to make it clear how these people, eating their potatoes under the lamplight, have dug the earth with those very hands they put in the dish, and so it speaks of *manual labor*, and how they have honestly earned their food."

Most interesting of all is Van Gogh's statement: "I have wanted to give the impression of quite a different way of living from that of us civilized people. Therefore I am not at all anxious for everyone to like it or admire it at once." At this point any affinity that we may have felt between Van

120. VAN GOGH: *The Potato Eaters* (Amsterdam, V. W. Van Gogh Collection, photograph courtesy of The Museum of Modern Art).

238

Gogh and Millet disappears. There is no longer any question of glorifying and romanticizing the peasant as Millet had done but rather that peasant life represents a kind of primitive honesty and simplicity which the modern world needs very badly. In some ways Gauguin mirrors this viewpoint, as do certain later Expressionist painters. "To paint peasants," says Van Gogh, "is a serious thing, and I should reproach myself if I did not try to make pictures which raise serious thoughts in those who think seriously about art and about life. . . . "

Van Gogh shows no interest in presenting farmers as worth-while subjects or as picturesque themes but rather a moral obligation to explain that the farmer who produces our food supply often lives on boiled potatoes and tea. In the same way, his earlier drawings of the coal miners carried with them the implicit thought that their miserable shacks were heated by the meager clinkers gathered by women and children from the refuse heaps about the coal shafts. This more concrete and profound humanitarianism, differentiated from the still Romantic idealism of Millet, springs from the fact that Van Gogh approaches his subject from an emotional and sympathetic viewpoint rather than as an aesthetic experience. In spite of the fact that Millet came of peasant stock and Van Gogh of a middle-class clerical family, we are convinced of the inherent sincerity of the Dutchman's statement: "One must paint the peasants as being one of them, as feeling, thinking as they do. . . . " Van Gogh felt it necessary to "feel his way" into his subject, as did the later Expressionists, unlike the Impressionists of that day whose chief function was descriptive.

Up to this point in his life, the art of Van Gogh had been a starving, struggling thing, unrelated to the major currents of the nineteenth century. In his heroic attempts to master the painting medium, he had fought his way through various techniques of the past, starving himself to buy the tremendous quantity of paint necessitated by his furious activity. By the end of 1885 he was in a state of near collapse. In February of the following year, his brother brought him to Paris where he stayed for almost two years. Ultimately the excitement of the big city and its unfavorable climate forced him to go south for his health.

The Parisian period marks the final emergence of Van Gogh into the stream of modern painting. Through his brother, now an important art dealer and a protector of the Impressionists, Vincent met most of the members of this group. The wise and sympathetic Pissarro helped him as earlier he had helped Cézanne. Van Gogh's approach to the problem of brilliant color was affected by the neo-Impressionist manner either directly from Seurat or through Pissarro who, as we have already noted, gave their practices a trial for a brief period.

A typical work of the Parisian interlude (1886–1888) is the *Montmartre* (Otterlo) which shows how Vincent absorbed contemporary ideas. Although not so vivid and intense as his later work, it already has his characteristic and fairly regular spots of broken color that make it partly Impressionist and partly neo-Impressionist. Yet it is no mere pastiche by an artist searching for a means of expression but a painting that shows he has learned all the Impressionists have to offer—their dots of color elongated by a free-swinging wrist and a greater emotional drive. His acquaintances during this period included Degas, Lautrec, and Gauguin, but he was not interested in their subject matter as much as their method. From them he probably learned the usefulness of Japanese art as applied to modern themes, a fact already evident in the pictures of the Paris period but more visible in the next and final interval of his life.

In February of 1888 poor health made him leave for Arles in the south of France. There, overwhelmed by the brilliant sunlight and powerful colors of Provence, he produced the emotionally charged canvases that are his fame. During the two and a half years which were to mark the end of his life, he transformed the relatively unemotional art of the Impressionists into a vivid and exciting reaction to the things about him. His models and friends were chosen, as before, from the ordinary folk of the town, at least from those who were able to accept him as a human being. To most of the people of Arles he was as much a madman as Cézanne to the citizens of Aix. If small boys went out of their way to make life miserable for Cézanne, it was just as true in the case of the "crazy redhead" who was also pursued with stones and jeers.

The sun-drenched countryside of Provence, to him "as beautiful as Japan," lent itself admirably to his highly personalized method of applying

121. VAN GOGH: *The Bridge at Arles* (Otterlo, Rijksmuseum Kröller-Müller, photograph courtesy of The Museum of Modern Art).

pure color directly to the canvas. In some cases, as *The Bridge at Arles* (Fig. 121) or the equally well-known *Boats at Stes. Maries*, there is particular reference to the compositional effects of Japanese prints. Van Gogh himself said: "All my work is, in a way, founded on Japanese art. . . . Japanese art, in decadence in its own country, takes root again among the French Impressionist artists." *The Bridge at Arles*, in its simple theme and cut-off rendition of a hillock at the right, suggests similar subjects by Hiroshige. Neither the artists of Japan, however, nor contemporary French painters could give their work the amazing sensation of vivid sunlight contained in this painting that has not yet achieved Van Gogh's later intensity.

In addition to many still-life paintings (*Sunflowers, Shoes,* etc.) Van Gogh also did a number of interiors and figure studies during this period. The latter group are particularly revealing for what they tell us of his associations, as in *The Postman Roulin* or *The Peasant* (Fig. 122). Of the letter carrier, he says: "What a government and what times we live in! As for me, I have rarely seen a man of Roulin's temper, there is something in him tremendously like Socrates, ugly as a satyr, as Michelet called him, 'until on the last day a god appeared in him that illumined the Parthenon.'" About the peasant, Van Gogh writes: "You are shortly to make the acquaintance of Master Patience Escalier, a sort of man with a hoe, formerly cowherd of the Camargue, now gardener at a house in Crau."

When we look at the postman or peasant in terms of what Van Gogh has said of them, they take on an importance beyond mere representation. His chief interest is in their character rather than their appearance. Moreover, they have become types or symbols. For both these reasons, the painter's emphasis is on psychological rather than physical qualities. The monumental form and solemn attitude of *Maître* Escalier with his red-rimmed eyes and ruddy cheeks become a probing analysis of the human soul. Although Van Gogh seemed to be joking when he spoke of a "man with a hoe," his interpretation of peasant ruggedness and stark simplicity has a peculiarly modern emotional quality that anticipates such Expressionist works as the Modersohn-Becker *Old Peasant Woman* (Fig. 171).

122. VAN GOGH: *The Peasant* (London, Beatty Collection, photograph courtesy of Vizzavona).

Like the twentieth-century distorters of form and color, Van Gogh destroys our ordinary notions of intrinsic color. The face of the peasant is touched with spots of bright pigment which accentuate violet and greenish shadows of an almost frightening quality. He is no longer interested in the fugitive color sensations of the Impressionists but rather in color as a vehicle for strong emotions. Similarly, a new system for form de-

123. VAN GOGH: *Night Café* (New York, Stephen C. Clark Collection, photograph courtesy of The Museum of Modern Art).

lineation is presented here, so that recession of the eyes is conveyed by a series of concentric whorls composed of fairly regular lozenges of color. The outlines of the form itself are brutal and harsh, suggesting angularity, hardness, and force, giving the impression of frantic hurry and a slashing brush. Much of Van Gogh's painting was done in a great hurry, as though he did not have enough time to do all the things he wished, to show all the possible emotions of mankind and of himself. Yet, like the Orientals whose inspiration he admits, Van Gogh seems to have given a good deal of thought to many of his pictures. This is reasonably certain regarding those paintings of which he has left some sort of extended written record.

One other work of this period (September, 1888) clearly shows how far Van Gogh had drifted from the Impressionists and the neo-Impressionists. *Night Café* (Fig. 123), above all others, gives us the key to Van Gogh's attitude toward color. As he describes this scene in which he has "tried

243

to express the terrible passions of humanity by means of red and green," we feel an instinctive horror before the group of homeless night prowlers who crouch over the tiny café tables. "Everywhere," he says, "there is a clash and contrast of the most alien reds and greens in the figures of the little sleeping hooligans, in the empty dreary room, in violet and blue."

"In my picture of the *Night Café* I have tried to express the idea that the café is a place where one can ruin one's self, run mad, or commit a crime." When Van Gogh says: "It is color not locally true from the point of view of the stereoscopic realist, but color to suggest any emotion of an ardent temperament," we understand his wild desire to crawl into the very marrow of his subject. What he says of color distortion as a means to greater expressiveness also applies to form distortion in his painting as in any other.

Toward the middle of October, 1888, Gauguin arrived in Arles. He remained with Vincent until the end of the year when the latter, suffering from overwork and too much Provençal sun, had his first mental stroke. During their short period of companionship, Van Gogh, impressed by the other's greater worldliness and experience, tried to imitate his art. Vincent's own painting, already considerably stimulated by Japanese design, assumed an even greater simplicity at that time, reflecting the typical Gauguin flatly patterned and sharply outlined forms. An example of this phase is seen in the *Woman Rocking a Cradle* (Chicago, Chicago Art Institute), an intensely linear green figure with orange hair. Placed in a very shallow space against a green and pink-flowered background, this picture takes on some of Gauguin's rhythmical quality, but the color is entirely Van Gogh's, as is the lumpy, brutal handling of hands and face.

After the hospitalization following his breakdown in December (he had cut off one of his ears in a fit of despondency) and Gauguin's return to Paris, Vincent found it impossible to remain in Arles. In May of the following year he was taken to a nearby asylum at St. Rémy where, between fits of acute melancholia bordering on madness, he painted some of his finest pictures. One of these, *Cornfields at St. Rémy* (1889, Fig. 124), is best described in the painter's own words: "I am struggling with a canvas begun some days before my indisposition, a *Mower*, the study is all yellow, terribly thickly painted, but the subject was fine and simple. For I see in this mower a vague figure fighting like a devil in the midst of the heat to get to the end

124. VAN GOGH: *Cornfields at St. Rémy* (Otterlo, Rijksmuseum Kröller-Müller).

of his task, I see the image of death, in the sense that humanity might be the corn that he is reaping. So it is—if you like—the opposite of that sower I tried to do before. But there's nothing sad in this death, it goes its way in broad daylight with a sun flooding everything with a light of pure gold . . ."

" . . . It is an image of death as the great book of nature speaks of it—but what I have tried for is the 'almost smiling.' It is all yellow, except a line of violet hills, a pale fair yellow. I find it queer that I saw it like this between the bars of a cell."

The same agonized treatment, the same frenzied squeezing of thick little dabs of paint out of tubes directly onto canvas, is seen in his *Landscape with Cypresses* (Fig. 125). Once again nature reflects all the emotional contrasts struggling for possession of the painter's soul, the maddening southern wind agitating the landscape with its gaunt and frightening cypresses. This is no longer the gentle rustling breeze of Monet or Renoir but a cyclone of emotion that causes vegetation to writhe and clouds to pile up tumultuously.

During his stay at St. Rémy, Van Gogh made a number of copies of Millet, Delacroix, and Daumier—artists whose sympathetic attitude was bound to appeal to him—in his own highly individual style. After a year at the asylum he left St. Rémy for Auvers (near Paris and his beloved Theo) on May 17, 1890. Here, under the care of the extremely understanding Dr. Gachet, who had been one of the first admirers of Cézanne, Van Gogh was to spend the few months left him in painting his typical inward-searching landscapes and portraits. Of these, perhaps the most interesting is the *Dr. Gachet* (Fig. 126). In the sense that Van Gogh has reacted emotionally to his subject, this picture is a mate to the *Peasant* done two years earlier. But the artist has gone beyond that point in almost substituting himself for the melancholy and sensitive physician. "It has the same feeling," he says, "as the portrait of myself, which I took when I left for this place." Among all the portraits and figure studies of Van Gogh, we would have to look far to find so complete an expression of his own personality as we

125. VAN GOGH: *Landscape with Cypresses* (London, Tate Gallery).

see in the portrait of Dr. Gachet. This mingling of sensitive withdrawal and suffering that make up the story of Vincent's life are again summed up in his letter to Gauguin: "Meanwhile, I have a portrait of Dr. Gachet with the heartbroken expression of our time."

The debt of subsequent artists to Van Gogh has only been hinted at in this brief story of his life and art; its full effect will be seen later. In ten pitifully short years, between his beginning as an artist in 1880 and his suicide in July, 1890, he set down in words and paint some of the most sympathetic and moving ideas of any

126. VAN GOGH: *Dr. Gachet* (New York, Mr. and Mrs. Siegfried Kramarsky Collection).

artist anywhere. If we are amazed at his sensitivity to suffering and his tremendous emotional capacity, we must also remember that he was a rational human being, keenly aware of the problems about him. No mere subject for a romantic biography could have written: " . . . all the same they are building State museums, and the like, for hundreds of thousands, but meanwhile, the artist can go to the dogs."

The message of Van Gogh was not destined for the form-conscious Cubists but rather for the more intuitive Fauves of the early part of the new century, as well as the French and German Expressionists. Throughout his brief career, emphasis had been placed on expressiveness rather than structure. It was only during the brief contact with Gauguin that "modern" structural pattern ideas figured in his art. With the end of that relationship Van Gogh is once more himself, a painter trying to derive the essence of ideas, emotions, and things through broken form and color—feeling his way into a personality or substituting his own violent emotions for those of nature. Where the Impressionist looked at things from the outside, Van Gogh and his Expressionist followers looked at the world from the inside. That is his legacy for our times.

247

15. PAUL GAUGUIN

Like Van Gogh, Gauguin owes much of his fame to the romantic circumstances of his life. The *Noa Noa* which he wrote, W. Somerset Maugham's famous novel *The Moon and Sixpence*, and various editions of the painter's letters have all contributed to an exciting story that enhances the interest of the paintings.

For a long time critics said that the work of Gauguin was not so important as the example it set for later artists to follow: that of going away to primitive civilizations and absorbing their forms and colors. Yet the only genuine example of a painter inspired to follow Gauguin's precedent and go off to the South Seas is Max Pechstein. Moreover, the "primitive" tendencies of much modern painting have less to do with the influence of the romantic and world-weary Frenchman than with specific "aesthetic" and "museum" experiences. These self-conscious searches for expressive forms and violently colored arrangements in the older nonclassical arts are not escapist so much as attempts to strengthen and rejuvenate modern art.

Yet the influence of Gauguin's point of view has been of considerable importance in the formation of Matisse's style. Together with Van Gogh and the Norwegian painter Edvard Munch, his work also has some bearing on the development of the early Expressionist school known as *Die Brücke*, which included Pechstein, Nolde, Kirchner, Schmidt-Rottluff, and others. In his own time, Gauguin was a typical example of post-Impressionist revolt against the purely representational character of Impressionism. Like Van Gogh, he tried to give his art a certain emotional and even philosophical meaning; like Seurat and Cézanne, he tried to control nature rather than to record it. His patterned and rhythmical arrangements lead us logically to the art of Matisse; his expressive colors in their large flat areas lead us in the same direction and even beyond to the Expressionists.

Ever since the eighteenth century, French painters had been interested in exotic material, particularly from the Far East. During the following century, starting with Delacroix, artists began to visit Near Eastern countries such as Algiers, Morocco, and Turkey. Toward the end of the nineteenth century, the Impressionists had become involved with Chinese and Japanese art in ways already seen. Given this continuous tradition of borrowings from the Orient, the appearance of the art of Gauguin is not too surprising. If we look upon it as an expression of the expansion of European nations into newer Pacific areas, it is not too different from the excursion of Delacroix to Algiers.

To the average person unfamiliar with the Polynesian background from which Gauguin is supposed to have drawn his inspiration, it would appear, especially in view of the primitive subjects, that he based his art on what he found there. Actually, however, the island of Tahiti and to a lesser extent the Marquesas Islands, where Gauguin spent only his last few years, have no extensive plastic tradition. Even if it were argued that he borrowed from Polynesian art in general, the plastic expression of that area is hard and angular, considerably different from Gauguin's soft method of modeling, his gracious and flowing line. Robert Goldwater, who has concerned himself with the question of primitivism in modern art, says: "Nowhere in Gauguin's art is there any direct copying from Oceanic art"—except in one rather unimportant example.

Of what, then, does the so-called primitivism of Gauguin consist? Actually, it is primarily a question of theme and expresses itself through the many simple naïve subjects portraying the islanders. In some instances it involves more imaginative and romantic concepts, such as *The Spirit of the Dead Watching* (Fig. 127). There is a long narrative account of this picture in the painter's autobiographical *Noa Noa* (Fragrance) which ends with: "Otherwise it is simply no more than a study of the nude in Oceania." As for the Spirit in this painting, it is derived from the painter's imagination rather than from any specific work of art in the islands.

It becomes increasingly clear, as we unfold our story of Gauguin, that his is an extremely sophisticated and civilized technique with many borrowed elements from a variety of highly developed cultures. Gauguin himself often said: "Have always before you the Persians, the Cambodians, and

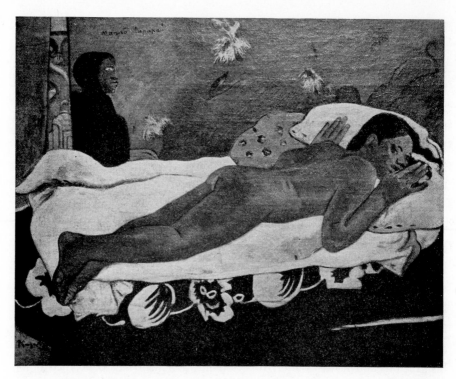

127. GAUGUIN: *The Spirit of the Dead Watching* (New York, A. Conger Goodyear Collection, photograph courtesy of The Museum of Modern Art).

a little of the Egyptians. The great error is the Greek, however beautiful it may be." This diffuse and exotic approach described Gauguin's art very well.

The exotic was part of his inheritance and environment. His father was a journalist from Orléans, his mother a beautiful Creole of noble background. When Paul was only three, the family moved to Peru (the father died en route) where they lived for the next four years in a curious sort of luxury, attended by Oriental and Negro servants, and amusing themselves in the sleepy and strange manner of Spanish grandees. At seventeen Gauguin shipped as a pilot apprentice on a South American trade boat and began his lifelong interest in travel and women. Three years later he was in the French navy as a stoker but after a few years of this life he settled in Paris and took a job in a stockbroker's office. Within a relatively short time he made a good deal of money, married a beautiful Danish girl, and they had five children.

The restless strain in his temperament and his early adventures made this routine life uninteresting. Gauguin became involved in a number of outside activities, among them painting. For a while he was satisfied to collect pictures but gradually he began to paint. His earliest work was done under the influence of Pissarro, that remarkable and saintly figure who had befriended Cézanne, Van Gogh, and many others. Gauguin participated in the Impressionist exhibitions of 1880, 1881, and 1882 with a series of pictures that, although the least satisfactory of his entire production, reveal his original contact with the Impressionist color tradition which he soon outgrew.

By 1883 his interest in painting reached such proportions that he gave up his business career, the last factor in the breakup of his already disintegrating family life. To save expenses he moved to Rouen for a while and from there to Copenhagen to his wife's family. The "crazy" notion of abandoning a lucrative business for art, together with his somewhat casual attitude, did not make him overpopular with his relatives. Taking one of the children, he returned to Paris to work at whatever odd jobs he could find, including bill posting, scenic decoration, and the like, and endured great hardships.

In 1886 he showed about twenty paintings without success and finally left in disgust for Pont-Aven in Brittany, where he would not have to contend with civilization, where people were more natural, and where, he thought, money was less important than in Paris. After only one year, however, he was back in Paris, for he never seemed able to resist the lure of the civilization which he hated so much but which could offer him the applause he needed. Although he did a good deal of talking about his art and met the Van Gogh brothers, success was as far away as ever, and he took himself off to Panama on a job and then to Martinique to paint. Dysentery and a terrible climate soon drove him back to Paris, still unhappy and difficult to get along with.

Another exhibition proved as disastrous as the earlier ones, and in 1888 he accepted Van Gogh's invitation to go to Arles. Although the personal relationship between the two men during their brief companionship has never been satisfactorily explained, the period culminated in Van Gogh's first serious attack and Gauguin's quick return to Paris. Yet the experience served to heighten Gauguin's color sense a step beyond its strong Martinique base.

The Women of Arles (1888, Fig. 128), from which Van Gogh borrowed the foreground figure, shows the progress made by Gauguin during this period. In a nonrepresentational manner typical of the anti-Impressionist approach, he combined the broad color areas of medieval stained glass with the elegant outlines and unusual perspectives of Japanese art. Instead of giving his figures realistic volume, he has rendered them abstractly in line and flat area. People and nature are distorted here into a carefully arranged and rhythmic pattern similar to the work of the contemporary Norwegian, Edvard Munch. At this stage the objective and stylized manner of *The Women of Arles* makes Gauguin a collaborator of Cézanne and Seurat in their attempts to control nature. Gauguin called this Synthesis.

128. GAUGUIN: *The Women of Arles* (New York, Estate of James W. Barney).

The next step in his development involved the symbolic element, through which he tried to make his people represent actual ideas, emotions, or both, somewhat in the fashion of the Symbolist poets. A good example of this attitude is *The Yellow Christ* (Fig. 129) or *Jacob Struggling with the Angel* (Edinburgh, National Gallery). These pictures were done shortly after *The Women of Arles*, when Gauguin had gone off to Pouldu in Brittany. In this new environment among simple archaic people whose customs had not changed for centuries, Gauguin experienced their simple religiosity and felt the rigid angularities of their religious art.

129. GAUGUIN: *The Yellow Christ* (Buffalo, courtesy of the Albright Art Gallery).

The paintings of the Breton period are supposed to reflect a state of mind solemn and concentrated, in which the women coming from church see in retrospect the sermon just preached, or sit down by the side of the road and meditate on the Passion of Christ. Gauguin is just as non-Realistic in *The Yellow Christ* as in *The Women of Arles*, but the new combination of contemporary women and the Crucifixion (like the women and the struggle between Jacob and the angel) creates an emotionally charged atmosphere. Colors take on the shiny enamel-like quality of medieval cloisonné, while contours become sharp and well defined. Though all these pictures retain the vantage point perspective and the cut-off figures, these are only vestigial remnants of the Impressionism with which Gauguin had started.

The flaming yellow of the Christ is already Expressionistic in the manner of a Franz Marc or Chagall painting—or perhaps better, *fauve* in the sense of a Matisse: "A metre of green is greener than a centimetre of green." Distortions in this kind of painting serve a double purpose. On the one hand, they enable the artist to create his form pattern or rhythmic effect, to subordinate his figures to a general aesthetic idea. Beyond that, they permit a certain emotional expressiveness, necessary in this instance for the religious and mystical purpose of the artist. The form of the Christ is that of Romanesque medieval art rather than folk art of the area, a change as justifiable as the other alterations of reality which the painter needs. Here, as in his later Tahitian subjects, Gauguin deliberately chose aesthetic forms from older cultures that would best express his ideas.

During this period Gauguin had a number of followers imitating his Synthetist procedures but within a short time he disavowed them. The philosophical basis for his primitive viewpoint during this Brittany phase is the general back-to-nature idea or pantheism of the so-called *art nouveau* movement. According to this method of thinking, a symbolically flowing and curving line expressed the fact that the art was based on natural forms. In the works of the *Jugendstil* painters in Germany, Munch in Norway, and Gauguin in France, these ideas found their expression.

In 1889 Gauguin was back in Paris, penniless, and parading about in Breton costume as he was to do later in Tahitian clothes. The young Symbolist poets of the time, feeling they had found a comrade, held a benefit for him and Verlaine at the Vaudeville where one of Maeterlinck's early plays was produced for the first time. This event, together with a public sale at the Hôtel Drouot, enabled Gauguin to go off to the tropics that he had read about in a book.

He left for Tahiti in 1891 armed with a document from the Ministry of Public Instruction that made him part of an "art mission." The rest of his life was to be marked by wanderings between those islands and France. At no time could he settle himself permanently in his beloved tropics where life was still "unspoiled," partly because of his restlessness but more because he needed a kind of applause and appreciation that he could not get from the natives. The ostensible reason for leaving civilization was a desire to get back to nature, to improve himself and his art; nonetheless, Gauguin never became part of a primitive environment that was no longer unspoiled. The Parisian sophisticate, ex-stockbroker, and adventurer was as out of place as his painting gear. Renoir put it very well on the occasion of Gauguin's departure when he said: "One can paint so nicely in the Batignolles."

In Tahiti Gauguin lived with a young native woman. Because of the antipathy of the local French residents he was forced to move a considerable distance inland, where for a time he went completely native with his young love. Many of these events are told in his poetic and evocative *Noa Noa*. After a while, however, he became weary of the place and since his money was running low, decided to return to Paris. The sale of a few pictures back home had netted enough to get him as far as Marseilles, when a fortunate legacy from an uncle facilitated a rather spectacular entry into Paris.

An elaborate exhibition of his paintings took place at Durand-Ruel's, the titles in Tahitian and the artist conspicuous in exotic costume. He set up a very unusual studio with brilliant yellow walls and primitive carvings on the doorways with such mottoes as "Here one makes love." In spite of its extraordinary character, the exhibition was a failure, and after his money was gone, Gauguin went off to Brittany again—this time with a new Javanese mistress. In an unfortunate incident the burly Gauguin tried to protect some of his artist friends from a group of drunken sailors and had his ankle broken by a kick from a wooden clog. By the time he was back on his feet, the Javanese lady had dismantled his studio in Paris.

Thoroughly discouraged, Gauguin sold everything he owned, held a final auction of his pictures, and, now a very sick man (from a casual adventure with a streetwalker), left civilization for good. His last years, from 1895 to 1903, were spent in Tahiti and the Marquesas Islands to which he moved later. Although life there was far from pleasant with the constant worry over money, severe illness, and incompatibility with the French residents, he did a good deal of painting. Some of his finest works date from this last period.

For a time he worked as government clerk at a few francs a day, then started a newspaper which got him into trouble and, in general, was pretty miserable. Money in small sums was sent by a sympathetic friend in Paris— most of it going to pay hospital bills. When he was able to walk again, he left for the Marquesas Islands, one of the few "unspoiled" spots remaining. There he died in 1903. Within a very short time his pictures became a valuable commodity.

The works of Gauguin during the last phase are marked by a broader, more resonant color that represents one of the great triumphs of modern decorative painting. Yet it is reasonable to suppose that he would have developed along these lines even had he not gone to Tahiti, for basically his painting was not affected by the surroundings. His art at this time represents a combination of European (French) elements with Indian, Egyptian, Javanese, and other forms, the whole saturated with a preconceived and romantic idea of life in the South Seas. Occasionally, as in the *Ia orana Maria* (We Adore Thee, Mary), we find him taking a Christian subject and refurbishing it in Pacific costume. All in all, his aesthetic is one of the most eclectic manifestations of the century, aided as it was by a variety of alternative style choices that only the modern artist could command. Yet it is a fully original and personal phenomenon of considerable consequence to the future development of painting. Although colors recede and advance with a feeling for depth, his work is less spatial in the plastic sense than the painting of Seurat and Cézanne. Yet its very decorative quality gives it importance for the Fauves of the next generation.

One of his most apparent borrowings from French painting is found in the *Woman with Mangos* (Moscow, Museum of Modern Western Art), a nude lying down out of doors against the foliage of Tahiti and holding a fan behind her head. She looks at us with the calm assurance of Manet's *Olympia* (Fig. 82), actually copied by Gauguin earlier that year in the Luxembourg and of which he had taken along a photograph. Gauguin's picture must be looked on as "simply no more than a study of the nude in Oceania."

Paintings like *Ta Matete* (The Hague, Museum of Modern Art) or *The Day of the God* (1894, Fig. 130) demonstrate his Egyptian and other Oriental borrowings as well as the basically decorative character of his art. There is little question but that Gauguin is primarily two-dimensional in his interests, that in suppressing background and perspective vistas, he gives the feeling of strange and exotic fabrics covered with beautiful designs. Yet it would be a mistake to overlook the integration of the various forms and the movement of colors. Nor should one omit the fact that Gauguin was interested in a special kind of space, even though it was more limited than that of

130. GAUGUIN: *The Day of the God* (Chicago, Chicago Art Institute, Birch Bartlett Memorial Collection).

Seurat. For the most part, it is true, he minimized modeling of forms, yet there are enough examples of articulated figures to prevent this from becoming an absolute rule.

While the *Ta Matete* (In the Market Place) borrows forms somewhat mechanically, *The Day of the God* uses the same kind of material much more imaginatively. In the first picture the extremely stylized outlines of the women and their careful precise gestures suggest Javanese dancing, while the patterning of the figures across the surface recalls ancient Egyptian art. Certain of the women are actually frontalized with the upper and lower parts of the body in disassociated perspective. ("Have always before you the Persians, the Cambodians, and a little of the Egyptians. . . . ") In *The Day of the God* the figures are less stylized and the general space arrangement less two-dimensional. Here the composition suggests the carefully recessed planes of Puvis de Chavannes. Although Puvis was not very popular with

Gauguin, at least publicly, there is reason to believe that the "painter who thinks" helped here, as in Gauguin's famous *Where Do We Come From? What Are We? Where Are We Going?* (Boston, Museum of Fine Arts). The upward tilted, spatial arrangement of *The Day of the God* and its arcadian mood suggest the work of the great academician. As to details, the tiny figures at the left derive again from the offering bearers in ancient Egyptian temples. The almost atavistic attitudes of the curled-up women in the foreground anticipate similar arrangements by Matisse in the next decade or two, as in his *Joie de vivre* (Fig. 139). A nonrealistic, stained glass patterning of the water into irregularly shaped and broad areas of vivid color should be considered from the same point of view.

The "museum" nature of Gauguin's borrowings can be shown again and again in many of his works and include such additional sources as Buddhist and Aztec art. A good example would be the *Contes barbares* of 1902 (German Private Collection) in which a typical Buddha of the classical period of Indian sculpture has been transcribed into Gauguin's sinuous curving lines. The arbitrarily elongated and crossed legs are arranged in the sacred position from which the left hand "calls on the earth to witness" in a typical ancient Indian gesture. Neither the wide-shouldered, narrow-waisted Indian figures nor the ideology have very much to do with twentieth-century Polynesia, but they can be used—and indeed often are— to create an exotic mood.

This need for creating mood is basic in most of Gauguin's works, Breton or Polynesian, and one might almost use the degree of effective communication of such an emotion as one criterion of success. The best known of Gauguin's story pictures is *The Spirit of the Dead Watching* (Fig. 127), famous primarily because of the long account in *Noa Noa*. This book, parts of which appeared during Gauguin's lifetime, tells us about his going off one day on a fishing trip, leaving behind his little Tahitian companion. Upon his return he found the hut dark, and lighting a match, he saw little Tehoura lying face down on the bed as in the picture—terror stricken. Her fright, compounded of night noises and the unknown spirits of darkness, communicated itself to the Frenchman. Finally, he was able to reassure her, but she said, still half fearfully: "Never leave me again without light."

This is the picture which the critic of the London *Times* in 1910 cited as an example of Gauguin's anarchism.

It is questionable to what degree Gauguin has succeeded here in rendering the narrative of *Noa Noa;* but the specific content of his pictures or their primitivism are of less importance than their stunning color arrangements and orchestrations or the Oriental poise and harmony of his landscapes. The fact that he struck a mighty blow against representational art with his large expressive areas of brilliant color, that he used deformations of form and color for emotive purposes, loom as the vital things in his legacy for the future.

"How does that tree look to you? Green? All right then, use green, the greenest green on your palette. And that shadow, a little bluish. Don't be afraid. Paint it as blue as you can!" As regards form, he said: " . . . why not stress even to the point of deformation the curve of a beautiful shoulder or conventionalize the symmetry of a bough unmoved by breath of air." Added to the famous: "A metre of green is greener than a centimetre of green," these statements furnish the basis for a new aesthetic. The painters of the first decade of the twentieth century, going to the museums in their

131. GAUGUIN: *Women at the River*—color woodcut (New York, The Museum of Modern Art).

turn for Persian, Byzantine, and other colorful and rhythmic forms, were to fulfill his prophecy.

A great deal of the emotionally inspired art of the early twentieth century owes something to the example of Gauguin. From the decoratively organizational Fauves to the less form-conscious German Expressionists, the stream of the expatriate Frenchman's influence is visible. One cannot overlook, in this connection, the powerfully drawn and starkly composed woodcuts of Gauguin. Less cursive and lyrical than most of the paintings, these graphic works (Fig. 131) create the modern art of wood-block cutting and in their strong black-and-white contrasts offer a direct link to the Expressionists—especially Nolde, who was clearly influenced. While the Expressionists would be generally attracted by the *art nouveau* quality of Gauguin (or Munch), a sense of violence and primitive strength implied in the deliberate roughness of surface and outline in such prints as the *Women at the River* have an immediate appeal for artists of the twentieth century.

16. HENRI ROUSSEAU

The simple and unpretentious story of Rousseau the man is easily told. Although lacking the drama and glamour of the life of Van Gogh or Gauguin, his career must be evaluated in parallel fashion. Like those emotionally responsive anti-Impressionists, Rousseau marks a specific revolt against the Realist point of view and a further step toward the emotional directness of modern painting.

Rousseau is generally spoken of as an untrained amateur, a Sunday painter. Whether or not this is true—and it would seem rather unlikely in view of his amazing technical facility and color sense—his art does have a spontaneous and frequently naïve quality. Certainly his approach was influenced by the immediate emotive situation confronting him rather than any complicated art theories. No artist before or since Rousseau achieved his unself-conscious quality and sincerity. More than anyone else, he illustrates the remark of another unsophisticated and sincere painter, Van Gogh, about one of his own works: "It resembles, if one wishes, a cheap color print. The people who buy the color prints and who love the barbarously sentimental songs of the organ grinder, follow the right path." Rousseau, in the final analysis, was the only real primitive of that era.

Himself the incarnation of the *petit bourgeois*, his art reflects in many ways that class of society. Most art during the nineteenth century is middle class in its origins and motivations, although in an oblique sense that shows a reaction, Bohemian or otherwise, against social restrictions imposed by the group. In the case of Rousseau, we find a man who likes to paint simple and modest things: the small man's wedding, excursion, patriotic celebration, and his aspirations. Like many middle-class folk, he had a respect and admiration for "culture" often expressed in a naïve and even humble fashion, as the later literary and musical séances at his home testify. Completely unaware that he was doing anything extraordinary, he approached most of his painting problems with a simplicity and directness which baffled self-conscious primitivists in the first decade of the twentieth century.

The essential facts of Rousseau's life are neither long nor complicated. For our purposes it is important to note that he was born at Laval in 1844, that he joined the army in 1859 and served in the Mexican campaign as a military musician from 1862–1867. The army service was to have considerable effect on his later painting of exotic and fantastic subjects. Rousseau appears to have been a sentimental person throughout his life. As a young man, he was deeply in love with a Polish girl named Jadwiga who appears in *Le Rêve* (Fig. 132), the best-known picture of his last year. Twice married and outliving his second wife, at sixty-four Rousseau was prepared to marry a third time.

Just when he began to paint is not known, but it is certain that he had practically no formal teaching except a few hints from Gérôme and Clément. The job he had taken in the Tollgate Department after his Franco-Prussian War service gave him enough leisure to pursue this interest in painting,

132. ROUSSEAU: *Le Rêve* (New York, Sidney Janis Collection).

which only became serious after Rousseau turned forty-one. *Le douanier* (tollgate keeper), as he was affectionately known, began to exhibit regularly from 1886 at the Salon des Indépendants, where his work was noticed by a few discerning ones. Renoir, Toulouse-Lautrec, Gauguin, and the mystical Redon were among the first painters to appreciate what he was doing. It is even possible that Gauguin was influenced by his boldly patterned and unrealistically decorative canvases. The fact that Gauguin's synthetist phase begins in 1888, only a short time after Rousseau began to exhibit regularly, may not be without significance.

The importance of the Salon des Indépendants for Rousseau and other nonschool or unattached artists cannot be overestimated. By 1889, the same year that Lautrec began, Van Gogh was sending some things to these annual exhibitions. Gradually, almost everyone of consequence in the art world of Paris, as well as the incompetents, crackpots, and other peculiar types of that Bohemian society—everyone except Picasso, that is—began to show here. This was due partly to the general lack of exhibition space in a very crowded artistic milieu, so that even a few pictures at the Independents meant something. The other reason, just as with our own Independents show in New York City, was the moral support for liberal art implied when an already established man contributed. If size means anything in this connection, we may note that by the turn of the century there were more than one thousand exhibits in the annual show. By 1906 the number had gone over five thousand.

After a while Rousseau was firmly established in Paris, where he opened a little shop in which Mme. Rousseau sold paper articles and her husband's pictures. From 1886 to the year of his death in 1910, Rousseau continued to send pictures to the Independents, and during 1905–1907 he sent works to the Salon d'Automne as well. Recognition spread from the limited circle of Rousseau's appreciators to include many others. Rémy de Gourmont, the novelist, ordered a lithograph, *Horrors of War*, from him, while a goodly number of young painters and writers (Picasso, Derain, Vlaminck, Marie Laurencin, Apollinaire, Duhamel, Max Jacob, René Acros, Jules Romains, and others) were friendly and sympathetic. Matisse at this time was still too "pedantic" to appreciate the directness and simplicity of Rousseau's approach, just as in 1908, as a member of the jury of the Salon d'Automne, he was to vote against Braque's early Cubist pictures.

In addition to painting, Rousseau practiced other arts: playing the violin, cornet, mandolin, and flute, and writing vaudeville sketches at the same time. At his home he established an academy, the Association Philotechnique where he taught music, drawing, diction, and other edifying subjects to the young ladies of the *quartier* at eight francs per month. Together with these activities, he also carried on a small business in public writing and legal advice for the good folk of the neighborhood. For a while he was even a drawing teacher in a city school, for which he was apparently awarded the Academic Palms decoration.

During 1908 and 1909 he held the famous literary-musical soirées at his home, where he and his pupils played together as an orchestra for the neighbors and his new friends of the art and literary world. For these distinguished painters and writers there was: "a little bad music worse played, a little declamation, a glass of wine and democracy untainted with the least suspicion of snobbery. There was a delicious absence of culture, on the one hand, and of romantic squalor on the other. The whole thing was solidly and sympathetically lower middle-class. The '*soirée tant familiale qu'artistique*' closed with a performance of the Marseillaise and the intelligentsia retired to bed feeling that life was full of beauty and significance."

Without attempting to read any profound significance into these little parties, the evidences of a slightly jaded artistic society are too clear to be ignored. The sincerity and honesty of Rousseau in this connection are beyond question, but the self-conscious simplicity of Picasso, Derain, Vlaminck, Braque, Delaunay, and the rest is very interesting. In 1908 Picasso gave a banquet at his studio in honor of *le douanier* in an environment somewhat different from the simple bourgeois home of Rousseau.

Rousseau sold his paintings to the people of the quarter, and often did their portraits; the pictures he showed at the various *salons* brought him further orders. An indefatigable painter, he worked day and night, sometimes with as many as three or four pictures going at once. When he died in 1910, his epitaph was written by Guillaume Apollinaire. The first retrospective show of Rousseau's work was held at the Salon des Indépendants in 1911, demonstrating for the first time the complete range of his painting.

In addition to individual portraits of his neighbors and group portraits such as *Père Juniet's Cart*, *The Wedding*, and *The Family*, Rousseau had done a number of suburban landscapes. Ranging from the banks of the Seine and Oise rivers to Montsouris Park and the outskirts of the city, these pictures may be exemplified by the *Boulevard Malakoff* (Fig. 133).

Although Renoir introduced us to the outskirts of Paris, his paintings tell relatively little of the actual life or sentiment of that part of the city. His suburbanism, like that of other Impressionists, is part of a slightly romanticized version of contemporary life. On the other hand, *Boulevard Malakoff*, like many of Rousseau's interpretations of his *petit bourgeois* environment, is an attempt by an unsophisticated and naïve person to render the *feeling* of the milieu in which he finds himself. Very few Impressionists in the 1890's would have thought of including such elements as telephone poles in a composition. To the simple and unspoiled Rousseau, however, these details appeared perfectly proper as part of his desire to convey the stiff and solemn feeling typical of the less crowded corners of Paris. Such an interpretation of the mood of a street—in which humanity plays a negligible

133. ROUSSEAU: *Boulevard Malakoff* (New York, Max Weber Collection).

part—is well in advance of similar efforts by Utrillo and others later in our own century.

If the *Boulevard Malakoff* had imparted something of the psychological quality of an unimportant street, Rousseau's treatment of people in that

134. ROUSSEAU: *The Wedding* (Paris, Mme. Jean Walter Collection).

environment is equally striking and unique. The individual and group portraits are even better suited to his direct method of visualization. In all of these works there is a systematic attempt to decorate the picture surface, to flatten the forms into arbitrary patterns which convey their meaning by the simplest possible means. A typical example is *The Wedding* (Fig. 134), a picture derived from the painter's own life. Built up in two-dimensional fashion, the darks move around the white of the bride's dress, while the foliage bending over accommodates itself to the flattened arrangement.

Such a method bespeaks either the trained craftsman or an artist with instinctive responses to the problems of formal organization. The claims that Rousseau was a "Sunday painter," an untrained amateur, gain little support from such paintings as this or *Le Rêve*. In each of his pictures, apart from the all-important psychological content, there is a sense of decorative arrangement which is again a reaction against the formlessness of Impressionist painting; here Rousseau joins the ranks of Gauguin, Seurat, and Cézanne. Drawing plays an important part in Rousseau's art as a direct expression of his imaginative reaction to what he sees and feels. Everything is set forth with straightforward clarity, as in the case of all untrained artists, because there are no learned studio tricks to get in the way. Yet his pictures are carefully planned and monumentally arranged; the coloring, even when at its boldest and simplest, always has a decorative sensitiveness, a feeling for pattern that again shows Rousseau's importance to modern painting.

There is a curious intensity in such a painting as *The Wedding* which disturbs until one becomes accustomed to this approach. The eyes of the characters have a peculiarly wide and staring quality (also the judiciously placed dog) that conveys a primitivistic form of fear. Everything Rousseau touches assumes this inward psychological meaning because he himself felt so powerfully the things he painted.

With Rousseau as with Gauguin, we find a strong imaginative sense applied to immediate or romanticized subjects. Early in his career, *le douanier* ventured into the field of exotic subject matter to express his almost childish imaginings. One of the first of these was *The Sleeping Gypsy* (Fig. 135), in which the curiously distorted figure of the sleeping woman is arranged to offer a fine compositional contrast to the simply drawn but menacing lion that stands above her. In such painting the naïve, almost otherworldly mentality and approach of this artist become obvious. He is telling the sort of story that would immediately be apparent to the simplest mind. That it is associated with sleep and the dream is an interesting evidence (although not proof) of his subconscious motivation.

135. ROUSSEAU: *The Sleeping Gypsy* (New York, The Museum of Modern Art).

Here Rousseau becomes one of the first and perhaps the best of the Surrealist artists. This combination of a direct statement with an imaginary and impossible situation, viewed against the intense brilliance of an endless landscape, is one of the earliest examples of Surrealist procedure. In the words of Jean Cocteau: "It is perhaps not without significance that the painter who never forgot details does not mark the sand around the sleeping feet with footprints. The gypsy did not come here. She is here. She is not here. She is in no human place. She lives in mirrors. . . . " Before Chirico, before Chagall, Rousseau created a marvelous dream atmosphere in subtle and delicate color tonalities.

During the course of his experiences in Mexico, Rousseau had stored up vivid and exotic impressions. Between 1904 and 1910 he painted a good many reconstructions of this environment in terms of his own powerful imagination. It is to such paintings as the *Snake Charmer*, *The Flamingos*, or *Le Rêve* that we turn for illustrations of the oft-quoted remark of Rousseau's friend Apollinaire: "He had such a strong feeling of reality that when he was painting a fantastic subject he often became frightened and, trembling,

268

was obliged to open the window." These pseudo-tropical landscapes convey a sense of real-unreality, a feeling of the supernatural that, for as direct an emotionality as Rousseau's, must have been really frightening. The *Snake Charmer* (Paris, Louvre), like *The Sleeping Gypsy*, conveys a fear-charged atmosphere against an exotic night scene. The mysterious and menacing native woman in the clearing of Rousseau's complex but imaginative jungle attracts long and dangerous-looking serpents from every side.

Although one is tempted to make an analogy between the primitivism of Rousseau and that of Gauguin, especially since they were contemporaries, there are profound differences. Gauguin's so-called primitivism stems from a self-conscious dissatisfaction with society and an inability to fit into that system. In the case of Rousseau, his primitivism, or exoticism, springs from a highly geared inner emotionality and imagination that has nothing to do with sophistication, learning, or other civilized devices. Moreover, from what evidence we have, Rousseau was a well-adjusted person socially, a sentimental family man, an individual with appreciative friends, who was able to pursue his chosen path with relatively little trouble. The art of Gauguin, with its specific museum borrowings from various high-level cultures, tended inevitably toward the Romantic rather than the primitivistic. Rousseau's art is primitive even where he does not deal with exotic material; it springs directly from the imagination and depends entirely on the artist's ability to create his decorative color patterns and tight architectural unities, while keeping intact the strong and even stark feeling motivating the work. It is significant that the art of Gauguin led so directly to the rhythmic and decorative painting of Matisse, while the work of Rousseau was one of the direct stimuli toward the primitivism of the period immediately preceding the First World War.

If we compare a typical Rousseau landscape with one by Gauguin, for example, *The Flamingos* (Fig. 136) with *The Day of the God* (Fig. 130), the Polynesian product immediately shows its synthetic origin and decorative basis. *The Flamingos*, on the other hand, is a basically imaginative concept. Although just as significant from the decorative point of view, it has the additional merit of personalizing the elements to such an extent that we would almost call the picture *The Lilies* instead of *The Flamingos*. Put some-

136. ROUSSEAU: *The Flamingos* (formerly Berlin, Mendelssohn Collection).

what differently, the relatively academic procedure of Gauguin gives way before Rousseau's extremely animistic handling of the various parts. Nature as seen by Rousseau has a more powerful and frightening quality than anything found in Gauguin, in spite of the latter's literary explanations.

Further, contrast *Le Rêve* with Gauguin's *Spirit of the Dead Watching* (Fig. 127), and again Rousseau gives us a more imaginative approach. The very title, *Le Rêve* (The Dream), brings into play entirely different forces and greater inventiveness, while in the work of Gauguin we feel a transcription of European expression into a synthetic and romanticized Oceanic background. We may observe, too, that in *Le Rêve* Rousseau was reproducing the face and form of an early beloved, Jadwiga. He was moving back into the realm of the subconscious, like the later Surrealists. It is interesting, also, that Rousseau places her in that part of his inner consciousness which to him is the most expressive and emotionally significant, the purely imaginative.

The tropical painting of Gauguin was done on the spot and to some

270

extent, therefore, represents a more realistic approach. Rousseau's works are pure fantasy, in spite of the fact that he had been stimulated early by the lush vegetation and color of Mexico. His paintings are not reproductions of Mexican scenery nor are his characters taken from that environment. In other words, they have no direct reference to models other than those indicated to him by his vivid and fertile, if slightly feverish imagination.

When a critic spoke of the nude on a couch in the jungle as naïve, Rousseau answered that: "The woman asleep on the couch is dreaming that she has been transported to this forest and that she can hear the enchanter's music. . . . If I have preserved my naïveté it is because M. Gérôme, who was professor at the École des Beaux-Arts, and M. Clément, Director of the École des Beaux-Arts at Lyons, urged me never to lose it. The time will come when you will no longer think this strange. I have been told that my work is not of this century. As you will understand, I cannot now change my manner which I have acquired as the result of obstinate toil. . . ."

Without taking the artist too literally, even though there is no real reason here why we should not, this statement seems very significant. Although it does not detract from the imaginativeness and spontaneity of Rousseau and certainly not from his ability as a designer and colorist, it does betray a certain awareness of what he was doing. Even though he may have been frightened by the effects he created, he seems to have striven for them consciously and not under some hypnotic or dream compulsion. One finds it hard to believe that the former drawing teacher and holder of the *Palmes Académiques* was just a "Sunday painter" working without knowing where his ideas derived from.

Unquestionably, Rousseau was the first and one of the best primitives of modern painting. That this should have attracted first Gauguin and then the twentieth-century Africanists and general purveyors of primitivism is not surprising. If we are not entirely sure to what extent his primitivism was unmotivated, we must remember that after all he was a small shopkeeper living in a *petit bourgois* environment. Under these circumstances his accomplishment must appear doubly remarkable.

17. TOWARD THE ABSTRACT: MATISSE AND THE FAUVES

In the decade before the First World War, events unrolled in the pattern laid out during the previous century. The factors which had created anarchism and other forms of social unrest were to reach their climax in the war itself. In the same way, the precarious situation of the artist in society and his developing isolation from that society became more and more aggravated. Every manifestation of new art—and there were many during this period—was an added shock to a public that had not yet absorbed post-Impressionism. But the artist, responding to the explosive character of the time, could not wait for acceptance. He was compelled to proceed with an expression of violent reaction against the increasingly unsettled and dangerous environment in which he found himself. In no period of the world's history do we find an art of such apparent dislocation in which dissociation from the social milieu seems so clear. Yet, in spite of its attack on all forms of realism, its denial of the form, color, and general character of the world around it, the abstract painting of the early twentieth century is as clear a response to that time as one could wish.

In France the period was marked politically by increasing agitation from both extremes that disturbed the Liberal government trying to carry out a reform policy. The thorniest domestic problem was the legal separation of Church and state, finally accomplished in 1906 after a terrific struggle. Symptomatic as always was the racial attitude. Although Captain Dreyfus was finally rehabilitated, the funeral of Émile Zola in 1902 brought the anti-Revisionists into the streets with hysterical rejoicing.

The rapid growth of syndicalism was world-wide with its accompanying strikes and other disturbances. Typical anarchist gestures of individual protest occurred in response to repressive brutalities in Czarist Russia and in Spain. These acts produced a prompt reaction from the Right. In 1908 a very provocative antidemocratic book by Georges Sorel predicted that the middle class could be manipulated by anyone using force and the threat of Red revolution. As background material for the continuing strikes of the next few years, Sorel's book makes interesting reading.

The most disturbing element in the psychology of that time, and perhaps the decisive factor in formulation of its art, was the increasingly explosive war situation. The average artist, although perhaps unaware of the economic and social causes of war, could not help reacting to such obvious signs as the "Agadir incident" in 1911, when the French refused to accept the challenge of the Kaiser's gunboat. Between the violence of Right and Left and the frightening imminence of war and destruction, the artist was forced into a new creative position.

Even during the previous epoch, his isolation from society had been an accepted fact; art had become less concerned with visible reality than with method. During that period we had found motif replacing subject. Under the new and more aggravated conditions of the prewar epoch, these factors were intensified and brought to their logical conclusion. Method and motif were supreme. The post-Impressionists, however, had generally succeeded in controlling and interpreting reality in terms of serenity and balance, whereas the men of 1905–1914 under the impact of their increasingly disturbed situation produced an art of agitation. In 1905 the followers of Matisse extended the colors and rhythms of Gauguin, Cézanne, and Van Gogh into something very intense and unrealistic. With the additional stimulus of the art of the African world—into which a greedy and expanding Europe had recently moved—the paintings of both the Matisse and the Picasso groups assumed a wildness appropriate to that time.

It is not without significance that this same period produced the first facet-cubist pictures in 1908. Whatever the stylistic derivation of these works, they were violent reactions against ordinary representational art, but even more they were prophecies of an already disintegrating world. Picasso and Braque (the joint fathers of Cubism), like Matisse and the

Fauves, represented an intensification and variation of post-Impressionist formalism because the period in which they lived demanded it. Matisse's pictures become *fauve* or wild in comparison with those of Gauguin and Cézanne, just as those of Picasso become cubist or form-disintegrating in comparison with those of Cézanne. Between 1908 and 1914 the art of the Cubists is progressively nonrepresentational and flat-patterned as a retreat from unpleasant reality or a reaction against it. The very dynamism and increasingly fragmentary character of this art, together with the wildness of the Fauves, are the artist's description of his times.

In 1909 the first Futurist manifesto appeared. Within a year a number of Italian artists joined this patriotic, machine-glorifying, war-exalting movement. By 1912 they held their first exhibition of Cubist-influenced but much more violent and dynamic works. Certainly these artists were responding to the age of the machine and the stimulus of oncoming war. In 1913 a similar group of Cubist-Futurists in London under the leadership of Wyndham Lewis exhibited as Vorticists. During the year of the "Agadir incident" (1911) there was the simultaneous development of flat-patterned Cubism by Picasso and Braque, and also the first intimations of Surrealism. This retreat into the mind was heralded by Apollinaire's use of the term *surnaturel* in connection with the work of Chagall. The war years saw perfection of the Synthetic Cubist approach, production of the so-called ready-mades, using machine parts in a spontaneous and disjointed fashion, and finally anarchic reaction against the senselessness of war through the various emanations of Dada.

These are some striking points in the picture as we view it from the beginning of the century to the end of the First World War. To the public of this period, Fauve art and Cubist art were infinitely more shocking than anything they had experienced before. Although there had been exhibitions of Cézanne, Seurat, Gauguin, and Rousseau during the last decade of the previous century, their work had not yet been accepted. Collectors for the most part were still hostile, and the exhibition of Impressionism at the Centennial Exposition in 1900 only served to canonize that form of art but did not help the newer painters. Not having accepted post-Impressionism, the public was still less prepared to favor later developments.

274

The popular artists of that decade of anarchy and corruption (1890–1900) had been the Symbolists led by Serusier, a follower of Gauguin. Together with Odilon Redon and his mystic group of so-called Rose-Croix painters, they foreshadowed to a certain extent some of the characteristics of later Surrealism. During their own period they produced the painting of Redon, James Ensor, Hodler, and Munch, the music of Debussy and Satie, and the writings of Maeterlinck, Mallarmé, and Verlaine.

One event contributing to the appearance of Fauvism was the 1901 exhibition of Van Gogh's work at Bernheim Jeune's Gallery. Derain, Vlaminck, and Matisse—later Fauve leaders—were very much impressed. Two years later, these young men and a few others began to exhibit as a group. In 1903 they organized the Salon d'Automne, as a generation earlier the neo-Impressionists had started the Salon des Indépendants. Their first venture was a Gauguin memorial show, an event of great distinction and even greater artistic influence. Rousseau was among the other contributors to this exhibition. The following year, 1904, this *salon* presented forty-two paintings by Cézanne, another climactic event in the development of modern painting.

It was at their 1905 showing that the term *fauve* was coined by a critic who described the exhibition as a *cage aux fauves* (wild-beast cage). Braque, the future Cubist, was one of the Fauves at this show. By 1906, the modern movement had reached such a point that the Salon des Indépendants with its more than five thousand pieces was a veritable artistic League of Nations, especially since it featured its foreign section. Like the Salon d'Automne a few years earlier, it also had a Gauguin presentation, a tremendous display that established him once and for all as a master—three years after his death.

The following year, the 1907 Memorial for Cézanne at the Salon d'Automne and a concurrent showing of his water colors at Bernheim's gave the final touch to that master's influence. All the progressive painters of the prewar period felt the impact of Cézanne's constructive genius: first, the young rebels grouped about Henri Matisse, and soon after, another group revolving about Pablo Picasso. Both schools, we shall see, were primarily interested—as Cézanne himself had been—in the formal and constructional aspects of painting.

The participants in the first Fauve *salon* of 1905, Matisse, Marquet, Derain, Vlaminck, Rouault, Dufy, van Dongen, and Friesz, affected the public even more violently than their post-Impressionist forerunners. Their deviation from ordinary concepts of photographic realism, from the things that people expected to find in pictures, was much more disturbing. If Cézanne had been severe in his constructional schemes, Matisse became even more abstract; if Gauguin had applied large areas of intense color, Matisse raised the key even higher. Van Gogh's use of broken expressive forms and colors was transformed by members of the Fauve group into a decorative but emotionally stimulating series of jagged, interrupted shapes. The directness and spontaneity of Van Gogh or Rousseau, the barbaric splendor of Persian ceramics, Byzantine mosaics, and even primitive African sculpture became influences in the development of this new school of painting.

Twentieth-century artists in search of useful precedents for their own emotional or aesthetic needs were in a better position than many of their predecessors. The expansion of world markets, together with increased facilities for travel and education through museums and reproductions, brought them into contact with all types of contemporary and older cultures. What had been true for Gauguin's freedom of style-choice was even truer in the following generation.

During the wild or *fauve* period this group was chiefly influenced by the bold patterns and broad color areas of Near Eastern ceramics and manuscripts seen at the Mohammedan Exhibition of 1903. As important a factor in their (and early Cubist) wildness was the sculpture of Africa, available through the formation of private and then public collections of this material in France and Belgium following expansion into the Dark Continent. From the sophisticated art of Persia, men of the early twentieth century took abstract design elements that fitted their needs; from African sculpture came a brute strength and power, as well as simplification of form, a shearing away of nonessentials. Yet at no time can it be said that the painting of the Fauves is uncontrolled or unarranged. It is always within the logical and rational tradition of French painting, no matter how much stimulated by outside elements.

Although the school was ultimately to become a decorative and charming expression suitable for the homes of the wealthy, its initial character was startling. The reaction of a critic on seeing a room full of these paintings, with a little Renaissance statue in the middle, is quite understandable. When he exclaimed: "Donatello among the wild beasts!" he was voicing the feelings of an outraged public, much as Albert Wolff had done in the 1870's. Gradually the pain and shock wore off, and today Fauvism is a very respectable form of painting.

Henri Matisse, titular leader of the group, was the son of a middle-class family from the north of France. Born in 1869, he came to Paris at eighteen to study law. For a short time he practised that profession near home but soon gave it up to go back to Paris and become an artist. His first instruction was in the studio of the well-known academician Bouguereau where he made innumerable drawings from plaster casts of ancient sculpture. From there he went to Gabriel Moreau's class, where he received fine teaching and encouragement to paint in tone and color. It was here that Matisse met some of his future Fauve collaborators: Dufy, Rouault, and Marquet. One Moreau routine was the study of Old Master pictures in the Louvre, and Matisse soon became quite expert at copying. Some of his copies were so good that they were bought by the government. Other paintings, done under the influence of Chardin, were shown in 1894 and 1896 and received much favorable criticism.

Amidst this academic background and experience with older painting, Matisse remained unaware of more recent movements. As late as 1896 he knew little, if anything, of the Impressionist furor, the death of Seurat and Van Gogh a few years earlier, and the disappearance of Gauguin from civilized society. At this point Paris seethed with quarrels between the neo-Impressionists under Signac and Cross and the Synthetist followers of Gauguin: Serusier, Maurice Denis, Bonnard, and Vuillard. Only gradually did Matisse realize what was happening. Then by 1897 his *La Desserte* caught up with Impressionism. Shortly afterward he met Pissarro, as well as some of the Synthetists. These contacts finally turned Matisse toward contemporary expression.

The change meant a considerable sacrifice on his part, since he was terribly poor—so poor, in fact, that his two children had to be sent to grandparents for a while. Only the skillful management of his wife saved him from even greater hardships.

For the next few years a series of experiments followed each other in rapid succession. During 1898 he painted in the manner of Cézanne with large flat planes of blue that some critics—notably the painter Marquet—consider the beginning of the later Fauve style. *Carmelina* (1901, Boston, Museum of Fine Arts) is a good illustration of the early influence of Cézanne on Matisse and a clear symptom of his basic interest in structural problems. His color range during this period, although powerful and clean, was still not so violent as either Van Gogh or Gauguin.

For a while he tried working with relatively sober colors, and about 1902 his *Notre Dame* (Fig. 137) struck a midway point that can serve as a beginning for Fauvism. In this picture we find broad and relatively even planes of color in darkened tonalities which deny the brightness of his earlier work. It is a kind of simplification that conveys emotional disturbance. Matisse was still not satisfied, however, and continued to experiment. Two years later his one-man show at Vollard's was neo-Impressionist in character.

During the period 1904–1906 Matisse became associated with Marquet, Vlaminck, Derain, Dufy, Rouault, Braque, Friesz, and van Dongen. Some of the group, notably Vlaminck and Derain, worked in the Van Gogh manner; Vlaminck's *Bridge at Chatou*, Derain's *The Port*, and Matisse's *Pastorale* exemplify this trend. The borrowings from Van Gogh were not so much emotional as decorative and exuberant, utilizing to the full the purely visual possibilities of his color. Certainly the paintings of Vlaminck and Derain during that phase were still representational, devoted to portraying the scene from which they were made. Within a short time, though, both these artists were to turn to Cézanne for inspiration, modeling in planes but freer in manner and generally more calligraphic in quality. Derain, who is perhaps the most eclectic of the group, went through a Negroid and Cubist phase in 1908. As for Rouault, he was not Fauve in the Van Gogh-derived decorative sense just described. He went his own way, emotional and profound in the manner of Daumier, whose modern Expressionistic counterpart he became.

278

137. MATISSE: *Notre Dame* (Buffalo, courtesy of the Albright Art Gallery).

Matisse himself went further than most of his colleagues in antirepresenta-tional ideas. Like Gauguin, he felt the need for color and pattern as pure aesthetic devices expressed in a primitive manner—but with the carefully premeditated design devices of the Orient. Clear formulation of his style occurs in the years 1905–1906, beginning with the famous 1905 Salon d'Automne. In such paintings as *The Young Sailor* (1906, Fig. 138) the Fauve painters claimed they were breaking with the rather ineffectual methods of the neo-Impressionist or Divisionist artists. Certainly this picture, by its bold and striking flat planes of color, is in serious conflict with careful and precise color-spot placing.

Although to the critics and public the work of the Fauves represented a riotous and even revolutionary point of view, the fact remains that most of these "wild beasts," and particularly Matisse, were very much interested in the problems of surface and structural design. *The Young Sailor*, for

279

all its broadness of color and brutality of outline, is a carefully designed work that cannot be regarded as mere surface decoration. Like the painting of Gauguin, it emphasizes precisely indicated outlines and bold flat color areas

138. MATISSE: *The Young Sailor* (Basel, Hans Seligman Collection, photograph courtesy of The Museum of Modern Art).

but adds a different form element, the conscious modeling of planes of color as in Cézanne.

Nevertheless, it is clear here that we are no longer interested in representational ideas, for there is no way of telling what the original young sailor looked like. The use of one red lip and one green lip, the ultragreen trousers and very blue shirt have little to do with the local color of those items. Proceeding from an everyday fact, the artist has simplified to a point where he uses a purely conventional outline to describe it and equally arbitrary colors to decorate and to model the form.

The following five years of Fauvism, from 1907 on, continue the influence of Gauguin's linear rhythms and Cézanne's organizational methods. Matisse's aesthetic during this period is particularly Oriental in its insistence on organically growing and flowing forms. As for the other members of the group, Dufy at that point is charming and light with a delicate design quality and free-flowing line suitable for textile designs. Van Dongen utilizes his own individual interpretation of Fauvism to describe beautiful women; while Laurencin is the most attenuated and pale of the entire circle.

Matisse's *Joie de vivre* of 1907 (Fig. 139), emphasizing the relationship with Gauguin in theme and cursive linear rhythm, is the product of two years of work and innumerable sketches. It illustrates the basic premise from which we must start in any Matisse painting, that the colors bind

139. MATISSE: *Joie de vivre* (Merion, Pa., courtesy of the Barnes Foundation).

281

together the various parts. We also see here a flowing arrangement of lines (as in Cézanne and Gauguin) that joins the divers elements from the front plane to the deep background where a group of dancers express the joy of living. The tense and powerful character of Matisse's line is especially evident in the group on the lower right.

Joie de vivre, like most of Matisse's pictures, attempts to distort willfully the original character of color and form in the interest of greater pictorial unity, to re-do nature in terms of art. To put it somewhat differently, the artist alters the shape and color of given parts of his picture in order to fit them into a pattern that will have movement, rhythm, a backward and forward pull of color, and an exciting allover decorative effect.

During the winter season of 1907-1908, Matisse opened a studio where he taught painting to a considerable number of followers. A good many were apparently attracted by his *succès de scandale*. One young woman, when asked by Matisse why she had come to him, answered: "I am looking for something new." To the infinite credit of Matisse, he did not encourage wildness for its own sake, even though he was nominal chief of the Fauve group. The first day he came to the atelier, he was confronted by a mass of students busily working at all sorts of distorted shapes and colors. The story goes that he brought a cast of Greek sculpture into the room, set it in the middle of the floor, and advised the too ardent *fauvistes* to turn their canvases to the wall and copy the cast for a while.

On another occasion he said: "In the beginning you must subject yourself to the influence of nature. After that you can turn back, motivate nature and perhaps make it more beautiful. But you must be able to walk firmly on the ground before you start tightrope walking. . . . " Since many of the people who flocked to him were not looking for serious training, his school was discontinued after the following season. Nothing could indicate more clearly the artistic soundness of Matisse's approach than this incident of the school.

As Cézanne had done, Matisse set out consciously to rebuild nature in careful arrangements of form and color. To do this, it was necessary to deviate from photographic representation in favor of a pictorial integration, a compositional unity. We are told, for example, that a woman once re-

140. MATISSE: *Women by the Sea* (Essen, Folkwang Museum).

proached Matisse with the fact that a hand he had drawn only had three fingers. Matisse pointed out that he had been unable to put in the other two without throwing the original three out of drawing. "It would," he said, "destroy the composition and the unity of my ideal. Perhaps some day, I may be able to get what I want of sentiment, of emotional appeal, and at the same time draw all five fingers! But the subjective idea is what I am after now. The rest can wait."

Matisse's chief paintings of the next few years are *Women by the Sea* (Fig. 140) and two great decorations for the wealthy Russian tea merchant Sergei Tschoukine, *La Danse* and *La Musique.* Like most of the work between 1908 and 1910, they are marked by extreme simplification, especially *Women by the Sea*, with its ochre-colored figures outlined by powerful violet lines. Most vivid is the reduction of earth, sea, and sky to a series of

283

three violently colored background bands of varying width, reminiscent of ancient Minoan painting. The reduction of forms to a series of flattened silhouettes is less significant here than the sturdy power of the figure playing with a turtle or the curiously bent posture of the seated woman. Matisse's attempts to bring out the most characteristic attitudes of his forms through these violent and symbolic simplifications differentiate his work from that of Gauguin. Design and spontaneity are no longer ends in themselves—at least in the paintings of this period.

Matisse's primary interests lie in the most significant aspect of a particular form. His effects are achieved through careful control and distortion of linear outlines, a distortion which necessarily emphasizes the most important and outstanding aspects of these shapes. We are told that Matisse tried to paint as though he had never seen either a picture or a nude before. Although he could not possibly hope to forget everything he had learned—or even wish to—he tried to ignore set patterns or rules, to react to the present problem after studying it carefully.

The distortions of *Women by the Sea* also involve color. Like Gauguin before him, Matisse intensified the most characteristic aspect of each object's color as he saw it and applied it in the broadest and flattest areas possible. The dazzling harmonies and extreme tastefulness of Matisse's paintings owe a great deal to the art of the Near East. His impeccable sense of color plays the double role of subtle decoration and skillful organization of forms and their composition.

For the most part, Matisse's figures are static to a high degree. One of the few exceptions is found in the famous *La Danse* (Fig. 141), one of the two decorative panels done for Tschoukine's eighteenth-century palace in Moscow. This work and its preliminary sketches, such as *Nasturtiums and La Danse*, possess an unwonted degree of animation and vital force imposed by the necessities of the subject. The tightly designed and dynamic group circling about the heaving landscape is derived from the background of his slightly earlier *Joie de vivre* (1906–1907, Fig. 139).

Although the inspiration for this painting came from an actual dance, a *farandole* which Matisse had witnessed in the same Moulin de la Galette that Renoir had painted, the new treatment shows how far we have come

141. MATISSE: *La Danse* (Moscow, New Museum of Modern Western Art).

from Impressionism. To Renoir, the dancing of simple people had been an opportunity for brilliant treatment of broken and diffused color embellishing his lyrical response. Matisse's dancers have been transformed into arbitrary but highly organized symbols of humanity expressing by their agitated forms and continuously flowing rhythmical lines the *sense of movement* imparted by the dance. One art is descriptive; the other is analytical.

This is not Matisse's usual practice, for that same year he painted *La Desserte* (Fig. 142), a repetition of an earlier Impressionist treatment of the theme, which is entirely different. Under the influence of Persian design, the treatment has become completely static, combining the rhythms of wallpaper designs and foliage outside the window with the lines of the woman laying the table and patterns on the cloth itself. This picture serves a useful purpose as evidence of how, in the lifetime of one artist, the direction of modern painting had changed so markedly. From the gentle and sensuous version of Matisse's 1897 Impressionist treatment of the subject, we move to a deliberately abstract representation under the influence of the sophisticated art of the Near East with its vividly patterned manuscripts, fabrics, and pottery.

One of the most lyrical of Matisse's prewar decorative pieces is the well-known *The Blue Window* (Frontispiece), an arrangement of rounded forms alternating with strong horizontal and vertical accents. The distribution of color areas throughout the canvas so as to relate a blue in one section with another blue elsewhere and similarly with the other colors gives this picture a strongly unified and organized character.

The paintings of Matisse during the First World War lost a good deal of their decorative charm and became more sombre in tone, even austere. *The Italian Woman* (California, Maitland Collection) exemplifies the influence of Negroid Cubism on him at that time. One may readily believe that this temporary quality was the result of general depression and fear in the

142. MATISSE: *La Desserte* (Moscow, New Museum of Modern Western Art).

capital. When the painter moved to a studio at Nice in the south of France, away from the tumult and unrest, his style became charming and gay, more decorative in content, and more realistic in method. During the latter part of the war and after, bitter years for Europe, Matisse took refuge again in a series of unworldly but this time attractive subjects.

Poppies (Fig. 143), for example, has a conscious, almost Impressionistic joyousness, a dashing handling of paint that runs through most of his work from 1917 to 1925. For the most part, these pictures are suffused with the

143. MATISSE: *Poppies* (Grosse Pointe, Mich., Robert H. Tannahill Collection).

warm sun of the Riviera and bring to mind the work of Matisse's Fauve colleague Dufy. Time and again we are shown the bright interior of a room, the beach itself, or a dazzling white road seen through the windshield of a car. Most of these paintings, although gay and effectively decorative, have little of the great organizational qualities Matisse had displayed earlier and to which he would soon revert.

Since 1926, Matisse has turned back to serious problems of formal organization, like the large *Decorative Composition—Odalisque* of that year (Fig. 144). Here the artist has placed a rigidly sculpturesque Odalisque against a vivid and almost riotous background of color. In a sense it is a reaction against the relatively pretty things of the previous period with a remarkable boldness eminently suited to large-scale decoration. During 1931 Matisse was invited to the United States to plan a series of mural decorations for the famous Barnes Foundation at Merion, Pennsylvania. The result of this assignment was a group of panels covered with a new *La Danse* and influenced by early Greek vase painting.

The story of Matisse is the story of the struggle of contemporary art to find its place in the sun. Long before Dr. Barnes commissioned the

Foundation murals, Matisse's work had been shown in a 1908 exhibition in New York at "291," gallery of the pioneering Alfred Stieglitz; but this caused scarcely a ripple. Two years later there was a retrospective show of his work at Bernheim Jeune's in Paris—at almost the same time as the original *La Danse* and Matisse's visit to Moscow. After the latter event came a steady trickle of the Frenchman's paintings to the mansion of Tschoukine. These pictures, seen today under the roof of the Museum of Modern Western Art in Moscow, represent one of the finest Matisse collections in the world. Although Matisse's pictures began to find their way into museums (non-French), his contributions to the famous 1913 Armory Show in New York occasioned a good deal of ill-bred hilarity. Two years later the Montross Galleries in New York gave him a show, and in 1921 the Luxembourg finally acquired its first Matisse.

The shift in American taste may be estimated by Matisse's capture of first prize in the 1927 Carnegie International Exhibition and his invitation to judge the same event during 1930. Success in this country reached a high-water mark the following year. Besides the Barnes commission, there were two simultaneous retrospective exhibitions in New York: sculpture at the Brummer Galleries and painting at the Museum of Modern Art. Similar exhibitions were held that year in Paris and Basel.

144. MATISSE: *Decorative Composition—Odalisque* (Paris, The Museum of Modern Art).

In addition to his outstanding reputation as a painter, Matisse has achieved considerable fame as a sculptor, lithographer, and general designer. Many lithographs show his sense of form and color even in the black-and-white medium. The amazingly sensitive drawing of such examples as *Model Seated* (Fig. 144a) reminds us once more that Matisse is one of the most

288

skillful and economical draftsmen of the twentieth century. Even nonabstract-minded people can appreciate the sinuous simplicity of such drawings. Proceeding from a traditional basis, the artist has been able to simplify and reduce the necessary lines to an absolutely bare minimum and still keep the essential qualities of the form. With no more than nine lines (including four for the hand), Matisse reveals all the graceful sensuousness of this young woman's body, its intrinsic character. From this point the next step is more understandable, the step leading to the kind of deformation that, although much less traditional, brings out the more characteristic aspects of shoulder or hip as they are to be called to our attention.

144a. MATISSE: *Model Seated*—lithograph (New York, E. Weyhe).

There can be little doubt of the secure place which Matisse holds among the connoisseurs and art lovers of our generation—or among the professional purveyors of art. That his work, after the Fauve period, became basically decorative rather than emotionally stimulating is due to many factors: personality, hard-won success, the art market and its demand for pleasing rather than disturbing pictures, etc. As important as anything else in this connection is the French tradition, a factor that the academically trained Matisse understood better than most men of his generation. The decorativeness, the balance, and the serenity of a great part of his art is as much due to this force as to any other.

Although it is customary to think of Matisse as chief of the Fauve group, his leadership rests upon the magnitude of his ability and reputation rather than any direct derivation from him. Other members of the group were as much influenced by brilliant and "wild" color as he, but each in his own way.

From the viewpoint of reputation, one of the most outstanding names is
André Derain (b. 1880), today acknowledged as a leader of "the school of
Paris." In the beginning he followed the "significant line" attitude of Matisse
and for a time allowed himself to proceed in a direction parallel with the
even more abstract art of Picasso and the Cubists. The basis of Derain's
Fauve art is found in expressive use of color to heighten emotional intensity
in his landscapes and figures.

The tonalities of his painting are never as outspoken as those of Matisse,
but with this relatively sober palette he infuses a high degree of visual and
tactile conviction into his work. Neither does decoration as such play an
important part, although his works, because of an intense study of other
art expressions, are always carefully and scientifically composed. Like all
members of the so-called "group," Derain has been attracted by the archaic
arts of Greece, Crete, Byzantium, the Romanesque period, and Negro

145. DERAIN: *Landscape: Southern France* (Washington, Phillips Memorial Gallery).

Africa. In this way, much of his early Fauve work calls violently to the eye, almost roars its message of expressive color and form.

His early painting, under the influence of Van Gogh, has been noted previously, as have the pictures done with the inspiration of African sculpture and early Cubism. More typical, perhaps, of the organizational tendencies of Fauvism and exemplifying the constant underlying influence of Cézanne are such paintings as *Landscape: Southern France* (Fig. 145). Although subdued in tone and carefully arranged in a series of receding planes from object to object, this picture has a uniquely emotive quality and mild distortion that bring it into the "school."

146. DERAIN: *Woman with Shawl* (Paris, Mme. Jean Walter Collection).

Derain has achieved his greatest contemporary popularity in figure painting, showing a powerful solidity mingled with a charm that sometimes brings to mind the work of Renoir. Such a painting as the *Woman with Shawl* (1930, Fig. 146) has a rich and plastic handling of paint that betrays the artist's study of Chardin, Corot, Manet, Courbet, and Renoir. In deviating from the theoretical abstractness of most of his contemporaries, Derain has brought back to painting the solid values of traditional art. Like his nineteenth-century predecessors, he has adapted these to the modern method. Apart from his interest in the plastic arts, Derain is a well-informed person with a deep knowledge of both modern and ancient literature and is a fine musician as well.

Of all the original members of the group perhaps the most interesting is Georges Rouault (b. 1871), if only because he stands so clearly apart from the rest. With him the promise of Fauve emotionality and primitive wildness is fulfilled. He has never become a decorator. Although a product of the Moreau school with Matisse and others in the group, and one of the founding fathers of the movement, Rouault stands much closer to the German Expressionists than to his fellow Fauves. Like Kokoschka, Nolde, and Beckmann among others, his primary concern is with humanity and its emotional possibilities. These are expressed in a tremendously vital type of distortion, in the sheer fury and misery of his interpretations rather than in decorative arrangements.

Two important influences helped to form Rouault's art. The son of working-class parents, he derived his interest in art from a grandfather who had a pronounced taste for Courbet, Manet, Daumier, and even Callot— and who took him to the Louvre as a child. The second factor to be noted is a long period of apprenticeship to a stained glass maker. The first circumstance helps explain Rouault's preference for the small man, the "works and days" of the circus people, the misery of prostitutes, and the pitiful horror of war. As for the second, it accounts for the expressively archaic and medieval treatment accorded many of these themes and the use of heavy black lines to divide one section from another, as in stained glass.

The art of Rouault is primitivistic in the best sense of the word, with a directness of sensation that leads him to the most fundamental emotions in the world. His use of older arts, unlike most Fauve painters, is for spiritual reinforcement, for a kind of pathos that one finds in medieval art and that becomes useful for his own sympathetic purposes. The emotional strength which others sought was a much more generalized thing, and one that ultimately conveys only a diffuse kind of agitation. What they derived from older sources was useful enough in the expression of the insecurity of the age, in showing the necessary restlessness. Rouault, on the other hand, acquired from these same sources a powerful stimulus toward the understanding of the misery of man, an ability to feel his way into the personality of his unhappy subjects and to express their inner character.

His *Portrait of Mr. X* (Fig. 147), therefore, is neither purely descriptive nor abstracted in the decorative manner of Matisse. Form and color are brutalized in a new way which makes us concerned with the personality of the subject, with what he is thinking and feeling. As the distortions take effect, they disturb us in the same way that the artist was disturbed in his conception of the spiritual meaning of the man. Part of the brutality and strength of this figure comes from the inspiration of medieval art, indicated here in the harsh lines dividing one section from another, as in early Gothic stained glass. Occasionally, we find Rouault using *cloisonné* surfaces, especially in religious subjects. The simulated texture of enamel adds to the

147. ROUAULT: *Portrait of Mr. X* (Buffalo, courtesy of the Albright Gallery, Room of Contemporary Art).

feeling of something old and holy, taking us out of the ordinary world into the world of the spirit.

The great significance of Rouault's work lies in the fact that he is so directly affected by what he sees and experiences. Unlike the Fauve or Cubist painters, he devotes himself to his subjects—they are seldom motifs—with a genuine sympathy and high pathos. Pictures like *The Condemned Man* (formerly Paris, Van Leer Collection) stem from the tradition of Daumier and Forain, but Rouault is more brutal and impressive than either of these earlier painters, more forlorn and directly tragic to the degree that his figures are emotionally heightened symbols of man's despair.

Rouault's nudes reek of the same atmosphere so assiduously cultivated by Toulouse-Lautrec in the 1890's, but the delicate nuances of vice have no particular fascination for this passionate artist. He is more concerned with human degradation and utter misery, with hopelessness, and the abuse of fundamental human rights—all expressed in his personal form distortions and Expressionistic colors.

One of the most interesting evidences of his humanity is the series of etchings called *Miserere and War*. In these prints, by means of violently emotional religious representations, he expresses the Romanesque frenzy of his despair at the inhumanity of man. The two groups of grinning skulls leading to a huge cross with another skull at its base form Rouault's version of the modern Golgotha on which mankind has been crucified. *Miserere and War* was done in 1922 at about the same time as the sunny and charming Riviera paintings of Matisse and coincident with Picasso's change from his Colossal period to Curvilinear Cubism. While the majority of French painters were concerned with painting as such, with decorative forms or complicated theoretical abstractions, Rouault was aware of his world and painted it.

The Fauve school as a whole, apart from Derain and Rouault, has produced an art eminently suited to decoration of the modern home. Its slightly daring quality, its chic, and its coloristic charm have taken the place of Impressionist painting in the hearts of the modern sophisticated public. For those who can afford the luxury of original paintings, the art of Matisse, Dufy, Marquet, Marie Laurencin, Vlaminck, and their various derivatives lends just the right touch to the home. Others have to be content with color reproductions. In either case, this style has achieved an acceptance greater than any other modern art form. It was Matisse himself who described his own creations as "an art of balance, of purity or serenity devoid of troubling or depressing subject matter, an art which might be for every mental worker, be he businessman or writer, like an appeasing influence, like a mental soother, something like a good armchair in which to rest from physical fatigue."

18. FROM PICASSO TO ABSTRACT ART

The formalized and abstract painting of Matisse, so typical of the theoretical interests of twentieth-century art, marked the first step in a process that became more accentuated as the century progressed. Simultaneously with the appearance of the Fauve school, there came into being a group of so-called Cubist painters, led by Picasso and Braque, that turned modern art even further in the direction of theory and its application.

Both groups were influenced to a certain extent by the formal interests of Cézanne, but the studies of the Fauves led them to rebuild compositional values in terms of flat color and expressive line. In their work the romanticized exoticism of Gauguin played a considerable part as well. This stream of half-intellectual, half-intuitional organization was later to influence not only Expressionism proper but the abstractly Expressionistic painting of Kandinsky and finally the Surrealist point of view.

The Cubists, on the other hand, were much more intellectual and theoretical, depending equally upon Cézanne in his most formal aspects, particularly such things as the later water colors. To this they added the profoundly austere approach of Seurat. Instead of thinking in terms of Fauvist compositional and rhythmical reorganization, the Cubists were interested in the study and analysis of objects in a formal, logical, architectural, and structural fashion that ultimately led to such machine-age movements as Constructivism, Suprematism, de Stijl, Purism, and other similar manifestations. Both movements, however, in the sense that they reflect Cézanne and Seurat, were bound up with the original theoretical approach inherent in Impressionism and what grew out of it. As we shall see further on, some aspects of Cubism were comparable to the Impressionist attitude.

The essentially "wild" or Fauve elements in the work of Matisse and his followers were also to be found in certain early painters of the Cubist movement: Picasso and Braque. The latter, in fact, actually had painted for a time in the manner of Matisse. It is evident, further, that both Braque and Picasso, through their interest in the powerfully distorted sculpture of the African Negro, were part of the general Fauve sentiment of the period.

The exceedingly theoretical, personal, and Bohemian character of the background against which Cubism was born cannot be shown better than in the recollections of Vlaminck, who tells us of meeting Derain (both of them of the Fauve group) in a little Montmartre restaurant frequented by chauffeurs and masons at the end of the rue de Ravignan, where Picasso and van Dongen had a studio together. Here such people as the inseparable Picasso and Max Jacob, Apollinaire, Derain, Braque, and André Salmon met to have their meals together on credit.

"At two o'clock in the morning," he tells us, "the air was unbreathable. The thick smoke from pipes and cigarettes, alcohol and white wine and the general excitement made these already over-heated spirits almost delirious. It is in this room that Cubism was born. Negro sculpture and the efforts at reconstitution of light through planes, to be seen in the later work of Cézanne, were joined to respond to the needs of a new formula."

Of the four important painters in this little salon, two, Derain and Vlaminck, went along the path of Fauvism; the other two, Picasso and Braque, founded the most influential phase of modern painting thus far: Cubism.

Since Picasso occupies so important a position in both the movement itself and the mind of the public, it is interesting to examine his career and influence. He was born in Malaga, Spain, in 1881 of a Spanish father and Italian mother. His mother's supposed Jewishness plus the artist's friendship with Max Jacob and others has given some critics an excuse to attack the character of Picasso's art. However, Alfred H. Barr, Jr.'s study, *Picasso: Fifty Years of His Art*, quotes Picasso as denying regretfully the possession of any Jewish blood.

After a short period of apprenticeship with his drawing-teacher father, Picasso studied at the School of Fine Arts in Barcelona during 1895 and then spent some time (1896–1897) at Madrid. Influenced by the tradition of Goya and Velásquez, his work of the period between 1895 and 1901 emerged in the form of realistic portraits and still life.

In 1901 young Picasso came to Paris and immediately fell under the spell of the most recent post-Impressionists, particularly Van Gogh and Lautrec. At this time he also became interested in the long skeletal forms of El Greco that, combined with the *fin-de-siècle* romanticism of Toulouse-Lautrec, produced the painting of his Blue Period. A typical example of this work can be seen in the well-known *Absinthe Drinker*

148. PICASSO: *Absinthe Drinker* (New York, formerly Gershwin Collection).

(Fig. 148) and the *Guitarist*. These pathetic-sentimental paintings reflect some of the background or inherent tendencies of Picasso's Spanish ancestry (Goya had done such subjects as the *Guitarist*), now combined with the subtle flowing line of Lautrec and the long exaggerated figures of El Greco. For a few years Picasso continued in this vein, changing from Blue painting to Rose, when in 1907 the first great retrospective Cézanne exhibition at the gallery of Bernheim Jeune struck the art world of Paris.

During the previous year, 1906, Matisse had brought Negro sculpture to the attention of the young Spaniard, who immediately became an ardent collector of this form of art. The two circumstances were destined to bring about the new movement but not before a number of necessary adjustments could be made.

In the first place, so different and powerful a style as African sculpture would not be very easy to assimilate in the sense of deriving the greatest benefit from its structural possibilities. The early efforts of Picasso in this direction (1906–1907) show a more than Fauve type of Expressionism in

297

149. PICASSO: *The Dancer* (New York, Walter P. Chrysler Collection).

such a figure as *The Dancer* (1907, Fig. 149), where there is an obvious degree of simplification and nonessentials are shorn off in a quasi-African sense. Comparison of an African piece with the Picasso figure[1] would indicate that a difference still existed between the African and the "civilized" approach of Picasso, since the former work is simpler in its organization and even more abstract than the figure of the modern painter. Picasso availed himself of the emotional possibilities of staring eyes, oblique nose, and bent legs frequently found in these sculptures, but finally and essentially *The Dancer* remains part of the Fauve spirit of the time.

Yet it is evident that Picasso and Braque were interested more in the direct and crude expressions of primitive African art with its possibilities of formal plastic organization than in the relatively sophisticated and older Persian art that had attracted Matisse. It follows from this that they would find it easier to absorb the specific interest of Cézanne in delineation of plastic volumes in almost architectural fashion. One may add the less significant fact that the year marking the great retrospective show of Cézanne's painting, 1907, also saw publication of a letter by that painter to Émile Bernard in which we find the oft-quoted sentence: "You must see in nature the cylinder, the sphere, the cone." Although later writers on Cubism have exaggerated the importance of this sentence to the painters of 1907, it is yet true that Braque,

[1] For typical examples of African sculpture the illustrations in the Museum of Modern Art catalogue *African Negro Art* should be consulted. Note there especially Figs. 379 and 465, in connection with Picasso, as well as Figs. 99, 101, 414, 462, and 514, for Africanism in general.

for example, had been working in the manner of Cézanne before he met Picasso (1908–1909), and that his work already had assumed a willfully geometric quality. The *Seaport* (1908–1909, Paris, Flechtheim Collection) of Braque shows a systematic attempt to break up the boats and other objects in the scene into a series of diamond-like facets, the background fused with the foreground as in some of the late work of Cézanne.

This painting, with its distinct reference to the work of Cézanne, is parallel in development with the *Head of a Woman* by Picasso (1908–1909, Fig. 150), which also suggests some of the ceremonial masks from the Belgian Congo. Picasso's sculpture of this period repeats the same formal concepts and the same disintegration of forms into small faceted surfaces with the edges cutting into one another.

Although it is fashionable to give Picasso more than his due share of credit for this development, the fact that Braque had worked out cubical analyses, deriving in style from Cézanne, earlier than the dates above, would seem to indicate that this phase of Cubist development would have come into being had he never met Picasso at all.[1] With their meeting and their collaboration, however, the analytical propensities of the movement became more surely defined and, during the first five years of their friendship, Cubist painting moved even further toward the abstract.

Whereas the *Seaport* of Braque and the *Head of a Woman* by Picasso were still predominantly sculpturesque in quality, the work of 1909–1910 shows, as in Picasso's *Portrait of Braque* (Fig. 151), a tendency for the clearly and sharply separated facets to slip, to become transparent, and to merge with the background of the painting (compare Cézanne's *View of Gar-*

[1]It seems fairly certain that Braque was the first to exhibit a Cubist picture.

150. PICASSO: *Head of a Woman* (Paris, Mme. Jean Walter Collection).

danne, Fig. 115). In the slightly later *L'Arlésienne* (Fig. 152) Picasso has caused the flat and even more transparent planes to overlap one another. In this picture we first become aware of one of the most important theoretical

151. PICASSO: *Portrait of Braque* (New York, Edward A. Bragaline Collection).

contributions of the Cubist group, the principle of simultaneity of vision, in the fact that the painter has superposed front and side views of the face of his subject.

All through the history of art, painters had taken it for granted that their picture frame acted as a sort of window through which the object was to be seen. According to Cubist theory, this limited the painter in his approach, since he could only survey that object from one standpoint and consequently did not represent all of the form but only the front or side. In their extremely theoretical and personalized approach to painting, the Cubists felt that this traditional method would have to be discarded, giving

152. PICASSO: *L'Arlésienne* (New York, Walter P. Chrysler Collection, photograph courtesy of The Museum of Modern Art).

themselves the right to walk into the picture space, as it were, and look at the object from all sides. Theoretically, this should have brought about a fuller and more solid vision of the object, since all sides and views were to be taken into consideration, but if we look at the further evolution of this practice in Picasso's *The Violin* of 1912 (Fig. 153), exactly the opposite has taken place.

It is true that we find here a great variety of points from which the object has been seen: the sound holes, the scroll, the lines of the strings, the sides, etc.; but the fact remains that the Cubist style, in its too ardent desire to analyze, changed from a sculptural and still realistic form of art to a flattened

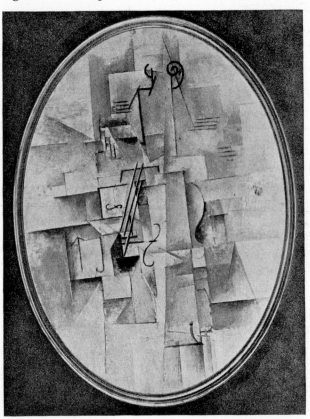

153. PICASSO: *The Violin* (Otterlo, Rijksmuseum Kröller-Müller, photograph courtesy of The Museum of Modern Art).

and nonrealistic type of representation, moving closer and closer to geometricized and abstract shapes. *The Violin* gives us an impression of form in almost the same sense that the earlier Impressionist paintings had given us an impression of the color surrounding form. The visual effect, apart from its demonstration of Picasso's designing skill, is to break up recognizable shapes into a series of rhythmical and pleasant form patterns.

We refer to this period of Cubist development as analytical, precisely because it was the painter's aim to break down, to disintegrate, to tear apart what we ordinarily call natural forms. In the efforts of the two leaders, Picasso and Braque, color had diminished in intensity, giving way to a strict application of purely formal principles rendered in such neutral terms as grays, browns, and olives.

The transition from the analytical to the synthetic phase of Cubism is so gradual as to be almost imperceptible without further explanation. We have seen how, in the development of analytical Cubism, the painter tended to move in the direction of almost purely geometric forms that lost their immediate relationship to the object from which they were derived. In other words, the spectator logically may have the reaction that the painter is improvising on a theme or series of themes suggested by the original object—that he has walked around it and chosen those parts which seemed to him most suitable for juxtaposition on his canvas. In the new phase it appears that the painter no longer tore down forms or disintegrated them, as in the *Portrait of Braque*, *L'Arlésienne*, or even *The Violin;* he now began to build up purely arbitrary and willful arrangements that did not even have to be suggested by the "walking around" process of visualization. How did this almost complete divorce from representation come about?

In the period between 1912 and 1914, the very inventive Braque had begun to practice his paint simulation of the textures of such materials as wood and marble, parts of a newspaper, or a sheet of music. These things, of course, had an independent existence or reality of their own apart from their connection with any sort of representation in a specific composition. He then began to use what are known as *papiers collés*, or pasted papers, that consisted of matchbox fragments, bits of playing cards, parts of newspapers or rags, all pasted to a canvas or board and sometimes aided by a bit of color or a fragmentary line. It will be seen that in work of this sort the emphasis was increasingly on surface textures and the ordinary notions of plasticity were decreased even further.

It became evident almost immediately that these nearly fortuitous associations of forms and colors had a compositional value of their own, and the fact that they had no immediate connection with ordinary reality was looked upon as a definite advantage to artists who attempted to emancipate themselves from the last naturalistic tie binding them to the past. Braque's collage, exemplified in *Le Paquet de tabac* (The Package of Tobacco) (1913, Fig. 154), is an interesting indication of the fact that the broken and fragmentary elements of analytical Cubism have been left behind for a new type of synthesis.

In the years between 1914 and 1917, the synthetic Cubists, proceeding from the type of *papiers collés* just cited, brought that form to its logical conclusion in the work of Picasso, Braque, Gris, and others. Here again, it is fashionable to assign the major role to Picasso, but the facts seem to indicate that Braque played an important part in the development and that Juan Gris managed to maintain himself even against those two. Such a painting as the Gris *Still Life* (1917, Fig. 155) is a typical example of the more sensitive type of synthetic Cubist painting with its opposed masses of now bright colors and almost completely geometricized forms.

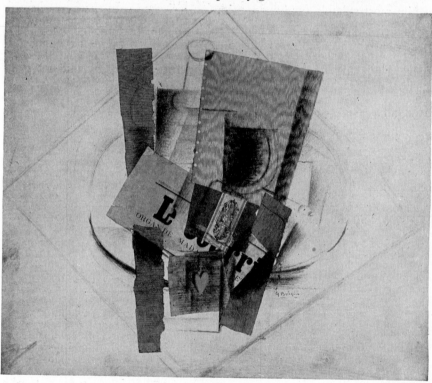

154. BRAQUE: *Le Paquet de tabac* (Philadelphia, Philadelphia Museum of Art, Gallatin Collection).

155. GRIS: *Still Life* (New York, George L. K. Morris Collection).

We must not consider compositions of this sort interesting merely from the viewpoint of surface pattern (it is true that they no longer have the depth of older painting) but also in the sense that actual motion in design is indicated by the way the parts are arranged about a central area. This latent dynamic quality in Cubism, particularly apparent in its earlier phase, appears to have been the basis from which so-called Futurist painting derived its impetus during the period from 1909 to 1914.

Although still regarded by a great section of the public as slightly ridiculous, the movement known as Futurism contained within itself not only the roots of later developments in the arts down to the present day but in its specifically aggressive, dynamic, machine-exalting, war-glorifying character, the ideological germs of later fascism, especially in the Italian sense. It was, in fact, an Italian movement, although later Frenchmen and Russians were to adapt its plastic technique to their own purposes. From a political point of view, the Futurist advocacy of the dangerous life and of the aesthetic beauty of war and patriotism was an undesirable but understandable symptom of the prewar period. Artistically, however, what they had to say was of prime importance because their attitude, and whatever art they

156. SEVERINI: *Armored Train* (New York, Mrs. Charles J. Liebman Collection).

produced during their short existence, was a reaction against the static inelasticity of Cubism, its relative formlessness, and its lack of emotional drive. It seems clear that, although there were certain resemblances between analytical Cubism and Futurism as seen in Severini's *Armored Train* (1915, Fig. 156), the total effect of the latter work is almost frenetic activity, a form of dynamism that was the basis of Futurist expression, even considered apart from the implications of a really significant subject matter.

Obviously, the Futurists used the Cubist device of simultaneity but in their hands it took on a dynamic rather than a static character. They maintained that the Impressionists had destroyed form and substituted fragmentary light and color in its place, just as the Cubists had broken down form into a series of fragments. Neither approach, then, gave to the object the solidity that it should have; but they felt a combination of the two methods might succeed in restoring that quality. In their further theoretical explanations of procedure, it was pointed out that just as adjacent colors under the Impressionist system influenced each other, so the juxtaposition of forms would have a similar mutual effect. The only thing to do, therefore, would be to break up form just as the Impressionists had broken up color, the work to be unified by the underlying dynamic rhythm whose purpose would be to indicate movement of a powerful and emotionally exciting sort.

Russolo's *Automobile*, subtitled *Dynamism*,[1] uses arrow-shaped "lines of force" behind which the dimly seen automobile rushes at breakneck speed—or should be rushing. It takes no more than one glance to show that the painter really has set down a series of symbols of movement rather than movement itself. Without the so-called lines of force we have merely a dimly painted automobile. In any of the plastic arts, the sensation of movement can only be conveyed by interacting volumes that oppose one another.

The defect in the Futurist approach is seen even more clearly in its most famous work (but also the most amusing), the *Running Dog* of Balla (Fig. 157), a pictorial evidence of the Futurist maxim that "a running horse has not four legs, but twenty." The treadmill effect of the multiplied legs is here in distinct opposition to the static quality of the upper part of the dog and its master, a serious defect for a work dedicated to dynamic movement.

In spite of its big talk, the Futurist movement was important only for a series of experiments that tried to carry out ideas for which its members, unfortunately, were not equipped. Its greatest value for the student of art history may be found in the fact that it represented a form of revolt against what they called, perhaps exaggeratedly, the academic passéism of Cubist

[1] Illustrated as Fig. 250 in *Cubism and Abstract Art* by Alfred H. Barr, Jr., New York, The Museum of Modern Art, 1936.

painting, and what we might better call its lack of emotional and social meaning. This alone would entitle Futurism to consideration as a link in the chain leading to the more intuitional and spontaneous movements of the twentieth century. Moreover, their cult of the machine was to have repercussions in Cubism, Dadaism, Constructivism, and Purism.

The first *Manifesto of Futurism* was published in Paris in 1909, and crystallization of the movement took place the following year with adherence to that document by the five members of the group—Carrà, Russolo, Severini, Balla, and Boccioni—in the presence of its author and their future publicist the poet Marinetti, later a Fascist senator. Their work began to appear in 1911 and had a considerable effect in many European and American centers. The French painter Marcel Duchamp, for example, in his celebrated *Nude Descending a Staircase*, which created such a furor at the famous 1913

157. BALLA: *Running Dog* (New York, A. Conger Goodyear Collection, photograph courtesy of The Museum of Modern Art).

308

158. LÉGER: *Luncheon, Three Women* (New York, The Museum of Modern Art).

Armory Show in New York, was influenced by the simultaneous dynamism of the Futurist painters. Duchamp, like Fernand Léger, was very much interested in the machine aesthetic promulgated by the Futurist group, showing specific evidence of this interest in some of his compositions during that early period, 1912–1913.

Léger, probably the most important of the machinistic painters, brings us back to Cubism, for, although influenced by the dynamic Futurist attitude, he is essentially derived from the earlier tradition. The most typical aspect of his work after emerging from simple analytical Cubism is found from 1917 on, in such paintings as the *Luncheon, Three Women* (1921, Fig. 158). With the monumental and mechanical rigidity of its tubular forms, it has a quietness foreign to some of the more dynamic compositions, as, for example, the *Élément mécanique* (1925, Fig. 159) or *The City*, which show the thrust and counterthrust of abstracted but obviously mechanized sections. Using the synthetic Cubist approach, Léger has conveyed here a Futuristic dynamism reflecting the aesthetic of the machine. It is perhaps significant to mention that in 1924 he participated in making the film *Ballet mécanique*.

The effects of such imposingly mechanical characters as we find in the *Luncheon* are occasionally seen in the literature of that period, *e.g.*, the play *R.U.R.* (Rossum's Universal Robots) by Karel Čapek, 1923. It is not so important for our purposes here to note which anticipated which, as it is to observe the considerable and henceforth continuous effect of the machine age on the plastic 'arts: painting, sculpture, architecture, stage design, cinema, poster illustration, and photography.

With such movements as Suprematism, Non-Objectivism, Constructivism, and *de Stijl*, we enter the final stage of modern abstraction, that stage in which the connection with objective reality is finally severed. The most abstract work of the Cubists, as we have already seen, was still bound to its subject matter; there was a definite element of recognizability even in their geometricized manner of rendering the object. Further, it might be said that Cubist efforts at analysis were reactionary in the sense that they took very little, if any, direct cognizance of the world about them. This was true, first, because they immersed themselves in purely abstract problems of technique; second, because they appeared to be almost completely unaware of the most vital and influential factors in modern civilization, *i.e.*, science and the machine in their exact context; and finally, because they concerned themselves completely with nonsignificant subject matter, such as the things they found in their studios. The Cubist, or the small group to which he belonged, was a world unto himself, out of touch with the general situation.

159. LÉGER: *Élément mécanique* (New York, Walter P. Chrysler Collection).

310

The purely abstract painters belonging to the movements enumerated above, although they dared to take the final step of divorcing painting from any realistic or photographic context, were yet specifically animated by the fineness of line, the smoothness of design, and the impersonal precision of the highly developed modern machine. In the sense that they have had a salutary effect upon many of the so-called useful arts, such as typography, poster illustration, and architecture, they justify their existence. Although they reflect the machine age more directly than do the Cubists and other near-abstractionists, the fact remains that as painters

160. MALEVICH: *Suprematist Composition* (New York, The Museum of Modern Art).

many of them, especially the later ones, are primarily impressed by the aesthetic and not the social possibilities of the machine.

The first great impulse toward pure abstraction came out of Russia with the Suprematism of Malevich, who anticipated the Dutch *de Stijl* artists in such a painting as the *Suprematist Composition* (1914, Fig. 160), a conscious arrangement of completely nonobjective forms in which geometric shapes and flat color areas are juxtaposed for their own intrinsic value. This art did not spring from the native tradition of Russia but was a logical development of the close connections with Paris maintained by collectors like Tschoukine and Morosov, who had bought a considerable number of Picasso and Matisse paintings.

By Suprematism, these painters mean the supremacy of "pure feeling or pure perception in the pictorial arts," meaning pure of associative, subjective, and other connotations. The best known of this early group of Russian abstractionists is Lissitzky, whose work is an interesting transition from a primarily two-dimensional painting to a more plastic, architectural type of expression that was to affect postwar Germany.

311

Another important Russian contribution to the abstractionist movements of the period from 1910 to 1918 is known as Constructivism. This may be connected directly with the later collages of Picasso in which that artist (during 1913) had constructed a number of reliefs with more solid and tangible objects than he had used in the first examples. Instead of the earlier pieces of playing cards, newspapers, and simulated textural finishes, Picasso used spools, pieces of glass, and wooden fragments, still appending, however, the usual Cubist "realistic" titles such as *Still Life*, etc. With such Constructivists as Tatlin and Rodchenko, this technique was elaborated and extended into the realm of pure abstraction and applied to all sorts of purely machinistic materials, such as sheet metal, concrete, and wire.

This kind of work increased in importance at the time of the Russian Revolution, and even for a while afterward, because of the industrial significance of these media that appeared to be plastic symbols of the aims of the new Russia. A developed example may be seen in Pevsner's *Relief Composition* (Fig. 161), which still shows its relationship to the Cubist collage method.

The possibilities of Constructivism were realized to greatest advantage in the Russian and German theater, in furniture, and other practical things; but as early as 1920–1921 a reaction had set in against this type of purely abstract art, at least as far as Russia was concerned, for the simple reason that it was not understandable to the great masses of the people. The

Revolution in the midst of a most serious crisis could not afford the luxury of an "art for art's sake" doctrine and either turned these efforts in a more practical direction, as indicated above, or withdrew its support. By 1922, the pure abstractionist movement in Russia was almost completely over, but the work of some of its members, such as Pevsner and Gabo, continued in other European centers, notably Germany and France.

161. PEVSNER: *Relief Composition* (New York, The Museum of Modern Art).

A second early source of machinistic abstract art in the twentieth century was Holland, its contribution being the well-known *de Stijl* school, made up of the painter Piet Mondrian, the architect Jacobus J. P. Oud, and the extremely versatile theoretician of the group, Theo van Doesburg, who was painter, sculptor, architect, writer, and many other things at once. In whatever medium these men expressed themselves, the fundamental theoretical basis of their work was, first, the simple form of the rectangle and, second, the primary colors: red, blue,

162. VAN DOESBURG: *Simultaneous Counter Composition* (Meudon-val-Fleury, Mme. Petro van Doesburg Collection).

and yellow. This states the problem almost in its final form. Actually, Mondrian and the others went through a long period of development, and it is interesting to observe that here again the initial impulse appears to have been Picasso and Cubism. In 1911 Mondrian was in Paris under that influence and in 1913 he proceeded, as did the Constructivists of the same date in Russia, to adapt it to his own purposes of geometricization.

After the evolution of this style and the crosscurrents effected upon it by mutual influence of the various members, we find emerging a typical example of a fully developed work, such as Mondrian's *Composition* (1917, Otterlo). Pictures of this type, in which the vestigial remnants of the fragmentary methods of Cubism can still be discerned, are similar to the work of Malevich (Fig. 160). In later examples from 1920 on, this method is elaborated into much larger areas of color and form but naturally still retains the complete antipathy to objective or naturalistic form that marks the final transition from a recognizable object to an entirely "pure" art; for instance, *Simultaneous Counter Composition* by van Doesburg (1929–1930, Fig. 162).

The *de Stijl* point of view had an almost immediate effect on the Bauhaus school of architects in Germany as early as 1919. The many visits of van

Doesburg to Weimar influenced Gropius and his designers toward the asymmetrically arranged, but clear and precise, geometrical façades and plans of that school. A simple comparison of almost any angular, non-objective painting of the *de Stijl* type with a typical Bauhaus building shows the relationship very clearly. The 1923 *de Stijl* exhibition in Paris stimulated Le Corbusier and others toward Purism. Along the same line, the influence of *de Stijl* on European and American typography is very strong.

We must remember that *de Stijl's* effect on the useful arts is combined with a strong current emanating from Russia. Lissitzky spent a good deal of time in Germany between 1922 and 1926. His design for the Hanover Museum in 1925 was a practical combination of *de Stijl* and Russian methods. Another evidence of Russian influence is found in the career of the Hungarian-born designer Moholy-Nagy (1895–1946), who began under Constructivist influence and became a professor at the Bauhaus. His pedagogical methods, which included practical testing of building materials through actual use in experimental structures and interiors, were essentially due to the influence of such men as Gabo, Pevsner, Tatlin, and Rodchenko. The development of this method by Moholy-Nagy and his associate Josef Albers and their later teaching in the United States have proved of considerable importance to industrial design in this country.

Another organized and reasoned attempt to relate painting to the machine aesthetic is found in the work of the Purists. Whereas the Futurists had attacked Cubism for its static qualities and lack of emotional drive, this new group under the leadership of Amédée Ozenfant and Le Corbusier (Charles Édouard Jeanneret) objected to the capricious and personal, unorganized and spontaneous character of synthetic Cubism. Just as the neo-Impressionists through the theoretical work of Signac had attempted to reform and systematize the loose methods of Impressionism, so the Purists now attempted to regulate and regularize the practices of Cubism. They wished to transform what they felt was the purely "decorative" character of Cubism (Ozenfant's specific criticism of Braque as published in the magazine *L'Élan* in 1916) into something architectonic and classical, to substitute for the casually found studio objects a series of forms that would be so universal in their significance as to be understood by any European.

Here again we see the analogy with the codified practices of Signac, as set forth in his *From Delacroix to Neo-Impressionism*, where not only colors but compositions also would be so prescribed as to make it possible—as a logical and somewhat hopeful conclusion—for anyone to be able to practice the art of painting.

Ozenfant then proceeded to stipulate the kinds of forms that were universal in their significance. First, there were what he called the organic type, which were based on such natural forms as the egg and best represented aesthetically by the subtle sculptures of Brancusi. More important from the viewpoint of this discussion were the so-called mechanical forms that stem from man-made or machine-made objects. Theoretically, of course, objects fashioned after these two admittedly universally known and understood groups should be both significant and understandable. The theoreticians of Purism went one step further and stated that the aesthetic products of twentieth-century living should be able to compete with machinery in such qualities as precision and craftsmanship. The *Still Life* (Fig. 163) of Le Corbusier or the *Accords* of Ozenfant (Boston, F. C. Bartlett Collection) can be taken as typical of the work produced under this school around 1920. In their meticulous drawing, machine-smooth coloring, and scrupulous joining of parts, pictures of this type have a direct relationship to the machine age of which they are definitely a part.

The importance of Purist paintings, as well as the earlier Dutch *de Stijl* and Russian Constructivist styles, lies in their rapid assimilation by architects, designers, typographers, furniture makers, poster makers, stage designers, and other practitioners of the more "useful" arts. It is in this direction that Purism fulfilled itself: first, in its practical application to architecture and the allied arts by Ozenfant's collaborator Le Corbusier, and then in its adaptation by other and less skillful artists. Even though Purism declined in importance as a pictorial movement soon after 1925, its influence in France during the twenties and thirties is of paramount significance.

It may be of interest to point out that the almost simultaneous appearance of Purism and Russian Constructivism gave the conservatives in France a wonderful opportunity to attack the former group as Bolshevistic. The fact that the movement soon fell into disfavor in Russia and continued for

315

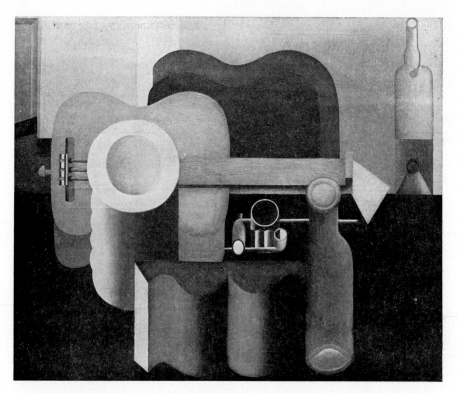

163. LE CORBUSIER: *Still Life* (New York, The Museum of Modern Art).

almost two decades in the rest of Europe in one form or another, that many of the practitioners of Purism, Constructivism, and other similar techniques were exiles from Soviet Russia (*e.g.*, Gabo, Pevsner, Lissitzky, etc.) made very little difference: another modern movement had been discolored with Red paint.

Considering Constructivism, *de Stijl*, and Purism as variants of the same approach toward unification of pictorial art with the methods and materials of the machine age, we may note two important results. First, the increasing emphasis on nonobjectivity, especially in the first two groups, meant not only ultimate obliteration of subject matter in art but the concomitant as well, that there was no longer any reason for painting in the old sense. In fact, the Bauhaus, even though it enlisted the aid of painters such as Klee, Kandinsky, and Feininger to help train designers, thought of painting as an art of the past, an art that had outlived its usefulness. If one granted the initial premise of the school, the desirability of machine-like buildings without ornamentation of any sort, painting as such was passé.

A second and more fortunate consequence of the machinistic point of view, in addition to its influence on the useful arts, is found in the field of industrial design generally. Here, under the popularized description known as "streamlining," objects of everyday utility, from kitchen clocks to locomotives, have undergone a smoothing out and simplification process that swept away much outdated design and ornament. In spite of the usual commercial misapplication of this cleaner approach, the new trend has been extremely healthful.

If, as many critics have insisted, abstract art's greatest contribution to modern life lies in just that sort of influence, no tears need be shed, for it is a significant and useful contribution. At the same time, it makes meaningful the various experiments from analytical Cubism to Purism, in the same sense as abstract scientific research that ultimately helps people to live better.

This account of the development of structurally abstract art began with Picasso and Braque, whose joint efforts in analytical and synthetic Cubism affected Futurism in Italy, Constructivism in Russia, *de Stijl* in Holland, and Purism in France. While Europe as a whole reacted as we have seen to the original stimulus of Cubism, the inventors pursued their own courses.

Since the First World War, the art of Picasso has undergone many changes. In some years it is possible to catalogue as many as four or five distinct styles, all valid and all exciting in their way. Up to 1925, he was still interested in synthetic Cubism and often produced strikingly colored variants of the original angular method alternately with a newer and more rounded type of flat patterning.

In this latter category, the later work of Braque is more fully developed, as in his *Still Life, The Table* (Fig. 164). Here Braque in an individualistic, half-Cubist, half-realistic, curvilinear style gives us one of the finest decorative results of the Cubist approach. The painting is still basically flat, with brown and green colors applied in rich patterns that vary in complexity. For the segment of the public which is interested in Cubism, these free-

317

flowing and richly colored paintings have a very satisfying quality; for artists tired of the geometric quality of Purist and related styles, this more Fauve than Cubist art has offered a way out. In fact, it seems to have offered Braque himself a variety of decorative possibilities during the past decade in which at times the Cubist manner disappears entirely or is at best only vestigial. This is especially true of the pictures executed during the occupation of Paris by the Nazis. Here the artist reaches a richness of color perhaps unsurpassed in the entire range of twentieth-century painting.

164. BRAQUE: *Still Life, The Table* (New York, The Museum of Modern Art).

Parallel in time with Picasso's synthetic creations until 1925 are Picasso's various classical styles between 1920 and 1925. Here we are particularly impressed by certain exaggerations and intensifications of modeling that make these monumental forms so different from the originals. One of the best-known "antique" paintings is the *Woman in White* (Fig. 165), whose plastic impressiveness and dignity is in such violent contrast to another Picasso category of this period, his pre-Surrealist pictures exemplified by *Femmes effrayées au bord de la mer* (Frightened Women near the Sea— also called The Race) (1923, Fig. 166). These ponderously sculpturesque forms are designed to create a sensation of unreal terror and impending violence. Within the next three years Picasso produced more specifically

Surrealist pictures but still in keeping with his personal idiom. At the same time the change from angular Cubism to flowing curved lines was completed, although the artist was not necessarily committed to that type of Cubism for longer than he cared to be.

In 1931–1932 Picasso introduced his famous "stained glass Cubism" in which flowing and powerful outlines enclosed strikingly toned and relatively flat color areas; while in the five years following we find a variety of Surrealist approaches, black-and-white illustrations for classical books, and a number of Romantically

165. PICASSO: *Woman in White* (New York, The Museum of Modern Art).

Baroque pictures. It is in this period from 1933 to 1937 that his bullfight types began to appear in their somewhat Surrealist fashion, perhaps as indications of the artist's uneasiness about what was happening in his mother country.

In 1936 with the Fascist intervention in Spain the curtain had gone up on the first act of the new world conflict. Picasso's series of symbolic etchings, *Dream and Lie of Franco*, were soon followed by his monumental black-and-white Cubist-Surrealist mural, *Guernica* (Fig. 167). It is perhaps futile to compare the figurative style of Goya's *Disasters of War* with the abstract paintings of the modern Spaniard but the same impact of horror and violence, the same fury of the patriot defending his country and defying the invading enemy are there in full measure. Even those unfamiliar with Picasso's method came away from the *Guernica* stirred by his turbulent distortions.

Although this monumental work attracted a great deal of attention to the Loyalist cause, it was severely criticized in some quarters because it was not as intelligible as a subject of this type should perhaps have been. There is no denial that the possibility of understanding it is limited to those attuned to Picasso's sophisticated and personal method of expression, but the fact remains that Picasso is that kind of painter. To attack him for this reason is to attack him for being himself. One may perhaps wonder if an expressive and legitimate form of art should have been cast aside at that time in favor of a more objective style, more immediately understandable. In view of the painter's versatility with other types of painting, a more illustrative manner is certainly possible, although it does not seem altogether consistent with the artist's development during the decade preceding *Guernica*. There can be no question of sincerity involved here for the subsequent behavior of Picasso during and after the occupation shows very clearly just where he stood with regard to the Nazis.

Another point which was raised about the *Guernica* was that the artist in his allegory had shown the Spanish people in an undignified way and

166. PICASSO: *Femmes effrayées au bord de la mer* (The Race) (New York, The Museum of Modern Art, owned by the artist).

167. PICASSO: *Guernica* (New York, The Museum of Modern Art, owned by the artist).

that the only impressive part of the picture was the monstrous bull, the symbol of the oppressor. It would seem, however, that Picasso's conception of the calmly victorious bull and the undignifiedly mangled people of Guernica was justified by subsequent events, by Rotterdam, Warsaw, Kharkov, and Coventry. The prophecy of *Guernica* was fulfilled in Picasso's art by his *Charnel House*, a seven- by nine-foot picture, begun in the summer of 1945 and representing in a manner reminiscent of the earlier work the horribly quiescent corpses of the Nazi concentration camps.

Picasso's inventiveness does not cease with the *Guernica*, for in the few years between that point and the Second World War there were still more modulations of his outstanding creative ability. These further developments, mostly abstract Surrealist, only emphasize the extremely personal nature of Picasso's evolution as an artist, particularly during the past twenty years. The kind of mentality that could produce in the same year several different types of painting, poles apart in their sources of inspiration and modern application, is typical of the modern creator's search for means of expression. It signifies, further, the very loose relationship between the artist and society, for it is only at occasional points and in exceptional circumstances, as *Guernica*, that the painter responds directly to contemporary stimuli.

This does not mean that the artist is no longer related to society, for the very developments we have been considering in abstract art have shown us that the most extreme forms of abstraction and nonobjectivity, such as Suprematism and *de Stijl,* are still results of contemporary life. Moreover, they also have had an effect on the useful arts of our time, just as Renaissance design affected furniture, costume, and other things. The significant change in viewpoint which we must grasp is that the abstractionists do not portray the world around them, as, for instance, the Impressionists did; but they do react to life about them. In a lesser measure this is also true, we shall see, of the more intuitive, emotional abstract movements, such as Expressionism, Surrealism, and others.

The modern nonrepresentational artist reacts to life about him in a very personal nonsocial manner, especially since there is no exact standard imposed by specific social necessities, such as religion, royalty, and the like. The shift back and forth from style to style of such painters as Matisse and Picasso does not occur, for example, in the art of the Renaissance. We are able often in the art of Raphael or Michelangelo to judge on the basis of style the date of one of their works; but it is almost impossible with a modern master, unless we have the actual documentary evidence to help us.

Without attempting to decide the merits or demerits of this situation, it is fairly evident that the modern painter is not an integrated part of society. If he turns to a capricious, highly personal art, if he is more interested in experimentation and theorizing on the best means of formal expression rather than concerning himself with subject matter, it is the result of the conditions that brought his art into being.

19. EXPRESSIONISM: REVOLT IN GERMANY

With the beginning of the twentieth century there emerged one of the most significant movements in modern art: Expressionism. Cradled in Germany during a period of intense militarism and Junkerdom, it moved forward parallel with the great industrial expansion and strenuous search for markets that led to the First World War—and reached its climax in the postwar period.

But the explanation for the disturbed quality of Expressionist art, its search for inner meanings, is much more complex. Similar conditions existed in France and England, Germany's two great rivals, who had the same economic aims and ambitions. In those countries, however, industrial expansion and imperialism were already well advanced, whereas in Germany they represented recent additions following the unification of that country after 1870. The transition from a group of loosely federated states to a highly unified and autocratic military monarchy was so abrupt as to cause social and spiritual shock.

The new Germany was little more than an enlarged Prussia, a state that had been an absolute monarchy until after 1850. In spite of the industrial developments of the period following the Franco-Prussian War, Prussia remained an agrarian country dominated by its landowner or Junker class. The predominance of Prussia in the highly nationalistic, newly industrialized Germany of the late nineteenth century meant the predominance of the most reactionary elements. It was the struggle between these conservative forces and the liberal middle class and class-conscious workers that conditioned the rise of the new state. Unlike England and France, Germany in the course of its meteoric rise to international importance had not had the time for gradual and comfortable democratization. Although it acquired a constitutional parliamentary system, the chancellor and cabinet ministers were still responsible to the Kaiser rather than to the Reichstag.

As far back as the seventeenth century, while other countries were engaged in building up powerful monarchies, Germany had been a continuous theater of religious war or the helpless victim of aggression. When in the following century the new middle classes in England and France gradually substituted their power for that of the already decadent aristocracy, Germany became a series of independent principalities led by Prussia and culturally dependent upon foreign nations. The impact of the Industrial Revolution meant relatively little to the federated German states and their princely rulers. While England and France went about the business of perfecting their industrial and commercial mechanisms during the first half of the nineteenth century, a certain old-world provincialism was still evident in the character of the small German nations whose court arrangements, dating from the eighteenth century, still exercised a profound influence upon the cultural autonomy of each group.

The background of Germanic culture, then, was one that led inevitably to cultural separatism, to the individual existence of centers each of which produced universities, music, and literature on a consistently high level. Art, on the other hand, deprived of the patronage furnished by a powerful and centralized monarchy, remained dependent upon the French tradition, not only during the Rococo eighteenth century but also through the nineteenth century.

Germany's historical and cultural heritage, as we can see, effectively prevented the formation of any single and dominant urban center such as Paris or London. In the sense that the Germanic states were dependent artistically upon Paris, they tended to reproduce, parallel, and sometimes excel the movements in French art. Yet it must be pointed out that the literary neo-Classicism of the late eighteenth century and the Romanticism of the early nineteenth were anticipated in Germany by such authors as Lessing and Winckelmann in the former case and Herder, Klopstock, Schiller, and Goethe in the latter. As we saw earlier, Mme. de Staël and Chateaubriand, who may be credited with initiating the Romantic movement in France, owed a great deal to the mystical Christianity that came from the Germany of that period.

In spite of the apparent parallelism of development, there were fundamental differences that must be noted. Germany, as a culturally separatist country, was bound to produce an art or literature that would reflect this quality well into the nineteenth century. When finally attacked by the economic and military autocracy of the 1870–1914 period, it was just as much fated to rebel individualistically. This may help to explain why German art and literature have tended to express themselves in the subjective and emotionally profound terms that we now recognize as their characteristic.

It is perhaps too much to say that, because German culture emerged from centers which were relatively provincial as compared with Paris, it had to assume a more naïve and emotional nature. Although we may admit such provincialism and consequent separatism as possible factors in the more emotional character of German civilization when compared with the studied formalism of France, there are other points that should be considered.

The turbulent religious background of seventeenth-century Germany, the struggles of the Reformation and counter-Reformation, left their indelible marks upon German thought and feeling. This is not a matter of race or blood but rather of social and historical causes. The emotionality of German culture and the academic and formalistic character of French culture cannot be explained on the basis of inherent differences.

The emotional and psychical conflicts in Germany's religious background, expressed in the dramatic music of Johann Sebastian Bach in the early eighteenth century, were related to the development of the neo-Christian movement at the end of that century, as well as that movement's general striving and idealistic yearning. Undoubtedly, religion has colored the development of German culture; as late as the end of the nineteenth century it was still an important problem whose implications emerged in much of the literature of the time.

The factors we have noted so far are cultural separatism, an apparent provincialism, and a religious and spiritual yearning. Add to these the retarded economic development of nineteenth-century Germany and the sudden breath-taking industrial shift indicated above, and the background for modern Expressionism with its inward searching and emotional qualities is almost complete.

From a specifically aesthetic point of view, German art during the early nineteenth century showed Romantic qualities analogous to those of France, but differing in important particulars. Although it manifested a similar interest in the Middle Ages and classical antiquity, both of these fields in the hands of German artists were vehicles for the simple and homely middle-class emotionality of the late eighteenth century. The French Romantics, in reverting to earlier techniques and subject matter, chose either the relatively cold ideals of the Renaissance or medieval material expressed in a Baroque technique. In France one feels that classical material, like medieval, is often a symptom of Romantic "harking back," but in Germany it becomes a relative certainty. Schiller and Goethe, for example, were in many ways Classicists, yet fundamentally they remained Romantics either in their upper middle-class emotionality, individuality, or mysticism. When German neo-Classical architecture produced at Regensburg a building fashioned after the Parthenon, it was given the curiously medieval and Germanic title of Valhalla.

In the same way, the many Romantic landscapes of the first half of the nineteenth century in Germany are filled with Italianate ruins and back-grounds and peopled with picturesquely dressed characters. We are reminded of that nostalgic Italianism so dear to the German school of poetry and illustrated in Goethe's *Wilhelm Meister:* "Know'st thou the land where the lemon trees bloom. . . . "

Even more startling is the fact that all the so-called Romantic painters were the products of academies in Germany, a striking evidence that this form of expression was taken for granted, that it was the rule rather than the exception. To be sure, there were a good many neo-Classicists in painting, sculpture, and architecture during the nineteenth century in Germany, but the purposes to which they put their studies were almost invariably emotive or sentimental.

The down-to-earth emotionality of the German school of painting is indicated not only in choice of subject matter but, which is more significant and different from the French, in adoption of the meticulous and detailed realistic technique of later medieval painting. In such a work as *Hermann and Dorothea* by Julius Oldach (1804–1830) we find a direct carry-over of Goethe's early sentimental middle-class tragedy by that title, with the

326

painter disclosing the same lumbering *Gemütlichkeit* as the dramatist. This Romantic Realism is evidenced throughout the course of the century by such painters as Moritz von Schwind (1804–1871) with the cozy intimacy of the *Morning Hour*, or Karl Spitzweg (1808–1885) with such titles as *Stargazer, Suspicious Smoke*, or *Farewell*, of much the same character.

The neo-Christian attitude mentioned earlier can be found in both subject matter and technique in the work of painters like Franz Pforr (1788–1812), Julius Schnorr von Carolsfeld (1794–1872), or Alfred Rethel (1816–1859). It is understandable that this art form would be of great interest in Germany, because religion always played such an important part in the lives of its inhabitants, and also because the actual art is derived from the native traditions of Germany itself (late fifteenth and early sixteenth centuries).

Neo-Germanic painters in the first half of the nineteenth century used that material out of Germany's past which lent itself to a sentimental, pious, and relatively gentle feeling. During the early twentieth century, this source was tapped again by the Expressionists, but their spiritual necessities led them to adopt the more expressive and violent art of Grünewald rather than that of Lochner or Schongauer.

What were the steps by which German art changed so radically from academic Romanticism to dynamic Expressionism? While the revolutionary events of the earlier part of the century had left Germany relatively untouched, its internal political and economic development eventually made it more susceptible to newer influences. Thus the painting of the later part of the century is generally divided into Realism and Impressionism paralleling the somewhat earlier French development, although not comparable in vigor or freshness. Many Barbizon-like landscapes, old-fashioned portraits (*e.g.*, Anselm Feuerbach), romantic Italianate scenes, and sentimentally academic shepherd boys and gypsies responded halfheartedly to the cleaner colors of Impressionism. Most of the painters were products of academies and only utilized those elements from French painting that made their pictures more appealing and up-to-date.

This first breach in the wall of conservative painting was the least important step in the progress of that era after the middle of the century. Stronger and more individualistic responses to French progress are found in the realism of Wilhelm Leibl (1844–1900), who eventually came under the influence of Manet, and Wilhelm Trübner (1851–1917), a disciple of Leibl, who shows not only realistic strength and forthrightness but an increasing clarity of color as well. An important spiritual element in the art of this time is the otherworldliness of Arnold Böcklin (1827–1901) and Hans Thoma (1839–1924), whose art shows certain analogies with that of the pre-Raphaelites in England. The idealism and nature worship of Hans von Marees (1837–1887) is comparable to similar qualities in the painting of Gauguin.

With the linear spiritualism and the identification of the artist and nature found in the work of the Swiss-German Ferdinand Hodler (1853–1918), we arrive at a kind of expression seen in many countries at the end of the century. The stained glass quality of his design, its strong linear and rhythmic effects, and its attempt to symbolize the forces of nature rather than to represent them are more directly comparable to the art of Gauguin than was the case with Marees. Like the painting of the Norwegian Edvard Munch, who was destined to be so influential in the formation of Expressionism, the work of Hodler is part of what the Germans call *Jugendstil* (Youth Style) and the French *art nouveau*. In its abstract qualities (Hodler referred to it as parallelism) it brings part of German painting level with the "modern" attempts of the French. Like French art of that period, it is also a reaction against the increasingly ignoble and brutal world in which the artist found himself.

As a symptom of the economic changes following the Franco-Prussian War, the *Iron Foundry* (1875) of Adolph von Menzel, although academic in coloring and photographic in arrangement, is a clear indication of the new industrial life of victorious Germany. This abrupt transition was violent enough to catch the attention of even so conservative a painter as von Menzel. The period to which this painting belongs also saw the rise of social democracy as a political movement reflecting the increasing awareness of the nascent proletariat.

Working people during this era suffered not only their usual disadvantages but just as much from the fact that handicraft workers in many instances were being replaced by machinery. One of the great social dramas of the period, Hauptmann's *The Weavers* (1892), was written as a protest against the earlier tragic unemployment of many Silesian weavers, caused by the introduction of machinery. The following year Germany's great woman artist Käthe Kollwitz (1867–1945) began her famous series of black-and-whites

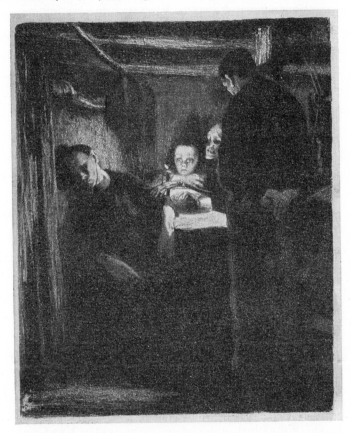

168. KOLLWITZ: *Death, Weavers' Revolt Series*—print (photograph courtesy of Hudson D. Walker).

inspired by this play and called the *Weavers' Revolt* (1893–1897). It included such subjects as *Need, Death* (Fig. 168), *Betrayal, Weavers' March, Storm,* and *End,* each of which expresses not only the horror of its theme but also a dark, almost tortuous striving for inner emotional meaning. Kollwitz in the late nineties is already an understandable product of the social and artistic environment of that time.

Growing up in a period influenced by the new social philosophies of Ferdinand Lasalle, Friedrich Engels, and Karl Marx, Käthe Kollwitz was the daughter of a man who had forsaken his law studies to become a worker, and the sister of Konrad Schmidt, who often wrote articles for Germany's leading radical newspaper, *Vorwärts*. With such literary influences as Zola, Ibsen, Dostoevski, Arno Holz, Freiligrath, and Hauptmann, as well as a keen consciousness of the increasing economic misery of Germany (where three-quarters of the population "lived" on about seventy-five dollars a year), it is only natural that she would turn to the subject matter of the *Weavers' Revolt*.

Kollwitz came to Berlin at the age of seventeen to study art. A short time later the dark and mystical Norwegian Edvard Munch (1863–1944) made his presence felt in the changing art world through the famous exhibition of 1892, where he was howled down because of the unconventionality of his subject matter and the frightening quality of his formal and coloristic distortions. Such a painting as *The Dance of Life* (Fig. 169) is typical of Munch's intense mysticism and sense of impending doom. It represents his rebellion against the crassness and brutality of earthly existence and may be seen as an effort both to escape and to protest it. The vivid swirls of brilliant terrifying color together with the tortured linear symbols constitute a background for his morbid picture of humanity. Undeniably the protest here is implicit rather than explicit but it was to offer, along with the work of Van Gogh and Gauguin, a suitable program and technique for the artists of the next few decades.

The painting of Munch, Van Gogh, and Gauguin, although typical of the last decade of the nineteenth century (expressed in Van Gogh's portrait of *Dr. Gachet* (Fig. 126): " . . . with the heartbroken expression of our time"), was symptomatic of a serious change from objective to subjective analysis. During the following generation Germany was destined to turn toward the analysis of inner truths, toward the expression of a higher form of reality that could not be voiced in fleeting and transient color values.

Munch and these other artists, then, must be reckoned among the ancestors of the Expressionist movement. Van Gogh with his tortured mysticism, his ardent yearning expressed in writhing colors and twisted

169. MUNCH: *The Dance of Life* (Oslo, State Art Museum).

forms, is unquestionably one of the great antecedents of the Expressionists. One has only to compare a typical Van Gogh portrait with a similar work by Kokoschka to see the derivation in both style and mood. Gauguin, with violent but simple tonalities, an instinct for the beautiful, and feeling for primitive virtues, must also be considered as an anticlassical, anti-Impressionist ancestor of the movement. His symbolic linearism is further support of Munch's point of view. When we add to the implicit influence of these two men the simultaneous impact of the work of Munch and the furor created by his Berlin exhibition in 1892, the way was clear for an artistic revolt.

The *Seʒession* movement led by Max Liebermann (1847–1935), although a first step in the German artistic revolution, was still under French influence and primarily naturalistic and Impressionist in character. As a movement, its greatest virtue lay in its assertion of the right of German artists to follow the French school in their more daring innovations.

In his pre-*Seʒession* pictures, Liebermann had presented simple themes expressed in terms of a slightly earlier French Realism. Such paintings as the *Net Menders* (1889) are manifestly stimulated by Millet and to some extent by the Dutch painter Josef Israels. Combined with these virtues, however, we find insistence upon the use of clear and sharp, almost Impressionist colors for this glorification of simple peasant types. The analogy with his contemporary, the American painter Winslow Homer, is too striking to be ignored.

With the *Sezession*, however, the painting of Liebermann and his group became more and more Impressionist in technique, although still related to the simple and direct Realism of the German tradition. The revolutionary character of this movement was not obscured by elaborate but fundamentally distracting analyses of method and procedure, as happened in France. Because the Germans absorbed from the French what was most useful to them and adapted it in a characteristically German manner, their art avoided the relatively abstract post-Impressionist art of Cézanne and Seurat. They went directly from Van Gogh and Gauguin—add perhaps the mystic qualities of Henri Rousseau—to the distorted and inward-searching art known as Expressionism.

Contemporary with Liebermann we find such a painter as Max Slevogt (1868–1932) who immediately shows a more imaginative and brutal Impressionism. In his *Pacing Lioness Caged* (1901) we have a typical example of the violent nontheoretical approach. The same thing can be said of the work of Lovis Corinth (1858–1925) whose *Self-portrait* (Fig. 170) has some of the stark and emotional brutality of Van Gogh. He is closest, among members of the *Sezession* group, to what the Expressionists do later but still must be regarded as a transition between the objective, descriptive qualities of the first movement and the more subjective forces of the second.

The Expressionist movement proper, beginning in 1905 (about the time that the most Expressionistic Fauve, Rouault, was doing some of his best work), was in sharp contrast with the almost contemporary French movement headed by Matisse. The French and the Germans derived entirely different influences from the work of Gauguin and Van Gogh in the exact degree to which their respective backgrounds differed. Gauguin gave the Germans an outstanding feeling for lyrical primitivism and expressive color;

German painters such as Nolde and Pechstein made the pilgrimage to the Pacific islands he had visited. The French brought forth the linear style of Matisse and the Fauve decorative sense. Van Gogh gave the French a free technique and a brilliance of color such as we find in Dufy. The Germans took from him his heavy passionate quality and his frenzy.

Both the French and German groups of the first decade of the twentieth century were influenced by the primitivism of African Negro sculpture. Kirchner had come upon this type of work in the Dresden Ethnological

170. CORINTH: *Self-portrait* (private collection).

Museum in 1904, about the same time that Vlaminck and Derain, and shortly afterward Matisse, had uncovered the specimens at Chatou. The French benefit from this type of art is perhaps best expressed in the pastiches of Picasso, the elegant stylizations of Modigliani, or the generally arbitrary handling of forms in some of Léger's more rigid paintings. With the Germans, on the other hand, it was a question of utilizing the brutal force and unspoiled qualities that Negro sculpture possessed. The fact that the Germans used first-rate examples from the Dresden Museum, while the French were influenced by things they saw in curio shops, may have something to do with the difference.

In essence, we may say that the Germans go back to their own "native" tradition, to the spirit of Cranach, Grünewald, and Baldung, as they had done earlier in the nineteenth century in a more Romantic fashion. The French always remain members of the "school," inheritors of an academicism dating back to Poussin's seventeenth century and continued in the modern world with Cézanne, Seurat, and abstract art.

In 1905 Kirchner, Schmidt-Rottluff, and Heckel formed *Die Brücke* (The Bridge) group at Dresden; shortly afterward Nolde and Pechstein joined them. By 1913, with the Expressionist movement definitely launched, *Die Brücke* was dissolved.

From 1905 on, the gap between the Germans and the French becomes inevitably wider, the French tending toward Cubism and plastic forms, while the Germans move in the direction of *Einfühlung*, infusing the object with inner meaning, attributing to that object an interior life, an emotion. Instead of glorifying form, the German breaks it down. He becomes more and more interested in color used to shock and to express. It is not the color of the average Fauve (Matisse, Dufy, Marquet) but rather the color that indicates "interior" qualities, the color of Rouault and the German Expressionists. The difference between the Expressionist and the Fauve again brings to mind Matisse's statement as to what he wished his art to be: " . . . an art of equilibrium, tranquillity, without disturbing or pre-occupying subject matter. . . . " The contrast between this attitude and the "soul" conflict involved in Expressionistic painting is evident, for the latter is not so much concerned with organization as with expression of inner qualities and usually with transcending obvious appearances. Although there are undeniable evidences of influence from Fauve paintings among some of *Die Brücke* artists, notably Pechstein, in the main the two schools develop side by side along the lines most characteristic of their own countries.

The inevitable development of Expressionism in Germany out of its social and artistic background is shown by the fact that certain painters appeared at this time who had not the slightest connection with *Die Brücke*. Among these may be mentioned Paula Modersohn-Becker (1876–1907) who died before the Expressionist movement was really under way. Her contact with Paris had exposed her to the influence of Cézanne, Gauguin, and Van Gogh (1900 and 1903), among whom the latter two had a marked effect on her.

When we compare such a painting as her *Old Peasant Woman* (Fig. 171) with Van Gogh's *Peasant* (Fig. 122), we return to that same concept of the stark and simple emotion, the extremely expressive colors that give to the figures of Van Gogh their peculiar intensity. The breadth of her coloring, however, and the relative simplicity of outline must be attributed to

Gauguin's influence. Her interest in what she liked to call "poor little humanity" undeniably drew her in the direction of Van Gogh's eminently sympathetic art. She concerned herself with all sorts of profound but human sentiments, especially motherhood, and her many treatments of these themes are to be paralleled with those of Käthe Kollwitz, whose lithographs and etchings of the subject are among the most beautiful and sympathetic things the latter artist has done.

Modersohn-Becker was a very young woman when she died, ironically enough, in childbirth, but her feeling for humanity, her ability to project herself into a situation in a psychologi-cally sympathetic manner, is another reinforcement of the nascent Expres-sionist tradition.

171. MODERSOHN–BECKER: *Old Peasant Woman* (Grosse Pointe, Mich., Robert H. Tannahill Collection).

A second painter whose Expressionist efforts must be considered apart from the development and organization of *Die Brücke* is Oskar Kokoschka (b. 1886). He appears to have developed an entirely personal manner of rendering humanity and nature in a profoundly psychological way. The almost Baroque intensity of his painting, analogous to the inward searching efforts of an El Greco or a Van Gogh, may have something to do with his Austrian background. In his portrait of *Dr. Schwarzwald* (Fig. 172), the dis-tortion of form and color, the character portrayal of a consistently analytical and emotionally disturbed quality in his subject, permits a comparison with Van Gogh's *Dr. Gachet* (Fig. 126). Unlike Van Gogh, however, Kokoschka has little direct connection with the Impressionist tradition and does not use small spots of regular writhing color. To be sure, his color has a tortuous quality but applied in such a loose and haphazard fashion that it gives an impression of emotional spontaneity, of a feeling poured out on the canvas.

It is one thing to impart a high degree of inner psychological meaning to a portrait and another to attempt such a rendition of inward meaning for the representation of nature. Nevertheless, in addition to Kokoschka's highly individualized portraits, he also did a series of intense coloristic

172. KOKOSCHKA: *Dr. Schwarzwald* (Pittsburgh, Carnegie Institute).

and formal distortions that sum up from within the characters of great metropolises of Europe: London, Paris, Amsterdam, Constantinople, Lyons, Naples. In a sense, he may be considered the painter who extended German Expressionism into the world at large by application of this technique to large vistas of its great cities.

The infusion of inner meaning into objects without human animation is one of the peculiar atmospheric and psychological devices of Expressionism.

336

To render in broken and jagged terms the irregular beat of a city's pulse, or its full-blooded industrial pounding, is what Kokoschka accomplished in his *Jerusalem* (Fig. 173). The mood is not one of melancholy Romanticism nor yet is it one of matter-of-fact Realism, for he has increased the tempo, he has raised the beat to such a point that we feel the overmastering power of the city in his flashes of colored lighting.

Expressionism, then, as we have seen from the early efforts of Paula Modersohn-Becker and Oskar Kokoschka, differs from Impressionism in the sense that the color it uses is entirely emotional in character. It loses the superficial and objectively realistic quality of Impressionist painting and attempts to probe into the symbolic and psychological truth concerning the persons or things described. Where Impressionism is descriptive, Expressionism is deductive; where Impressionism is lyrical and gentle, Expressionism becomes excited and powerful.

Die Brücke, the first coherent group of Expressionist painters in 1905, turned artists' minds to the study of primitive art from which they hoped to derive a more expressive language. Their fundamental down-to-earthiness is indicated by the fact that practically every member of this group was an artisan of some sort. Many were engravers and in this sense paralleled the efforts of German artists of the late fifteenth and early sixteenth centuries, the most expressive of whom, like Cranach and Grünewald, they rediscovered and adapted to their purposes. Some made stained glass windows achieve an intense color that was to have a symbolic value analogous to the contemporary efforts of Rouault in France. Their ambition was to become primitive and strong, either through the health-giving qualities of artisan work or through steeping themselves in the traditions of the past where that type of expression had been fostered.

The period of 1905 to 1914 in literature also marked an increase of Expressionistic effects. The tendency to produce more and more highly naturalistic efforts, combined with inner analysis and an extremely sensitive subjectivity, is marked first in the rebellious poetry of Arno Holz or the socially conscious efforts of Richard Dehmel. Early in the twentieth century, the sympathetic novels of Heinrich Mann emphasize this realization that the social order is tyrannical and unfair to the underdog. From here, as in

337

173. KOKOSCHKA: *Jerusalem* (Detroit, Institute of Arts, photograph courtesy of J. B. Neumann).

338

painting, there developed a highly personalized, introspectively lyrical art in poetry, such as the work of Stefan George and Rainer Maria Rilke. The former poet with his *Come into the Death-doomed Park* reveals the same mystical identification of man with nature as we have seen above in the painting of Kokoschka, although in a more gently lyrical sense. This Romantic submergence of the individual in the moods of nature is characteristic of many Expressionists and is another evidence of Gauguin's influence.

More powerful Expressionistic literature is found in the novels and poems of Franz Werfel, the plays of Ernst Toller, Georg Kaiser, and Kokoschka himself, whose *The Burning Bush, Murder—Hope of Women*, and *Job* are among the earliest experimental dramas of the twentieth century. In the same connection may be mentioned the plays of Ernst Barlach, one of the most important Expressionist sculptors.

We seen now that both literature and the plastic arts reacted almost simultaneously against the arbitrariness and logical positivism of the early twentieth century in Germany. In the same way that the public of that day hissed the Expressionistic drama, it also refused to have very much to do with its pictorial analogue. The objections, as always, were twofold, for not only was the public annoyed by the disturbing quality of Expressionistic technique and its brutality but there was also a great distaste for some of its subject matter.

Part of the artistic reaction against the mechanization and industrialization of that day took the shape of naturalistic criticism of social conditions, as found in Heinrich Mann or Käthe Kollwitz. The best possible index of the period may be the fact that Kollwitz' 1906 poster for the Home Work Exhibition was suppressed personally by the Empress (the Kaiser himself had previously referred to her work as "the art of the gutter"), and in 1912 a poster she did for a children's playground was forbidden by the police. Under these conditions it is natural that various forms of artistic rebellion had to take place. Some of it was social in content, like many plays and novels, some lyrical and escapist in a mild and spiritual manner; but the great bulk of the material produced out of this reactionary, warmongering atmosphere took the shape of a highly disturbed and tumultuous art with

339

broken forms and expressive colors conveying the psychological difficulties of the period.

Emil Nolde (b. 1867), for example, manifests a highly visionary temperament, reminiscent in his religious paintings of the later Middle Ages from which he, like so many of the Expressionists, derived considerable inspiration. It was only after he joined *Die Brücke* in 1906 that he achieved a

174. NOLDE: *Magicians* (New York, The Museum of Modern Art).

personal style of extremely violent character. In 1909 his specifically mystic works began to appear with Biblical and other subjects. An example of this phase is seen in his *Magicians* (Fig. 174), where a high degree of plastic and coloristic deformation is accompanied by a primitive and medieval intensity. The heads are large, the eyes stare, while the gestures take on a curiously spasmodic, almost Romanesque quality. In addition to the influence of the Middle Ages on his painting, Nolde responded sculpturally with more tangible evidences of influence from that source, but these are not so immediate in their emotional appeal.

175. NOLDE: *Masks* (Essen, Folkwang Museum, photograph courtesy of J. B. Neumann).

The necessity for strength and direct force that led the Expressionists into deformations of form and color naturally brought them in touch with the art of primitive peoples. Like the Frenchmen of that day, Nolde was influenced by primitive arts, and as early as 1911 we see such painting as the *Masks* (Fig. 175) in which a free but psychotic adaptation of Oceanic sculpture is fairly evident. All the painting of Nolde is touched with the brush of intense emotionality, with a feeling so strong that it becomes barbarically frightening. For this reason, perhaps, it is possible to think of his work as too insistently dramatic, whereby it occasionally loses the force of its intention.

In 1914 Nolde (whose graphic work had been influenced by Gauguin) made a pilgrimage to the South Seas that confirmed him in his latent decorative tendencies. This phase of his painting is most clearly seen in the water colors, where a feeling for bright, delicate, and almost Fauve coloring is combined with a slightly decadent and at times macabre quality that impresses the spectator as a combination of Marie Laurencin and Soutine.

Ernst-Ludwig Kirchner (1880–1938) was a cofounder with Heckel and Schmidt-Rottluff of *Die Brücke*. It was in his studio, fixed up in a store on the Berlinerstrasse in Dresden, that their sessions were held. In his review, *Chronik der Brücke*, written in 1913, he shows the important part played in the formation of his style by the German wood engravers of the fifteenth and sixteenth centuries, Negro sculpture, and the art of the Pacific islands.

341

During the early part of his career, he underwent the influence of Van Gogh, Gauguin, and Munch, which undoubtedly turned him in the direction of extreme spirituality on the one hand and a preference for realistic subject matter on the other. An interesting evidence of this relationship is found in Kirchner's *Peasants' Meal* (Fig. 176), a work that is more overt than Van Gogh's *Potato Eaters* (Fig. 120) but stemming from the same sympathetic and spiritual source. One may also point out in this connection that Kirchner often chose subjects from the more lugubrious novels of Dostoevski and other psychologically naturalistic writers.

The work of Karl Schmidt-Rottluff (b. 1884), like other members of this group, developed out of an early Impressionist phase to a more powerful spiritual form of expression under the influence of Van Gogh and Munch. His style emerged fully about 1910 with such paintings as the *Evening on the Sea* (Fig. 177) in which the exceedingly primitive quality of his art is clearly seen. Every line and tone has a shock of its own, a violence exceeded only by the quality of his woodcuts. The forms of Schmidt-Rottluff are

176. KIRCHNER: *Peasants' Meal*—woodcut (private collection).

177. SCHMIDT–ROTTLUFF: *Evening on the Sea* (Detroit, W. R. Valentiner Collection).

almost invariably brutally cut off at the edges in the fashion of Negro sculpture, a fact equally visible in his treatment of people or landscapes.

Erich Heckel (b. 1883), like Schmidt-Rottluff, had been associated with Kirchner in the founding of *Die Brücke*. His work is characterized by a rather Romantic attitude toward nature, instead of the brutal inheritance of Van Gogh so important in the development of his two colleagues. Heckel found himself drawn toward the Romantic Gothicism of the nineteenth-century painter Thoma and the sixteenth-century Cranach. His relationship to painters of the past and their emotional simplicity may be seen in such a painting as the *Praying Figure* (Fig. 178) where, in spite of the characteristically forceful colors and forms of Expressionist painting, the sentiment remains distinctly mild and unviolent. During the war he painted in Flanders; the *Madonna of Ostend* that comes from this period is reminiscent of fifteenth-century madonnas.

Max Pechstein (b. 1881), although full of power and vitality, is probably the least primitive member of this group in spite of the fact that he went off to the South Seas during 1914 in the wake of Nolde. For about ten years he was among the best known of the Expressionists and did more than anyone else to spread their ideas. The probable sources of his inspiration may be inferred from the fact that he did a considerable number of mosaics and stained glass windows. He was able to derive benefit from every artistic contact: the exotic influences of the South Seas, the mosaics of Ravenna (1917), the art of Matisse, or the Eastern and Pacific objects in the Paris Trocadero. A typical example of his work may be found in *The Idol* (1917, Fig. 179) where, in one of the many subjects of the Palau period (described, like Gauguin's *Noa Noa*, in the *Palau Diary*), his exotic lyricism is given free play. Pechstein and Nolde are sometimes considered part of a neo-Romantic branch of the Expressionist movement.

178. HECKEL: *Praying Figure* (collection of the artist, photograph courtesy of Carl Nierendorf Gallery).

Among the many members and associates of *Die Brücke*, we have discussed those who were the psychological and formalistic base of the group. The early period of both Fauvism and Expressionism (in France and Germany respectively) was followed by an abstract movement in each country. France produced Cubism in its various phases, while Germany brought forth nonfigurative Expressionism.

In 1912 a group known as *Der Blaue Reiter* (The Blue Rider), with headquarters at Munich, had been formed about the personalities of Wassily Kandinsky (a Russian) and Franz Marc. Although undoubtedly stimulated to a certain extent by Cubism, this movement was essentially emotional in its purpose and means of expression. Its members were joined by such men as Paul Klee, who must be reckoned among the important predecessors of modern Surrealism. If we examine these three men, we find that the com-

179. PECHSTEIN: *The Idol* (private collection, photograph courtesy of Carl Nierendorf Gallery).

mon basis of their work was a certain lyrical spontaneity, a feeling of subconscious motivation from which so much of their art appeared to spring. In this sense they are all to be considered precursors of our contemporary Surrealist painters.

Franz Marc (1880–1916), who died at the Battle of Verdun, may be regarded as a link between the emotionality and expressiveness of *Die Brücke* and the gentler, more poetic mood of *Der Blaue Reiter*. Unlike either Kandinsky or Klee, Marc remained invariably bound to the subject matter and its specific form. We always recognize immediately the things to which he has reference. His connection with the other two was reinforced by the specifically introvert tendencies through which he removed himself from everyday life, taking refuge in a relatively abstract attempt to probe into the reactions of animals.

These animals, for which Marc is famous, are a substitute subject matter enabling him to express in a highly mystical fashion what purports to be the animals' reactions to things but what is actually the painter's own feeling. It is by no means farfetched to consider the painting of Franz Marc as a plastic form of what the Germans called *Einfühlung*, the psychological term describing an attempt to feel one's way into the emotions of other beings. This attitude is exemplified by an incident in Marc's life when he sat with his wife and dog on a promenade. As the dog held itself in its characteristically still and alert position, Marc wondered what he was thinking and feeling, and painted the *Dog before the World*.

In such paintings as *The Dream* where he shows a female nude seated cross-legged in the midst of a landscape peopled with wild and tame animals, we see a melancholy gentle lyricism in keeping with the expression of such poets as Stefan George.

The art of Marc tended to become more violent and visionary in the flamingly brief course of his life. In the *Yellow Cow*, that animal dominates the tumultuous landscape over which it leaps in a highly "emotional" manner. The colors in their violent blues, reds, and oranges, apparently deriving from the Fauves but psychologically more significant, are combined with an increasingly broken and agitated form such as we find in *Resting Animals* (1913–1914, Fig. 180) or *The Gazelle* (Plate III). Here, in Marc's own words: "One is no longer concerned with the reproduction of Nature, but destroys it in order to show the mighty laws that surge from behind the beautiful appearance of things." From the trenches in 1915, Marc wrote home: "Very early in life I already found man ugly, and animals seemed to me cleaner and more beautiful. But even in them I discovered much that was unacceptable and ugly, so that my art instinctively became more schematic and abstract."

These pictures unquestionably have a Cubistic dynamic character that brings to mind Duchamp, and it is in works of this type that the relationship between Marc and contemporary abstract painting becomes clear. As a product of the early twentieth century in Germany, however, it follows almost inevitably that he would adapt this technique to the depiction of what has been called "the state of souls."

Wassily Kandinsky (1866–1944) and Paul Klee (1879–1940), the one from Russia and the other from Switzerland, are also part of the Abstract Expressionist movement. More abstract than Marc, they are saved from the limbo of purely nonfigurative art by their spontaneity and impulsiveness, their dependence upon interior and almost automatic compulsion, as well

Plate III. MARC: *The Gazelle* (Museum of Rhode Island School of Design, color plate from Stites, *The Arts and Man*, Whittlesey House, courtesy of the author)

180. MARC: *Resting Animals* (Berlin, Bernhard Koehler Collection, photograph courtesy of J. B. Neumann).

as a certain lyrical form and color found in Kandinsky or a fantastic humor in Klee.

Although, like Marc, stimulated by Cubism in the direction of the abstract, their purpose is entirely different. Both Klee and Kandinsky may be said to give us a fragmentary view of the universe, in terms of "free associations" that can almost be classified as spontaneous writing. Kandinsky's fugal and lyrically automatic method of painting is illustrated in his *Little Balls* (1921, Fig. 181), where the lines and colors sing across the page.

The geometric character of Kandinsky's painting is explained by his Russian background and the exceedingly formalistic work done in that country since the first decade of the century (Rayonism, Suprematism, and Constructivism). Generally speaking, Kandinsky was trying to teach the spectator "to look at the picture as a graphic representation of a mood and not as a representation of objects. . . ." Somewhat in the same fashion as Marc, although more musically, he wished to express the spiritual essence of materiality through painting. His approach is tinged with a mysticism that appears to come from states of trance, the subconscious playing a much greater part than is immediately apparent. Thus he may be said to rank as one of the forerunners of Surrealism, particularly in his earlier improvisations where the geometrical influence of such Russians as Malevich and Rodchenko is not yet evident.

The automatic point of view in composition and drawing is even more obvious in the work of Paul Klee, who seems to have derived a good deal of inspiration from the art of children, the art of the insane, and other primitive and direct sources. One of the most original and clever artists in the modern world, Klee is perhaps our first real evidence in twentieth-century art of the preoccupation with the subconscious.

As a matter of art history, it is maintained that the entire Abstract Expressionist movement is related to the mystical and subconscious art of Odilon Redon (1840–1916). Whether entirely true, this is difficult to prove, but the emergence of an almost psychiatric art, such as that of Klee in his *Fool in a Trance* (Fig. 182), is surely a significant symptom of modern dislocation. The artist's interest in this form of expression, his ability to think himself into the naïve state of mind demanded by the subject, is still part of the general *Einfühlung* seen previously but here devoted to digging out the more bizarre aspects of human consciousness, the symptoms of social disorder.

181. KANDINSKY: *Little Balls* (New York, Solomon R. Guggenheim Foundation).

348

In general it may be said that while the French had retained in Picasso, Braque, and Gris a strong sense of organization, the Germans had allowed their intuitions and sensibilities to play a greater part, thus foreshadowing the Surrealist developments of the next decade.

One of the most important modern Expressionists, the Russian Marc Chagall (b. 1890), was also part of the prewar French Surrealist development but may be considered here as a parallel phenomenon to the efforts of the *Blaue Reiter* group. He spent the four years before the war in Paris and then went back to Russia, whence he returned shortly after the Revolution since he

182. KLEE: *Fool in a Trance* (Wiesbaden, Willy Strecker Collection, photograph courtesy of Buchholz Gallery).

had been unable to accommodate his mode of thinking to the requirements of a new collectivized society. After that he lived for a long time in Paris, considered by many a French Expressionist; he has lived recently in the United States.

Chagall's Russian-Jewish background, the reactionary character of pre-Soviet Russia, and the turbulent hectic quality of the Revolutionary period he witnessed, are undoubtedly all contributions to the disturbed and introspective feeling of his painting. Whatever forces of revolt are felt in Chagall's art are entirely personal, in the fashion of most Expressionists. Even before the events of 1914–1918, Chagall was already pointed in a highly emotionalized subjective direction touched with the somewhat sardonic and melancholy humor characteristic of him. One of the best-known paintings of his prewar period, *I and My Village* (Plate IV), shows a huge figure of a man confronting an equally large, lugubrious cow on whose head we find outlined a scene of milking that may indicate the course of that animal's thinking at the moment. Both the human beings and the animal are presented

349

in such a manner as to emphasize the inward elements; but with all this, Chagall has arranged the figures in a characteristically bold decorative manner with violently charged reds and ochres pitched in a key lower than those of Marc, though equally insistent upon the emotional function of color.

In a pleasantly nightmarish fashion, Chagall exercises his prolific fancy, causing people to float mournfully over the little Russian towns he knows so well, as in *Over Witebsk* (1916, Fig. 183), a painting reflecting the melancholy and poverty of the prewar period in old Russia. Here the large sad figure of an old Jew with the traditional pack over his shoulder flies out from behind a provincial old-style church. The unexpectedness of this typically Eastern European character, appearing in so illogical a fashion, has a quality of shock augmented by the broad, powerful color contrasts.

During his stay in Russia, Chagall painted a great many subjects reflecting the customs of his coreligionists in the tiny villages of that land, conveying their melancholy travail and traditional suffering in a far from "picturesque"

183. CHAGALL: *Over Witebsk* (Germany, private collection, photograph courtesy of C. J. Bulliet).

350

fashion. He became Director for the Academic Jewish Theatre in Moscow, where his decorative talents and humor served him well.

It cannot be doubted that Chagall is one of the greater Expressionists, in spite of the fact that it is difficult to tie him to any specific school or group. His highly developed individuality, produced by an unusual background and equipment, place him well in the forefront of both modern Expressionism and Surrealism. As a unique picture of a certain environment and period, his work has even further value to the student today.

With the end of the war in Europe, a period of successful and unsuccessful revolutions followed in Russia, Germany, and Hungary—in those countries that had suffered more than others. In 1919 the revolution in Germany was suppressed, the leaders of the movement assassinated, and the short-lived and hungry Republic brought into being. For us this period in Germany's history may be initiated with the passionately expressive woodcut by Käthe Kollwitz dedicated to the great revolutionary leader Karl Liebknecht (Fig. 184) who, with Rosa Luxembourg, had been assassinated. It is a prophetic note sounding the future suffering of Germany, the postwar inflation period with its moral and economic despair, its futility and hunger.

Very few countries during the postwar period (besides Russia) underwent the strain suffered by Germany at that time. The results in the latter country were to produce a specifically antisocial feeling and an antiaesthetic movement, both reactions against existing conditions. On the one hand, there appeared a movement since classified as *Neue Sachlichkeit*, or New Objectivity, begun in 1920 by Otto Dix and George Grosz; on the other, a tendency or group of tendencies going from Dadaism to Surrealism. Both movements had as their existing basis the same spiritual lassitude and hatred of the existing order, but New Objectivity was much more specific in its impatience with artistic and social reform. The painters Dix and Grosz, sympathetic to communism as were the French Surrealists, attacked the profiteering middle classes with a fierce and bitter satire that was also applied to all so-called modern artistic movements.

They were often fined and jailed for their efforts, another indication of the reaction against the abortive revolution of 1919 that, although politically unsuccessful, helped to build up a vast pro-labor movement and a serious

351

increase in proletarian consciousness and organization. The artists of this period returned to a dry realism that was narrow, cold, and distinctly unhappy, more negative than positive in character since it appears to have sprung from no conviction and certainly no aesthetic necessity—hence the term Objectivity.

The despair which brought about this attitude was tied up with a search for underlying social and moral causes for the sorry condition of the day, in spite of the apparent "objectivity" of the art. Fundamentally, it can be said that the psychological revolt of the period implied in Freud, Surrealism, and subconscious literary forms of all sorts is also seen in the painting of Dix, Grosz, and the early Beckmann. The dry realism of these men, let it be remembered, was paralleled in England by painters such as Edward Wadsworth, in America by Charles Sheeler and Arnold Friedman, and in France by Pierre Roy. The emotional strain in the art of the three Germans derived partially from Expressionism but changed in such a way that clear light is

DIE LEBENDEN DEM TOTEN . ERINNERUNG AN DEN 15.JANUAR 1919

184. KOLLWITZ: *In Memory of Karl Liebknecht*—woodcut (New York, Erich Cohn Collection, photograph courtesy of Hudson D. Walker).

352

focused on all parts of the painting with distortion of the most characteristic and significant parts of a person.

Otto Dix (b. 1891) is one of the masters of this "veristic" method of exaggeration. He had been disgusted with his experiences in the war, the same disgust reflected by such writers as Remarque, Renn, and others, and Dix's own 1924 series of etchings called *War*. He turned in his memoirs and paintings to the most vicious satiric attacks on the bourgeoisie that he could fashion, a satire so effective because of its restraint, its objectivity. The cold biting realism in such a work as his *Portrait of Hans Bredt* (Fig. 185)

185. DIX: *Portrait of Hans Bredt* (Germany, private collection, photograph courtesy of Carl Nierendorf Gallery).

is a simple instance of the determined way in which the artists of this group set out to show the emptiness and despair of that day. This realistic objectivity has been compared with that of Dürer and perhaps Baldung, but the comparison fails when viewed in the light of the social purpose of Dix's painting and its specific emotional results.

Max Beckmann (b. 1884) also reflects modern Germany in the morbid tenseness of most of his paintings. They are not so cold in the beginning as those of Dix and Grosz and remain more in the orthodox Expressionist tradition. It will be seen, however, in such a painting as *The Night* (1918–1919, Fig. 186), that the artist in objectively quiet but terrifying fashion has set down accurately the sentiments of that horrible end-of-the-war period, the nightmarish quality of a time when Germany was starving and when sadistic impulses were more overt than imagined.

George Grosz (b. 1893) is the best known of this group primarily because he has lived for a long time in America and his work has become known to a wider public. Even before the First World War, Grosz was doing proletarian illustrations and water colors. In the latter medium he was for a long time among the most important painters in Europe. During the revolutionary period he gave free rein to his resentment against feudal, military, and bourgeois Germany, and participated in the founding of various satirical reviews. For a while he was even associated with the extremely negativistic Dada movement in Berlin.

Even more than Dix, Grosz was accused of indecency, sacrilege, treason, and other crimes because of his attitude that made him then one of the most powerful social critics and artists in the world. His well-known *Mirror of Philistines* is a strong indictment of the moneyed oligarchy which profited from the war, that group whose greed (originally confined to profiteering in edibles) ultimately led to their complete dominance. Similarly, in *Metrop-*

186. BECKMANN: *The Night* (Frankfurt, Staedel Institut, photograph courtesy of Buchholz Gallery).

354

187. GROSZ: *Metropolis* (New York, The Museum of Modern Art).

olis (Fig. 187) the artist has set out to show the viciousness of the big city, the brutality and cunning of its clearly portrayed inhabitants.

The fierce despair of which the *Neue Sachlichkeit* of Grosz is a reflection, the period of hunger and helplessness, was in the final analysis a moral and psychological swamp from which the fanaticism of the Third Reich was destined to emerge.

20. ESCAPE INTO THE MIND: DADA, SURREALISM, AND NEO-ROMANTICISM

The prewar period that saw the rise of Fauvism and Cubism also produced another direct psychological reaction to the times: Surrealism. Although artists like Rousseau, Chagall, and Chirico had been Surrealist and the later "school" was to claim them, they were not part of any formal programmatic movement. What these men had to say was unpremeditated and personal, responding directly to the strong psychical stimuli inherent in their environment and their own sensitive imaginations.

These things we have seen in the fear-laden and real-unreal compositions of Rousseau or the fancifully distorted and psychologically symbolic work of Chagall, already described as *surnaturel* by Apollinaire in 1912. Their art, together with the inward-searching, romantic, and possible-impossible dream ideas of Giorgio di Chirico, formed the basis for the later and less significant Surrealist movement. When the "school" finally crystallized during the postwar decade, Rousseau was already dead and neither of the other two were to belong to it. Before considering organized Surrealism— and the pioneering contributions of Chirico, Chagall, and Rousseau— we must turn to the war period itself.

By 1916 it was already clear that the ideal of the war to make the world safe for democracy was slightly tarnished; at least it seemed that way to some of the younger artists. A group in Zurich including the Rumanian Tristan Tzara, the Alsatian Hans Arp, and the German Hugo Ball led the Dada movement. As this nonsense word almost tells us, Dada implied a high degree of irrationality. It was in essence an attempt to ridicule all existing standards, both artistic and social. The great deception that was the war, man's inhumanity to man, the specious values that were exploited, and the behavior of industrialists and profiteers, were all under serious and passionate attack.

In its origins and development Dada was basically literary, producing hardly anything of significance in the plastic field—a logical result of its own premises. Proclaiming themselves anti-painting and anti-poetry, a group of young men in various parts of Europe, without any well-defined aims, produced completely negativistic and nihilistic ideas. In 1917 a magazine called *Nord-Sud* was founded in Paris with Apollinaire, Max Jacob, André Breton, Philippe Soupault, and Louis Aragon among its contributors. The last three were to organize the Surrealist movement in 1924 but at this point they were Dadaist in tendency. In 1917 also a Dada group appeared in Berlin with George Grosz as its leader. The following year the Cologne group, including Max Ernst and Hans Arp, came into being. What were these groups trying to say?

Perhaps the only authentic Dada works, in the true nihilistic sense of the term, were the famous copy of the *Mona Lisa* with a moustache or the simple marble urinal called *Fountain* that Marcel Duchamp sent to the Independents in New York in 1917. From the viewpoint of trying to break down all previously held aesthetic values, the significance of such work is clear. At the same time the complete rejection of every ordinary value, as implied in these "creations," could lead logically to only one conclusion, suicide, but that would have been too logical.

Since the only possible form of action at that time of world-wide madness was war, it followed that a policy of inaction was better. In the same way that life appeared ridiculous to the Dadaists, art and aesthetics, as part of the emptiness of modern thought with its academic poverty, were put into the category of stupid and useless. Dada represented a protest that attempted to destroy logic and substitute a pretended madness. At some of their meetings poetry was recited to the accompaniment of absolutely deafening music. As part of this planned confusion it was customary for some of the poetry to be composed from words picked at random out of a hat. This hysterical retreat into the recesses of the mind can be understood against the frantic background of the end of the war and the two years following. But since Dada had nothing else to offer, it disappeared; by 1920 its own adherents had laughed it out of existence.

The shock tactics of the group in the 1916–1918 period, together with its partly anarchist, partly communist orientation (especially in Berlin), added to the disrepute in which modern art was held. Although Dada was the first group to become so directly involved in politics—even for this short period—the damage was done. The later adherence of the Surrealists to Communism, equally meaningless since the Communists refused to have them, only served to strengthen the unfavorable impression.

In a way, the existence of Dada in Berlin, Paris, and Zurich during the war years was symbolic of an internationalism which in that period tried to devise a means of preventing a recurrence of 1914–1918. During the prewar years this internationalism had been represented by the School of Paris, whose artists had come from all parts of the world to learn and to exchange ideas. The thousands of paintings they brought to the *salon* of the Independents represented a supranational feeling that was to grow in other ways after the war.

The alternative to Dada's nihilistic program, and there had to be an alternative if it was to continue in any form, was the fashioning of works that would be more positive or creative in approach. Paradoxical though it may seem, artists like Max Ernst, Kurt Schwitters, and Hans Arp were able to find a new direction for Dada. During 1916–1920 they turned to a new set of values, more positive in character, that through their emphasis on chance associations and spontaneity were to lead to Surrealism.

Since by definition Dada was antiartistic, it could not produce works of art in the accepted sense; it had to be constructively Dada. Kurt Schwitters (b. 1887), for example, although one of the original Dadaists, took an important step in this direction. Almost in spite of himself, the new work seems a more spontaneous version of Cubist collage. His so-called *Merzbilder* (Rubbish Pictures) (Fig. 188), with all their contempt for traditional art media, are still related to the procedure of putting together everyday materials, such as bits of newspaper, wood, etc., developed by Picasso and Braque. Schwitters' work is also collage but with the range of substances increased to include pieces of wire, old rags, buttons, and various other types of rubbish. Since, however, this kind of creation was looked upon as reactionary by Dadaist standards, it soon ceased to be of importance.

A more successful attempt to direct Dadaism into positive channels is found in the work of Max Ernst (b. 1891). Originally a member of the *Blaue Reiter* group in Germany, Ernst also turned his attention to the "constructions" and collages of Picasso, but to these he added an element of fantasy and humor more in line with the aims of Dadaism. By 1919 when Dadaism had turned from its completely nihilistic attitude toward a more specifically plastic form of expression, Ernst and Hans Arp (b. 1888) worked out a new type of collage. Their *Fatagaga* creations (Fig. 189) show the connection between Cubism and the newer fantastic direction. The mysterious character of these pictures, with their absurd title derived from the preposterous phrase "*Fabrications de tableaux garantis gazométriques,*" is something new in the plastic field. These elements have a puzzling and piquant quality that, combined with the mixture of recognizable and unfamiliar forms in the painting, foreshadows Surrealism.

188. SCHWITTERS: *Rubbish Picture—Merzbild* (Philadelphia, Philadelphia Museum of Art, Gallatin Collection, photograph courtesy of The Museum of Modern Art).

The otherworldly quality of the *Fatagaga* combination of painting and collage stimulates the mental participation of the spectator, sets him to wondering, and even amuses him, whether the work is fully understood or not. Although recognizable elements and normal associations are few, the difference between this approach and the formal attitude of the Cubists is great enough to constitute a real change.

Ernst's love of the marvelous and the spontaneous results from his association with the more extreme *Blaue Reiter* artists, especially Paul Klee. The latter painter's simulation of the child mind for many of his fantasies, his description of things almost as they occurred to him, were foreshadowings of this later movement.

Hans Arp, after his Purist period under the influence of the Paris abstractionists,

189. ERNST: *Fatagaga—Here Everything Is Floating* (New York, The Museum of Modern Art).

shows the same contempt for conventional material as Schwitters and Ernst. His creations are bas-reliefs rather than paintings, usually in wood, saw-cut into fantastic and spontaneously conceived shapes such as the *Relief 1930* (Fig. 190). Emancipating himself from the more formal qualities of Schwitters and Constructivism generally, he lets himself go in a free expression of apparently casual forms, anticipating the lyrical Joan Miró among the abstract Surrealists.

Surrealism, like Dada, is primarily a literary movement and only secondarily artistic. Divorcing itself even more violently from everyday reality than the Dadaists or the later neo-Romantics, it has been doomed from the outset to a certain sterility and impotence. Some of the neo-Romantics, for example, were to assume the role of prophets of despair, but they did

'190. ARP: *Relief, 1930* (New York, Mrs. George Henry Warren Collection).

express an understandable nostalgia and depression suitable to the postwar epoch. As for Dadaism, it could claim the distinction of having protested violently against the deception of the war period. Although primarily destructive, it had served a useful function by showing up much of the sham of that time, both artistic and political. Surrealism is more oblique in its approach than either of these movements.

In Germany, Dadaism's lack of a positive program had led artists to switch to the more active procedures of the New Objectivity movement. The French, on the other hand, following a more romantic line of thought, extended the subconscious and physically inactive elements of Dada— in fact, made virtues of them. Taking the very things the Dadaists had opposed: logic, reason, traditional art, life, and the world in general, the Surrealists, many of whom had belonged to the earlier movement, organized these ideas into a positive artistic and literary program. What they now attempted to portray was the illogical, the irrational, the spontaneous, the unreal, and the untraditional. The psychological was to be opposed to the everyday thing; the intensely subjective to the objective.

Freud's newly developed psychology was brought into play as the activizing mechanism of their program. One may question the degree of understanding achieved by the average practitioner of the terminology so glibly used. Nevertheless, this combination of art and psychoanalysis is symptomatic of its age as had been the earlier joining of neo-Impressionism and optics. To put the matter in its simplest form, the basis of the Freudian proposal (and after him Jung and Adler) was that the motivating factors of human conduct and thought were submerged in the unconscious. The human mind, it was maintained, consisted of two portions that could be

362

compared with the two parts of an iceberg. One-fifth was above the surface and visibly active, the other four-fifths was below the surface but of paramount importance in determining our thoughts and actions.

Although the first *Manifesto of Surrealism* did not appear until 1924, typical activities such as automatic writing emerged as early as 1919. By following this procedure which suppressed the conscious mind and allowed the subconscious to rise to the surface, André Breton, literary leader of the movement, and Philippe Soupault wrote *Les Champs magnétiques* (Magnetic Fields). It was in this book that the unreal and mysterious beauty of the dream world was first opened for the intellectual public. The authors showed how the submerged four-fifths of the mind was always trying to communicate something to the exposed upper section. Because the conscious was continually interfering and distorting the message, it was necessary to divert its activities or seal it off for a time so that the efforts of the subconscious could be communicated. This was the basis and *raison d'être* of automatism.

The Surrealists maintained that through the age-old occurrence of various objects and ideas in familiar or taken-for-granted relationships, these things and thoughts were accepted on their slightly blurred face value. No attempt was made to identify these concepts with newly evoked images or to broaden their significance through identification with other and not so easily recognizable elements. The Surrealists proposed to overcome this difficulty by restoring to words, things, and ideas a new meaning through wider and newer associations coming from the subconscious mind. These revitalized meanings effected through the coloration of the subconscious would necessarily be tinted with unreal as opposed to real meanings, with a "marvelous" as against a commonplace quality. But the real of the everyday world and the unreal of the dream world would be combined in a new realism, a super-realism.

Reason and ordinary concepts of aesthetic practice were automatically destroyed by this approach. One further factor remained to hinder the absolute freedom of expression, the automatic responses of the subconscious for which they strove—morality. Like the Freudians, the Surrealists maintained that many of our psychological difficulties are the result of conflict between "natural" desires and the many layers of morality and social behavior imposed by custom and religion. The abnormalities of behavior brought to light by Freud, Krafft-Ebing, Steckel, Jastrow, Myers, and others were *ipso facto* proof of the part played by suppressed desires shunted off into the subconscious. Ordinary concepts of morality and ethics were to blame for the unhappy state of mind of many so-called abnormal individuals.

By 1924 Breton was able to define Surrealism as: "pure psychic automatism by which it is intended to express verbally, in writing, or by any other means, the real process of thought. It is thought's dictation, all exercise of reason and every aesthetic or moral preoccupation being absent." Although Breton, who was a neurologist, was able to formulate a fairly clear program for Surrealists to follow, carrying out these ideas was to prove a more difficult problem if intelligibility and communicability were to be maintained.

The feeling for the supernatural, the marvelous, and the intuitive has always existed, but without program. Moreover, although organized Surrealism gave the accolade to some of its contemporaries like Chirico, Miró, and Roy, these men were unaffiliated and independent outgrowths of the same subconscious escapism. Neither they nor Chagall and Rousseau were aware of any elaborate theoretical reasons for their artistic behavior and to that degree perhaps they are more genuine manifestations of prewar fear and postwar cynicism. Yet the existence of a program had the beneficial effect of clarifying ideas for many people.

We have already seen how the intensely psychotic *Neue Sachlichkeit* painting in postwar Germany contained some elements of Surrealism. More than once these pictures convey a certain emotional intensity frozen into immobility by the searching and critical glance of the painter. In almost the same way, the art of Pierre Roy (b. 1880) offered a contemporary but unaffiliated Surrealist quality in the evenly spread quality of its light on beautifully and exactly drawn associative objects. Works like the *Musique #3* (Fig. 191) may be credited with having set an example for the later Surrealist objects with erotic content, while the seemingly disparate groupings of forms are sentimental reminiscences. Yet they have little of the violence and moral revolt inherent in Dali's later arrangements.

Roy's emphasis on the associative meaning of objects makes him a precursor of the Surrealist movement as early as 1919, but his approach is quite different. *Musique #3* shows none of the violent dislocation and turnabout meanings so cherished by the average Surrealist. Each item in this painting is specifically associated with music or sound. The point of contact between Roy and his time, if not with the Surrealist movement, lies in the romantically retrospective quality of his art, searching the memory for things loved as a child. The same fastidious delicacy exists in his work as in the sensitive probing into bygone time

191. ROY: *Musique #3* (New York, James Thrall Soby Collection).

of Marcel Proust's novels. Extensions of Roy's style may be found in America through the paintings of Georgia O'Keeffe and Arthur Dove.

Another more important precursor of the Surrealist movement, with greater direct influence than Roy, is Giorgio di Chirico (b. 1888) whose nostalgic perspectives and attenuated shadows evoke the past in a particularly effective manner. The childhood of Chirico, spent in Greece among the ruins of classical antiquity, had a permanent effect on his later evocative feeling for the past. This type of Romanticism, comparable to the neo-Classical phase of early nineteenth-century escapism, was turned toward dream world fantasy by the influence of the morbid art of Arnold Böcklin. The combination of two such forms of turning from the world resulted in a series of important associative works between 1911 and 1920 designed to have considerable influence on Dada, Surrealism, and neo-Romanticism.

Like Pierre Roy, Chirico's interest in the past—indicated by exaggerated perspectives, lengthened sunset shadows, and use of older architecture and sculpture—provided one of the mechanisms that helped the Surrealists and neo-Romantics to unhinge reality. His influence is no less significant than the fine quality of his work. There are two main categories in the early painting of this artist: the purely romantic association of past and present, and the more fanciful type that brings together apparently dissociated ideas out of the subconscious—both, however, foreshadowing doom.

As an example of the first category, *Souvenir d'Italie: The Joys and Enigmas of a Strange Hour* (1913, Fig. 192) is the attempt of a twentieth-century individual living in the age of the locomotive to find his way into the past. The painter achieves this evocation through the unusually long perspectives of the arched loggia and its walk, the medieval tower, and the long oblique shadow cast by the setting sun. Distance is emphasized by the tiny men in the background contrasted with the huge restless classical sculpture in the foreground. The sleeping posture of this figure is similar to later forms in the neo-Romantic pictures of Picasso, Tchelitchew, or Berman, not only because of the position but also in its implications of uneasiness. The distances in Chirico's painting have influenced both neo-Romantics and Surrealists; his attempt to escape from everyday reality into the realm of memory or the subconscious prefigures the work of the

192. CHIRICO: *Souvenir d'Italie: The Joys and Enigmas of a Strange Hour* (Santa Barbara, Calif., Wright S. Ludington Collection).

366

latter group. Chirico's 1914 statement: "What I hear is worth nothing to me; there is only what my eyes see when they are open and *more often when they are closed*," parallels the Futurist concept of landscapes which the artist carried about in his mind.

In his second type of early painting, Chirico adds a number of completely unforeseen elements out of the subconscious, as in *Les Muses inquiétantes* (Fig. 193). Here, in addition to classical ruins, the painter offers the interesting Surrealist device of bringing together objects that ordinarily do not belong together. In a manner reminiscent of Hieronymus Bosch, he shows a huge seated figure with thighs growing out of column sections and a "head," represented by a type of shiny

193. CHIRICO: *Les Muses inquiétantes* (New York, Mrs. Jonathan Tichenor Collection).

handle, contained within encircling arms. The standing columnar figure at the left with a draped torso growing out of it is capped by a form of beehive or military balloon. The relatively simple nostalgic ideas of the *Souvenir d'Italie* have been overlaid by newer dream elements. Incongruity, as in the dream state, is minimized and counterbalanced by the clarity with which this series of illogicalities is shown, but uneasiness remains.

In an actual dream (and this explanation can stand for a good deal of Surrealist art) we see ourselves performing acts or experiencing events whose juxtaposition is completely illogical. We are aware—and sometimes remember—that item A and item B do not belong together. They may date from different periods or stem from different relationships in our experience. Yet so clear and definite is the portrayal of our subconscious so-called dream mechanism that we are forced, in spite of ordinary logic, to believe what we see.

Everyone can remember the type of dream in which he has traveled at impossible speeds or dropped from incredible heights without damage to himself. While dreaming these amazing things, wondering all the time how they are accomplished, one sees a number of everyday details so clearly as to be reassured of the truth of the whole event. When, for example, we dream of stepping from a speeding automobile with a brief but crystal-clear view of our shoe as it leaves the vehicle, it is difficult not to believe. The recognizability of elements such as the shoe destroys any reservation as to whether the realistic shoe and the unrealistic action belong together. This fusion of the real and the unreal, according to Surrealist reasoning, tends to create a higher form of realism, a super-realism or Surrealism.

Chirico's art, however, has none of the elaborate theorizing that marks so much of Surrealist painting. His work springs from no manifesto or program but rather from a conscious aesthetic desire to organize ideas plastically. In that sense he is more important than the Surrealists themselves, who are generally first Surrealists and then artists.

The work of Chagall during the period 1911–1918 is crucial for the development of the Surrealist idea. Nevertheless, we must remember that Chagall is a real poet without any pretentious posing. Moreover, his art, in spite of its influence on the later Surrealist "school" painters, lacks the qualities of cruelty, self-conscious exploitation of sex, or delight in other "forbidden" things for their own sake. Venturi quotes him as saying of his own pictures: "I don't understand them at all. They are not literature. They are only pictorial arrangements of images that obsess me. . . . The theories which I would make up to explain myself and those which others elaborate in connection with my work are nonsense. My paintings are my reason for existence, my life and that's all."

The early works of Chagall in Paris during the last years before the war show a combination of the real and the unreal, the typical dream experience. In *I and My Village* (Plate IV), previously examined for its Expressionistic characteristics, we find an image recorded within the head of the cow while a man in the background walks along preceded by a woman walking upside down. Similarly in *Over Witebsk* (Fig. 183) the disproportionately large figure of the Jewish peddler floats over the city in a quiet, clear, yet fanciful

Plate IV.   CHAGALL: *I and My Village* (New York, The Museum of Modern Art).

manner. Apollinaire referred to pictures of this type when he used the term *surnaturel*, shortly changing it to *surréaliste*. The frequent occurrence of irrationally combined forms, like a violin-playing fish, or equally irrational uncombined forms, with the head of a man in another part of the picture or attached upside down, place Chagall in the pre-Surrealist category. To be sure, there are other elements in Chagall's painting, his Expressionistically distorted landscapes or his various Cubist forms, but by and large he looms as one of the more vital influences on the growth of Surrealism.

A final contributor to the subconscious strivings of the Surrealists was Henri Rousseau. His interest in the marvelous, his evident spontaneity and naturalness, had held a profound appeal for artists in the early part of the century. This attraction, it will be remembered, extended to the most sophisticated circles of the day. But Rousseau's paintings had been genuine reactions to the way he felt, whereas the men of the prewar period, like those of the twenties, were self-consciously primitive and potentially fabricators of a cult.

In Rousseau's work, as in *Neue Sachlichkeit*, we often feel a certain psychological strain resulting from the intense clarity with which details have been rendered, as in *The Wedding* (Fig. 134). Other works are more romantic and even psychotic in quality. *The Sleeping Gypsy* (Fig. 135), for example, has a definitely morbid feeling caused by the fantastic character of the subject and its specific dream quality. Rousseau's account of the fear that seized him when painting such themes, although possibly to be taken with caution, is an interesting commentary. *Le Rêve* (Fig. 132) suggests the subconscious of the painter, since the nude is supposed to be his first wife—long since dead—while the tropical vegetation and wide-eyed animals relate to his youthful experiences in Mexico. Pictures like this clearly foreshadow the subconscious juxtaposition of incongruous elements and the love of the marvelous and surprising so often found in Dali and Tanguy. The idea of a sofa in the jungle is parallel to Chirico's postwar indoor-outdoor pictures in which the meaning of an indoor object is heightened by changing its milieu to the outdoors.

From the abstract side, Surrealism is perhaps best expressed in the painting of Joan Miró (b. 1893). His work, though without specific subject matter, shows a certain intensity and imaginativeness in its scrawled and humorous figures that suggest living yet unreal beings. His wit and charm are well suited to the collage method in which he has been outstanding. Under the influence of Hans Arp, he has done such abstract forms as the *Composition* (1933, Fig. 194) where humor is added to pure plasticity and where we feel below-the-surface psychological motivation. Decorativeness of color and movement make this picture stimulating as well as rhythmic; the suggestion of a subject—possibly a bullfight—excites the imagination even further. This lyrical and apparently spontaneous interplay of forms and colors in the work of Miró is in sharp contrast to the more objective arrangements of Dali and Tanguy.

The light spirit and generally humorous attitude of Yves Tanguy (b. 1900) may be compared to Miró, but Tanguy's technique stems from the more concrete art of Chirico. He adopts the Italian painter's deep perspectives and sharp reduction of scale in background figures to achieve an analogous endless extension of the immediate world. If Tanguy's milieu is the dream world, it is a rather pleasant and often humorous place filled with incongruities whose lack of normalcy and logic tie them to Surrealism. But he is free of the usual obsessions found in the work of Dali and rather imbued with the kind of imagination that is frequently intriguing and entertaining. A typical example, *Papa, Maman est blessée* (Fig. 195) shows a series of amoeba-like forms designed to convey the somewhat ludicrous message: "Papa, Mama is wounded." This fantastic and illogical story against a deep background suggesting the recesses of the subconscious relates Tanguy to the movement as a whole. With all its charm and humor, however, the work of Tanguy, because of specific painterly limitations, cannot be placed

194. MIRÓ: *Composition* (New York, private collection).

370

on a very high plane of accomplishment comparable to Chirico, Chagall, or even Dali.

Salvador Dali (b. 1904), best known of the organized Surrealists, brings their ideas to a logical if fantastic climax. Since apologists of the movement have used Dali's creations as an evidence of what Surrealism can accomplish, our argument may well revolve about him.

According to Dali, his paintings are produced in a state of psychological delirium. In view of the relative lack of communicability of Surrealist painting, we have to rely upon the "medium" himself who says: " . . . these

195. TANGUY: *Papa, Maman est blessée* (New York, The Museum of Modern Art).

ideas, delirious at the moment when they are produced, present themselves as already systematized." In other words, there is no necessity for altering the initial dictation of his subconscious. He goes on to say that in many cases he has no idea what he has painted until he has recovered from the delirium, a fact that does not quite jibe with the extreme minutiae of his technique or the ordered character of the compositions.

Dali and the Surrealists maintain that since the emotional and psychological problems shown in their art are common to almost everyone, their art should be more communicable than most. Yet, the very fact of its emergence from the subconscious of separate individuals suffering from various delusions or obsessions (classified as paranoia) makes Surrealist art as individualistic as any other modern expression. To this diversity of individual mental backgrounds has been added a pseudoscientific jargon, in itself difficult enough to understand. Granting for the moment that Dali and his group know what they mean by the various manifestations of paranoia, there are many others who do not. The latter, who undoubtedly have similar if less intense obsessions, cannot always translate their dreams or "paranoiac processes of thought" into the symbols of Dali or Tanguy. Compared with earlier automatism, Surrealism is much more communicable but even to the literate public it remains obscure.

Dali's *The Persistence of Memory* (1931, Fig. 196), with its limp watches (symbolizing the relativity of time and the artist's ability to bend time to his will), insects that suggest decay, and a sleeping monster, is a highly meaningful and evocative picture. But to this statement must be added certain reservations, for to some people symbols from an artist's subconscious, without a "leading" title, are as obscure as any others. Of all the images evoked by Dali, this picture is the most translatable. Whether or not we take his elaborate psychological explanations into consideration—and one should not have to use so many program notes—many of Dali's paintings, although beautifully detailed and mysteriously lighted, attract us by their obscurity rather than their clarity. We are drawn to these things out of a desire to find out what is going on. Meanings are debated when, the Sur-

196. DALI: *The Persistence of Memory* (New York, The Museum of Modern Art).

realists would maintain, we should attempt to place ourselves in a receptive mood and allow the picture to suggest further images.

In psychological terms, the painter working through images from his subconscious has been acting as his own medium, since he did not know what he was doing at the time. With the picture painted, he then attempts to communicate these ideas to the spectator and suggest further ideas to him. In this rather curious and unscientific reversal of roles, the spectator becomes the medium and the painter the doctor.

Some critics have felt that the elaborate program and the various apologia, although often necessary for clarification, have helped, more than anything else, to create a feeling of ungenuineness about Surrealist effort. We are told, for example, that Dali's *The Enigma of William Tell* (1934) is a reappraisal of that legend in terms of incest, apparently through the processes of his own obsessions. René Crevel, the authority for this statement, cites other instances of similar obsessions of Dali, especially as regards the *Mona Lisa*, who has acquired modern fame through Freud's somewhat exaggerated book on Leonardo. On the other hand, another critic has it straight from the artist that what he had in mind with the *William Tell* was an allegory on political liberty. In Surrealist terms, the face of Tell becomes the face of Lenin, even to the rough worker's cap, thus substituting the modern revolutionary leader for the defender of Swiss liberty. The possible reason for this particular association of ideas may lie in the fact that Lenin and his group were waiting in Switzerland to cross into Russia at the very time the Dada revolution was beginning. Very interesting, to be sure, but what becomes of the picture without this little "intermission talk?"

It is useless to argue whether Dali or any Surrealist is capable of executing such fine and minute paintings under the influence of the subconscious— although psychoanalysis would seem to rule against it. One way or another, this extremely personalized and individualistic form of expression has opened the way toward an investigation of the vast unexplored realm of the subconscious, a worthy and exciting task that still remains to be carried out.

Although escapist in character, like many other contemporary movements,

Surrealism tried to ally itself with Communism. The attraction stemmed from presumably similar aims: hatred of organized religion, war, and the bourgeois point of view generally. In spite of many Surrealist gestures toward the Left, nothing serious came of it, partly because of the typical radical distrust of "intellectualism" but more because the artistic gentry were willing to come in only as Surrealists, not as Communists. Such a position could scarcely appeal to a group with a definitely active and non-escapist program.

Basically, Surrealism is a form of Romantic escape into the mind. It used Freudian psychological techniques to express the brutality and cynicism brought about by the First World War. Dali's paintings, although part of nineteenth-century representational art, are the clearest possible reflections of twentieth-century civilization.

In the beginning the Surrealist movement was part of a reaction against the rather austere logic of Purism and its associated movements. Later effusions were tied up with the hatreds and cruelties, the tortured repressions of political ideologies in the post-depression period. Surrealism has a dual character. Even though there is the association with revolt and even with Communism (*c.* 1925) and in spite of the antifascist character of some of Dali's and Peter Blume's pictures, Surrealism takes a leading place in the expression of politically stimulated sadism, lust, and filth. It brings to the surface in plastic form the very things the Nazis and Fascists expressed more tangibly. Just as Cubism in the prewar years had foreshadowed the imminent fragmentation of the world, Surrealism at the end of the twenties foresaw the degradation of the age of Fascism.

During the middle twenties Chirico had contributed to the movement his indoor-outdoor method of association. This procedure placed objects belonging within the house outdoors against a street or landscape, a device that inevitably sharpened taken-for-granted associations. The 1926 exhibition of many Rousseau pictures at the Independents (including *The Sleeping Gypsy*, Fig. 135) must have had some bearing on the development of Surrealist and similar ideas.

Surrealism in the thirties was marked by the use of Chirico's name in its exhibitions as well as by Picasso's contributions. The path the latter artist had marked out for himself in his early *Femmes effrayées au bord de la mer* (1923, Fig. 166) was to be climaxed in the abstractly Surrealist *Guernica* (Fig. 167). Picasso's Surrealism, like the postwar efforts of Chagall and Chirico, remains within the compass of the modern abstract movement, different from the representational art of Dali and Tanguy.

Toward the end of the postwar decade a new type of mental escapism appeared in the form of neo-Romanticism. As a movement it began during the middle twenties with a nonabstract but literary and emotive kind of painting. Since the neo-Romantics were all very young men, they escaped the powerful influence and prestige of Cubist art as such, but the overwhelming personality of Picasso was still a factor. Going back beyond the abstract phases of his art, they returned to his Romantic Blue and Rose Periods with their highly spiritual and psychological themes.

In neo-Romantic art it was no longer a question of appealing to the intellect as Picasso, Braque, and Gris had done with their architectural and austere work. What interested the younger men was achievement of a poetic and even mournful intensity of feeling. In one of the most remarkable reactions of modern art (although understandable after Expressionism and Surrealism) the neo-Romantics turned with unashamed frankness to exploitation of the pathetic and the poignant. Their art is sentimental in such a touching fashion and with such mysterious implications that it is impossible to be offended.

In a sense, both neo-Romanticism and Surrealism return to the pre-Cubist and rather traditional ideals of an understandable and more readily communicable art. This is truer of the former than the latter, but it can be said for both that they are more approachable as media of communication, certainly for the average person, than the formalized and abstract art of the Cubists. To a certain extent both forms of expression refresh our confidence in painting to the degree that they deal with psychological concepts in time and space and not with the mechanical forms of Cubist art.

In the beginning the neo-Romantics, because they felt they were poets, allowed themselves to be overcome by a dark and tenebrous kind of color, like the Romantics a century earlier. Their painting was restricted in color but deep in quality, owing its greatest debt to the intense unvarying blue of Picasso's early work. Like the Surrealists they were definitely escapist, taking refuge in forms of mystic suspension of animation. Both movements were antirational, in which sense again they may be contrasted with the "painting as architecture" of the Cubists. Painters like Bérard, Tchelitchew, and Berman deal with a sense of futility, with sadness rendered in terms of inactive bodies and thoughts, with somber backgrounds of a timeless character. Their personages (the Cubists had painted still life for the most part) are found asleep or hiding in mysterious places. Sometimes they stare at the spectator in a fixed and immobile manner, but there is always a feeling of sadness or nostalgia, a world-weariness expressed in accents of lyrical despair.

During their short-lived existence as a group, they helped steer modern painting back to a consciousness of its own emotions. Although centered in Paris, the movement is basically non-French, the only exception being Christian Bérard (b. 1902).

Bérard is generally more emotional in approach than the other neo-Romantics, deriving his color, as many of them do, from Picasso's Blue Period, but working it over in the typically smudgy manner of the younger artist. Although it took him longer to arrive at his art than the others, he is probably a better painter than they and able to communicate feelings more directly, vague and disturbed though these feelings are. He is not particularly concerned with ordinary notions of form or composition, willfully disturbing the balance of these elements in the interest of greater expressiveness but not greater formal strength. The unbalanced quality of his art helps to create an air of mystery that is inevitably intriguing. By dislocating the composition or drawing of a particular form, he helps remove his subject to a distant world, as in *The Sleeper* (Fig. 197). Here the back of the head is cut off in a most unconventional fashion and proportionately distorted as well, but a melancholy, even morbid impression is distinctly conveyed.

Another indication of Bérard's psychological quality is found in his extraordinarily interesting portraits. These works, in spite of their sensitive withdrawal, are only successful when the painter knows the subject intimately and is able to respond to his personality. In the portraits as in his

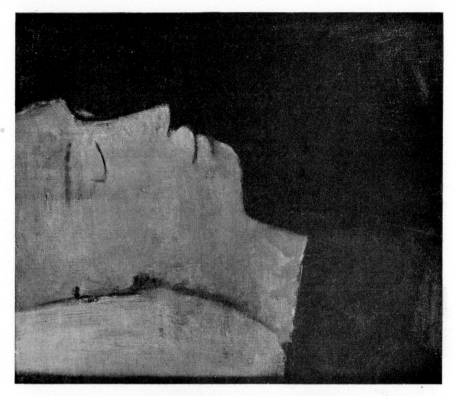

197. BÉRARD: *The Sleeper* (private collection).

other paintings and in most neo-Romantic art, we are oppressed by a feeling of suspended animation, as though the figures were restless and uneasy, about to move, and yet held quiet.

Among the neo-Romantics the name of Pavel Tchelitchew (b. 1898) is important not so much for the typical quality of his work as for his intellectual leadership of the group. Less emotional than Bérard, he often gives the impression of approaching his subject metaphysically in a thoughtful and reasoned manner that differentiates his work from the others. Where Bérard, for example, conveys the feeling of oppressiveness, of the weight under which mankind labors, this painter projects a carefully thought-out nostalgia. The emotional possibilities of his more formalized suspension of animation are not fully realized because of an often dry and uninspiring color. Tchelitchew's skill lies in his clever drawing, in the unusual photo-

377

graphic effects achieved in such paintings as *The Bull Fight* (Fig. 198). Its unconventional and disparate perspectives—anticipated in Picasso—are combined with a contrasted quality of vivid action and restrained emotionality.

Eugène Berman (b. 1899), like Tchelitchew of Russian birth, proceeded from the same technical and emotional basis as the other neo-Romantics. Like the others he uses a very sombre tonality, developed from the original blueness of Picasso, as well as the familiar nostalgic references to the past. In the course of his travels in Italy he had absorbed many impressions that were to become the subjects of his deeply perspectivized canvases. This attempt to project himself into the past like the original early nineteenth-century Romantics is related to the efforts of the twentieth-century Surrealists like Chirico. But Berman's "search for times past" is a muffled and static thing, clouded by a heavy, almost sensual feeling of immobility. It is a freezing of the mind and body, weighted down by enveloping murky colors or draperies that actually restrain the thought and action.

The Magic Circle, Venice (1932, Fig. 199) combines the bright color

198. TCHELITCHEW: *The Bull Fight* (Charles Henri Ford Collection, photograph courtesy of J. T. Soby).

378

feeling of the Venetians Tintoretto
and Veronese with an increased interest in deep perspectives. This unusual depth, together with the figures
sprawled across the open square, emphasizes the relationship to modern
Surrealism, especially to Dali and
Chirico, in spite of strong neo-Romantic unwillingness to be included
in that orbit. The difference between
such a picture as the *Venice* and one
by Chirico is not great, at least in
psychological method. Technically,
however, neither this painting nor
other products of the "school" can be
compared with the work of Chirico in
his success at evoking a nostalgic past

199. BERMAN: *The Magic Circle,
Venice* (Chicago, Ruth Page Fisher
Collection).

with expressive but controlled color and limitless spaces. In figure painting, a chief interest of the neo-Romantics, unfortunate comparisons arise
again, this time with their avowed ancestors, the Blue and Rose pictures
of Picasso.

The neo-Romantic painters remain interesting to the student as a symptom
of the revolt against Cubist formalism and as evidence of the psychotic
interests of much modern painting; from the purely aesthetic side, however,
their work has not been of too great significance.

The postwar period that saw the end of Dada and the growth of Surrealism and neo-Romanticism was an era of great prosperity for modern
art. During the decade following the war (up to 1929) those dealers who
had backed modern painting finally came into their own with all categories
of modernism. The fact that it was an unprecedented period of prosperity
for France undoubtedly had something to do with this. By 1923 the ravages
of war had been overcome to a great extent. With the "pegging" of the
franc at one-fifth its prewar level, business leaped forward and tourists
came in droves. Cheap French money and world-wide prosperity both
contributed to the boom in French art. People now bought modern pictures

379

as investments, a safe thing with most of the already canonized artists, and a reasonable gamble in the case of many living men, who were considerably helped by this development. In America the establishment of the Barnes Foundation, the Museum of Modern Art, and the Museum of Living Art were tangible indications of the same sort, stemming from the personal interests of wealthy backers of these institutions.

During the postwar decade there were also a number of interesting attempts to break down ordinary nationalistic barriers. The fraternal feeling of the Swiss, Rumanian, French, and German artists belonging to the Dada movement continued in the realm of international architecture, painting, and sculpture. The School of Paris with its many non-Frenchmen (an irritating thing to conservative critics, for some reason) was the most effectively international movement the modern world had produced. Artists from Russia and Holland went to Germany; others came to Paris from Spain, Italy, Poland, Hungary, Rumania, and other places. For the nationalistic-minded Nazis a decade later, the art produced by this school was understandably undesirable.

The postwar aesthetic of the Purists is part of the same desire to stabilize things, to achieve a series of universal values. It is during this period that critics attempted to discover an underlying artistic principle for the art of all nations and periods. Although this so-called "oneness of art" overlooked the different cultural and social forces producing the various components of their common denominator, it was another important evidence of universalism. In the same way, the further development of the pre-Surrealist art of Rousseau, Chirico, and Chagall during this period was a symptom of the general attempt to break down the ordinary barriers of thought.

Neo-Romanticism was perhaps the last organized movement. During the thirties we are more conscious of important individuals rather than important groups: Ozenfant, Léger, Chagall, Chirico, Rouault, Matisse, Bonnard, Picasso, Derain, Dali, and Dufy are among the many productive artists of this period. Even after the "crash" of 1929 the momentum of the twenties carried the modern movement forward. In terms of money and fame the situation of the artist was still good—at least in France. In the United States, the events of 1929 had immediate repercussions; whatever progress had been made during the boom period was almost completely stopped.

Politically the French were unable to respond to the needs of the emergency; five administrations succeeded each other between 1932 and 1933. It was in 1932 that the ultimately victorious coalition against the Republic was formed. The Stavisky scandal of 1934, like its famous Panama predecessor of 1892, gave the Right (*Croix de Feu* ex-soldier groups advocating the leadership principle) an opportunity to blast the government's slowness in prosecuting. The tumultuous night of February 2, 1934, in the Chamber of Deputies, with the *Croix de Feu* attempting to drive the Deputies out of the Chamber and the police fighting back, ended in the fall of Daladier's government. His successor, Doumergue (backed by Pétain, Laval, and Flandin) was openly fascist. During the next fifteen months, with Laval's hand on the Foreign Office portfolio, Germany marched into the Rhineland, while Ethiopia and Austria went by the board.

The Popular Front government of Blum that followed in 1936 may have known what it wanted to do but it did not have the strength to carry out its ideas. In spite of outlawing the *Croix de Feu* and trying to nationalize the munitions industry so as to weaken the *Comité des Forges* (financial backers of the Right), Blum's government could not hold on. Big business struck back by shipping gold out of the country to weaken the franc. Reliance on the British for leadership in the Franco crisis weakened Blum's position with his own coalition, which broke under the strain. The important thing to note is that the anti-Popular Front group was strengthened by recruits from the middle classes, now increasingly nervous because of the threat of Leftism. George Sorel's prediction some thirty years earlier on intimidating the middle class with the Red menace had been fulfilled. By 1940 the Right had won and France was on the verge of another German invasion.

During the turbulent thirties, the Surrealist group had been especially active in politics. Their magazine at this period was called *Surréalisme au service de la révolution*, and Aragon, a chief organizer and theoretician of the movement, attended the Revolutionary Writers Congress at Kharkov. Yet, as we have seen, the Surrealist painters were not accepted by the Communist Party for reasons indicated earlier. Although their Leftism was not sufficiently orthodox for organizational purposes, their art reflects the already evident brutality and sadism of fascism.

Before the First World War, the Surrealism of Chagall, Chirico, and Rousseau had manifested psychotic fear reactions and romantic escape mechanisms. In the postwar period this art had been redolent of disillusionment and cynicism. By the end of the twenties and the beginning of the thirties it responded to the menace of the new world terror. It is to this period that the bulk of Dali's work belongs, after he joined the movement in 1929. At this time he became their outstanding propagandist and leading artist with films, so-called Surrealist objects, and double-image paintings.

His films, done in collaboration with Luis Buñuel in 1929 and 1930, are masterpieces of their kind. The much less interesting "objects functioning symbolically" consist of ordinary things from everyday experience: shoes, kitchenware, etc., to which the artist gives special meaning by slight changes. Thus a fur-lined teacup or an antique slipper trimmed with lamb-chop papers should create a feeling of uneasiness or shamefulness. Where the obscenity is more than usually evident, such a result doubtless occurs.

Most significant from the creative point of view are Dali's later paintings during the thirties, especially those involving double images that express his "paranoiac criticism" (representation of his personal obsessions and the like). In this procedure a form or object can also be taken for another form, either by concentration or by shifting position, adding thereby to the sense of disturbance which Surrealism constantly seeks.

This final stage of Surrealism is as much a protest as the earlier phases, but its cries are still muted and indirect, its revulsion a turning in on itself as though to find out why people act as they do. Picasso's Surrealism, which also belongs to this period, although abstract in form, is direct and violent in its strident cries of anger, its powerful accents of suffering and torture. In Cassandra-like tones of imminent doom it stands out in bold relief against the tortuous self-examinations of the orthodox Surrealists.

Although by and large the period preceding the fall of France produced little in art that is particularly new, the work of Dali outside the framework of modern painting and the work of Picasso within its compass foretell the not too happy future.

21. AMERICA TODAY

America is young—we realize just how young when we consider that there are Americans still living who saw the Civil War. In that short time the modern industrialized world has come into its own.

Under the fluid and restless conditions of the boom era following the Civil War, the period of westward expansion, art would necessarily be relegated to a minor position. The earlier landed gentry, patrons of the arts in their day, had disappeared a long time before this. It was only when the restless land-hungry Americans had settled into their various parts of the country that there was a breathing space. In an impressively vulgar fashion the newly rich bought ornaments for their homes, stuffy furniture, and sentimental illustrative pictures as part of the insignia of their recently acquired power. Although this was true of the majority of potential art patrons, there were still artists who persisted in painting.

Some, like Whistler and Mary Cassatt, went off to Europe and allowed themselves to be absorbed in the rich and powerful art movements of the second half of the nineteenth century. Others, like Winslow Homer, Thomas Eakins, and Albert P. Ryder, refusing to run, stayed on in America to be ignored for the most part or neglected. It may be reassuring to say that the roughness and crudeness of post–Civil War America is summed up in the vigorous sincere work of Homer and Eakins, or that Ryder represents the finest spiritual emanation of that time, but the fact is that artistic isolation, the feeling of speaking to oneself, was as prominent during this period of American industrialism as in contemporary Europe.

On the positive side we find the establishment of such groups as the Art Students League and the Society of American Artists. After the great Philadelphia Centennial Exposition in 1876, where many foreign pictures were shown, painting in this country received considerable impetus. With that kind of stimulus, however, a good deal of American painting developed

383

according to the various styles of Paris or Munich—usually on the conservative side. During the last quarter of the century, many Americans underwent European apprenticeship.

Although Homer and Ryder cannot be looked upon as European in quality, Eakins was fully aware of developments abroad, responding to them in an entirely personal fashion. Many others, however, allowed themselves to imitate almost completely, a perhaps natural reaction during a period of learning. Among the artists who brought European influences to this country were the Romantic landscapist William Morris Hunt, friend and fellow student of Millet in Couture's studio, and the Renaissance-inspired John La Farge. The latter was an important influence on art through his writing and lecturing. Frank Duveneck and William Merritt Chase were both disciples of the Munich type of painting with its heavily loaded brushwork and bravura effects, while John Singer Sargent became the most fashionable portraitist of that era.

Finally America began to respond to more recent movements such as Impressionism. J. Alden Weir, John Twachtman, Ernest Lawson, Childe Hassam, and Mary Cassatt were the leaders. With the exception of Cassatt, who had been in close contact with Degas and others, most of the American Impressionists were more derivative than original.

An interesting offshoot of Impressionism is found in the work of a handful of American Realists, a "reportorial" group many of whose members had been newspaper illustrators. This type of painting, deriving from Manet's directness of visualization, included among others Robert Henri, John Sloan, George Luks, and William Glackens. From these newspaper-trained men, whose work had accustomed them to the directest observations and most everyday events, a great stimulus toward a Realistic school of American painting was to come.

They were not the first to concern themselves with commonplace subjects, for they had been preceded by Homer and Eakins as well as by the sentimental genre painters of the nineteenth century. They were, however, in the first organized group, the earliest protagonists of the artist's right of free expression; as such, they made history. Not only were they concerned with relating art directly to life, but they were also interested in the major social trends of their day. Some were liberals, while others tended further to the left.

By this time academic painting was well entrenched in America and when the rebellious group held their first group show in New York in 1908, epithets like "The Ashcan School" and "Revolutionary Black Gang" were freely hurled. Robert Henri, leader of the movement, although technically of the same stamp as Chase and Duveneck, was a person with tremendous enthusiasm for the everyday world. The effect of his powerful example is still felt in American painting today. It was from this rich source that the Realists of the early twentieth century—the painters of city life—stemmed. Henri, his pupil George Bellows (perhaps the most vigorous of the group), and John Sloan are primarily responsible for the doctrine of painting "American." Although put forth as an antiacademic device, it was to have great influence on the various later types of Americanism in art, especially on regional painting.

Other artists of that day who may be classified loosely with the Henri disciples are Jerome Myers, Glenn Coleman, George ("Pop") Hart, and Rockwell Kent, all part of that same rebellion against the reactionary policies of the Academy. After organizing an independent show (without benefit of Academy or dealers) in 1910, the Henri group supported the epoch-making modernist Armory Show of 1913 as well as the Society of Independent Artists which was set up in 1917. The reception accorded their paintings in 1908 and 1910, together with the abusive criticism of the Armory Show, taught these artists that if their work was to receive any kind of recognition, it would only come through their own efforts. Like the Impressionists and other groups in France, the progressive Americans of the early part of the century had to make their own opportunities. What the "Black Gang" had begun in 1908 with their analyses of contemporary life was to be continued in the postwar period, but another vital influence intervened to play an increasingly important role in the fight against the conservatives.

Even before the Armory Show of 1913, a number of Americans had come into direct contact with the post-Cézanne painting of Paris. Max Weber (a pupil of Matisse and friend of Henri Rousseau), Abraham Walkowitz, Alfred Maurer, Samuel Halpert, Marguerite Zorach, Bernard Karfiol, and John Marin came back with varying personal interpretations of the modern movement. The photographers Alfred Stieglitz and Edward Steichen brought works by different modern painters to this country for exhibition. As far back as 1908, Stieglitz in his influential gallery at 291 Fifth Avenue had shown some of Matisse's pictures. Even though public reaction was far from favorable, it was an important beginning and for a long time "291" was the focal point of modern art propaganda in this country. Picasso, Matisse, Rousseau, Cézanne, and many others were first presented to the American public in this small gallery.

Perhaps the most consistently productive of this prewar group of American moderns have been Max Weber and John Marin. The former, although he has practiced most of the newer techniques, is basically and finally an Expressionist with a profoundly Romantic and mournful quality reflecting to a certain extent his own racial background. In John Marin we have one of the most talented form analysts of our time, an artist who is considered a leading American water-colorist (Fig. 200). Although the planes in his paintings suggest Cézanne, there is a dynamic force and explosiveness more akin to the Cubist-Futurist point of view; but in the final analysis, Marin's works are entirely personal. In the opinion of some critics, he ranks among the best America has produced.

Abraham Walkowitz' work was originally Fauve in a decorative and lyrical manner. Later he did a number of abstractions of city scenes and poetic interpretations of the life of the poor. His beautifully cursive and flowing abstractions inspired by the dancing of Isadora Duncan are among his best known accomplishments. Karfiol's work is somewhere between late Impressionism and post-Impressionism with suggestions of Renoir, Gauguin, and Cézanne. Halpert's painting is perhaps the most conservative of this early modern group, influenced to some extent by his work under Bonnat in Paris; while the painting of Maurer, originally Whistlerian in manner, toward the latter part of his life veered to Fauvism. Perhaps closest to the Fauve manner is the effectively decorative work of Marguerite Zorach, one of the important pioneers of modern painting in America.

These artists and many others became part of the Armory Show of 1913,

200. MARIN: *Mountain Top*—water color (Cleveland, Cleveland Museum of Art).

a history-making exhibition organized under the nonmodern and Romantic Arthur B. Davies with the help of Walter Pach and Walt Kuhn. Although the reaction of public and critics to the more than two thousand American and European modern works resembled a visit to a combined fair, circus, and vaudeville show, the effect on the younger artists was very important. Here for the first time was a really broad exhibition outlining the entire modern movement from neo-Classicism through Romanticism, Realism, Impressionism, and post-Impressionism to the most recent developments, Fauvism, Cubism, and Futurism.

The next blow for the cause of modern art was struck by the fiery critic Willard Huntington Wright, with the Forum Show he put together in 1916. He had recently returned from Paris, where his brother S. MacDonald Wright was an organizer of the Synchronist movement. The author of

Modern Painting (an outstanding pioneer book) was fired with tremendous enthusiasm for his subject and mercilessly attacked the conservative critics. This exhibition, with good sponsorship, was a moderate success critically although a failure from the financial point of view.

With the entry of America into the war the following year, the impetus gained by the modern movement was lost. The Realist reportorial artists were also set back by the war. Many of them had been contributors to the *Masses*, a liberal publication that now took an antiwar position. The ensuing trials and suppression of the magazine disorganized their movement considerably.

In the postwar period we begin to see the results of the Armory Show. All shades and varieties of modernism appear, some merely offshoots of

201. O'KEEFFE: *Ram's Head, Hollyhock, Little Hills* (New York, courtesy of the Downtown Gallery).

202. DAVIS: *Street and Bridge* (Houston, Tex., Mr. and Mrs. Robert Straus Collection, photograph courtesy of the Downtown Gallery).

the original stimuli and others individual to a high degree. These artists may be divided roughly into groups corresponding with their formal interests. In the verist or New Objectivity category we find such painters as Georgia O'Keeffe, Charles Sheeler, Niles Spencer, Francis Criss, and Stefan Hirsch. Of these the paintings of O'Keeffe are perhaps the most stimulating and original (Fig. 201), with a symbolism all their own and a thoroughly modern decorative quality allied to the Fauves but definitely individual. In some ways her painting, like that of Arthur Dove, is akin to Pierre Roy. Related to this group of artists we find Peter Blume, whose work is similarly precise but whose symbolism is much closer to the Surrealists.

In the Cubist line of influence we have Stuart Davis (Fig. 202), another very original artist whose point of departure from French art is not too obtrusive. His earlier affiliations with subject painting and his interest in people rather than motifs have given his type of Cubism an unusually personal quality as well as a firm basis in life. Also related to Cubism, the work of Charles Demuth goes one step further to include Futurist dynamics as well. Joseph Stella is another Cubist-Futurist and a painter whose roots reach into the very beginnings of modernism in our century.

Among those who follow the Expressionist method, Max Weber is perhaps the best known. Strongly influenced by Cézanne, Negro sculpture, and other forms, his work, although genuinely emotive, carries with it a certain eclectic quality. A more genuine and individualistic manifestation of Expressionism may be found in the violent distortions of Paul Burlin, whose art was originally stimulated by American Indian forms. One of the strongest and most moving of American painters, Burlin has run the gamut of subject matter from soda jerks to flop-houses and allegorical political commentary but he is no mere recorder of everyday events. Every one of his pictures has an intensity that raises it to the level of an emotional experience. If, occasionally, his satire seems a bit obscure, the picture remains a form experience nonetheless. Burlin is one of the few Americans who have absorbed the message of modernism without being overwhelmed by it (Fig. 203).

During the postwar period reportorial Realism was continued by Peggy Bacon, Reginald Marsh, Guy Pène du Bois, and others. Their work is limited in aesthetic appeal but it does show a generalized sympathy for people, although occasionally even that element is lacking. At the same time we get a type of American scene painting that foreshadows the Benton-Wood-Curry regional school. This earlier group, including Edward Hopper and Charles Burchfield, shows a genuinely Romantic and sincere feeling for America without flag-waving or histrionics. Hopper's firmly built architectural evocations of the Victorian past have a moving yet soothing quality that saves his painting from the morass of photographic illustration. Burchfield, less specialized in theme, is more overtly emotional, especially in his very early works (1916–1918) where he achieved a purely independent and uninfluenced Expressionism to which he has recently reverted (Fig. 204). Between these two periods he did a wide variety of American scene subjects which may still be differentiated in both feeling and form from the merely representational efforts of the conventional Americanists.

These latter are led by Thomas Benton, Grant Wood, and John Steuart Curry of Missouri, Iowa, and Kansas fame. Their glorification of these

203. BURLIN: *The Wandering Jew* (New York, courtesy of the Downtown Gallery).

areas is part of a pattern of self-conscious nationalism and chauvinism that condemns European modernism in favor of their own true emanation of "the American spirit." Most critics today will agree that the art of these highly touted masters of the American scene leaves something to be desired.

Benton, who has profited from some of the best publicity obtainable, shows a highly stylized method of painting and a constant formula for his spasmodic Tintorettesque compositions (Fig. 205). One cannot criticize a man's desire to paint—even self-consciously—his own country, but if the American spirit means a patronizing and cruel jingoism, something is wrong with our definitions. In the case of Wood we have a placid and even static decorator for whom the virtues of modern abstraction have been claimed. It is true that he has gone back to the same sources as many moderns: late Gothic painting, stained glass, and Swiss nineteenth-century mystical painting like Hodler's, but the results are quite different. Neither Wood nor the other self-conscious Americans avail themselves of our own traditional art. Although they profess to despise the decadent traditions of European art, they exercise quite freely the privilege of using it. The art of Curry offers an Impressionistically colored, almost academic kind of drawing employed in "interesting" bits of local color that include baptisms in Kansas, tornados, and acrobats.

The phenomenal success of this branch of regional painting encouraged

204. BURCHFIELD: *Beginning of a Snowstorm* (New York, Whitney Museum of American Art).

205. BENTON: *The Arts of the West*—mural decoration (New York, Whitney Museum of American Art).

many artists to follow suit during the late twenties and early thirties. For the most part, these artists have been illustrative in character, reverting to the photographic Realism of the nineteenth century with an Impressionist ingredient added. Fortunately there have been some, like Paul Sample of New Hampshire and Barse Miller of California, whose work, although regional in subject matter, has had enough structural components to place it within the modern tradition. Their painting, like that of other regionalists encouraged during the period of the Federal Art Project, combines a feeling for the American scene with the procedures of modern painting.

Mainly, however, the artists of the late twenties, the sincere American scene painters as well as the modern, did not prosper to the same degree as the highly touted Middle Western "masters" or the widely advertised French moderns. Although art in America profited from the boom as did art in France, the results were by no means comparable. As we have already seen, the tradition of the reportorial Realists was no older than 1908, while that of the modernist was as recent as 1913—with neither one really acclimated so far as the general public was concerned. Things had happened too rapidly for the situation to have settled itself when the depression of

393

the thirties finally hit. We can point to the establishment of the Museum of Modern Art in 1929 and the Whitney Museum in 1931 as encouraging signs, but by themselves they could scarcely be expected to solve the artist's problem of making a living.

Even though American painting has profited to an amazing degree from the stimulus of French and German art and although many artists in this country have tried sincerely and in many cases successfully to adapt themselves to these new developments, they have only succeeded in estranging themselves further from the public. To put the matter in its simplest form, our public was not prepared, even in the relatively slow way the French public had been, for the various developments since 1920. The modern French painters in the nineteenth century may have been hated and reviled but they were not ignored as were ours. Without the tradition of a Church or aristocratically sponsored art, without the slow but violent period of struggle the Europeans had undergone, without the opportunity or the leisure to develop a taste for the arts, it could not be otherwise.

The amazing thing in America is not that art is not appreciated but rather that it continues at all. Even conservative painting here does not get the support one finds in France and elsewhere at the hands of a Ministry of Fine Arts. When there are government or local commissions, they are generally given to the less modern artists, but these jobs are hardly enough to make a living for people in the profession. There apparently have always been more artists than our market could absorb, a necessary condition of modern individualistic economics.

When the depression took hold in the early thirties, the condition of the average—and even above average—artist in America was really critical. One of the shocking conditions revealed by the Federal Art Project set up in 1935 was the list of famous names on it, the men and women who had distinguished themselves in the field and who now had to undergo the Means Test to qualify for a job, i.e., to certify their destitution. We shall have more to say later concerning the specific accomplishments of this government-sponsored idea, its function in helping to prepare a new public, creating new artists and media, and bringing cultural opportunity to communities hitherto completely isolated.

From the point of view of our immediate story, however, we can take note of the decentralization of art in America that resulted from this development in various parts of the country. Men and women who would never have been able to devote themselves to art, certainly under depression conditions, were now given the opportunity to create. This was felt as early as 1936 in the Museum of Modern Art exhibition, "New Horizons in American Art." The 1939 retrospective showing of the M. H. de Young Memorial Museum in San Francisco revealed the emergence of a great many talents in all phases of modern painting, print making, sculpture, and other media. Moderns, "middle of the roaders," conservatives, all got their opportunity. New American scene artists were produced also: Mitchell Siporin and Edward Millman of Chicago, Herman Maril of Baltimore, Fletcher Martin of Idaho, Raymond Breinin of Illinois, Jack Levine of Boston, and others.

During the thirties also we see the further development of a rich school of abstract painting recognizably related to the main stream of French art. In this category we find the names of George L. K. Morris, Balcomb Greene, Arthur Carles, Byron Browne, Carl Holty, Charles Howard, and John Xceron among the leaders. Within recent years artists in this field have set up a Society of American Abstract Artists. The group does not generally include men outside of the Cubist and post-Cubist tradition. Other modern procedures such as Fauvism or Expressionism are not organized in the same way. The recent establishment of the Guggenheim Museum of Non-Objective Art has helped the abstract cause considerably.

Within the same period we see the further growth of a Romantic tradition. This is usually a kind of catchall category to include men and women with whom the cataloguers do not quite know what to do. Often for that very reason they are among the best talents the nation has produced. Some leading names in this group are Morris Kantor, Henry Mattson, Marsden Hartley, John Carroll, Darrel Austin, Franklin Watkins, Yasuo Kuniyoshi, and Hobson Pittman. If we try to reduce their apparently diverse styles to some kind of common denominator, keeping in mind what is generally meant by Romanticism, we find that each of these painters shares in some way the characteristics of the genre. Thus, Mattson and Hartley represent the mood-evoking power of nature, Darrel Austin its mysterious qualities. Sensibility is projected by John Carroll, fear-inspiring atmosphere by Hobson Pittman and Watkins, and imaginative fancy by Kuniyoshi (Fig. 206) and Austin.

206. KUNIYOSHI: *Deliverance* (New York, Whitney Museum of American Art).

The economic depression that produced the Federal Art Project in response to the superfluity of artists in a declining market (small number of dealers, few museums accepting work, etc.) also brought forth Social Realism. This movement, although a continuation of the socially conscious work of the prewar artists associated with the old *Masses*, was now raised to a new level because of aggravated economic conditions and the imminence of a second world war. Moreover, its members were now organized in groups whose aim was to make art a weapon in the struggle against their own poverty as well as to "combat war and fascism." The Artists Union, formed in 1934 primarily of unemployed artists, was one of the first of these groups. As the crisis deepened, organizational activity among artists increased. In 1936 the First American Artists Congress was held in New York. Although the orientation of this conglomerate meeting was radical in the Popular Front sense, it did contain enough elements from different artistic camps to give a good idea of what was bothering artists in those depression days.

The delegates at the Congress felt that art, a dispensable luxury, had been affected by the world crisis more seriously than anything else, that private galleries, museums, and patrons could no longer give even their usual meager support. Further, the various types of government art projects were giving only temporary employment to a small fraction of artists. Finally, the artist was faced with constant attacks on his freedom of expression, attacks that intensified as the coming world struggle made the Left and Right more self-conscious. The destruction of Rivera's mural in Rockefeller Center was one of a series of incidents in which public or private patrons took action against what they felt was an unnecessary intrusion of political material. On the other hand, artists to whom the world danger was a very real thing felt they could not paint otherwise. Even though some of the above "incidents" involved the Federal Art Project, in the main this activity was liberally administered and offered much more freedom of expression than official jobs ordinarily have. This loosening of strictures added to the dynamics of the situation.

There can be little question of the social awareness of the Congress as a whole or that of other organizations such as the United American Artists, the Sculptors Guild, and many others. Basically, they responded to the world-wide economic imbalance and the increasingly dangerous political situation in which they felt they had to play a role. As the lines were more sharply drawn between the Left and the Right, artists' groups, particularly those on the Left, came out strongly in defense of the things that seemed to them important.

This wholehearted participation by large numbers of artists in politics is a rather unique spectacle. We can no longer claim that the public misunderstood the modern painter's attitude at that point, as had been the case during the latter part of the nineteenth century or in the sporadic communism of the Berlin Dadaists and the French Surrealists. Not since the short-lived antimonarchist *Artistes Républicains* of 1848 or the Artists Federation of the 1870 Commune had there been such an open and avowed political stand taken by artists—and in such numbers. Whatever one may think of this kind of activity for artists, there was surely no money and little fame to be derived from such a position.

Although the bulk of Social Realist art produced under these auspices is as indecisive as most other branches of modern American painting, there are a few positive accomplishments. Some of its adherents—notably Philip Evergood, William Gropper, Ben Shahn, Mitchell Siporin, Jack Levine, Mervin Jules, Robert Gwathmey, and Joseph Hirsch—turned out work comparable to the best in other areas of our art. Others, even without the specific subject matter of imminent war, fascism, and depression, managed by virtue of their interest in what was going on around them to produce an art expressive of their time. Where the French moderns offer only an occasional name like Daumier or Courbet in this field, twentieth-century America has produced an entire school.

The difference between the Social Realists and the American scene painters is not merely one of political viewpoint, though often they do represent opposite poles. Where the Americanists are basically representational and picturesque in their approach, the socially conscious painters, instead of avoiding modernism, learn whatever they can from it. Their most frequent source of influence is Expressionism, whose distortions meet the needs of contemporary artists of protest as they did those of pre-Hitler Germany. It has been said that Expressionism is one of the dominant modes in American painting today.

One of the most effective Social Realists in America today, and one of the frankest in his convictions, is Philip Evergood (b. 1901). Painting every aspect of modern life, the scenes of struggle as well as the others, he works with a consistently veristic intensity that relates him to one branch of

Expressionism. Evergood is more important than most members of the "social conscience" group to the degree that he has found more adequate volumes, tensions between volumes, and sufficiently expressive colors to

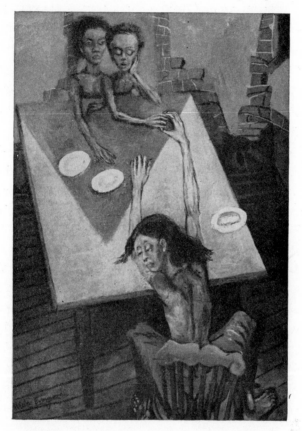

207. EVERGOOD: *Don't Cry Mother* (New York, The Museum of Modern Art).

convey his feelings in a given situation. His *Don't Cry Mother* (Fig. 207) is typical of the controlled violence of his color, the passionate protest of his social message.

Equally noteworthy in this general area is Ben Shahn, the most widely accepted by critics as representing a fusion of modern techniques and social themes. Whatever he paints, there is a uniformly high emotive quality in his ideas. Shahn expresses himself best with monumental figures moving in lonely fashion through a stark and empty world (Fig. 208). Experience as a muralist on the Federal Art Project, photographer for the government, poster designer for the Office of War Information, have all contributed to the boldness of his forms and their emotional directness. The large masses of relatively thin color are related to poster work. Although dealing with the most concrete subjects, Shahn's art is the result of careful planning, of "many sketches from which the figure is abstracted." Like Evergood, Shahn has found an objective technique suitable for his expression of the world as he sees it. Very few contemporary artists have been so much and so effectively of their own time as he.

Jack Levine (b. 1915) is one of the younger Social Realists and, like many others, a product of the Federal Art Project. The rich and somber tonalities of his work and its powerful personal Expressionistic distortions constitute one of the most original and effective modern techniques developed in this

208. SHAHN: *Scott's Run, West Virginia* (New York, Whitney Museum of American Art).

209. LEVINE: *Feast of Pure Reason* (New York, The Museum of Modern Art).

country (Fig. 209). William Gropper (b. 1897), although the best known
of the social consciousness painters, is at his finest in the black-and-white
medium. For many years an illustrator for the radical press, he has fought
consistently against all forms of inequality. Like many other members of
the group, his art often suggests the inspiration of Daumier. Other well-
known Social Realists are Joseph Hirsch, a painter of solid high-colored
representational forms; Robert Gwathmey, whose Cubist-derived abstractions are decoratively and sympathetically applied to Negro themes;
and Mervin Jules, a bold experimenter with tempera, silk screen, and other
media.

For better or worse, Social Realism was one of the outstanding contributions of American painting in the thirties. Responding to a set of circum-

stances as severe as they were unique, these men and women have left a moving record of our times. Whether or not one agrees with their general political viewpoint, many of the painters in this group have received critical approval of a high order. Shahn has been given a one-man show at the Museum of Modern Art. That same institution's exhibition of "Americans 1942" included the work of Joseph Hirsch, Jack Levine, and Mitchell Siporin. The paintings of Evergood and Gropper have been acknowledged by museum acquisitions.

Although the tendency in modern art criticism is to try to divorce the painter from the content of his work, to "give him his due" in spite of an often overtly expressed radical viewpoint, many of these men would not wish to be judged that way. If we feel, as many will, that we cannot sympathize with their position, we still have the obligation to decide, if we can, with what degree of success they have fused their ideas with the techniques of modern painting. Whether their point of view will bear fruit remains to be seen.

Up to about 1933 the modern movement in this country had only partially been absorbed. Between the lack of preparation and interest of the public and the very powerful competition of American scene painters, modern art as such did not stand much of a chance. To be sure, there were the continuers of the tradition of 1913, the early American moderns following the Armory Show. With them we may also group other painters of the post–First World War decade who branch off into a series of not too original variants of modernism, with exceptions as noted. Toward the end of the thirties, also undoubtedly stimulated to a certain extent by the economic security offered by the Federal Art Project, as well as in reaction against both Regional and Social Realist art, we get a goodly number of Romantics of the type already listed, along with abstract artists.

It is only fair to acknowledge that the modern movement has been helped considerably by arrival on these shores of many leading European artists fleeing from the Nazi terror. From the post-Cubist tradition we received Fernand Léger; from the Purist and Constructivist side there came Ozenfant, Moholy-Nagy, and Gropius. The Surrealist school contributed Marc Chagall, and other schools, other people. All in all, a tremendous number of Europe's outstanding creative artists came to the United States, many of them to engage in teaching or to start their own schools. Between their transplantation here and the canonization of this general form of art in the Guggenheim Museum of Non-Objective Painting, we have undergone a swing to the abstract again.

The trend toward Non-Objectivism within the past few years has a double character. A number of skillful but slightly esoteric practitioners of Abstract Expressionism and Constructivist-type pictures have carried the modern movement into one of its unfortunate obscurantist blind alleys. On the other hand, some of this same material in the hands of the Bauhaus people: Moholy-Nagy, Gropius, Ozenfant, and their adherents, through the force of their teaching even more than through individual works, has had a most interesting effect.

In various parts of the country, schools under their influence are beginning to emerge for the purpose of bringing together the modern artist and contemporary business requirements in product design, typography, advertising, photography, film, and architecture. The Harvard Department of Architecture, Chicago's Institute of Design, the Brooklyn Museum Design Laboratory, and others indicate an effort to integrate art into the machine age. As in the case of the original Bauhaus, this new school of thought hopes through the experimental handling of tools and materials to break down the barriers between fine and applied arts, to allow the creative imagination of the artist or designer to express itself in keeping with contemporary needs.

Although such interests may have little to do with the traditional conception of painting and sculpture, they might well offer one avenue of enrichment for the contemporary scene. As we have already seen in connection with the general development of post-Cubist or Purist, Constructivist, and other forms, they have had a salutary effect on modern architecture, furniture design, typography, etc. This important beginning during the twenties was renewed and refreshed through the work of the schools and men listed earlier. Instead of the frustrating retreat into a maze of non-intelligibility, some abstract artists are beginning to find an outlet for their design impulses in useful things of greater or less importance.

Although both types of Non-Objectivism represent a retreat from content and to that extent from the traditional function of painting, there have been many other painters who during the past few years have also enriched the American art world. The abstract Surrealism of Morris Graves has a challenging kind of humor and emotion which may be compared with the work of Europeans like Miró and Masson in terms of originality of expression. An interesting and aesthetically exciting variant of the Surrealist viewpoint is found in the often Romantic work of Rico Lebrun (Fig. 210).

210. LᴇBRUN: *The Tattered One* (New York, courtesy of Julien Levy Gallery).

Though there are many recognizable echoes from Dali and Picasso, this amazingly powerful draftsman has managed to combine various elements of the modern tradition into something quite personal and unique.

From the Expressionist side, one of the most sensitive contributions has been the painting of Loren MacIver (Fig. 211). Her *Shack* is typical of the humor and delicacy of her approach, her unusual and even fantastic way of looking at things. Whether she treats a series of flickering, iridescent offering lights, a child's view of a hopscotch game, or the flattened version of the shack with its walls neatly laid on the ground, MacIver is sometimes as subtle and as delicate in tonality as Paul Klee.

More overtly Expressionist has been the highly emotive work of Abraham Rattner. His glowingly mysterious and jewel-like canvases (Fig. 212) have an emotional starkness comparable to the work of Rouault. The intensity and sincerity of feeling in Rattner's pictures, their skillful combination of different phases of modernism, place him in an unusually high position in American art today.

Artists like Graves, Lebrun, MacIver, and Rattner are symptomatic of a significant change in American painting. The post-Armory modernists had been too busy ingesting new ideas to strike off on their own very much. Throughout the twenties and even into the early thirties—with important exceptions like Paul Burlin and Stuart Davis—this condition persisted.

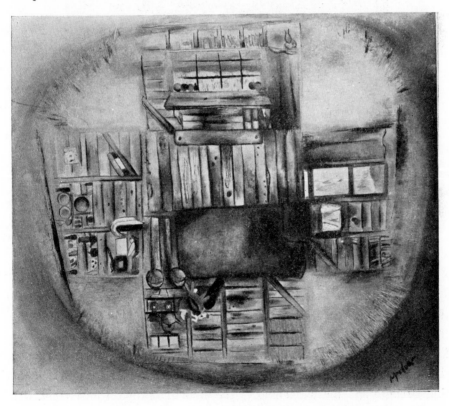

211. MacIVER: *Shack* (New York, The Museum of Modern Art).

Perhaps the best indication of the disease is the plethora of Picassoids and even lesser fry that have called themselves abstract painters, especially in the Non-Objective group. But the last decade has begun to yield a crop from the many modern seeds planted since 1913. Contemporary European art has

212. RATTNER: *The Emperor* (New York, Whitney Museum of American Art).

at last been absorbed and made part of American culture; we go on from there to something new. Finally, we are beating our own path to the future.

Within this same period American art has become increasingly decentralized away from the largest cities to many smaller places. Between this growing strength and the weakening of the modern European movement, the world center of art productivity has shifted toward the Americas.

406

22. THE MODERN ARTIST AND SOCIETY

Our story of modern painting began at the point where feudal society had just disappeared, taking with it art's oldest and best customers: the Church, the monarchy, and the nobility. Since then the artist has wandered about at the mercy of a newer and much more difficult client. Less sure of himself than his predecessors, the new middle-class patron of the arts was bound to be far more conservative. Holding on with deathlike grip to the established styles of the past, he stubbornly refused to admit any kind of innovation. This intellectual uneasiness in bourgeois leaders of finance and government was combined with a parallel political conservatism that made new ideas—artistic or otherwise—highly suspect. In fact, artistic liberalism soon became synonymous with political liberalism.

The post-Revolutionary artist in France, trying to express the exciting age in which he lived, soon ran afoul of the authorities, the Academy, the official *salon*, and other symbols of established order. Whereas in previous centuries artistic styles had developed in response to the needs of those periods, nineteenth-century art evolved as a reaction against the era. Yet, while the art of men like Géricault and Delacroix refused to be bound by officially accepted academic standards, it still reflected traditional styles. Although far from unintelligible, it was nonetheless unacceptable.

Throughout the Romantic development from Delacroix to Barbizon, the cautious public, held down by conservative critics and official attitudes, refused to accept individualistic ideas. The Realist movement, still based on art of the past, was equally unwelcome. Its vulgarity was objected to, its glorification of the commonplace derided. By the middle of the nineteenth century the artist was completely isolated. The defensive aggressiveness of Courbet and his group betrays their position as nothing else could.

Sitting about café tables mulling over their problems and ambitions, they become the living symbols of the artist's estrangement from society.

As we have already seen, the artist's right of free expression implied not only the freedom to choose subject matter but also the liberty of individual technique. From the Impressionist period on, the rhythm of mutual rejection between artist and audience increased. Now it was a question of techniques that were not understood, that deviated sufficiently from the traditional to make them unintelligible to the public of that day. If they didn't like it, it was too bad, reasoned the artist during the second half of the century. Rejected and refused, he became more than ever the Bohemian unconventional stereotype.

Through all this, however, the painter pursued his course of finding the proper motif to express his "little sensation" of form, whether or not the public cared or bought. From active attack the public passed to indifference and apathy, offset by the attempts of art dealers, museums, and publications to change the situation. Art in our own day has become more than ever something for the instructed few, for those with the leisure to interest themselves, to take the trouble to understand. The older functions of art as a vehicle for religious fervor or a device for glorifying nations or important individuals have long since disappeared. Even the traditional job of setting down the likeness of those with the ability to pay has yielded to the mechanical proficiency of the camera. What has remained has been a mounting individuality, a searching of one's own mind, one's own little world of studio and bedroom, instead of the world at large. Since the manner of this expression has long since ceased to interest the general public, it matters relatively little how this is accomplished.

But the problem of making a living still remains. Even though the modern artist no longer fits into our society, he has to come to it for his subsistence through dealers, publicity methods, and other devices which have very little to do with art. Some have managed to be accepted as decorative, as suitable for the so-called modern home; others lend themselves to various advertising schemes, to the glorification of tobacco, jewelry, and other commercial products. Fads are created through cleverly placed articles in newspapers and magazines, and reputations enhanced by books and favorable criticisms. Through this limbo the artist wanders like some lost soul hoping to be saved, waiting for the kind of luck or help necessary for fame and success.

So long as these conditions prevail, there is little hope for the survival of painting as a profession—or even as an art. With the loss of his standing as a craftsman, with the loss of standards of craftsmanship, the artist has become a kind of special being, a mysterious "creator" encouraged to think of himself as unusual in every way. Some have become inverted and uncommunicative in the process, others have studiously cultivated un-intelligibility. In either case the results are bad in that they have deprived the artist of an audience. Some means must be found to bridge the tremendous gap that has grown up between the painter and the public, some midway point at which the creative person and the literate spectator can meet. Within the past twenty-five years the Western Hemisphere has seen two significant experiments in that direction: the Mexican Renaissance and the government-sponsored art activities in the United States.

In modern Mexico the end of eleven years of revolution and intervention (1910–1921) brought about a new situation. Under the beneficent administration of General Alvaro Obregón, the exiles returned, among them the distinguished anthropologist Manuel Gamio. As an instigator of the new Mexican movement, Gamio tried to explain the racial background that was to form one of the bases for contemporary Mexican painting. What he proposed was not the conventional ideal of civilizing Mexico's enormous Indian population but rather the reeducation of the so-called educated ones.

To rule well, the new government would have to understand the nature of Mexico's many component races. It should realize, for example, the importance of the fact that a tremendous number of inhabitants have Indian blood, that to express properly the character of the country there would have to be a return "to native values, spiritual and artistic." Although this concept was violently at odds with the unoriginal and becalmed European academicism of previous Mexican art, it was from contemporary Europe that the new stimulus for the revival was to come.

Like a good deal of modern art, the Mexican Renaissance also sought structural values in terms of simplification. Many of its leaders have spent years in Europe; all are innovators in a modern and abstract sense. Among the earliest to point the way, David Alfaro Siqueiros and Carlos Mérida were the most abstract and clearly show the relationship between Mexico and Europe. Mérida, for example, who is of pure Mayan stock, worked in Paris with Modigliani (noted for his Africanist painting) and Picasso. Although unaffected by the elaborate "isms" of the period, his primitivistic simplifications are part of the general feeling of the time but stronger in color than those of Modigliani or Picasso (Fig. 213).

The significance of Mérida's work derives from his subtle relationships of color and line, together with the formal strength of his murals, and the brilliant delicacy of the effective water colors. Although he paints peasant subjects, he is never picturesque but reverts to the monumental art of his Mayan ancestors in a quiet and thoughtful way.

213. MÉRIDA: *Peasants* (1924, Mexico, private collection).

410

The earliest stirrings of artistic revolt in Mexico preceded the political upheaval. In 1909 Dr. Atl, an important pioneer figure in the history of Mexican art, had begun to preach nationalism. The following year, with the outbreak of the Revolution against Porfirio Díaz, the students at the Academy of Fine Arts (including the young Siqueiros) struck against the obsolete methods practiced there and walked out, never to return.

They rented a house in a small village outside the capital, painted out of doors, and called themselves the Mexican Barbizon, although they were really Impressionists. Yet for Mexican art this movement, much like the *Neue Sezession* of about the same time in Germany, was a proclamation of the artist's right to paint in a modern unacademic fashion. During the same period, there were produced the social paintings of Francisco Goitia, one of Gamio's earliest collaborators in gathering folk material, and the brothel scenes of José Clemente Orozco, already an independent at this point.

In 1913 with the initiation of Huerta's dictatorship after the murder of President Madero, the artists Atl, Orozco, and Goitia were joined by a large group of art students, including Siqueiros, in a revolt against the dictator. This was the period of Pancho Villa, the "bandit" soldier, and Emiliano Zapata, the great agrarian leader whose slogan "Land and Liberty" was not fulfilled until many years later. Intellectuals like José Vasconcelos became involved also, either as propagandists or as soldiers. During that time Orozco did political caricatures, while the print maker José Guadalupe Posada produced his famous *corridos* (illustrated songs on colored paper) dealing with events of the day and engraved in a morbid primitive fashion that made them popular in the streets and camps.

In 1919 a government of Revolutionary artists in the state of Jalisco, under the painter Zuno as governor, set up a congress of "soldier-artists" with the aid of de la Cueva (a later collaborator of Siqueiros). Its purpose was to plan the new directions and purposes of art and culture generally. One of its accomplishments was to send Siqueiros and Carlos Orozco-Romero off to Europe for study. Shortly afterward, Siqueiros and Rivera met in Paris, presumably to their mutual advantage.

In the meantime things in Mexico began to move very rapidly. Carlos Mérida returned from Guatemala to have his first exhibition of paintings

411

with genuine folk motifs integrated aesthetically and not merely as picturesque illustrations. The following year (1921) was the turning point; with the end of political Revolution upon the accession of Obregón, the artistic revolution really began. José Vasconcelos, the friend of Zapata and once a soldier under Pancho Villa, was appointed Minister of Education with a new program in which art was to play an important role. That same year Siqueiros, probably as a result of his exchanges with Rivera, proclaimed in a manifesto from Barcelona that the art of the Mexican Revolution should be based on native vitality and not on outworn European ideas. Adolfo Best-Maugard arranged a magnificent fair in Mexico City's Chapultepec Park with real native dances and music as a feature. Rivera returned after three Cubist years via Italy where he was much impressed by early Italian frescoes and Byzantine mosaics. Orozco-Romero came back from Europe at this point and Jean Charlot (part French, part Mexican) arrived to join the movement. Artists came to Mexico City from various parts of the country, as did de la Cueva and Guerrero from Guadalajara; Orozco had been there all the time.

Under Vasconcelos' newly announced policy of education for everyone, which brought back the artists, intellectuals became organizers and propagandized both workers and artists. A tremendous development in building, painting, planning, publishing, and other cultural and social activities soon followed. All ideas, experiments, and projects were welcome.

The stimulus given to art by this policy was simply incalculable. Everything seemed to express itself through this medium, even the education of children. Beginning in 1922, vast painting projects were carried on with furious day-and-night activity, although opposed by those who were unconvinced of the value of decorating public buildings. Experiments in painting spread from school walls to the classrooms themselves. Under the leadership of Adolfo Best-Maugard a series of pedagogical ideas based on familiar folk art were now projected. This vital connection between everyday experience and the ideas taught in school was to prove very useful in creating a public for the next generation. Art became so popular during this period that open-air schools for children were founded. Unusual talents such as the fourteen-year-old Pacheco, mural assistant to Rivera, and the brilliant but prematurely deceased Abraham Angel were developed.

In view of the richness and variety of Mexico's folk art, it is not too surprising that these things should have happened. The Mexicans, living in a handicraft culture, make their own pottery, mats, furniture, blankets, and serapes with taste and feeling for decorative ornament. Their toys, jewelry, lacquer work, and ceremonial objects are all witness to a continuous tradition of artistic workmanship dating from earliest times. Every district in Mexico has some specialty for which it is known. With this background the public had long been prepared for the development of other art forms.

In speeches and newspaper articles, artists came forward with the idea that murals in public buildings would give back to art a certain social function. It would restore a meaning it had once possessed in both Europe and Mexico —in pre-Spanish temples, Baroque church decorations, and other forms.

While in Spain, Siqueiros had already foretold this artistic revolution. Yet in view of other "modern" theoretical approaches, it is not too surprising that he thought in terms of Renaissance technique and modern abstract art. Although the latter remained his final qualitative yardstick, by itself it did not have the largeness of style to cover the walls the government-sponsored Syndicate was to paint.

The revolutionary character of Siqueiros' approach, and its ultimately antiaesthetic quality, is found in the fact that he believed subject to be as important as style. This idea, although greeted with amazement by his "arty" Spanish friends, was soon to dominate Mexican painting. Siqueiros believed that his painting should derive its formal and emotional strength from the model itself, but the model must not be chosen merely as an opportunity for artistic juggling. This, he pointed out, was merely "the sterile behavior of pedants, prima-donnas and dilettantes."

Although he advocated the study of older Mexican art, he warned against the fallacy of "lamentable archaeological reconstruction," advocating, rather, a participation in our "marvelous dynamic age." "Like the classic artists," he said, "we must achieve our purpose within the inviolate laws of aesthetic balance. We must, like them, be good craftsmen, and like them, too, we must have a constructive base and great sincerity."

In 1922 the Revolutionary Syndicate of Technical Workers, Painters, and Sculptors was formed, and toward the end of the year the first govern-

413

ment contracts were signed for the decoration of public buildings. Not only did the Syndicate ally itself with labor in its action as an organized group but it proclaimed in forceful and vibrant terms the "fallacy" of the "art for art's sake" credo. Although its artists were primarily interested in the creation of a new art with a social purpose, they did not believe that mass art, to be useful or revolutionary, had to be subservient to prescribed ideas. "A panel sincerely and forcefully conceived from pure emotion, and portrayed according to the aesthetic laws of the craft, will generate its own morale."

The focal point of this new mural activity was the National Preparatory School in Mexico City. There, by 1923, Rivera and his assistants (Leal, Revueltas, de la Canal, Guerrero, Siqueiros, and others) had already completed a number of important panels. Here Orozco did his most important early work reflecting the artist's rich Revolutionary experience. Siqueiros' painting in the *Preparatoria* is one of the few important examples of his mural painting in Mexico. The largeness and simplicity of effect achieved by Rivera's *History of Philosophy* in these early frescoes was due to his adaptation of early Italian wall paintings and Byzantine mosaics.

The spectacle of artists in overalls receiving the same wage as the masons preparing the plaster, the feeling of friendliness, the lack of snobbery, was something unique. This solidarity of sentiment and genuine friendship between the artists and their fellow workers did not prevent the middle-class public from objecting violently to what they were doing. Both press and public attacked furiously, but the painters were determined to carry through the still fluctuating Mexican artistic revolution. Petitions and committees flowed through the office of the Minister of Education, who was accused of wasting the public's money. Ultimately, some murals in the Preparatory School were defaced by the children of these same committee members and others. For a time the artists worked with revolvers strapped to their waists but they continued to paint.

A political shift to the Right under Calles brought with it a new Minister of Fine Arts and Education and almost the entire group, except Rivera and Roberto Montenegro, were dismissed. Even though the Syndicate as such no longer existed, its example was by no means dead. A second generation of muralists was to come into being, as well as painting schools, craft centers, weaving and embroidery classes, and sculpture workshops. The success achieved by the Mexican painters outside of Mexico later helped to convert another Secretary of Education to public murals. In Guadalajara and Vera Cruz the tradition of the Syndicate was continued during this interim period and paralleled in a vital school of literature.

In the United States, the modern Mexican movement contributed enormously to the development of the mural idea even before there was any question of government-subsidized art in this country. The murals done in

214. RIVERA: *Soldier, Peasant, Worker* —mural section (Mexico City, Secretariat of Education).

the United States by Rivera, Orozco, and others served as a strong stimulus to the Social Realists here.

The best known of the Mexican group of painters is undoubtedly Diego Rivera (b. 1886), whose first group of murals has already been mentioned in connection with the National Preparatory School. His prolific contribution includes other elaborately descriptive and historical works in the Ministry of Public Education (Fig. 214), the library of the Agricultural School at Chapingo, and countless other places—something like three hundred murals in Mexico alone. In addition, there are the many frescoes in San Francisco, Detroit, and New York City. The incident of the Radio City wall paintings that were destroyed because the artist had dared put a figure of Lenin into one section created world-wide interest. Although banned from Rockefeller Center, the entire composition was later reproduced in the Palacio de Bellas Artes in Mexico City.

As a personality, Rivera has always been overwhelming. A social lion in every sense of the term, this declamatory figure has had a long history of Left and ultra-Left revolutionary activities. Although he is necessarily a painter of ideas, these ideas lack the emotional fire found in many of his colleagues; but his comparatively static arrangements are splendid decorations in the traditional sense.

What Rivera lacks in emotional fire is found in full measure in David Alfaro Siqueiros (b. 1898), a real product of the Mexican Revolution. From drummer boy at the age of sixteen, Siqueiros worked his way up to a staff officer's position. When the Carranza government came to power, the young man was sent abroad to study, returning to edit *El Machete* (The Scythe), organ of the newly formed Artists Syndicate of which he became general secretary. It was during this period that he decorated the stairway of the National Preparatory School—a work which was never completed.

When the Syndicate was dissolved, Siqueiros, who had been its leading spirit, went off to Guadalajara in the state of Jalisco with de la Cueva and Romero to work on the state capitol and university buildings. But he became increasingly involved in labor work, spending most of his time on strike committees and organizing the Jalisco Miners Federation. A forceful labor leader, he worked even more at these activities than at painting. He spoke of himself as a "conscious artist, and to be a conscious artist one must also be a workman, and workmen nowadays must sit on strike committees."

Siqueiros became "delegate at large" of Mexico's artistic revolution. He went to California in 1932 to head a group of artists decorating exteriors in Los Angeles. His political viewpoint finally caused his expulsion from the United States, but he continued to preach his message on the social function of decorative mural painting in Buenos Aires. Returning to Mexico in 1934, he began to work out his experiences up to that point in a series of striking and sculpturesque forms rendered in Duco paint. Typical of the works of this period is the *Proletarian Mother* (Fig. 215) in which the deeply modeled forms are combined with a feeling for abstract arrangement. The face of the mother, as in many other Siqueiros pictures, has a physical and spiritual largeness emphasized by the sharp sculptural undercutting of the features. It looms out of the painting with an intensity of feeling that sums up the artist's passionate reaction to one of his favorite subjects, the suffering of the lower classes. Rather than depicting a specific scene, however, these themes are often rendered in symbolic fashion. A more violent example is the Museum of Modern Art's *Echo of a Scream*, where the artist has let himself go in a powerful expression of protest against the murder of women and children in the Fascist attacks on Spain.

In 1935 this aggressively proletarian artist engaged in a furious polemic with Diego Rivera on the true nature of revolutionary art. Opposing the preachments in paint of his more famous rival, Siqueiros maintained that socially conscious art need not necessarily deal with the specific subject matter of the struggle between classes; nor must a painter or sculptor be judged significant on the basis of archaeological reconstructions but rather

215. SIQUEIROS: *Proletarian Mother* (courtesy of Miss Ines Amor, Mexico City).

"within the inviolate laws of aesthetic balance." He says further: " . . . we must have a constructive base and a great sincerity." Put somewhat differently, this attitude—so different from the viewpoint expressed in Rivera's murals—means that to be of your own time, you paint what you see with all the conviction at your command. The purpose of art, he implies, is not speechmaking or ideological complexities. Art should show the life, the feeling of the time. In doing this, it will convey much more clearly the burden of mankind.

This does not mean that Siqueiros had abandoned his revolutionary ideas; it was another approach to the problem. His activities on the political front continued uninterrupted. In 1936 he was delegated by the Mexican Artists Congress to the American Artists Congress in New York. The following year he was invited by the Loyalist government in Spain to help in their artistic propaganda. Like others of his social-minded colleagues,

Siqueiros preferred to enlist in their army and fight. His relative inactivity after the end of the Spanish war was the result of political difficulties with the Mexican government and a long period of absence from Mexico. Perhaps his most important work since then is the powerful mural done in 1944 on the same floor of the Palacio de Bellas Artes that already had the earlier murals by Rivera and Orozco.

Whatever one may feel about his various political involvements, Siqueiros has been true to his beliefs. Far removed from hothouse studio considerations, his art is the product of a profound feeling for people, a feeling that stems from his own direct experience.

Perhaps the most powerful and Expressionistic of the first generation of modern Mexican painters was José Clemente Orozco (1883–1949), called by admirers "the Mexican Goya." He was the only one of the original group who did not enjoy the benefit of French or other European training and only began to study painting in 1909. Where Rivera is distinctly philosophical in his approach, especially in his early work at the Preparatory School, Orozco from the very beginning was animated by his rich background in the Revolution. These experiences are reflected in a series of early wash drawings and lithographs (1913–1917) that can only be compared with the drawings and aquatints of Goya, particularly the *Disasters of War*. The terror and brutality, the horror of attack and mutilation, the war-stimulated excesses, stand out with a starkness of effect that is matched by the artist's economical and simplified line.

Lacking one hand, Orozco could not actually fight in the Revolution but made drawings for a regimental paper, the *Vanguardista*. After the war he spent a number of years doing newspaper caricatures of Mexico's underworld and political corruption. Although the genre scenes were attacked as immoral, the political cartoons helped expel a number of the many opportunists in the administration.

As Orozco turned from underworld types and prostitutes to political caricature, his social consciousness was ripening, but he did not reach his full maturity until a few years later. Taken as a sort of afterthought into the National Preparatory School work, his contribution turned out to be the most important part of its decoration. Some of the sections he did here

(Justice and the Law, Father God, Reactionary Forces, etc.) are caricatures rather than murals, although still part of his ripening political attitude. Others, especially the monumental and plastic *Maternity*, *Cortez and Malintzin*, *The Strike*, and *The Trinity* (Fig. 216) although experimental

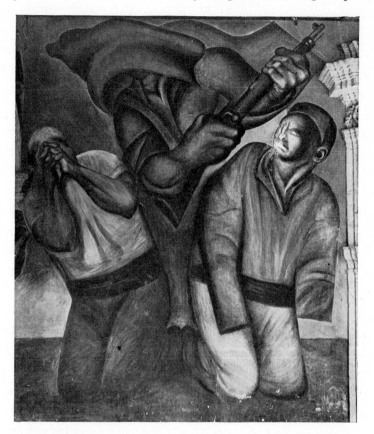

216. OROZCO: *The Trinity*—mural section (Mexico City, National Preparatory School).

in character, have a quality of three-dimensional power rivaled only by Siqueiros. His fully formed manner emerged in such sections as *The Return to the Battlefields*, *Franciscan and Indian*, or *The Mother's Farewell*, where a certain amount of distortion and a high degree of simplification achieve a somber and tragic symbolism. This phase remains evident in his work through his American period and until his latter-day work at Guadalajara.

419

Although Rivera had done the first mural in the Preparatory School's central courtyard, his philosophical paintings (the Creation; Woman and the Fine Arts; Hope, Faith, and Charity; Drama; Tragedy; the Sciences) were never completed. While Orozco was laying out his vast scheme of revolutionary subject matter in this building (1923–1926), Rivera moved over to the Secretariat of Education where his decorative murals told a similar story (1923–1930).

Shortly after the completion of the Preparatory School murals, Orozco and the other organizers of the Syndicate, except Rivera, found themselves out of work. Orozco had a rather difficult time until a wealthy admirer exerted some influence and had him recalled to decorate the Industrial School at Orizaba. In 1927 he went off to the United States where he received commissions to decorate walls in Pomona College, California, the New School for Social Research in New York, and Dartmouth College in New Hampshire. After his return to Mexico in 1934 he did such important government jobs as the fresco in the Palace of Fine Arts (1934), the dome in the state university at Guadalajara, the decorations in the Hospicio (Orphanage) and state capitol in the same city, and the lobby of the Supreme Court in Mexico City. More recently his murals in the Hospital of Jesus and in the open-air theater of the new Normal School, both in Mexico City, mark a final stage in the growth of this master.

There is probably more overt power expressed in an Orozco painting or lithograph than in the work of most of his colleagues. Although he did not have the decorative facility of Rivera, the controlled monumentality of Siqueiros, or the delicate primitivism of Mérida, he showed in such paintings as the *Zapatistas* (Plate V) a completely modern and personal Expressionism. While the painting of Rivera is almost always aesthetically appealing, it sometimes tends to become slick. Orozco's work, for the most part, shows an uncontained and wild tragedy, an almost blind force suggesting Goya in the smaller things but completely his own in the murals. The difference between Orozco and Rivera is underlined in their murals at the Palace of Fine Arts. Rivera's *Man at the Crossroads* is a well-ordered and thoughtful presentation of the evils of the contemporary world and their cure in the ideal society of Socialism. Orozco's man is a suffering

Plate V.   OROZCO: *Zapatistas* (New York, The Museum of Modern Art).

creature floundering around in a world torn by chaos. He offers no hope or remedy.

One of the most important personalities of our time, Orozco was unrelated to either the orthodox Leftism of Siqueiros or the ultra-Leftism of Rivera. Similarly his art, although basically Expressionist, came from the man himself rather than from any influence by modern European art. His philosophy —if one can use such a term about an artist who refused to explain his work —was purely that of the Mexican who has seen his people suffer. The subject matter of his murals in the state capitol in Guadalajara includes the *Phantasm of Religion in Alliance with Militarism* and the *Carnival of the Ideologies*, condemning both communism and fascism. Between them, as it were, stand the *Outcasts*, the tortured, unheard people of Mexico. Looming majestically in the vault is the awesome figure of the patriot priest *Miguel Hidalgo y Costilla* (Fig. 217), father of the Mexican Revolution. One hand raised in the traditional gesture of judgment, the other holding a flaming torch, he points the way to Mexico's future.

Although the thirties gave an impression of less activity in Mexican mural painting, this period produced a new generation of artists. In 1933 the progressive Secretary of Education Bassols initiated a policy of decorating all newly built schools in the Federal District (Mexico City and suburbs). Pacheco, O'Higgins, Zalce, O'Gorman, Guadarrama, Castellanos, Galván, and others have been involved in this work. The major paintings of Orozco, as we have seen, also belong to that period. Nor was Rivera idle during this time. Beginning with the 1930 murals in the Palace of Cortez in Cuernavaca, sponsored by the late U.S. Ambassador Dwight W. Morrow, and continuing with the mural in the Palace of Fine Arts, Rivera was constantly productive. As recently as 1945 he decorated the first-floor corridor of the National Palace in Mexico City. Many younger artists, some originally pupils and assistants like Pacheco, have carried on his ideas.

One of the most interesting projects of that decade involves the murals done for the Abelardo Rodriguez Market in Mexico City (1934–1935). Here in an environment of fruits, vegetables, and other edibles, a number of United States and Mexican adherents of the mural movement have left an interesting monument to the desire for a real people's art. Grace and

Marion Greenwood, Pablo O'Higgins, the sculptor Noguchi, the new artists Antonio Pujol, Bracho, Tzab, and Rendon, are responsible for a fine piece of decoration that blends admirably with its surroundings.

217. OROZCO: *Don Miguel Hidalgo y Costilla*—mural section (Guadalajara, State Capitol).

The Rodriguez Market murals mark a new trend in Mexican art, a departure from such formal backgrounds as the Secretariat of Education, the National Preparatory School, and the National Conservatory of Music. During the early thirties the LEAR (League of Revolutionary Artists and Writers) had pointed out that a good deal of earlier mural production had been in relatively inaccessible places, at least as far as the masses of the people were concerned. Moreover, they felt that some of the original murals

422

had tended to become picturesque and "touristy," as the force of the Revolution had waned and American "imperialism" (the perpetual bugaboo of Latin America) reared its head again.

As a result of this tourist quality and the apparent monopoly of Rivera and his pupils during the early thirties, (and for other reasons) many younger Mexican artists began to turn to purely aesthetic problems divorced from social content. Perhaps the most outstanding example of this trend is the work of Rufino Tamayo (b. 1910), formerly a muralist in the revolutionary tradition, now one of Mexico's leading easel painters.

One apparent result of LEAR's complaint that art had been removed from the people was the formation of a graphic arts workshop known as the Taller de Gráfica Popular. Here a number of younger men, including Pablo O'Higgins, Alfredo Zalce, Leopoldo Méndez, and Antonio Pujol, dedicated themselves to the graphic arts, particularly the woodcut and lithograph. For the masses they revived Posada's art of the colored broadsheet, wherein illustrations of current events were combined with popular songs and made to sell for a few centavos each. Although without sponsorship or financial support, the Taller has produced some extraordinarily graphic and sympathetic scenes from the life of the people. Of these, Méndez' moving accounts of the government's attempt to institute popular education in the face of violent Church opposition are among the most effective. The prewar conflict between the labor movement and the rising Sinarquist or fascist groups is also part of the material in their *corridos*.

From the point of view of murals, what had earlier been federal sponsorship became more or less a local matter, often depending on the interest in art of a particular administrator. Thus the work of Orozco in Guadalajara was due to the patronage of the then governor of the state of Jalisco, Don C. Everardo Topete. Orozco's black-and-white mural in Jiquilpán is similarly a gift to the people of that town by ex-President Cárdenas, who was born there.

It is unquestionably true that some murals of the later thirties had become picturesque and "touristy." One of the best—or worst—examples is the decoration inside the gigantic hollow statue of Morelos on the island of Janitzio in Lake Pátzcuaro. Here the story of the liberator of the Morelia area is unwound along the staircase in a decidedly tiresome and uninspired fashion.

Yet the mural movement in Mexico is far from dead, in spite of picturesqueness and lack of a well-defined government policy. In the middle thirties the trade unions had resolved to assess their members a small monthly sum for cultural activities. Although this program was hampered by the imminence of war, the unions did sponsor a few significant mural projects. Perhaps the most interesting is the staircase decoration in the main headquarters of the powerful Electrical Workers Union in Mexico City. Though the space is small, Siqueiros and his assistants have done a very worth-while job, taking advantage of every trick of perspective to give an impression of greater area. Antonio Ruiz has done the new building of the Cinematographers Union.

Although the modern movement in Mexico seems to be dominated by political-minded artists, it should be clearly understood that the art of Mexico is the product of a revolutionary period that necessarily conditions the character of its expression. Yet it must be remembered that this was not a communist revolution, that its orientation was primarily socialist. In spite of the orthodox Leftist views of some Mexican intellectuals, the majority were more or less pure socialists, depending on the seriousness of the situation before them. Essentially, the Revolution was an upsurge of landless peasants against the forces holding them down. However directed, this movement and its background are reflected in the art of the twenties and thirties.

On the other hand, one finds a group of nonpolitical artists: Julio Castellanos; Manuel Rodríguez Lozano and his pupil, the young Abraham Angel; Carlos Mérida, who has turned toward abstraction; and Antonio Ruiz, who has done important work in the children's theater as well as in the legitimate theater and motion pictures. Frida Kahlo (the former Mrs. Diego Rivera) is a well-known Surrealist; while Rufino Tamayo, an outstanding independent in the Picasso tradition, has already been mentioned. During the war period, evidences of Mexico's continued productivity are found in Rivera's National Palace murals in Mexico City, Siqueiros' mural in the Palacio de Bellas Artes, the work of the Taller, and many other instances.

424

After the war the most conspicuous feature of the Mexican movement was the new direction taken by the art of Orozco. His monumentally abstract outdoor decorations in the Normal School of Mexico City (1948) are perhaps among the outstanding contributions to the mural art of our generation. Also during this period the activities of the Department of Plastic Arts under the newly organized governmental Institute of Fine Arts promise a good deal for the future development of art in Mexico.

The second important experiment in government-aided art grew out of very different circumstances from those pertaining to Mexico. The economic crisis of 1929 with its world-wide repercussions brought the problem of the artist into sharp relief, especially in the United States. Existing heretofore in the most precarious way, the artist had been subjected to the capricious patronage of people to whom buying pictures was a sure and easy mark of culture. Now he was deprived of even this source of income.

During the first stages of the fight against depression, the artist was put on the dole. When it was realized that national unemployment was not merely a temporary setback and that living on charity was bad for morale, work relief was instituted. In an incredibly short time the Civil Works Administration under Harry Hopkins put more than four million people to work. But the inappropriateness of many of the jobs, together with failing government funds, forced the liquidation of this project.

The experience gained was not altogether useless. Early in 1935 it was channeled into a more useful and permanent form as the Works Progress Administration (WPA). Under this new arrangement the relief eligibles in each community were put into the kind of project needed there—taking into consideration the particular skill of the individual. It was still a work-relief project but far better than before, in that carpenters, for example, would not be assigned to office work.

One branch of the Works Progress Administration was the Federal Art Project constituted in August, 1935, and paralleling other programs in music, dance, theater, and writing. Within a relatively short time all these activities found large and responsive audiences, a fact as surprising to the so-called cultured public as to the artist himself. Whatever the shortcomings of the Federal Art Project under these admittedly difficult emergency conditions, it did produce before the astonished gaze of all beholders a mass public whose existence had never been suspected.

The chief problem for the Project's administrator, the capable and sincere Holger Cahill, was not merely to get the best artists for the best jobs. Under the stress of a relief program he was forced into taking on all sorts and conditions of artists, geniuses or not. As he himself once put it: "The organization of the Project has proceeded on the principle that it is not the solitary genius but a sound general movement which maintains art as a vital functioning part of any cultural scheme. Art is not a matter of rare occasional masterpieces. The emphasis upon masterpieces is a nineteenth century phenomenon. It is primarily a collector's idea and has little relation to an art movement."

To take up the slack between outstanding and average artists, a series of activities were organized that performed the double function of occupying those out of the "genius" class and, through their efforts, laying the groundwork for public acceptance and understanding. More than half the artists employed on the Project were given other than "fine arts" work: teaching, photography, posters, applied arts, stage sets, and similar forms. Out of this phase of the Project's activity there grew two important things: the Index of American Design, and Federal Art Galleries and Art Centers.

The Index set itself the tremendous task of recording in permanent form (oil paint or water color) the history of American decorative art from earliest times to the present day. More than seven thousand renditions of furniture, costumes, textiles, ironwork, wood carving, glassware, signposts, and other folk arts were produced. Although we cannot be sure that the Project's administrators had in mind establishment of the same kind of relationship between modern art and native forms as in Mexico, the analogy is rather striking.

More direct educational activity was undertaken in the many Federal Art Centers set up throughout the country. Whole areas that had never before been exposed to the arts, areas where even public libraries were lacking—and there still are such places—now had a cultural awakening. In these Centers (as in scores of settlement houses, churches, clubs, etc.) the public was offered free classes in painting, drawing, and sculpture, lectures by visiting and local art people, and circulating exhibitions. Although such a program seemed ambitious, especially for small cities, people were willing to look and listen. Not only did individuals and groups respond to the opportunity, but in many instances the local authorities encouraged the movement. The importance of this teaching activity lay in its preparing the foundations for an art-educated or art-acclimated generation. Had the Project continued beyond the brief half decade of its existence, this would eventually have been carried much further.

As for the "fine arts" Projects themselves, they were geared to a belief that an art tradition must be renewed from generation to generation to retain its soundness. The living tradition, it was felt, is contained in the work of present-day artists and not in the cellars of museums. Whatever it may have believed about itself, the fact is that the Art Project did unearth a considerable amount of new talent. Its artists won important prizes and their works were often acquired by museums. The response of the painters, sculptors, and others to the stimulus and security of government aid, to the idea of being useful and wanted, was very important.

From the viewpoint of direct public response, the mural section of the Project was necessarily the most effective, since its work was so readily seen. More than a thousand wall paintings were installed in hospitals, schools, colleges, courthouses, airports, and other public buildings, with the local authorities paying only the nonlabor or materials cost of the job. The mural design by Mitchell Siporin of Illinois (Fig. 218), who was "discovered" by the Project, is distinctly American in feeling but symbolically rather than in any superficially illustrative sense. Carl Sandburg, Edgar Lee Masters, and Vachel Lindsay, all poets of the Middle West, are shown singing to a drought-stricken family.

The majority of the Project's creative artists were engaged in easel painting, which produced relatively few studio subjects such as nudes and still life. Like the muralists, the easel painters showed a remarkably ready response to everyday problems that almost naturally expressed themselves in more understandable terms. With both groups, the fact that their work was to be placed in public buildings for people to look at made them turn to a more communicable artistic language. As a purely statistical fact, it is

427

218. SIPORIN: *Prairie Poets*—mural design (courtesy of WPA Federal Art Project).

interesting to note that there were far more requests for murals and easel paintings than the Project could fulfill.

With an intelligence and tolerance foreign to ordinary government-sponsored enterprises, the Federal Art Project permitted its artists the widest latitude, imposing the fewest possible restrictions in the expression of social attitudes. For the most part, this liberty was not abused but resulted in a very healthful and eye-opening process in the arts.

Although the end of the emergency and the oncoming war combined to kill the Projects, they had kept a considerable number of artists, writers, and musicians going during a period of great economic distress. New talents were uncovered. The "Americans 1942" exhibition of the Museum of Modern Art reveals that of the eighteen representative painters and sculptors chosen, four (Darrel Austin, Morris Graves, Joseph Hirsch, and Samuel Cashwan) had been helped by the Project, and six (Hyman Bloom, Raymond Breinin, Donal Hord, Jack Levine (Fig. 209), Fletcher Martin, and Mitchell Siporin (Fig. 218) received their best and in some cases first real opportunity under the same auspices. There are many other artists that could be added to this list.

From a historical standpoint, examining the position of the artist in society, the Art Project had furthered the idea of participation. Although the relative economic security given to Project artists was very important, the feeling of being part of the movement and life of their own time was even more important, especially to the younger artists. This in turn tended to give them a new conception of responsiblity to the public, a feeling far different from the individualistic approach of artists in previous years. For a brief period it seemed possible that there would be an end to the detached attitude that had led to a museum art.

In spite of this newly effected relationship with a widely interested public, the projects were abandoned. The question arose then—and still exists now—as to the future of government-sponsored art. Although there seems little immediate likelihood of the resumption of this activity, artists' groups are still working on the problem. In New York State (where one still finds the majority of artists), there has been constant agitation for a New York City art center and recently a bill was offered in the state legislature for a state project. Either one of these ideas would be very useful in reestablishing the prewar relationship of artist and public.

With the death of the Project and despite the so-called boom period during the war when people earned and spent more freely, the economic position of the artist reverted to its previous state of depression. A recent survey in the *Magazine of Art* by Elizabeth McCausland, "Why Can't America Afford Art?" reveals that out of two hundred leading artists answering her questionnaire "44 per cent depend largely or entirely on income from other sources than art to pay rent, buy materials, care for family, and exist." Even more startling is the fact that for the entire two hundred, with an average of four years' art training and twenty years' art practice, the average income from art sales to museums and collectors was $1,154—and this in the "boom" year, 1944. The survey found that forty-four per cent of artists teach and twenty-seven per cent do commercial work, a very small percentage have independent incomes, and a considerable number do odd jobs that have nothing to do with their craft.

Granted that the sampling might have been larger in this survey, but noting at the same time that the artists represented were people who had exhibited consistently at the leading museums, we must conclude that there is very little economic support for American art. Yet we have seen that under the government-sponsored Projects, a great many people (more than two million) came to exhibitions, classes, and demonstrations, that hundreds of tax-supported institutions received murals, paintings, prints, etc. Exciting though the Mexican government's program had been, it could not begin to compare in sheer weight of accomplishment with what the United States program had effected. It would seem, then, that in spite of the lack of private patronage in the two countries, government aid had helped to produce worth-while art movements.

Other ways of bringing art to the people or the people to art have been tried. Big business has taken the lead in an attempt to encourage contemporary painting through various promotional devices. The formation of collections in the name of the company may or may not result in a good grouping—depending on the taste of the individual in charge—but it necessarily becomes part of a cultural good-will advertisement. Although those men whose pictures are bought derive direct benefit, it is sometimes questionable if these collections represent the best in our art.

Another device used by business is the sponsorship of contests to stimulate interest in their product. The paintings produced may be reproduced as calendars or circulated in some other form. Where there is no relationship between the painting and the product, as in some competitions, the effect of such an annual national promotion is generally favorable. On the other hand, where contests are arranged or pictures commissioned in terms of the painter's direct representation of a specific product, the only one to profit from the arrangement is the company that gets a well-known name for relatively little. The effect on the artist is unquestionably bad, for instead of working creatively he has become a routine advertising man.

The field of advertising proper offers another possibility of employment for the artist. With very few exceptions, this has been the worst influence on the work of many promising young men and women. Admitting the seriousness of the temptation, the fact remains that the uniform representation of one cigarette company's product by a number of different artists is a corruption of these men's talents. The same is generally true no matter what the product, coffee, medicines, or cigarettes, since the purpose of the company's art director is to create a simple type of medium that will attract the greatest number of customers. As in the case of the magazine-cover artist, our museum or gallery man is forced to make his picture conform to the most elementary level of visual comprehension.

The inevitable result of all these procedures is not to bring art to the people but rather to degrade whatever taste they may have. Its effect on the artist is to put him at the mercy of a kind of patronage that, although new and wealthy, has certainly given no indication of developing art or any other form of culture. The vulgarization of artistic taste through this kind of advertising is part of a general pandering to the lowest intellectual standards, as seen in other fields as well. Instead of elevating taste, most of our media of mass communication so far have succeeded in the main in thinning quality to a point where it has almost disappeared.

On the other hand, certain agencies, notably the magazines, have done a very useful job of bringing art to the public. Although many of these efforts have been concerned with established contemporaries or Old Master artists rather than with the relatively unknown painters, their contribution has been very fine. The *Scribner's* American Painters Series, the *Vanity Fair* reproductions of French moderns, *Esquire's* color-illustrated biographies, *Life's* widely varied offerings in color, *Coronet's* efforts, and others show what can be done and, more important, that the public wants the material.

National and local radio programs have indicated that there are literally millions of people willing to listen and anxious to get the pamphlets, brochures, and prints accompanying these broadcasts. The 1939–1940 National Broadcasting Company program planned by this writer dramatized the lives and discussed the work of Old Masters, modern painters, and contemporary Americans for a weekly audience of three and a half million listeners. The networks and the museums expect that the further development of television will help even more along this line.

Yet these activities, although they undoubtedly stimulate interest in art and spread information, do not make a living for artists. Nor does the dissemination of color prints, which are the only things the average man can afford. The ordinary citizen, by definition, cannot be a patron of the arts, unless a very inexpensive original medium like the silk screen print (serigraph) becomes sufficiently popular to attract his attention. So far this has not happened, although progress has been made.

Most people will agree that something should be done about the arts. It is in the manner of solving the problem that disagreements arise. From those who oppose any form of federally sponsored cultural activity there are objections to what they call "socialism," "propaganda," etc. Another group objects that a Federal department of fine arts along the lines of European ministries of art would be so bureaucratic as to stifle art. Yet we have seen that for art to continue as a legitimate cultural activity in the traditional

431

sense, the contemporary painter and sculptor must be given more tangible encouragement and help. Lacking the patronage upon which he depended in the past—the Church, the monarchy, or a cultured aristocracy of wealth—and having developed along lines that isolated him from the public, an adjustment must be made. It would seem that only official aid in some form will do this. Whatever procedure is finally adopted, an open discussion of the problem of the artist in our society by all parties concerned will be an important step along the road of reintegrating art in the modern world.

During the course of the past century and a half, the artist has been driven in upon himself, changing from a socially useful being to a creature without function, since he no longer has an audience—or an audience that can give him a living. Unless we argue, as some have, that art in the traditional sense has outlived its usefulness, we are bound to do something about it. The fact that millions of people, when given the opportunity, responded to the appeal of art in its various forms means that there is still an audience, even if that audience is unable to buy.

Although the development of modern history has deprived the artist of his traditional support, it has done nothing to replace these patrons and the public they supplied. It is equally clear that the artist cannot survive in his historic role of creator under the mass production efforts of advertising and big business generally. The efforts of the modern design advocates, beneficial as they have been in architecture, product design, advertising, and related fields, have little to do with painting or sculpture as we ordinarily think of these arts. Whether or not their work will bring about an ideal joining of the artist and the modern industrialized world still remains to be seen.

It would seem, then, that modern democratic governments acting in the place of older monarchies or church administrations will have to solve this problem. The cultural returns on any investment of this sort, the positive good, socially and intellectually, are worth far more to the nation than any relatively small sum of money. Out of his ivory tower, away from the market place where elaborate program notes make his work palatable to a limited few, the modern artist can be brought back to a more communicable language, to a useful place in our society.

432

WHAT TO READ

Although the following titles have been restricted to works in English, the reader will find a very rich literature on modern painting in many other languages as well. Such books, even where the language is unfamiliar, are extremely interesting for their illustrations whose titles can usually be puzzled out. Since many modern painters and the movements they represent have not yet been adequately treated in English, merely the experience of leafing through the pictures of foreign books can give a useful bird's-eye view of that particular kind of work. For this reason a special list of picture books is appended to this bibliography.

MODERN PAINTING: GENERAL

Bell, Clive. *Since Cézanne*. New York: Harcourt, Brace and Company, Inc., 1922.

————. *Landmarks in Nineteenth Century Painting*. New York: Harcourt, Brace and Company, Inc., 1927.

Bulliet, C. J. *The Significant Moderns and Their Pictures*. New York: Covici, Friede, Inc., 1936.

Cheney, Sheldon. *A Primer of Modern Art*. New York: Liveright Publishing Corp., 1924.

————. *The Story of Modern Art*. New York: The Viking Press, Inc., 1941.

Craven, Thomas. *Modern Art*. New York: Simon and Schuster, Inc., 1934.

Dorner, Alexander. *The Way beyond Art*. New York: Wittenborn, Schultz, Inc., 1947.

Goldwater, Robert J. *Primitivism in Modern Painting*. New York: Harper & Brothers, 1938.

Gordon, Jan. *Modern French Painters*. Rev. ed. London: John Lane, The Bodley Head, Ltd., 1940.

Guggenheim, Peggy (ed.). *Art of This Century*. New York: Art of This Century, 1942.

433

Huyghe, René. *French Painting: The Contemporaries*. New York: French & European, 1939.

Lemaitre, Georges. *From Cubism to Surrealism in French Literature*. Cambridge: Harvard University Press, 1941.

Lewisohn, Samuel. *Painters and Personalities*. New York: Harper & Brothers, 1937.

Museum of Modern Art. *Art in Our Time*. New York: The Museum of Modern Art, 1939.

———. *What Is Modern Painting?* Alfred H. Barr, Jr. New York: The Museum of Modern Art, 1943.

Ozenfant, Amédée. *Foundations of Modern Art*. New York: Brewer, Warren & Putnam, 1931.

Pach, Walter. *Queer Thing, Painting*. New York: Harper & Brothers, 1938.

———. *The Masters of Modern Art*. New York: Huebsch, 1924.

Putnam, Samuel. *Paris Was Our Mistress*. New York: The Viking Press, Inc., 1947.

Read, Herbert. *Art Now*. London: Faber & Faber, Ltd. (The Scientific Press), 1948.

Richardson, Edgar Preston. *The Way of Western Art: 1776–1914*. Cambridge: Harvard University Press, 1939.

Rocheblave, S. *French Painting, XIXth Century*. New York: Hyperion Press of New York, Inc., 1941.

Rothchild, Edward F. *The Meaning of Unintelligibility in Modern Art*. Chicago: University of Chicago Press, 1931.

Rothenstein, John. *Nineteenth Century Painting*. London: John Lane, The Bodley Head, Ltd., 1932.

Sweeney, James Johnson. *Plastic Redirections in Twentieth Century Painting*. Chicago: University of Chicago Press, 1934.

Symons, Arthur. *From Toulouse-Lautrec to Rodin*. London: John Lane, The Bodley Head, Ltd., 1929.

Terrasse, Charles. *French Painting in the XXth Century*. New York: Hyperion Press of New York, Inc., 1939.

Venturi, Lionello. *Modern Painters*. New York: Charles Scribner's Sons, 1947.

Vollard, Ambroise. *Recollections of a Picture Dealer*. Translated by Violet M. Macdonald. Boston: Little, Brown & Company, 1936.

434

Wilenski, Reginald Howard. *The Modern Movement in Art*. Rev. ed. London: Faber & Faber, Ltd. (The Scientific Press), 1945.

———. *Modern French Painters*. London: Faber & Faber, Ltd. (The Scientific Press), 1944.

Wright, Willard Huntington. *Modern Painting*. New York: John Lane, The Bodley Head, Ltd., 1915.

THE FRENCH REVOLUTION

Antal, Friedrich. "Reflections on Classicism and Romanticism," *Burlington Magazine*, April, 1935.

Brown, Milton W. *The Painting of the French Revolution*. New York: Critics Group, 1938.

Dowd, David L. *Pageant Master of the Republic*. Lincoln: University of Nebraska Press, 1949.

Valentiner, W. R. *Jacques Louis David and the French Revolution*. New York: Frederic Fairchild Sherman, 1929.

GOYA

Calvert, A. F. *Goya*. London: John Lane, The Bodley Head, Ltd., 1908.

Gudiol y Cunill, José. *Goya*. New York: Hyperion Press of New York, Inc., 1941.

Mayer, August L. *Francisco de Goya*. Translated by Robert West. London: J. M. Dent & Sons, Ltd., 1924.

Poore, Charles. *Goya*. New York: Charles Scribner's Sons, 1938.

EARLY ROMANTICISM: GIRODET AND GROS

Addison, Agnes Eleanor. *Romanticism and the Gothic Revival*. New York: Richard R. Smith, 1938.

Antal, Friedrich. "Reflections on Classicism and Romanticism," *Burlington Magazine*, March, 1936.

Gaunt, William. *Bandits in a Landscape; a Study of Romantic Painting from Caravaggio to Delacroix*. London: The Studio Publications, Inc., 1937.

Gros–Géricault–Delacroix Loan Exhibition. New York: M. Knoedler & Co., 1938.

LATER ROMANTICISM: GÉRICAULT AND DELACROIX

Badt, Kurt. *Eugène Delacroix Drawings, with an Introduction Based on the Artist's Journal.* Oxford: Cassirer, 1946.

Berger, Klaus. *Géricault: Drawings and Watercolors.* New York: H. Bittner & Co., 1946.

Delacroix, Eugène. *The Journals of Eugène Delacroix.* Translated from the French by Walter Pach. New York: Covici, Friede, Inc., 1937.

Eugène Delacroix: 1798–1863. New York: Wildenstein and Company, Inc., 1944.

Konody, Paul George. *Delacroix.* Philadelphia: Frederick A. Stokes Company, 1910.

San Francisco Museum of Art. *French Romantic Artists: Gros, Géricault, Delacroix.* San Francisco: San Francisco Museum of Art, 1939.

INGRES AND THE ACADEMICIANS

David and Ingres. New York: M. Knoedler & Co., 1940.

Froelich-Bume, L. *Ingres: His Life and Art.* Translated by Maude Valerie White. London: William Heinemann, Ltd., 1926.

Mongan, Agnes (ed.). *Ingres: 24 Drawings.* New York: Pantheon Books, Inc., 1947.

Pach, Walter. *Ingres.* New York and London: Harper & Brothers, 1939.

THE ENGLISH CONTRIBUTION

Chamot, Mary. *Painting in England from Hogarth to Whistler.* London: Country Life, 1939.

Finberg, Alexander. *The Life of J. M. W. Turner.* New York: Oxford University Press, 1939.

Fry, Roger. *Reflections on British Painting.* London: Faber & Faber, Ltd. (The Scientific Press), 1934.

Gaunt, William. *British Painting from Hogarth's Day to Ours.* London: Avalon Press, 1946.

Leslie, C. R. *Memoirs of the Life of John Constable.* London: Medici, 1937.

Mauclair, Camille. *Turner.* Translated by Eveline Byam Shaw. New York: Hyperion Press of New York, Inc., 1939.

Ritchie, Andrew C. *English Painters.* Baltimore: Johns Hopkins Press, 1942.

THE ROMANTIC LANDSCAPE IN FRANCE

Hoeber, Arthur. *The Barbizon Painters*. Philadelphia: Frederick A. Stokes Company, 1915.

Lafargue, Marc. *Corot*. Translated by Lindsay Wellington. New York: Dodd, Mead & Company, Inc., 1926.

Museum of Modern Art. *Corot–Daumier*. Eighth Loan Exhibition. New York: The Museum of Modern Art, 1930.

Smith, Charles Sprague. *Barbizon Days: Millet–Corot–Rousseau–Barye*. New York: Wessels, 1903.

THE REALISTS: MILLET, COURBET, DAUMIER

Boas, George (ed.). *Courbet and the Naturalistic Movement*. Baltimore: Johns Hopkins Press, 1938.

Daumier, Honoré: 240 Lithographs. With an introduction by Bernard Lemann. New York: Reynal & Hitchcock, Inc., 1946.

Frantz, Henri, and Octave Uzanne. *Daumier and Gavarni*. Edited by Charles Holme. New York: The Studio Publications, Inc., 1914.

Gsell, Paul. *Millet*. Translated by J. Lewis May. New York: Dodd, Mead & Company, Inc., 1928.

Laran, Jean. *Gustave Courbet*. London: William Heinemann, Ltd., 1912.

Larkin, Oliver. "Courbet and His Contemporaries," *Science & Society*, v. 3, 1939.

———. "Courbet in the Commune," *Science & Society*, v. 5, 1941.

Lassaigne, Jacques. *Daumier*. Translated by Eveline Byam Shaw. London: William Heinemann, Ltd., 1938.

Metropolitan Museum of Art. *Loan Exhibition of the Works of Gustave Courbet*. New York: Metropolitan Museum of Art, 1919.

Phillips Memorial Gallery. *Honoré Daumier: Appreciation of His Life and Works*. New York: E. P. Dutton & Co., 1922.

Sadleir, Michael. *Daumier: The Man and the Artist*. London: Halton & T. Smith, 1924.

Tomson, Arthur. *Jean-François Millet and the Barbizon School*. London: George Bell & Sons, Ltd., 1903.

Wickenden, Robert J. *The Art and Etchings of Jean-François Millet*. Boston: Houghton Mifflin Company, 1914.

Duret, Théodore. *Manet and the French Impressionists*. Translated by J. E. Crawford Flitch. Philadelphia: J. B. Lippincott Company, 1910.

Mauclair, Camille. *Claude Monet*. Translated by J. Lewis May. London: John Lane, The Bodley Head, Ltd., n.d. (In Masters of Modern Art Series.)

————. *The French Impressionists*. Translated by P. G. Konody. London: Gerald Duckworth & Co., Ltd., 1911.

Museum of Modern Art. *The History of Impressionism*. John Rewald. New York: The Museum of Modern Art, 1946.

Rewald, John (ed.). *Camille Pissarro: Letters to His Son, Lucien*. New York: Pantheon Books, Inc., 1943.

Tabarant, A. *Pissarro*. Translated by J. Lewis May. London: John Lane, The Bodley Head, Ltd., 1925.

Uhde, Wilhelm. *The Impressionists*. New York and Vienna: Phaidon Press, 1937.

RENOIR

Barnes, A. C., and Violette De Mazia. *The Art of Renoir*. New York: Minton, Balch & Co., 1935.

Florisoone, Michel. *Renoir*. Translated by George Frederic Lees. London: William Heinemann, Ltd., 1938.

Fosca, François. *Renoir*. Translated by Herbert Wellington. New York: Dodd, Mead & Company, Inc., 1924.

Frost, Rosamund. *Renoir*. New York: Hyperion Press of New York, Inc., 1944.

Rewald, John (ed.). *Renoir Drawings*. New York: H. Bittner & Co., 1946.

LINEAR IMPRESSIONISM: DEGAS, LAUTREC

Manson, J. B. *The Life and Works of Edgar Degas*. London: The Studio Publications, Inc., 1927.

Mauclair, Camille. *Degas*. New York: Hyperion Press of New York, Inc., 1941.

Mehring, Walter (ed.). *Degas: 30 Drawings and Pastels*. New York: E. S. Herrmann, 1944.

Meier-Graefe, Julius. *Degas*. Translated by J. Holroyd-Reece. London: Ernest Benn, Ltd., 1923.

Chicago Art Institute. *Toulouse-Lautrec Loan Exhibition*. Edited by Daniel Catton Rich. Chicago: Chicago Art Institute, 1931.

Lapparent, Paul de. *Toulouse-Lautrec*. London: John Lane, The Bodley Head, Ltd., 1928.

Mack, Gerstle. *Toulouse-Lautrec*. New York: Alfred A. Knopf, Inc., 1938.

Symons, Arthur. *From Toulouse-Lautrec to Rodin*. London: John Lane, The Bodley Head, Ltd., 1929.

CÉZANNE AND POST-IMPRESSIONISM

Barnes, A. C., and Violette De Mazia. *The Art of Cézanne*. New York: Harcourt, Brace and Company, Inc., 1939.

Fry, Roger. *Cézanne, A Study of His Development*. New York: The Macmillan Company, 1927.

Jewell, Edward Alden. *Cézanne*. New York: Hyperion Press of New York, Inc., 1944.

Loran, Erle. *Cézanne's Composition: Analysis of His Form with Diagrams and Photographs of His Motifs*. Berkeley and Los Angeles: University of California Press, 1944.

Mack, Gerstle. *Paul Cézanne*. New York: Alfred A. Knopf, Inc., 1935.

Meier-Graefe, Julius. *Cézanne*. Translated by J. Holroyd-Reece. London: Ernest Benn Ltd., 1927.

Novotny, Fritz. *Paul Cézanne*. Vienna: Phaidon Press, 1937.

Rewald, John (ed.). *Paul Cézanne, Letters*. London: Cassirer, 1941.

Venturi, Lionello. *Paul Cézanne, Water Colours*. Oxford: Cassirer, 1943.

Vollard, Ambroise. *Paul Cézanne: His Life and Art*. New York: Crown Publishers, 1937.

NEO-IMPRESSIONISM: SEURAT, SIGNAC

Pach, Walter. *Georges Seurat*. New York: Duffield & Company, 1923.

Rewald, John. *Georges Seurat*. New York: Wittenborn & Company, 1946.

Rich, Daniel Catton. *Seurat and the Evolution of "La Grande Jatte."* Chicago: University of Chicago Press, 1935.

Seligman, Germain. *The Drawings of Georges Seurat*. New York: Kurt Valentin, 1947.

VAN GOGH

Meier-Graefe, Julius. *Vincent van Gogh, A Biographical Study.* Translated by John Holroyd-Reece. New York: Harcourt, Brace and Company, Inc., 1933.

Museum of Modern Art. *Vincent van Gogh.* Edited by Alfred H. Barr, Jr. New York: The Museum of Modern Art, 1935.

————. *Vincent van Gogh: Letters to Émile Bernard.* Edited, translated, and with a foreword by Douglas Lord. New York: The Museum of Modern Art, 1938.

Pach, Walter. *Vincent van Gogh: A Study of the Artist and His Work in Relation to His Time.* New York: Artbook Museum, 1936.

Van Gogh, Vincent. *The Letters of Vincent van Gogh to His Brother, 1872–1886.* London: Constable & Company, Ltd., 1927. 2 vols.

————. *Further Letters of Vincent van Gogh to His Brother, 1886–1889.* London: Constable & Company, Ltd., 1929.

Vincent van Gogh. With an introduction by Wilhelm Uhde. New York: Oxford University Press, 1941.

GAUGUIN

Burnett, Robert. *The Life of Paul Gauguin.* New York: Oxford University Press, 1937.

Fletcher, John Gould. *Paul Gauguin, His Life and Art.* New York: Nicholas L. Brown, 1921.

Gauguin, Paul. *Noa Noa.* Translated from the French by O. F. Theis. New York: Nicholas L. Brown, 1920.

Gauguin, Pola. *My Father Paul Gauguin.* Translated from the Norwegian by Arthur G. Chater. New York: Alfred A. Knopf, Inc., 1937.

Rewald, John. *Gauguin.* New York: Hyperion Press of New York, Inc., 1938.

Rey, Robert. *Gauguin.* Translated by F. C. de Sumichrast. New York: Dodd, Mead & Company, Inc., 1924.

ROUSSEAU

Museum of Modern Art. *Henri Rousseau.* Daniel Catton Rich. New York: The Museum of Modern Art, 1942.

Barnes, A. C., and Violette De Mazia. *The Art of Henri-Matisse*. New York: Charles Scribner's Sons, 1933.

Museum of Modern Art. *African Negro Art*. Edited by James Johnson Sweeney. New York: The Museum of Modern Art, 1935.

Museum of Modern Art. *Henri-Matisse Retrospective Exhibition*. New York: The Museum of Modern Art, 1931.

Museum of Modern Art. *Rouault*. James Thrall Soby. New York: The Museum of Modern Art, 1945.

Romm, Alexander. *Matisse, A Social Critique*. Translated by Jack Chen. New York: Lear Press, 1947.

Vaughan, Malcolm. *Derain*. New York: Hyperion Press of New York, Inc., 1941.

Venturi, Lionello. *Georges Rouault*. New York: E. Weyhe, 1940.

FROM PICASSO TO ABSTRACT ART

Apollinaire, Guillaume. *The Cubist Painters, Aesthetic Meditations*. Translated from the French by Lionel Abel. New York: Wittenborn & Company, 1944.

Art of Tomorrow. With an introduction by Hilla Rebay. New York: Solomon R. Guggenheim Foundation, 1939.

Cassou, Jean. *Picasso*. Translated from the French by Mary Chamot. New York: Hyperion Press of New York, Inc., 1940.

Janis, Harriet, and Sidney Janis. *Picasso— the Recent Years: 1939–1946*. New York: Doubleday & Company, Inc., 1946.

Kahnweiler, Daniel-Henry. *Juan Gris: His Life and Work*. Translated by Douglas Cooper. New York: Kurt Valentin, 1947.

Lozowick, Louis. *Modern Russian Art*. New York: Société Anonyme, 1925.

Mackenzie, Helen F. *Understanding Picasso*. Chicago: University of Chicago Press, 1940.

Martin, J. L., B. Nicholson, and N. Gabo (eds.). *Circle: International Survey of Constructive Art*. London: Faber & Faber, Ltd. (The Scientific Press), 1937.

Moholy-Nagy, L. *Vision in Motion*. Chicago: Paul Theobald, 1947.

Mondrian, Piet. *Plastic Art and Pure Plastic Art*. New York: Wittenborn & Company, 1948.

Museum of Modern Art. *Bauhaus*. Herbert Bayer, Walter Gropius, Ise Gropius. New York: The Museum of Modern Art, 1938.

————. *Braque*. Henry R. Hope. New York: The Museum of Modern Art, 1949.

————. *Cubism and Abstract Art*. Alfred H. Barr, Jr. New York: The Museum of Modern Art, 1936.

————. *Picasso, 50 Years of His Art*. Alfred H. Barr, Jr. New York: The Museum of Modern Art, 1946.

EXPRESSIONISM

Cheney, Sheldon. *Expressionism in Art*. New York: Liveright Publishing Corp., 1934.

Grosz, George. *A Little Yes and a Big No*. Translated by Lola Sachs Dorin. New York: Dial Press, Inc., 1946.

Hoffmann, Edith. *Kokoschka, Life and Work*. London: Faber & Faber, Ltd. (The Scientific Press), 1946.

Kandinsky. Edited by Hilla Rebay. New York: Solomon R. Guggenheim Foundation, 1945.

Käthe Kollwitz. With an introduction by Carl Zigrosser. New York: H. Bittner & Co., 1946.

Klee (ten reproductions in facsimile). With an introduction by Georg Schmidt. New York: Wittenborn & Company, 1946.

Museum of Modern Art. *German Painting and Sculpture*. Edited by Alfred H. Barr, Jr. New York: The Museum of Modern Art, 1931.

————. *Paul Klee*. Edited by Margaret Miller. New York: The Museum of Modern Art, 1945.

————. and Art Institute of Chicago. *Marc Chagall*. James Johnson Sweeney. New York: The Museum of Modern Art, 1946.

Thoene, Peter (pseud.). *Modern German Art*. London: Pelican, 1938.

Venturi, Lionello. *Marc Chagall*. New York: Pierre Matisse, 1945.

DADA, SURREALISM, NEO-ROMANTICISM

Dali, Salvador. *The Secret Life of Salvador Dali*. Translated by Haakon Chevalier. New York: Dial Press, Inc., 1942.

Gascoyne, David. *A Short Survey of Surrealism*. London: Cobden-Sanderson, 1935.

Levy, Julien. *Surrealism*. New York: Black Sun Press, 1936.

Museum of Modern Art. *Fantastic Art, Dada, Surrealism*. Edited by Alfred H. Barr, Jr., and Georges Hugnet. New York: The Museum of Modern Art, 1936.

————. *Joan Miró*. James Johnson Sweeney. New York: The Museum of Modern Art, 1941.

————. *Salvador Dali*. James Thrall Soby. New York: The Museum of Modern Art, 1946.

————. *Tchelitchew*. James Thrall Soby. New York: The Museum of Modern Art, 1942.

Soby, James Thrall. *After Picasso*. New York: Dodd, Mead & Company, Inc., 1935.

————. *The Early Chirico*. New York: Dodd, Mead & Company, Inc., 1941.

AMERICA TODAY

Barr, Alfred H., Jr., and Holger Cahill. *Art in America in Modern Times*. New York: Reynal & Hitchcock, Inc., 1934.

Benson, E. M. *John Marin*. Washington: The American Federation of Arts, 1935.

Boswell, Peyton. *Modern American Painting*. New York: Dodd, Mead & Company, Inc., 1939.

Charles Burchfield. Edited by Andrew C. Ritchie. Buffalo: The Albright Art Gallery, 1944.

Evergood, 20 Years. With an introduction by Oliver Larkin. New York: A. C. A. Gallery, 1946.

Gruskin, Alan D., *Painting in the U.S.A.* New York: Doubleday & Company, Inc., 1946.

Kootz, Samuel. *New Frontiers in American Painting*. New York: Hastings House, Publishers, Inc., 1943.

Larkin, Oliver. *Art and Life in America*. New York: Rinehart & Company, 1949.

Mellquist, Jerome. *The Emergence of an American Art*. New York: Charles Scribner's Sons, 1942.

Museum of Modern Art. *Americans 1942*. Edited by Dorothy C. Miller. New York: The Museum of Modern Art, 1942.

———. *Ben Shahn*. James Thrall Soby. West Drayton, Middlesex: Penguin Books, Ltd., 1947.

———. *Charles Sheeler*. With an introduction by William Carlos Williams. New York: The Museum of Modern Art, 1939.

———. *Contemporary Painters*. James Thrall Soby. New York: The Museum of Modern Art, 1948.

———. *Fourteen Americans*. New York: The Museum of Modern Art, 1946.

———. *John Marin*. New York: The Museum of Modern Art, 1936.

———. *Romantic Painting in America*. James Thrall Soby and Dorothy C. Miller. New York: The Museum of Modern Art, 1943.

———. *Stuart Davis*. James Johnson Sweeney. New York: The Museum of Modern Art, 1945.

New York World's Fair. *American Art Today*. With essays by Holger Cahill, William Zorach, and others. New York: New York World's Fair, 1940.

Pagano, Grace (ed.). *Contemporary American Painting*. New York: Duell, Sloan & Pearce, Inc., 1945.

Pearson, Ralph. *Experiencing American Pictures*. New York: Harper & Brothers, 1943.

Saint-Gaudens, Homer. *The American Artist and His Times*. New York: Dodd, Mead & Company, Inc., 1941.

Whitney Museum of American Art. *John Sloan*. Guy Pène du Bois. New York: Whitney Museum of American Art, n.d.

THE ARTIST IN SOCIETY

Brenner, Anita. *Idols behind Altars*. New York: Payson & Clarke, 1929.

Charlot, Jean. *Art from the Mayans to Disney*. London: Sheed & Ward, Inc., 1939.

Helm, MacKinley. *Modern Mexican Painters*. New York: Harper & Brothers, 1941.

José Clemente Orozco. With an introduction by Alma Reed. New York: Delphic Studios, 1932.

McCausland, Elizabeth (ed.). *Work for Artists.* New York: American Artists Group, 1947.

M. H. de Young Memorial Museum. *Frontiers of American Art.* San Francisco: M. H. de Young Memorial Museum, 1939.

Museum of Modern Art. *New Horizons in American Art.* With an introduction by Holger Cahill. New York: The Museum of Modern Art, 1936.

Museum of Modern Art (in collaboration with the Mexican Government). *20 Centuries of Mexican Art.* New York: The Museum of Modern Art, 1940.

Orozco's Frescoes in Guadalajara. Edited by Frances Toor with critical notes by Carlos Mérida. Mexico, D.F.: Frances Toor Studios, 1940.

Overmyer, Grace. *Government and the Arts.* New York: W. W. Norton & Company, Inc., 1939.

Schmeckebier, Laurence E. *Modern Mexican Art.* Minneapolis: University of Minnesota Press, 1939.

PICTURE BOOKS

The following titles, including many items in foreign languages, are suggested as typical of the rich material available in picture book or portfolio form. Their purpose is to offer the reader additional illustrative material—often in color—rather than textual criticism or history. The latter part of the list concerns itself with illustrations of paintings that may be found in American collections.

American Art Portfolios. New York: Raymond & Raymond, n.d.

Arte Italiano del nostro tempo. Edited by Stefano Cairola. With 100 plates in color, 200 plates in black and white. Bergamo: Instituto d'arti grafiche editore, 1946.

Die Kunst der Gegenwart. Mit einer Einleitung von J. Meier-Graefe. 42 plates in color. Munich: Marées Gesellschaft, R. Piper & Co. There are also individual artists published by this organization, e.g., *Renoir* (1920), *Cézanne* (1921), etc.

Éditions du Chêne, Paris. Portfolios with 12 to 16 color reproductions. Bonnard, Chagall, Cézanne, Braque, Picasso, Renoir, Vuillard, Vlaminck, Léger, Modigliani, etc.

Éditions de la Revue Verve. Richly illustrated color monographs on Picasso, Matisse, Bonnard, etc.

Einstein, Carl. *Die Kunst des 20ten Jahrhunderts.* Berlin: Propyläen Series, 1934.

Frescoes of Diego Rivera. New York: The Museum of Modern Art, 1933.

Gauguin, Paul. *Noa Noa.* With 36 full page facsimile reproductions and woodcuts by Paul Gauguin. Facsimile of Gauguin's original manuscript of his Tahitian voyage. Munich: Meier-Graefe, 1926.

Huyghe, René. *The Contemporaries.* With biographical notices by Germain Bazin. Translated from the French by Paul C. Blum. New York: French & European Publications, Inc., 1939.

——— *La Peinture actuelle.* Paris: Éditions Pierre Tisné, 1945.

Living Art. Twenty facsimile reproductions after paintings, drawings, and engravings and 10 photographs after sculpture, by contemporary artists. New York: Dial Publishing Company, 1923.

Raynal, Maurice. *Peintres du XXme siècle.* Genève: Éditions d'art, Albert Skira, 1947.

Read, Herbert, Maurice Raynal, and Jean Leymarie. *The History of Modern Painting.* With 200 color plates. Geneva: Albert Skira, 1949–1950.

Skira Portfolios of Color Prints, Geneva. Portfolios with 11 to 16 color reproductions. Matisse, Bonnard, Braque, Picasso, Dufy, Utrillo, Marquet, Rousseau, Derain, Vuillard, etc.

Uhde, Wilhelm. *The Impressionists.* Vienna: Phaidon-Verlag, 1937.

Vanity Fair's Portfolio of Modern French Art. 40 plates in full color. With an introduction by R. H. Wilenski. New York: Vanity Fair, 1935.

Zervos, Christian. *Histoire de l'art contemporain.* Préface par Henri Laugier. Paris: Éditions "Cahiers d'art," 1938.

The Adolph Lewisohn Collection of Modern French Paintings and Sculptures. With an essay by Stephan Bourgeois. New York, E. Weyhe, 1928.

The Cone Collection of Baltimore, Maryland. Catalogue of paintings, drawings, and sculptures of the nineteenth and twentieth centuries, with a foreword by George Boas. Baltimore: Etta Cone, 1934.

Jewell, Edward Alden. *French Impressionists and Their Contemporaries Represented in American Collections.* New York: The Hyperion Press, 1944.

Phillips, Duncan. *A Collection in the Making.* A survey of the painters in the Phillips Memorial Gallery, Washington, D.C. New York: E. Weyhe, 1926.

Shoolman, Regina, and Charles Slatkin. *The Enjoyment of Art in America.* A survey of the permanent collections in American and Canadian museums. New York and Philadelphia: J. B. Lippincott Company, 1942.

INDEX

A

Academic style, Directoire art as a transition to, 67, 68
  as a European phenomenon, 67
  and Ingres, 67
  neo-Renaissance aspects of, 67
  similarities of, to Romanticism, 66
  stereotypes of, 80, 81, 85
  struggle of, with Romantics, 48, 66, 67
  (*See also* French Academy)
Academy (*see* French Academy)
Alba, Duchess of, 27
Albers, Josef, 314
American Artists Congress, 397, 417
Apollinaire, Guillaume, 296
  and Surrealism, 358, 369
Aragon, Louis, 358, 381
Armory Show, 385–387, 402
  organization of, 387
  results of, 388–390
  sponsorship of, by Henri group, 385
Arp, Hans, 359; Fig. 190
  as coauthor of *Fatagaga*, 360
  as cofounder of Cologne Dada group, 357
Art, and business, 430, 431
  and magazines, 431
  as propaganda, 3, 4, 6, 9, 12, 40–43, 60, 70, 139, 396–402
  and radio, 431
Art nouveau, 252–254, 260, 328

Artist, and government, 412*ff.*
  modern, vs. society, 46–49, 315, 316
  and society, 4, 5, 15, 16, 18, 19, 24, 25, 30, 273, 274, 321, 322, 407–409, 429*ff.*
Artistes Républicains (1848), 131, 398
Artists Federation of 1870, 132, 398
"Ashcan School," 384, 385
Atl, Dr., 411
Austen, Jane, 33, 86
Austin, Darrel, 395, 396, 428

B

Bacon, Peggy, 390
Ball, Hugo, 357
Balla, Giacomo, 307, 308; Fig. 157
Barbizon school, 103–106, 108, 109, 115
  influence of, on Impressionism, 114, 115
  Mexican, 411
  opposition to, of society, 104, 111, 407
  relation of, to English art, 89, 93
Baroque style, and Courbet, 124, 127
  and Daumier, 135
  in David, 10
  in Delacroix, 55, 63
  in Géricault, 49–50
  in Girodet's *Pietà*, 32
  in Goya, 25
  in Gros' *Napoleon at Arcola*, 40

448